MW01700037

IELTS 考试技能训练教程

Listening Strategies for the IELTS Test

听　　力

（最新修订）

李亚宾 编著

北京语言大学出版社
BEIJING LANGUAGE AND CULTURE UNIVERSITY PRESS

（京）新登字 157 号

图书在版编目（CIP）数据

IELTS 考试技能训练教程·听力/李亚宾编著.（最新修订）.
—北京：北京语言大学出版社，2007 重印
ISBN 978-7-5619-1435-9

Ⅰ. I…
Ⅱ. 李…
Ⅲ. 英语-听说教学-高等学校-入学考试，国外-习题
Ⅳ. H319.6

中国版本图书馆 CIP 数据核字（2005）第 049029 号

书　　名：IELTS 考试技能训练教程·听力
责任印制：陈　辉

出版发行：北京语言大学出版社
社　　址：北京市海淀区学院路 15 号　邮政编码 100083
网　　址：www.blcup.com
电　　话：发行部　82303650/3591/3651
　　　　　编辑部　82303393
　　　　　读者服务部　82303653/3908
印　　刷：北京外文印刷厂
经　　销：全国新华书店

版　　次：2005 年 10 月第 1 版　2007 年 8 月第 9 次印刷
开　　本：787 毫米×1092 毫米　1/16　印张：19.25
字　　数：364 千字　　印数：45001—50000 册
书　　号：ISBN 978-7-5619-1435-9/H·05049
定　　价：34.00 元

修 订 说 明

《IELTS 考试技能训练教程》（以下简称《教程》）是北京语言大学出国人员培训部的教师积多年的 IELTS 培训教学经验、对 IELTS 考试进行细致分析后编写而成的。自 1997 年首版出版以来，《教程》以其内容丰富广泛、练习形式多样、编排科学实用、能恰到好处地把握考试的重点和中国考生的难点等特点，受到了广大 IELTS 考生和培训教师的好评，被公认为 IELTS 考试辅导书之经典。

这次修订主要做了以下工作：1）增加了针对 IELTS 考试新题型的内容；2）删除了上一版中内容陈旧的材料，代之以新材料；3）修改、补充、完善了保留部分，使之更便于使用；4）听力和阅读分册增加了具有高度指导意义和实用价值的讲解与练习辅导；5）对版式进行了重新设计。相信修订后的《教程》定能帮助广大考生高效、有的放矢地备考 IELTS，使考生的考试成绩有一个新的飞跃。

《IELTS 考试技能训练教程·听力》简介

《IELTS 考试技能训练教程·听力》是为参加 IELTS 英语听力测试的考生进行短期强化训练而设计的。它不但有助于短期内提高考生的应试能力，同时也可以作为广大英语学习者的听力专项训练用书。

本教程内容丰富，涉及广泛，取材于英语国家生活和学习的实际场景，内容按照先易后难、循序渐进的原则编排。全书分为“学生用书”和“教师用书”，便于自学。

一、学生用书

“学生用书”共分为七个单元，前六个单元提供了听力专项练习，它们是模拟 IELTS 听力考试的题型进行分类设置的。

第一单元以数字练习为主，选材于实际生活中与数字有关的对话和报告。例如：时间、旅行时刻表、地址、电话号码及科研学术报告中的数据等。

第二单元是注重听与写的专项练习，通过旅行住宿登记、电话记录和填写各类表格的形式，训练考生捕捉主要信息并记录信息的能力。

第三单元是视与听专项练习，以示图、图表等形式检测考生对听力材料的理解能力。

第四、五单元为综合性练习，要求考生在听懂和理解的基础上进行概括整理，并以扼要的短语回答问题、补全信息，或者做多项选择和是非选择题。

第六单元的练习强化训练考生边听边记的技能。

第七单元提供了四套模拟试题。四套试题是根据英国文化委员会近年来提供的不同的 IELTS 听力考题形式模拟设计的。

我们建议：考生在开始学习本教程前，可以先做一套模拟试题，检查自己的英语水平，找到自己听力上的弱点，以便有的放矢地进行本教程的专项训练。在训练进行的各个阶段，都可以选做第七单元的模拟试题，以便检验训练效果。

根据英国文化委员会提供的评分标准，满分为 9 分，及格线为 6 分。

IELTS 听力考试每套题一般为 40 题左右，答对 25 题就可达到及格线 6 分；答对 24 题以下的，建议要多做听力练习，以便进一步提高；若只答对 12 题以下，说明英语听力基础很差，需要参加英语基础培训，建议暂时不要申请参加 IELTS 考试。

二、教师用书

“教师用书”包括录音的全部书面材料及答案。

近年来，国外把英语短期强化教学作为专门的领域进行研究，总结出它特有的规律，形成了一整套教学理论，并根据这些理论不断更新、出版相应的教材。

希望本书的出版能够为广大学习英语的朋友提供一套实用的听力教材。本教程自 1997 年出版以来，深受 IELTS 考生和培训教师的欢迎。本教程在编写过程中得到在北京语言大学出国留学预备人员培训部工作的英国、美国语言专家的热情帮助，在此谨表示衷心的感谢。

由于编者水平有限，书中缺点、错误在所难免。诚恳希望广大读者给予批评指正。

编　　者

Contents 目录

Student's Book

Unit One
Letters, Numbers and Numeral Relationships

Unit Two
Form Filling and Table Completion

Unit Three
Description and Location

Unit Seven
Practice Tests

Teacher's Book

Tapescript

Answer Key

Appendix

Student ' s Book

Unit One

Letters, Numbers and Numberal Relationships

——Getting the Facts

在 IELTS 听力考试中，常会出现让考生拼写人名或者地名的考题。这就要求考生对英语的 26 个字母不仅要非常熟悉，而且要掌握其准确的发音。如果你自己的发音不准，就会影响听音的准确性。例如“Gill”中的字母“G”常被考生误听成“J”，而字母“W”也常被考生误听成“double”。

在 IELTS 听力考试中，还常常出现与数字相关的信息，如电话号码、时间、日期等，要求考生用最快的速度把这些信息抓住并准确地记下来。

本单元就是通过日常对话、报告等形式针对人名、地名、数字及与数字相关的信息进行训练。目的是：

1. 帮助考生熟悉日常生活中常见的人名、地名、数字及与数字相关的信息，并能在实际交流中准确地拼出人名、地名，记录下数字及其相关信息。

2. 通过字母拼写和数字练习培养学生边听边记的能力，改变只听不写的做法。

建议考生在做本单元练习的过程中，当听到人名、地名和数字时一定要跟着重复或默读。这样能加深印象，有助于准确地记住有关信息。在数字练习中，如果掌握了三位数数字的听和记，应付较大的数字就比较容易了。因为英文数字是以三位数为一组读出的。例如：321,321,321 读作 three hundred twenty one million, three hundred twenty one thousand, three hundred and twenty-one。

Listening Activity No. 1

In Britain, when giving or asking for telephone numbers, we don't say thousand, hundred or million, we say each number separately. So 421 6759 is *four-two-one, six-seven-five-nine*. The '0' is pronounced 'Oh'. 081 436 0872 is *oh-eight-one, four-three-six, oh-eight-seven-two*. These numbers are in groups. The groups are codes for areas in Britain. When we say the numbers, we pause between the groups. However, when the same number occurs twice the word 'double' is used with the number. 1994422 is *one-double nine, double-four, double-two*.

Listen to some dialogues between a caller on the phone and a secretary. As you listen write the telephone numbers and names in the spaces below.

1. Is that ____________________?
   Yes. Can I help you?
   I'd like to speak to ____________________, please.

2. Hi. Is that ____________________?
   Yes. Who do you want to speak to ?
   ____________________, please.

3. Hello. Is that ____________________?
   Who do you wish to speak to?
   ____________________, please.

4. Good morning. Is that ____________________?
   Yes. Can I help you?
   I'd like to speak to ____________________, please.

5. I'm sorry to disturb you, but is that ____________________?
   Who do you want to speak to?
   ____________________, please.

Listening Activity No. 2

In the UK the house number is given first and is followed by the name of the street. These two items are written on the same line. Next, the name of the city and county are written and are followed by the post code and the country if you are abroad.

Listen to the following short dialogues and fill in the missing information in the spaces below.

1. My new address is
   23A Smithfield Road
   Ealing W5
   London
   My telephone number is ______________________________.

2. My sister lives at
   ______________________________ Avenue
   Nottingham
   Her telephone number is ______________________________.

3. My friend Alan lives in London. His address is
   ______________________________ Road
   Ealing, London W5 5RF
   His telephone number is ______________________________.

4. My brother Larry's address is
   ____
   ____
   His telephone number is ______________________________.

5. My parents live at

____

____

Their telephone number is ____________________________________.

6. My uncle George lives at

____

____

His telephone number is ____________________________________.

7. Mrs. Harper lives at

____

____

Her telephone number is ____________________________________.

8. Mr. Johnson lives at

____

____

His telephone number is ____________________________________.

Listening Activity No. 3

In Great Britain, the British Council operates a voluntary scheme for the inspection of English language schools. The schools must comply with strict regulations regarding teacher qualifications and school facilities. EF international language schools in Cambridge, Hastings and Brighton are recognised as efficient by the British Council, and they are members of the Association for Recognised English Language Teaching Establishments in Britain.

Here are their addresses.

Look at this address list, tick (✓) if the information is correct, or write in the necessary changes.

1. EF Language School
   EF House ____________
   1 Farman Street ____________
   Hove, Brighton ____________
   Sussex BN3 1AW ____________
   Tel: 723651 ____________
   Telex: 77843 ____________

2. EF International School of English
   21 Hills Road ____________
   Cambridge ____________
   CB2 2RL ____________
   Tel: 240020 ____________
   Telex: 817713 ____________

3. EF International School of English
   1-2 Sussex Road ______
   Brighton ______
   Sussex BN2 1FJ ______
   Tel: 571802 ______
   Telex: 957005 ______

4. EF International School of English
   64/80 Warrior Square ______
   Hastings ______
   East Sussex TN7 6BP ______
   Tel: 432898 ______
   Telex: 957005 ______

Listening Activity No.4

Listen carefully to a conversation between Alison and Alan. Tick (✓) if the information is correct, or write in the necessary changes.

Alison wants to make a phone call. ______
It's cheaper to make a call before 6 pm. ______
Telephone directory provides gardening information. ______
Arrange an alarm call before 10:30 pm ______
Tuesday evening. ______
You would pay until you talk to the right person. ______
Alison will make a personal call. ______

Listening Activity No.5

Listen carefully to the tape and write down the following names and places.

1. ______________________
2. ______________________
3. ______________________
4. ______________________
5. ______________________
6. ______________________
7. ______________________
8. ______________________

Listening Activity No.6

Listen to the following dialogue between an operator and an enquirer. As you listen, write down the type of call, name and phone number in the spaces below.

Operator: Long distance. May I help you?
Caller: Yes. I want to 1. ______________________, please.
Operator: What is the name of the person, please?
Caller: 2. ______________________.
Operator: What is the number?
Caller: 3. ______________________.

Listening Activity No. 7

Listen to the following dialogue between an operator and an enquirer. As you listen, write down the name, address and phone number in the spaces below.

Operator: Directory Enquiries. What city please?
Enquirer: 1. ____________________
Operator: Name?
Enquirer: 2. ____________________
Operator: Thank you. And could you tell me his address?
Enquirer: 3. ____________________
Operator: The number is 4. ____________________.

Listening Activity No. 8

Listen to the following dialogue between an operator and an enquirer. As you listen, write down the name, address and phone number in the spaces below.

Operator: Directory Enquiries. What city please?
Enquirer: 1. ____.
Operator: Name?
Enquirer: 2. ____.
Operator: And her address?
Enquirer: 3. ____.
Operator: The number is 4. ____________________________.

Listening Activity No.9

You will hear a conversation between a secretary and a student. The secretary is asking the student for information in order to complete an application form for a course. As you listen, fill in the appropriate information on the form below.

Surname (IN CAPITAL LETTERS)	1.	________________
First name	2.	________________
Country	3.	________________
Age	4.	________________
Address	5.	________________
Telephone No.	6.	________________

Listening Activity No. 10

You will hear a conversation between a secretary and a student. The secretary is asking the student for information in order to complete an application form for a course. As you listen, fill in the appropriate information on the form below.

Surname (IN CAPITAL LETTERS)	1.	________________
First name	2.	________________
Country	3.	________________
Age	4.	________________
Address	5.	________________
Telephone No.	6.	________________

Listening Activity No. 11

You will hear a conversation between a secretary and a student. The secretary is asking the student for information in order to complete an application form for a course. As you listen, fill in the appropriate information on the form below.

Surname (IN CAPITAL LETTERS)	1.	______________
First name	2.	______________
Country	3.	______________
Age	4.	______________
Address	5.	______________
Telephone No.	6.	______________

Listening Activity No. 12A

Listen to some short dialogues. In each dialogue, you will hear someone ask a question about the time. When the answer is given, write down the time in the space below.

1. A: Excuse me. Can you tell me the time, please.
   B: Yes. It's ______________.

2. A: Do you have the right time, please?
   B: I think it's ______________.

3. A: Do you know what time the next bus is, please?
   B: Yes. It's ______________.

4. A: What time do you finish your work today?
   B: ______________.

5. A: When do the shops open, please?
   B: ______________________________.

6. A: What time does the London train leave, please?
   B: ______________________________.

7. A: What's the next train to Birmingham, please?
   B: ______________________________.

8. A: Excuse me, please. What time does the Liverpool train arrive?
   B: ______________________________.

9. A: When does the Paris flight leave, please?
   B: ______________________________.

10. A: What time's the next flight to Amsterdam, please?
    B: ______________________________.

Listening Activity No. 12B

You will hear a dialogue. As you listen, fill in the form below.

Time of Dr. Kent's Lecture

Monday 1. ______________ Room No. 2. ______________

Friday 3. ______________ Room No. 4. ______________

Length of each lecture 5. ______________

Listening Activity No. 13

You will hear some announcements from railway stations and airports. These announcements give information to travellers about trains and planes. For each announcement that you hear write in the box below the platform, flight number, time and destination.

Trains

	Platform No.	Time	Destination
1.			
2.			
3.			
4.			
5.			
6.			
7.			
8.			

Planes

	Flight No.	Time	Destination
9.			
10.			
11.			
12.			
13.			
14.			
15.			
16.			

Listening Activity No. 14

Listen to the tape carefully and write down the area and population for each city and region.

Table 1

Area	People /sq km
UK	
European Community	
England	
Greater London	
Scotland	
Wales	
Northern Ireland	

Table 2

City	Area (sq km)	Population (thousand)
Greater London		
Birmingham		
Leeds		
Glasgow		
Edinburgh		
Manchester		
Bristol		
Coventry		

Listening Activity No. 15

Listen to the tape and write down the numbers in the correct column.

Undergraduate Students at the University

	Men	Women
Total		
Science		
Social Science		
Engineering		
Arts		
Medicine		
Dentistry		
Law		
Veterinary Science		

Listening Activity No. 16

You are going to practise some percentages. We use percentages when we want to express a number more simply. Percentage means the number of X per hundred. For example, there are 46 students in a class. 23 of them are female students. We can say 50% of the students are female students. "Percent" is said after the number.

Skim the table below. Then listen to the tape and fill in the missing percentages in the correct column.

British Household Expenditure 1975-1985

Households	1975	1985
Car	1.	2.
Central heating	3.	4.
Television	94.8%	97.6%
Telephone	5.	6.
Home computer	7.	8.
Video recorder		9.

Listening Activity No. 17

You will hear a talk about British trade in 1987. As you listen, write down the numbers in appropriate places.

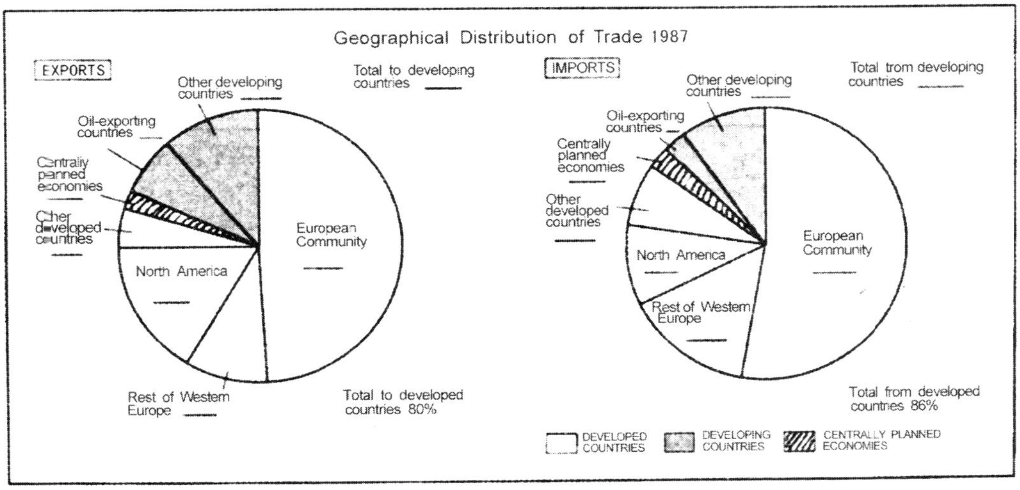

Listening Activity No. 18

You are going to listen to a talk. Look at the table below first, then listen carefully to the talk and fill in the percentages in the correct column.

Countries / Young people (%) who agree	China	Japan	Korea	Thailand
A women's place is in the home.	12%	6.	12.	19.
If a couple both earn money, both should share the housework.	1.	7.	13.	20.
Men and women should be paid the same for the same job.	2.	8.	14.	21.
Nursing is women's work.	3.	9.	15.	22.
Mining is men's work.	90%	10.	16.	23.
Cooking should still be done by women.	4.	82%	17.	24.
Washing clothes should still be done by women.	5.	11.	18.	25.

Listening Activity No. 19

You are going to practise some dates. Dates in Britain can be written in two ways. 1) In numbers only: day, month, year. So 6-3-94 is the 6th of March, 1994. 2) In numbers and words. For example, you can read day, month, year. or month, day, year. For example, 21-12-1994, you read 21st of December, 1994, or December the 21st, 1994.

Listen to the following dates. As you listen, tick the correct letter A or B.

1. When's Lincoln's birthday? A. February 12th B. February 20th
2. Do you know Valentine's Day? A. February 15th B. February 14th
3. When's Washington's birthday? A. February 23rd B. February 21st
4. Do you know when April Fool's Day is? A. April 1st B. April 3rd
5. When is Easter? A. April 3rd B. April 1st
6. When is Mother's Day? A. May 5th B. May 8th
7. What date is Memorial Day? A. May 13th B. May 30th
8. Do you know when Father's Day is? A. June 19th B. June 9th
9. Do you know when Independence Day is? A. July 5th B. July 4th
10. When is Friendship Day? A. August 17th B. August 7th
11. When is Halloween? A. October 1st B. October 31st
12. When is Thanksgiving Day? A. November 25th B. November 24th

Listening Activity No. 20

You are going to hear about the circulation of some British newspapers and when they were founded. Listen to the tape and write down the numbers in the correct column.

	When founded	Circulation in 2003
Quality Daily Newspapers:		
The Daily Telegraph		
The Times		
The Guardian		
The Financial Times		
Quality Sunday Newspapers:		
The Sunday Times		
The Observer		
The Sunday Telegraph		
Popular Daily Newspapers:		
The Daily Express		
The Sun		
The Mirror		
Daily Mail		
Popular Sunday Newspapers:		
News of the World		
Sunday Mirror		
The People		
The Mail on Sunday		
Sunday Express		

Unit Two

Form Filling and Table Completion

——Listening for Specific Details

本单元共有 20 个练习，内容选自国外日常生活场景的各种对话内容，如打电话、找工作、旅馆订房、去银行开户等。

在 IELTS 考试中，常常出现的基本题型就是表格填写（Form filling）或图表完成题（Table completion）。这些类型的试题要求考生根据所听内容填写表格中的信息，以测试其对所听内容的理解能力和准确性。本单元的重点是表格填写练习，目的是帮助考生了解和熟悉题型；通过日常对话，提高考生的实际听力能力，培养考生在听英语会话中捕捉重要信息的能力。

建议考生在听之前，一定要把表格中的问题、句子认真读一遍，养成认真审题的习惯。要学会横看和竖看图表上的已有信息和需要填补的信息，做到心中有数。这样在听的过程中才能有针对性地寻找所需信息，并准确抓住要记录的信息，填写到正确的栏中。

Listening Activity No. 1

You will hear a dialogue. As you listen, fill in the form below.

Family name	1.	________________
First name	2.	________________
Length of English study	3.	________________
Examinations passed	4.	________________
Score	5.	________________
Subjects needing help	6.	________________
Biggest problem	7.	________________

Listening Activity No. 2

You will hear a dialogue. As you listen, fill in the form below.

Which subject put first	1.	________________
Reasons	2.	________________
Second	3.	________________
Third	4.	________________
Fourth	5.	________________
Which subject put last	6.	________________
Reasons	7.	________________

Listening Activity No. 3

You will hear two telephone conversations involving an invitation. As you listen, fill in the forms below.

Conversation 1

Receiver's telephone No.	1.	______
Receiver's name	2.	______
Reason for phoning	3.	______
What will they do	4.	______
When will they do it	5.	______

Conversation 2

Receiver's telphone No.	1.	______
Caller's name	2.	______
Receiver's name	3.	______
Why can't they meet on Friday	4.	______
Why can't they meet on Saturday	5.	______

Listening Activity No.4

You will hear the BBC weather forecast. As you listen, fill in the missing information in the correct column.

Places	Weather	Temperature
S. England and Midlands		
	sunny spells, strong winds, rain	

Listening Activity No.5

A man is looking for a new flat. He is talking to an estate agent. Listen carefully and fill in the form below.

Rental Application Form

Caller's full name	1. ________	
Address	2. ________	Avenue
Telephone No.	3. ________	
Occupation	4. ________	
Employer	5. ________	

Listening Activity No.6

Listen to a conversation between a landlord and a tenant. Imagine you are the tenant. Listen carefully and fill in the form below.

Is the room available?	1. ________
Number of beds in the room	2. ________
Facilities to be shared with others	3. ________
Number of people who are sharing the facilities now	4. ________
Is there a phone in the house?	5. ________
Can the tenants make calls in the house?	6. ________
The rent	7. ________
The rent is due	8. ________
The first month's payment	9. ________
Telephone number	10. ________

Listening Activity No. 7

You will hear a conversation at the customs in Gatwick Airport. As you listen, fill in the form below.

Surname	1.	______
First name	2.	______
Sex	3.	______
Date of birth	4.	______
Nationality	5.	______
Occupation	6.	______
Reason for travel in the UK	7.	______
Address in the UK	8.	______

Listening Activity No. 8

You're a member of the staff in a lost property office in a department store. A woman comes to your office to report that she has lost something. As you listen, fill in the report form with the information she gives you.

Lost Property Report

Item		1.	______
Total value		2.	______
Description		3.	______
Last time noted		4.	______
Last place noted		5.	______
If found, notify:	Name	6.	______
	Address	7.	______
	Phone No.	8.	______

Listening Activity No.9

You will hear an interview between a young woman who has applied for a position with a company and the personnel officer of the company. As you listen, fill in the form below.

Name of applicant		1.	______
University attended		2.	______
Subject		3.	______
Year of graduation		4.	______
Work experience:			
	Last position	5.	______
	Years	6.	______
	Salary	7.	______
	Previous work	8.	______
	Years	9.	______
New job's salary		10.	______
Benefit of the job		11.	______

Listening Activity No. 10

You will hear four telephone messages. As you listen, write down the important information given by the callers.

Message 1

Caller's name	1.	______
Message for	2.	______
Message	3.	______
Ring back	4.	______

Message 2

Receiver's phone No.	1.	______________________
Caller's name	2.	______________________
Message for	3.	______________________
Message	4.	______________________
Phone No.	5.	______________________

Message 3

Receiver's phone No.	1.	______________________
Caller's name	2.	______________________
Message for	3.	______________________
Message	4.	______________________
Phone No.	5.	______________________

Message 4

Receiver's phone No.	1.	______________________
Caller's name	2.	______________________
Message for	3.	______________________
Message	4.	______________________

Listening Activity No. 11

You are going to hear an interview on transportation. As you listen fill in the form below.

Questions / Name	How do you get to school?	How far is it from your home to school?	How long does it take you to get to school?	Are you ever late because of transportation problems?	Suggestions for improving the transportation
Mike	*Example*: *By bus*	3.	6.	8.	11.
Liz	1.	4.	It depends.	9.	12.
Tom	2.	5.	7.	10.	

Listening Activity No. 12

You will hear a conversation. As you listen, fill in the missing information in the form below.

Reason for call	1.	______________
Personnel manager's name	2.	______________
Caller's name	3.	______________
Caller's college	4.	______________
Caller's subjects in college	5.	______________
Caller's work experience	6.	______________ ______________
What foreign languages can the caller speak?	7.	______________
Interview place	8.	______________
Interview time	9.	______________
Documents caller must take to the interview	10.	______________

Listening Activity No. 13

You will hear an interview. As you listen, fill in the form about Miss Wood.

Surname	1.	______
First name	2.	______
Country	3.	______
Marital status	4.	Married / Single
Education	5.	______
Present occupation	6.	______
Number of years for the present occupation	7.	______
How many languages can she speak?	8.	______
Interests	9.	______
Previous employment	10.	______

Listening Activity No. 14

You will hear a dialogue between a bank officer and a customer. As you listen, fill in the form below.

City to which money is to be transferred	1.	______
Name of the bank	2.	______
Recipient of the money	3.	______
Recipient's address	4.	______
Account number	5.	______
Amount of money to be transferred	6.	______
That amount in American dollars	7.	______
Sender of the money	8.	______
Sender's address	9.	______
Fastest method of sending money overseas	10.	______
Method chosen by customer	11.	______

Listening Activity No. 15

You are going to listen to a conversation between a student and a clerk at Barclays Bank. Listen carefully and tick (✓) if the information is correct, or write in the changes.

	Answer
Example:	
The student wants to open a bank account.	✓
He is going to London University in August.	*October*

The grant is paid by the British Council.	1. ______
A student account offers a cheque book	2. ______
and an account book.	3. ______
The card can be used 24 hours a day in the bank machine.	4. ______
It also can be used for a cheque book.	5. ______
Up to £500, interest is 6%.	6. ______
A student account offers a £150 overdraft.	7. ______
You need: a letter from some authority	8. ______
a library card	9. ______
simple forms about your course	10. ______
your previous work employment	11. ______
your address and signature	12. ______

Listening Activity No. 16

Listen to Jane on the tape talking about her relatives. Tick (✓) if the information is correct, or write in the necessary changes.

		Answer
Example:		
Aunt Elme is my father's sister.		*mother's*
She has got 2 grown-up children.		✓
She is a housewife.	1.	____________
Louise is a housewife.	2.	____________
She is divorced.	3.	____________
Uncle Tom is a bank manager.	4.	____________
Lewis lives in Paris.	5.	____________
Roger is Jane's uncle.	6.	____________
He is a sales manager.	7.	____________
Mark studies in Oxford University.	8.	____________
He is talking to his sister.	9.	____________

Listening Activity No. 17

Julia is a student at university. She is looking for a room to rent. She has seen an advertisement and has decided to phone the landlord. As you listen, fill in the form below.

Caller's name	1.	________________
Address of accommodation	2.	________________
Telephone No.	3.	________________
The rent	4.	________________
Type of room available	5.	________________
Rooms shared:	6.	A. living room
		B. bathroom
		C. kitchen
		D. bedroom
Deposit	7.	________________
House rules	8.	________________
		________________
Is it close to public transportation?	9.	________________
Appointment time	10.	________________

Listening Activity No. 18

You will hear a conversation. As you listen, fill in an accident report form with the information you hear.

ACCIDENT REPORT FORM

Name of casualty ________________ Age ____________ Sex ____

Address ________________________________

Occupation ____________________

Details of accident: Date ____________ Time ____________

Category of accident: Road ____ Domestic ____ Sporting ____ Other ____

Injuries sustained ____

Witness's name ____________________

Address ____

Action: Police notified   Ward ________________

Family notified

Employer notified   Casualty officer ________________

Listening Activity No. 19

You are going to hear a talk about some volcanoes. Look at the chart below. Listen carefully to the talk and write down the missing information in the correct place.

Name of the Place	Location	Date of Eruption	Number of People Who Died
Vesuvius		79 A.D.	
	Ecuador		1,000
Krakatoa			
	Martinique		
Mount St. Helens			60
Mount Tambora	Indonesia		

Listening Activity No. 20

You will hear a dialogue between a student and a landlord. The student has seen an advertisement and is phoning the landlord to find out more about it. As you listen, fill in the form below.

Telephone number	1.	______________
Address	2.	______________
Type of room	3.	______________
Rent	4.	______________
Shared rooms	5.	______________
Day rent due	6.	______________
Deposit amount	7.	______________
House rules	8.	______________
Public transport	9.	______________
When is the room available	10.	______________
Nearest tube station	11.	______________
Appointment time	12.	______________

Unit Three

Description and Location

——Identifying People/Items from Description

本单元共有 20 个练习。练习的重点是人物描述（Description）和找方位（Location）。这两项技能是我们日常生活中不可缺少的，而且与国外实际生活紧密相关。

本单元用图片、图表和图等形式，帮助考生通过对所听到的人物的描述，或对方位的指令和指引，选出要找的人或要找的地方。通过练习培养考生边听、边看、边记的综合能力。

建议考生在做图片练习时，要注意图片中人物的共同点和不同点，以提高答题的命中率。在做找方位的练习时，要认真看图上已有的信息，如街名、地名。这样，在做听力练习时即使没跟上指令，只要你记住了图上的地名，也有助于你找到位置，因为在给指令时常以图中已有的地名为参照，如：opposite the church，behind the school，or next to the post office.

Listening Activity No. 1

Task 1

You are going to listen to a conversation about how to make English-style tea. As you listen, put the missing words in the blanks below.

1. First, put ____________ water in a kettle.
2. ____________ the water.
3. ____________ the teapot.
4. Put ____________ into ____________.
5. Pour ____________ over the tea.
6. Let the tea ____________ for ____________.
7. Pour a little ____________ a cup.
8. Then pour ____________ into ____________ cup.
9. Add some ____________ to the tea.

Task 2

Listen to the conversation again. As you listen, put the following pictures in the correct order.

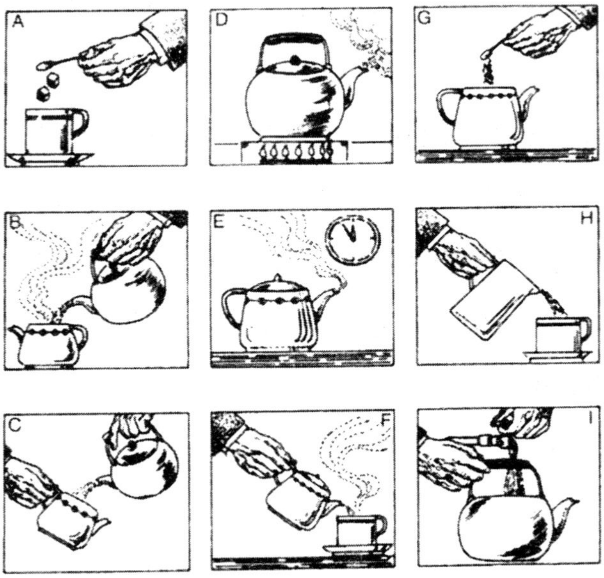

1. ____________
2. ____________
3. ____________
4. ____________
5. ____________
6. ____________
7. ____________
8. ____________
9. ____________

Listening Activity No. 2

Task 1

Listen to a conversation between Mary and her brother, Jack. As you listen, complete the instructions about how to use the water heater.

A. Plug in the ________________.

B. Close the ________________ tap which is the drainage tap.

C. The water tank takes about ________________ minutes to fill up.

D. Open the black one which is the ________________ tap.

E. About ________________ later, you should have ________________ water.

Task 2

Listen to the coversation again. Follow the instructions and put them in the correct order.

1. ________________________

2. ________________________

3. ________________________

4. ________________________

5. ________________________

Listening Activity No. 3

Task 1

Look at the following pictures and listen carefully to the news. As you listen, pick out the wanted man according to the description.

A

B

C

D

Task 2

Listen to the news again and complete the following statements.

1. Police are looking for the wanted man for ________________.
2. The man escaped with goods valued at around ________________.
3. They included items of jewellery, a stereo, ________________ and ________________.
4. The description was given by ________________.
5. The man has a ________________ face and a ________________ nose.
6. The man was wearing ________________.
7. The man has a ________________ on his left cheek.
8. Please contact the nearest ________________ if anyone can offer assistance.

Listening Activity No.4

Task 1

Look at the following pictures and listen carefully to the news. As you listen, pick out the wanted man according to the description.

A B C D

Task 2

Listen to the news again and answer the following questions.

1. Where did the man break into a factory? ____________________
2. How much money has been stolen? ____________________
3. How did he get away? ____________________
4. Why is the man dangerous? ____________________
5. What should people do if they see him? ____________________

Listening Activity No.5

Task 1

Listen to a conversation between Jim and Kathy. As you listen, pick out Kathy's sister according to the description.

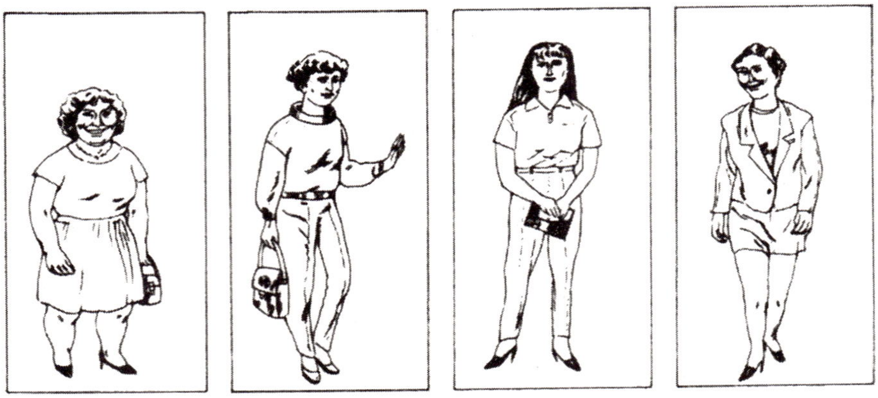

A B C D

Task 2

Listen to the conversation again and answer the following questions.

1. Where is Kathy going to meet her sister? ______________________
2. When will they meet? ______________________
3. Why can't Kathy meet her sister herself? ______________________
4. Has Jim met Kathy's sister before? ______________________
5. How old is Kathy's sister? ______________________
6. What does Diana usually wear? ______________________

Listening Activity No.6

Task 1

Listen to a conversation between a customer and a policeman. As you listen, pick out the man the lady described.

A B C D

Task 2

Look at the following statements. Tick (√) if the information is correct, or write in the necessary changes.

	Answer
1. A man just stole a lady's purse.	________
2. He was tall and thin.	________
3. He was in his twenties.	________
4. His hair is black.	________
5. He was wearing jeans and a jacket.	________
6. The purse was brown.	________
7. And it was made of leather.	________

Listening Activity No. 7

Task 1

You will hear a dialogue between a policeman and a lady who has lost her daughter. As you listen, work out who is the lady's daughter.

A　　B　　C　　D

Task 2

Look at the following statements. Tick (✓) if the information is correct, or write in the necessary changes.

Answer

1. Mary went to school this morning. ____________
2. She lives at 31st Bath Road. ____________
3. Mary is ill. ____________
4. Mary is 9 years old. ____________
5. She has long black hair. ____________

   She is wearing:

6. a white long-sleeved blouse. ____________
7. a pink and white striped skirt. ____________
8. long stockings and brown shoes. ____________

Listening Activity No. 8

You are going to listen to a conversation. As you listen, tick the right letter according to the directions.

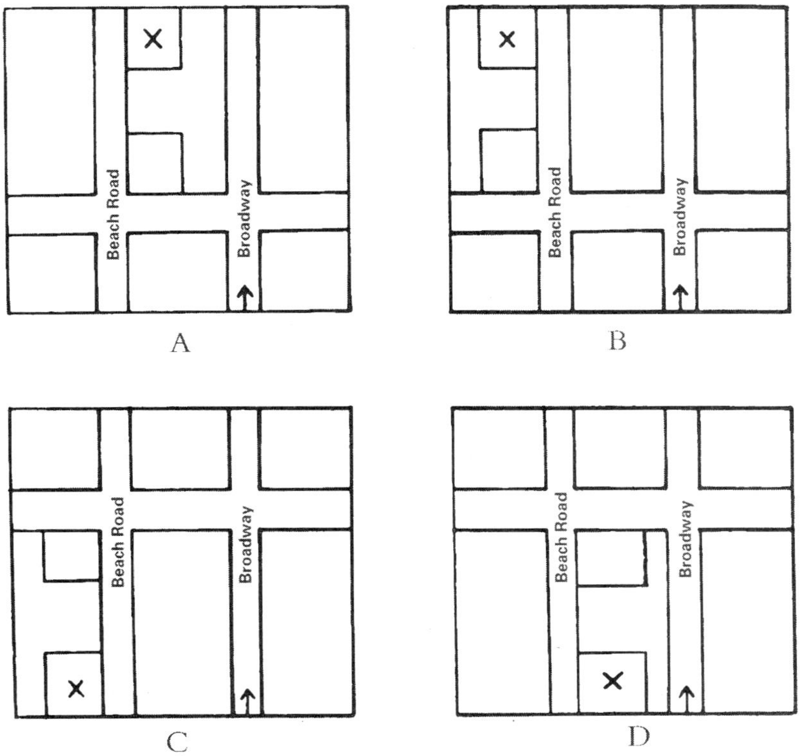

Listening Activity No.9

Look at the diagram below and listen to the directions. As you listen, follow the directions and then write the appropriate number beside the name of each place.

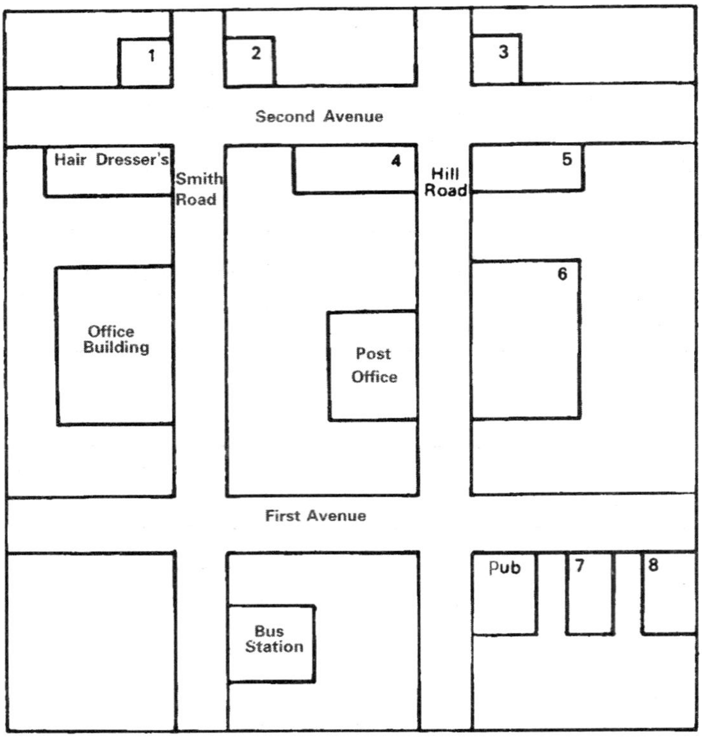

the university library __________

the supermarket __________

the hotel __________

the best bookshop __________

the Lloyds Bank __________

Listening Activity No. 10

Look carefully at the street plan below, follow the sets of directions and then answer the questions at the end of each set of directions.

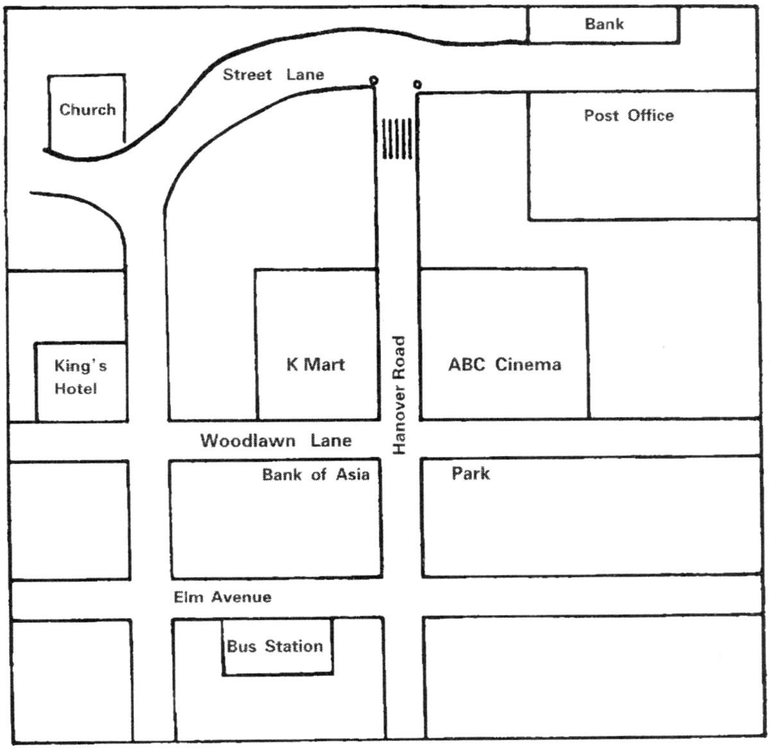

1. What's the building on your left? ______________

2. What's the building on your right? ______________

3. What's the building on your right? ______________

Listening Activity No. 11

Look at the map of Maple Town. You will hear five separate sets of directions to particular places on the map. As you listen, follow the directions carefully and write the letter beside the name of the place. Find the station at the bottom left first. Listen carefully to the directions.

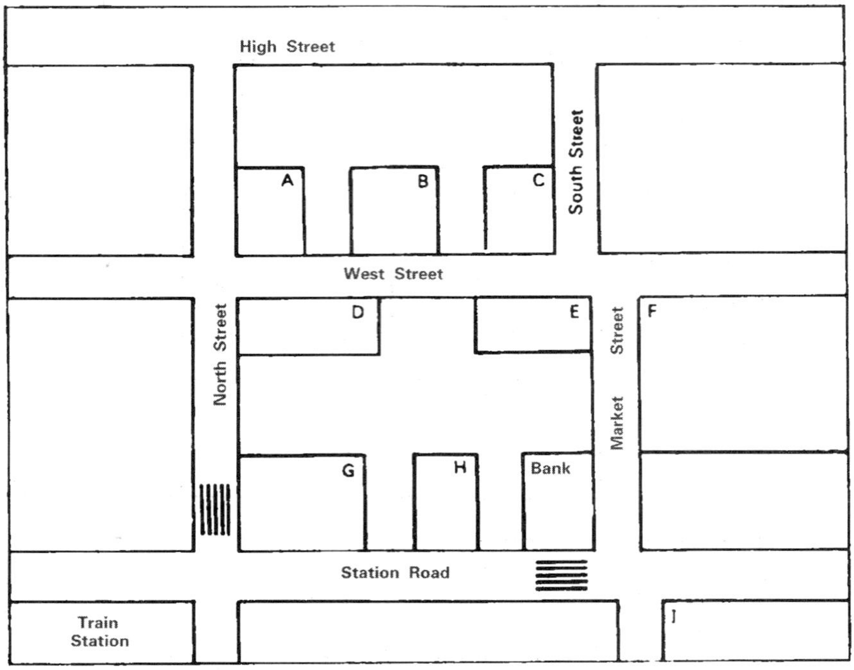

1. the bookshop ____________
2. the coffee bar ____________
3. the chemist's ____________
4. the hotel ____________
5. the art museum ____________

Listening Activity No. 12

Look at the map below. You will hear six separate sets of directions to a certain place on the street plan. As you listen, follow the directions carefully, then write the appropriate letters beside the names of the places below. The first one starts at the car park.

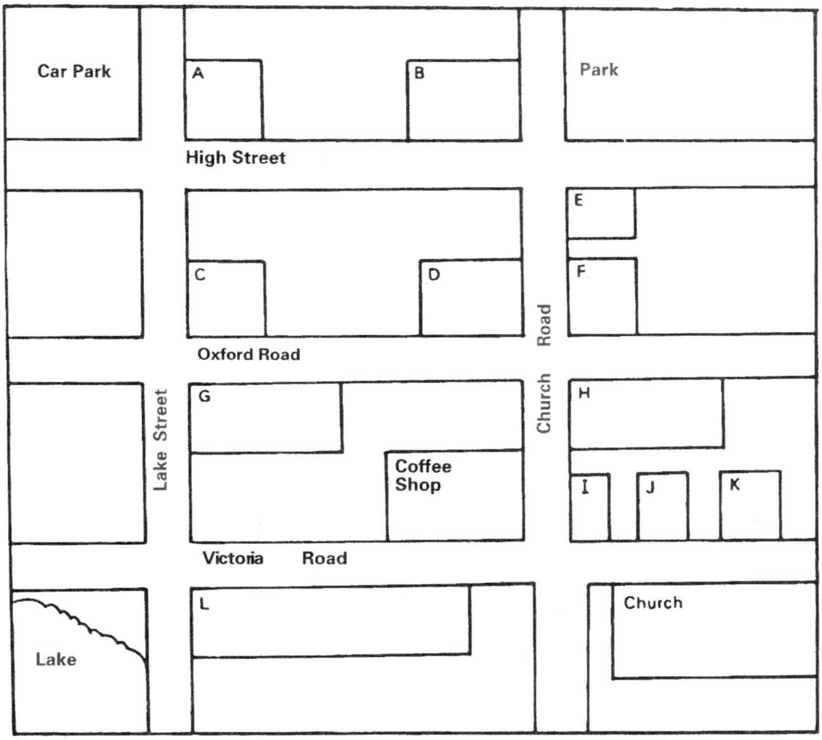

1. the post office ____________
2. the bank ____________
3. the Windsor Hotel ____________
4. the Chinese restaurant ____________
5. the newsagent's ____________
6. the grocer's ____________

Listening Activity No. 13

You are going to listen to a conversation between Janet and her friend. Janet is telling her friend about her holidays. As you listen, write down brief notes in the boxes below about her holiday.

Day	What she did
Saturday	
Sunday	
Monday	
Tuesday	
Wednesday	
Thursday	
Friday	
Saturday	

Listening Activity No. 14

Task 1

You will hear a dialogue between two students. One of them is describing a route on the map. Draw a line to show the route taken. If the student went inside any of that place named on the map, mark that place with a cross (×).

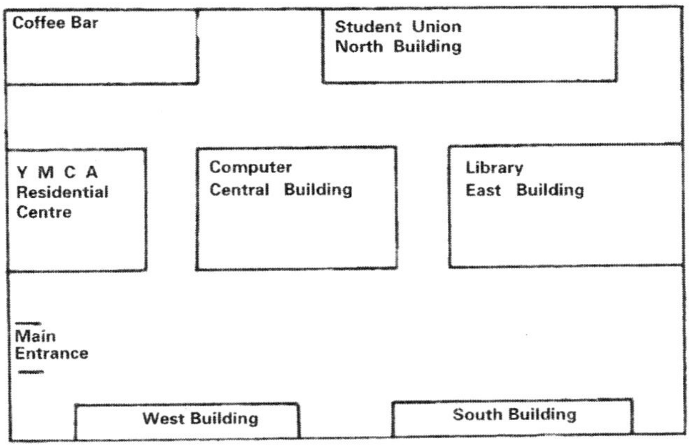

Task 2

Listen to the conversation again and list the places the student went to, and then write the reasons the student went to these places.

	Place	Reason
Example:	*West Building*	*to register*
	1.	
	2.	
	3.	
	4.	

Listening Activity No. 15

You are going to listen to a talk about children's safety at home. Look at the table below. Listen to the talk and fill in the missing information in the correct column.

	What children can see	What children can't see	What children can find	What children can do
At home	pan handles, lead on the kettle	panes of glass in doors or screens, things left on the floor	medicine, household cleaners	climb the stairs and don't know how to get down
The dangers		trip or fall over things	can't tell the difference	

What can you do:

1. You can help keep them safe by planning ________ and making the right ________.
2. You can ________ medicines and make it more difficult for children to ________ or grab hot things.
3. You should turn ________ away from the front of the cooker.
4. You'd better ________ all fires and heaters.
5. You should use ________ on stairs and teach them how to go ________ the stairs.

Listening Activity No. 16

Look at the picture on the sheet in front of you. This is Kevin's bed-sitting room. He is describing his room to his friend. As you listen, draw in the furniture in the right places in the picture, using a square or a circle to mark in the furniture as described. Just a quick sketch will do.

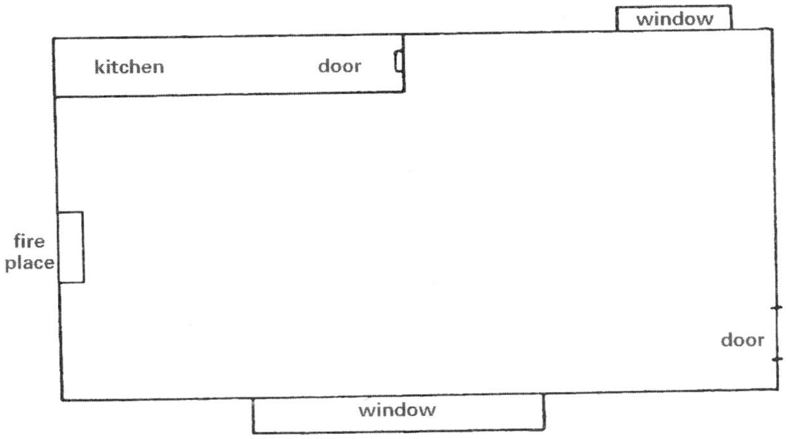

Listening Activity No. 17

Sally bought a new house a few days ago in a small village. She is phoning her friend Richard and inviting him for dinner at the weekend. Sally is giving directions to get to her house. Look at the map. As you listen, take notes and mark Sally's house with a cross (×).

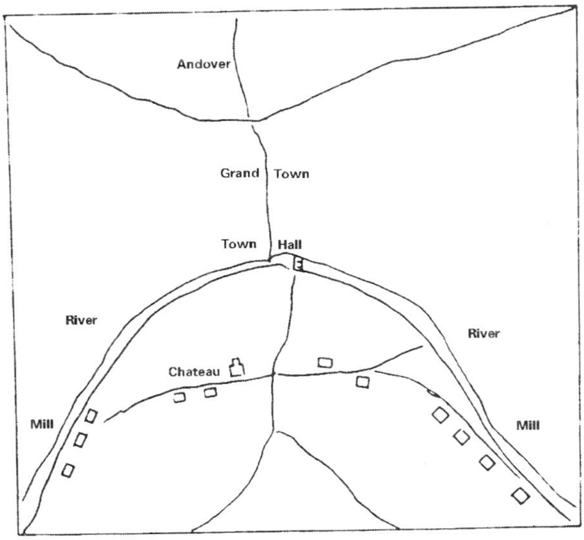

Listening Activity No. 18

Read the timetable below and study it by yourself for a few minutes. Find out what the following symbols and letters mean.

You are going to listen to five conversations between a new information officer and passengers. Look at the timetable and check whether the information officer provides correct information or not by writing T for true and F for false beside each number.

Conversation 1 ______________ Conversation 2 ______________
Conversation 3 ______________ Conversation 4 ______________
Conversation 5 ______________

INTERCITY
London→Nottingham
Principal train service 2 October 1989 to 13 May 1990

Mondays to Saturdays			Sundays		
	London St. Pancras depart	Nottingham arrive		London St. Pancras depart	Nottingham arrive
▲	0730 sx	0914	B	1030	1247
●	0730 so	0924	C	1030	1300
▲ ×	0830 sx	1009	B	1230	1450
	0900 so	1043	C	1230	1456
×	0925 sx	1113		1430	1652
	1030	1206		1635	1837
	1130 sx	1310		1735	1927
	1200 so	1342		1835	2031
	1225 sx	1409		1935	2126
	1330 sx	1507	●	2035	2227
	1330 so	1524	●	2205	0010
	1430 sx	1610		2305	0109
	1500 so	1654			
	1525 sx	1702			
	1630 so	1823			
■	1630 fsx	1824			
▼	1630 fo	1824			
■	1705 fsx	1849			
▼	1705 fo	1849			
■ ×	1725 fsx	1901			
▼ ×	1725 fo	1901			
	1730 so	1918			
	1830	2010			
	1930 sx	2113			
	2000 so	2159			
	2040 sx	2222			
D	2100 so b	2340			
A ●	2200 so	2352			
●	2300 sx	0023			
●	2330 sx	0124			
A ●	2330 so	0131			

Notes

A Until 16 December and from 31 March
B Until 17 December and from 1 April
C 24 December to 25 March
D From 23 December
b Change at Derby
fo Fridays only
fxs Fridays and Saturdays excepted
so Saturdays only
sx Saturdays excepted

All services shown in this timetable are InterCity unless otherwise stated.

InterCity services offer First Class and Standard accommodation, light food and hot and cold drinks and reserved seats.

× Service of meals including hot food to customers travelling first Class (and Standard, provided accommodation is available).

▲ OUTWARD portions of SAVER tickets are NOT valid on this train.

▼ RETURN portions of SAVER tickets are NOT valid on this train.

■ SAVERS are NOT valid on this train.

● NOT an InterCity service. First Class accommodation available.

Listening Activity No. 19

Look at the graph below. This graph shows the number of people who visited London Zoo, Kew Gardens and Regent's Park from 1978 to 1987. Mark in the names London Zoo, Kew Gardens and Regent's Park on the appropriate lines on the graph.

(Numbers shown in thousand)

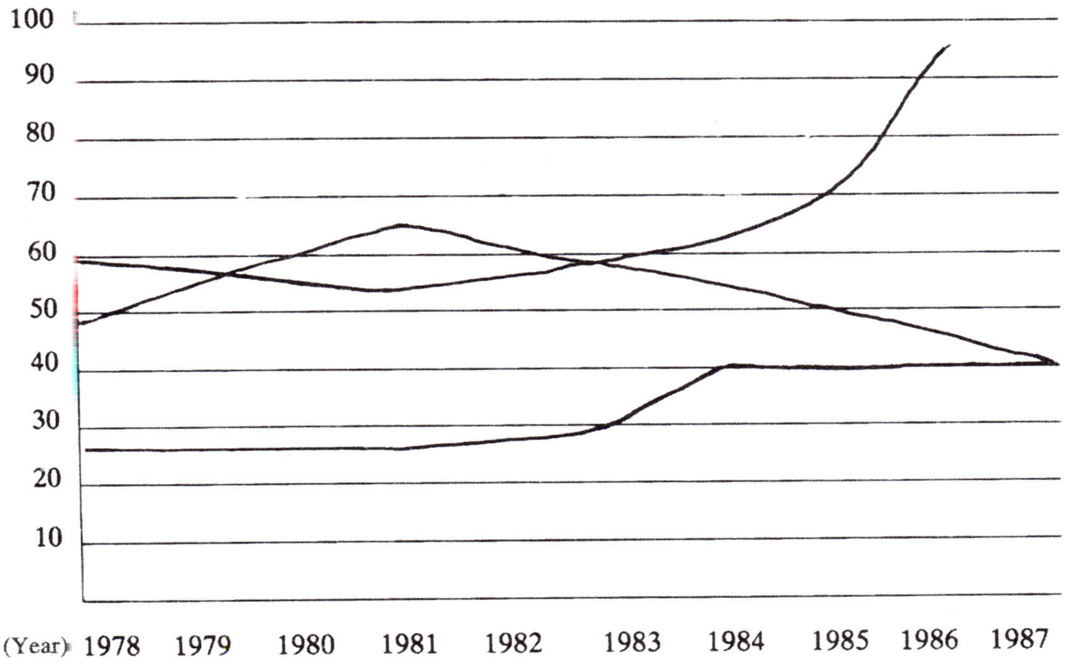

Listening Activity No. 20

Look at the graph below. This one shows the numbers of visitors to the Exhibition Center, the Museum and the Art Gallery. Mark in the names Exhibition centre, Museum and Art Galley on the appropriate lines on the graph.

(Numbers shown in thousand)

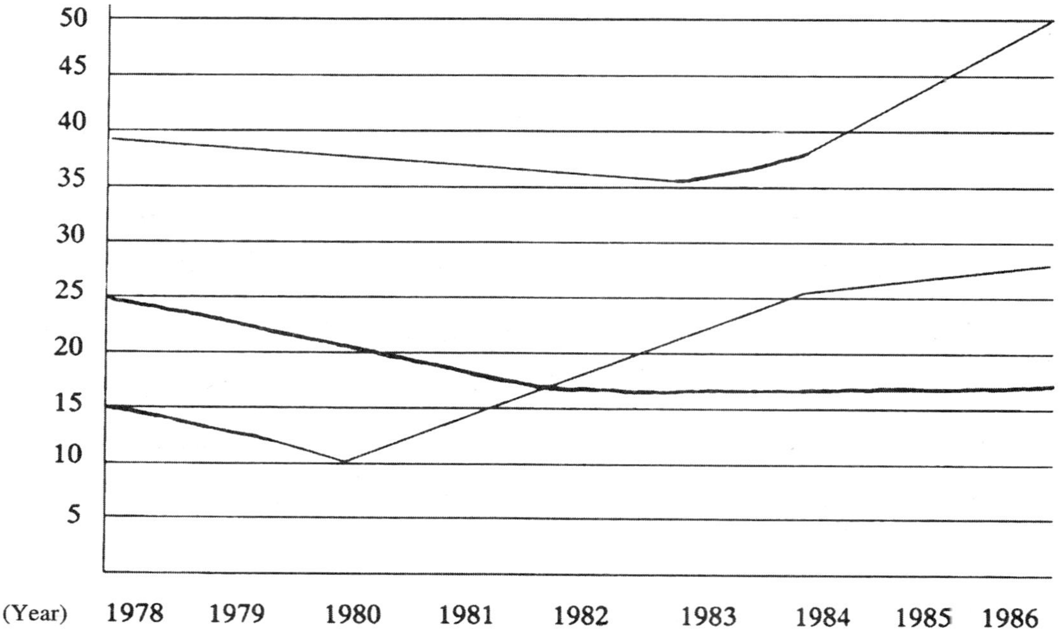

Unit Four

Answering Questions and Multiple Choice

——Listening for Meaning

本单元共有 20 个练习。内容多为国外生活中常会遇到的日常生活场景，如找工作、旅馆订房、去银行等；也有一些国外学习的场景，如与导师谈话、学校图书馆、学生会的职能等。

本单元的练习形式包括了雅思听力考试出现的多种题型，例如：完成句子（Sentence completion）、回答问题（Answer questions）、多项选择（Multiple choice）、判断句子准确与否或未提及（Accurate/Inaccurate/Not given）。本单元的每个练习都相当于 IELTS 听力试题的一个部分（Section），通过多种题型的变化来检查考生的听力理解能力。

本单元的目的是通过多样化的练习形式帮助考生了解和熟悉 IELTS 听力考试的不同题型，培养考生的应试能力以及在听英语会话、讲座和报告中捕捉重要信息的能力。

建议考生在听之前，要认真审题。根据 IELTS 听力考试的要求，每个部分之前都有 30 秒钟的读题时间。考生要充分利用这 30 秒钟时间。可用前 10 秒钟快速阅读该部分所有的题，以便了解该部分都有什么题；再用后 20 秒钟认真阅读前 3 ~4 道题，以求理解并记住，这样做题时就有针对性。此外，听力材料中的信息有时不按问题的顺序出现，如果能多记住几道问题，就不会漏掉问题点。同时，切记不要只盯一道题。

Listening Activity No. 1

Indicate whether the following statements are true or false by writing T for true, F for false and N if the statement is not mentioned.

1. A man is calling from home.
2. He has been phoning for about 15 minutes.
3. The man dialed a wrong number.
4. The man keeps making a funny noise.
5. The man hasn't put enough money in the phone box.
6. The operator said the lines were overloaded.
7. The problem is because of crossed lines.
8. The man got through after talking to the operator.
9. The man is calling a friend in Manchester.

Listening Activity No. 2

Answer the questions by writing up to three words or a number.

1. Which session of the conference is it?

   ____

2. Which room will the grammar session be held in?

   ____

3. Where should people return their keys?

   ____

Circle the appropriate letter.

4. What should be returned to the session chairpeople?
   A. Discussion handouts.
   B. Tape recorders.

C. Discussion records.

D. Section recorders.

5. By what time does the speaker want people to gather to take the 3:30 buses?

A. 2:30.

B. 3:15.

C. 3:30.

D. 3:25.

6. Where should people gather to take the buses?

A. Outside the airport.

B. Outside Room 203.

C. Outside the main building.

D. Outside Room 302.

7. Who is not asked to collect reprints from the conference desk?

A. Professor Hurst.

B. Professor Cole.

C. Professor Malnachurk.

D. Professor Olsen.

Indicate whether the following statements are accurate or not by writing

A for an accurate statement;

I for an inaccurate statement;

N if the information is not given.

8. Professor Olsen is from the Leeds University.

9. The sixth Annual Convention of EFL will be held soon.

10. All people have to leave their names at the conference desk.

Listening Activity No. 3

Answer the questions by writing a few words.

1. Whom is the letter for?

____

2. What does the mother complain about?

____

Circle the appropriate letter.

3. How much is the phone bill for 3 months?
   A. £30.94　　B. £140.44
   C. £130.94　　D. £300.44
4. The phone calls are more expensive
   A. between midnight and 6 am.　　B. in the evenings.
   C. after 6 pm.　　D. before 6 pm.

Indicate whether the following statements are accurate or not by writing

A　for an accurate statement;
I　for an inaccurate statement;
N　if the information is not given.

5. Jane works on Saturdays.
6. Jane has to use the phone box down the road.
7. The phone box down the road is expensive.
8. Jane has to pay half of the bill.

Listening Activity No.4

Complete the statements below.

1. Underground tickets are available at ________.
2. Ticket prices for the underground vary according to the travel ________.

Answer the question.

3. How many zones are within the travelcard area? ________

Circle the appropriate letter(s).

4. Where can you get travelcards?
   A. At travel agencies　　B. At train stations.
   C. At underground stations.　　D. At bus stops.
5. What time can the travelcards be bought?
   A. Anytime during the day.　　B. After 9:30 at weekends.
   C. Anytime at weekends.　　D. After 9:30 am on weekdays.

Indicate whether the following statements are accurate or not by writing

A　for an accurate statement;
I　for an inaccurate statement;
N　if the information is not given.

6. The easiest and most economical way to travel around London is with a travelcard.
7. You need a passport for a travelcard season ticket.
8. Smoking is allowed on the underground.

Listening Activity No.5

Complete the statements below.

1. They are talking about a job at a ________________.
2. The company is seeking ____________________.

Answer the following questions.

3. What does the company provided for people to travel in? ________________
4. What does the company offer in addition to a salary? ________________

Circle the appropriate letter.

5. The job offers excellent prospects for
   A. a retired person.
   B. a person who has a car.
   C. a young person with ambition and enthusiasm.
   D. a young person with ambition and experience.

Indicate whether the following statements are accurate or not by writing

A for an accurate statement;
I for an inaccurate statement;
N if the information is not given.

6. The applicant must write to the personnel manager.
7. The man is interested in the job.
8. The applicant has to be good on a team.

Listening Activity No.6

Answer the questions by writing a word.

1. Who is Mike talking about? ________________
2. What was the first complaint about Mike? ________________

Circle the appropriate letter.

3. Mike often talks about
   A. his difficulties at his house. B. finding a place to live.
   C. the parties he went to. D. his friend's house.
4. Mike wants to move, but he wants to live
   A. alone. B. in a quiet place.
   C. near the school. D. with his parents.
5. How many people live in Tom's house besides Tom?
   A. 2 B. 3
   C. 4 D. 5
6. The expenses which Tom and his housemates share do not include
   A. food. B. rent.
   C. light. D. heating.
7. If Mike goes to live with Tom, he will likely have
   A. more food. B. more expense.
   C. more noise. D. more freedom.

Write a word or a number in the spaces provided.

8. What day is it when Tom and Mike are talking? ________________
9. On what date will Jane vacate her room? ________________
10. When is Mike moving into the house? ________________

Listening Activity No. 7

Answer the questions by writing up to three words.

1. When did the researcher finish her survey? ____________
2. What do the science students complain about? ____________
3. Circle the complaints that students made about the library catalogues.
   A. They are too complicated.　　B. They are incomplete.
   C. They are really bad.　　D. They are out of date.

Circle the appropriate letter(s).

4. When the chief librarian heard the criticisms, he indicated it might be possible to
   A. buy some new books.
   B. change the librarians there.
   C. check all the cards and reprint them where necessary.
   D. change to a computer system.
5. How much would it cost to do the first option?
   A. About £1 000.　　B. About £6 000.
   C. About £60 000.　　D. About £600.

Indicate whether the following statements are accurate or not by writing

A　for an accurate statement;
I　for an inaccurate statement;
N　if the information is not given.

6. It would take about a year to change the catalogue system to a computer system.
7. The chief librarian suggested two possible ways to improve the catalogue system.
8. The chief librarian agreed to try to improve the borrowing facilities as well.

Listening Activity No. 8

Answer the following questions by writing up to three words.

1. Where does the student come from? ____________________
2. How long has the student been in this country? ____________________
3. What is the student studying at the moment? ____________________

Circle the correct answer.

4. What does the student worry about now?
   A. His English study hours.
   B. That her qualifications may not be accepted here.
   C. Her working experience in her own country.
   D. Her tutoring at school.
5. What kind of course does the counsellor suggest the student to apply for?
   A. Civil engineering diploma course.
   B. Master's degree in English.
   C. English diploma.
   D. Master's in engineering.

Write up to three words in the spaces provided.

6. Did the student study engineering at a university? ____________________
7. How long did the student work for a big company? ____________________
8. When does the counsellor suggest the student apply for a degree course?
   ____

Listening Activity No.9

Answer the questions by writing a few words.

1. Where are all student services to be found at the college?

____

2. Are all students automatically members of the Student Union?

____

3. What document do the students need to get their student cards?

____

4. Where do students go to get their student cards?

____

Circle the appropriate letter(s).

5. When is the student health centre open?
   A. From 9:30 to 8:45 on weekdays.
   B. From 9:30 to 5:00 on Fridays.
   C. From 9:30 to 5:00 on weekdays.
   D. From 9:30 to 8:45 Monday to Thursday.
6. Circle the days when Dr. B. Kearns hold a surgery in the Medical Centre.
   A. Monday and Tuesday mornings.
   B. All weekdays mornings except Friday.
   C. Either Wednesday or Friday afternoons.
   D. Thursday afternoons.
7. Whom do students have to register with if they stay in England?
   A. A college doctor. B. Dr. B. Kearns.
   C. A local doctor. D. A hospital doctor.

Indicate whether the following statements are accurate or not by writing

A for an accurate statement;

I for an inaccurate statement;

N if the information is not given.

8. The nurses will make appointments for you.
9. Dr. Kearns can be found at her surgery any time during the day.
10. Dr. Kearns' surgery is located at No. 2 Ascott Avenue, W5.

Listening Activity No. 10

Answer the following questions by writing a number or up to three words.

1. Who is Ms. Penny Rawson? ____________
2. What is Ms. Rawson going to discuss? ____________
3. How many counsellors are there in the college? ____________
4. Are counsellors full-time at the college? ____________
5. Circle the ways students are referred to the counsellors.
   A. By themselves.
   B. By their parents.
   C. By their teachers.
   D. By a tutor.

Circle the appropriate letter.

6. How do counsellors meet students?
   A. See the students only individually.
   B. See the students only in groups.
   C. See the students in any way necessary.
   D. See the students only in the courses.

Indicate whether the following statements are accurate or not by writing
A for an accurate statement;
I for an inaccurate statement;
N if the information is not given.

7. Counselling Service can solve all students' problems.
8. Counselling Service is a confidential service.
9. Counselling Service has a small fee.
10. No one, according to Ms. Rawson, ever has problems at this university.

Listing Activity No. 11

Complete the following statements by filling in the relevant words.

1. Susan will be a ____________ student.
2. She wants to keep her money in a safe place with easy ____________.
3. She is suggested to open an ____________ Account.

Circle the appropriate letter(s).

4. A current account provides the following facilities:
   A. a chequebook　　B. a cashcard
   C. a deposit book　　D. all of the above
5. If the balance is £500 or over the interest is
   A. 5.25%.　　B. 2.55%.
   C. 7.25%.　　D. 7.55%.
6. Money can be withdrawn with
   A. a chequebook.　　B. a cash card.
   C. an ID card.　　D. a passport.

Indicate whether the following statements are accurate or not by writing

A　for an accurate statement;
I　for an inaccurate statement;
N　if the information is not given.

7. The bank statement tells you how much money is in your account.
8. The bank statement provides you with a permanent record of income only.
9. You can ask your bank about your statement by telephone.
10. You can use a cashcard to check the balance.

Listening Activity No. 12

Complete the statements below. Use up to three words.

1. Mrs. Jane Smith is ________________.
2. Mrs. Smith would like to talk about ________________.
3. Where is Peter presently working? ________________

Circle the appropriate letter.

4. Peter has had his present job
   A. since 2002. B. for more than three years.
   C. for three months. D. since 2003.
5. The reason he wants a new job is
   A. for a change. B. to earn more money.
   C. to get a promotion. D. to have a new challenge.
6. The thing he likes most about his present job is
   A. the responsibility. B. good salary.
   C. his colleagues. D. working conditions.

Indicate whether the following statements are accurate or not by writing
A for an accurate statement;
I for an inaccurate statement;
N if the information is not given.

7. They are looking for someone prepared to work overtime.
8. Peter graduated from Leeds University.
9. Peter has a diploma in design.
10. Peter will get the new job.

Listening Activity No. 13

Complete the statements below.

1. In Britain a foreign student can get treatment from the British Medical Scheme if the student's course of study is for ________.
2. For a long-term student, treatment in British hospitals is ________.

Answer the following question by writing a short phrase in the space provided.

3. What should the student do first if he wishes to join the British Medical Scheme?

____

Circle the appropriate letter.

4. Where can you find lists of doctors?
   A. From the Student Union office. B. From local post offices.
   C. From the registration's office. D. From the university medical clinic.
5. Give two ways to find out a doctor's consulting hours.
   A. ________________
   B. ________________

Indicate whether the following statements are accurate or not by writing
A for an accurate statement;
I for an inaccurate statement;
N if the information is not given.

6. Casualty or emergency treatment is free for everyone in all hospitals.
7. A dentist can choose whether or not to accept a patient for NHS treatment.
8. A private patient will pay the full cost of dental treatment.
9. Dentists like to check patients' teeth once a month.
10. Basic dental treatment is a minimum of 17 pounds.

Listening Activity No. 14

Answer the following questions and complete the statements below. Use no more than three words for each answer.

1. The college's first aim is to be a ________________ institution.
2. The college judges people on their ________________ and commitment to study as much as ________________.
3. Circle the statements about the students that the director has mentioned.
   A. Some students are seeking specific skills.
   B. Some are learning about the latest scientific knowledge.
   C. Some are seeking to develop their artistic abilities.
   D. Some are stretching their bodies.
4. How many teachers and staff are there at the college?
   A. 500 B. 800 C. 1000 D. 1500
5. Which word best describes the director's speech?
   A. Informative. B. Depressing.
   C. Inspiring. D. Amusing.

Write a word in the space provided.

6. Is it a congratulation speech? ________________

Indicate whether the following statements are accurate or not by writing
A for an accurate statement;
I for an inaccurate statement;
N if the information is not given.

7. You may find a suitable course at the polytechnic college.
8. The college specializes in a narrow range of subject areas.
9. The college has a homogeneous student body.
10. The college has the longest history of any school in its community.

Listening Activity No. 15

Complete the following statements by filling in a relevant word or a number.

1. Bell College is one of a group of schools run by the Bell Educational Trust, a ______________ educational foundation.
2. The College offers an attractive environment for study and leisure for students aged ______________ or over.

Answer the following questions with a word or a number as required.

3. How many students live on campus? ______________
4. How many students live off campus? ______________

Circle the appropriate letter(s).

5. What areas of study do the courses offer?
   A. English for Industrial Training. B. English Programme.
   C. Teacher Training. D. Social Studies.
6. How many nationalities are there in the college?
   A. 13. B. 30 or more.
   C. 50. D. 50 or more.

Indicate whether the following statements are accurate or not by writing
A for an accurate statement;
I for an inaccurate statement;
N if the information is not given.

7. Teachers in the college are from many parts of the world.
8. According to the college policy teachers from Rwanda are presently not welcome.
9. The college has its own medical centre.
10. The college provides cultural and social activities only on weekends.

Listening Activity No. 16

Complete the statements below. Use up to three words.

1. Peter asks Anna to do him a ________________.
2. Peter is going to visit ________________.
3. Peter will be away for ________________.
4. Circle the animal that Anna is being asked to look after.
   A. rabbits　　B. birds
   C. cats　　D. dogs
5. Circle the things that Peter wants Anna to do.
   A. To look after a pregnant animal.
   B. To buy a box of cat food.
   C. To feed the animals.
   D. To wash the animals every day.

Circle the correct answer.

6. How many babies did one of the animals have last time?
   A. 2　　B. 4　　C. 5　　D. 6
7. When Peter mentioned that one of the animals is going to be delivering soon, Anna was
   A. happy.　　B. worried.
   C. sad.　　D. angry.

Indicate whether the following statements are accurate or not by writing

A　for an accurate statement;
I　for an inaccurate statement;
N　if the information is not given.

8. The mother cat eat only cat food. ________________
9. Peter will bring a box of cat food. ________________
10. One of the cats is a male. ________________

Listening Activity No. 17

Complete the following statements below.

1. Our health is affected by ____________________.
2. Safeway tries to help customers not only in the range and types of food offered, but also by providing up-to-date reliable ________________.
3. Circle the reasons given for using less sugar.
   A. For the sake of our eyes. B. For the sake of our body's weight.
   C. For the sake of our teeth. D. For the sake of our livers.
4. Which of the following attacks the tooth itself?
   A. Carbohydrates. B. Saliva.
   C. Acid. D. Plaque.

Write a short phrase in the space provided.

5. What is the worst thing you can do to your teeth?

   ____

Indicate whether the following statements are accurate or not by writing

A for an accurate statement;
I for an inaccurate statement;
N if the information is not given.

6. The speaker advises people to stop taking sugar at once.
7. The speaker suggests choosing snacks carefully.
8. The speaker suggests substituting yogurt for sugar.
9. The speaker suggests cutting back on the sugar you use in baking.
10. The speaker is a dentist.

Listening Activity No. 18

Complete the following statements by filling in a relevant word or a number.

1. An au pair is a single girl without any dependants who comes to UK to learn English and to live as ____________ of an English speaking family.
2. An au pair may help in the house for up to ____________ hours a day for pocket money.
3. Circle the suitable tasks that an au pair may do in the house.
   A. Dusting the house. B. Painting the house.
   C. Taking care of children. D. Mowing lawn.
4. How much money should be given as pocket money?
   A. 14 to 20 pounds a week. B. 15 to 20 pounds a week.
   C. 15 to 20 pounds a month. D. 50 to 60 pounds a month.
5. An au pair must be a single girl aged
   A. under 17. B. under 27.
   C. more than 27. D. between 17 and 27.
6. Circle the appropriate nationalities for an au pair.
   A. Japanese B. French
   C. Turkish D. Russia

Indicate whether the following statements are accurate or not by writing
A for an accurate statement;
I for an inaccurate statement;
N if the information is not given.

7. A girl who has been in the UK before as an au pair will be allowed to come to the UK again as an au pair even if the total period is more than 2 years.
8. An au pair who is from the Commonwealth or EC will have to register with the police if she stays longer than 6 months.
9. An au pair may change host families during her time in the UK.
10. Write 2 possible ways for an au pair to apply for a longer stay in the UK.
    A. ______________________________
    B. ______________________________

Listening Activity No. 19

Answer the questions by writing a word or a number.

1. Which month would the customers like to book a holiday for? ____________
2. Do they know exactly where they want to go for their holiday? ____________

Circle the appropriate letter.

3. When will both customers be free to travel?
   A. The first week of July.
   B. The whole month except for the last five days.
   C. From the first to the twenty-third of July.
   D. From the seventh to the twenty-third of July .
4. Which country did the two customers visit last year?
   A. Italy. B. Sweden.
   C. France. D. Portugal.
5. How long did the customers want for their holiday?
   A. A week. B. Ten days.
   C. Two weeks. D. Four weeks.
6. Why don't the customers want to go to Italy?
   A. Because there are too many young people.
   B. Because it would be too hot.
   C. Because they've been there.
   D. Because the dates don't suit them.
7. Circle the reason that they don't like to go to Sweden.
   A. Too expensive. B. Too hot.
   C. No beaches. D. Not enough facilities.

Indicate whether the following statements are accurate or not by writing
A for an accurate statement;
I for an inaccurate statement;
N if the information is not given.

8. The customers prefer to visit Portugal by flight from London.
9. It would be 385 pounds for them to visit Portugal.
10. The customers have decided where to go for the holiday.

Listening Activity No. 20

Answer the following questions by writing a few words in the spaces provided.

1. What was the name of the popular song during the 1930s mentioned in the talk?

____

2. When was tea first imported to Britain?

____

Circle the appropriate letter(s).

3. When did the first coffee house offer tea?
   A. In 1760. B. In 1716.
   C. In 1706. D. In 1786.
4. Who was the owner of Tom's Coffee House?
   A. Lloyds. B. The Golden Lion.
   C. An insurance company. D. Thomas Twining.
5. What was on the sign of the tea shop owned by Twining?
   A. The Golden Lion. B. The Strand.
   C. The Tea Shop. D. Twining.
6. Circle the items which a comprehensive eighteenth century tea-tray would consist of.
   A. Glasses and spoons. B. A teapot and stand.
   C. A sugar bowl and a milk jug. D. Cups and saucers.
7. Where was tea kept by the mistress of the house?
   A. In basins. B. In locked wooden commodes.
   C. In metal kettles. D. In locked caddies.

Answer the questions in the spaces provided.

8. How were late-afternoon hunger pangs alleviated?

____

9. When was tea first imported from India?

____

Complete the following statements.

10. Tea from Ceylon, India and ______________ gives the broad range of teas that are ______________ today.
11. There have been few changes in ______________ centuries of tea trading.
12. Twinings still has a shop on the site of the original coffee shop at ______________.
13. The name Twining has been linked with tea for over ______________ years.

Answer the following questions.

14. Who persuaded the Prime Minister to reduce the high tax on tea in 1784?

____

15. Who was the Prime Minster in 1784?

____

Unit Five

Note Completion and True/False

——Listening for Details

本单元共有 20 个练习。内容选自国外生活中常会遇到的日常生活场景及有关国外学习的场景。

本单元的练习形式包括了雅思听力试题中曾出现的两种题型。一种是摘要填空题（Summary or Notes Completion）。摘要填空题是根据所听文章内容或部分段落内容给出一段或多段留有空格的内容概要，要求考生根据所听内容填补缺少的信息，以测试其对所听文章的理解及捕捉具体信息的能力。答案常可从所听内容中直接找出。

另一种是正误判断题（True/False/?）这种题要求考生根据所听文章内容所提供的信息对一些陈述句做出正、误判断。如果句子内容与文章内容相符，答案是 TRUE；如果句子内容与文章内容不符，答案是 FALSE；如果句子内容根据文章中提供的信息不足以判断正误，就用问号（?）表示。

本单元通过大量练习帮助考生了解和熟悉考试的题型，培养考生的应试能力及在听英语会话、讲座和报告中捕捉重要信息的能力和边听边记的能力。

建议考生在听之前把题或短文读一遍，并根据上下文推断要填的词，这样才能在听的过程中有针对性地去寻找所需要的关键词。

Listening Activity No. 1

You are going to listen to a talk about Student Coach Cards. As you listen, fill the missing words in the banks.

If you are a student in 1. ________________ education or aged 2. ________________, you can get a Student Coach Card for only 3. ____________. It will save you 4. ________________ off standard fares throughout Britain on National Express and Scottish Citylink services. You even get this 5. ________________ on Midweek Returns. It also entitles you to 6. ________________ off some continental services and to discounts on some Oxford Citylink and Invictaway services. A Student Coach Card lasts for a full 7. ________________ months with no restrictions. Student Coach Cards can 8. ________________ at Student Travel 9. ________________, many National Express and Scottish Citylink agents or by 10. ________________ simply by completing the attached coupon.

Listening Activity No. 2

You are going to listen to a talk about telephone services. Listen carefully and fill the missing words in the blanks.

Alarm calls, to wake you up in the 1. ______________, should be booked before 2. ______________ the previous evening. Transferred charge calls are 3. ______________ where the people you want to speak to 4. ______________ to pay for your call to them. Transferred charge calls can also be 5. ______________ to many countries 6. ______________. Personal calls are those where you tell the operator 7. ______________ of the person you wish to 8. ______________. You are not connected if that person 9. ______________ found, though a message can be 10. ______________ for him or her to ring the operator later. This service is normally 11. ______________ for international calls as well.

For emergency calls, if you want the police, fire or ambulance services in an emergency, dial 12. ______________. Tell the operator the 13. ______________ you want. Give your exchange and number or all figure number as appropriate. Wait until the emergency 14. ______________ answers. Then give them the full address where help is needed and other necessary information. 999 calls are 15. ______________.

Listening Activity No. 3

You are going to hear a talk about bats . Listen carefully and fill the missing words in the blanks.

James Austin is a(n) 1. ________________ researcher. His talk is about bats. Bats are black creatures which hang 2. ________________ and fly in the dark. Now they become more 3. ________________ because they can eat mosquitoes up to 4. ________________ in an hour. So many people want them 5. ________________.

Indicate whether the following statements are true or not by writing

T **for a statement which is true;**
F **for a statement which is false;**
? **if there is insufficient information.**

6. People build bat houses on their roof in summer.
7. People don't really know what bats look like.
8. Bat houses should be dark and hot.
9. Bat houses should be 12 to 15 feet off the ground.
10. People prefer to use chemicals to get rid of mosquitoes.

Listening Activity No.4

You are going to hear a conversation between a salesman and a customer. Listen carefully and write down the missing information in the notes below.

Patricia bought a videocassette recorder 1. ______________ ago. She phoned the shop and told them that she has some problems with 2. ______________. One of the problems is that the VCR won't 3. ______________ when she sets the timer. The other one is that she can't find 4. ______________.

Indicate whether the following statements are true or not by writing

T for a statement which is true;
F for a statement which is false;
? if there is insufficient information.

5. The VCR has got a one-year guarantee.
6. Patricia has got the salesman's name.
7. The salesman knows the customer.
8. Patricia should bring in the receipt when she goes back to the shop.
9. The salesman has to report to his manager about it.
10. The salesman will be there when Patricia goes back.

Listening Activity No.5

You will hear a dialogue. As you listen, fill the missing words in the gaps in the notes below.

Mr. Smith comes to London for a 1. ______________. He will stay there for 2. ______________ of months with 3. ______________ pounds. He wants to open an account. He is suggested to open a Higher Rate Deposit Account which requires 4. ______________ to open the account. Its interest is 5. ______________ on net and 6. ______________ on gross.

Indicate whether the following statements are true or not by writing

T for a statement which is true;

F for a statement which is false;

? if there is insufficient information.

7. A Higher Rate Deposit Account is calculated and paid monthly.
8. He can get a special card to his cash money.
9. The rate of interest will go down to 5.52% if it has savings go below five hundred pounds.
10. the Higher Rate Deposit Account allows people to be five hundred pounds overdrawn.

Listening Activity No.6

You are going to hear a talk from a course director. As you listen, fill in the gaps below.

There is a variety of opinions about 1. ________________ that should exist within initial teacher education between 2. ________________ in school and the study of the disciplines of education. It is our conviction that beginning teachers need to 3. ________________ on ideas about the aims and methods of education, but we believe more strongly that 4. ____________ of teaching is best learnt in school, working with 5. ____________ teachers.

Indicate whether the following statements are true or not by writing

T for a statement which is true;

F for a statement which is false;

? if there is insufficient information.

6. The director provides a general introduction to the course at Sussex.
7. All of the teaching takes place in small group seminars and workshops.
8. The course director is one of the interviewers.
9. All applicants will be interviewed before places are offered.

Listening Activity No. 7

You are going to hear an announcement. As you listen, fill in the gaps numbered 1-5 in the notes below.

Ladies and gentlemen,

We are arriving at Cambridge now, and there are a few things you need to remember. First, remove all 1. ________________ from the coach because we can't guarantee their safety. Second, note 2. ________________ on the front of the coach, so it can be recognized in the coach park. Third, stay with your own 3. ________________. Don't wander off as the town is large and people can 4. ________________ get lost. Photographs can only be 5. ________________ at certain points, so obey your guide's instructions.

Indicate whether the following statements are true or not by writing

T **for a statement which is true;**
F **for a statement which is false;**
? **if there is insufficient information.**

6. The speaker is an airline flight attendant.
7. The speaker will be guiding a group of tourists through the town.
8. The coach will leave for the park at 6:15.

Listening Activity No. 8

Debby buys a newspaper and then goes to the cafe. she sits next to a man and they discuss the gales. As you listen to their conversation, fill in the gaps in the notes below.

Here is the news about the gales. It says gales reaching 90 mph swept 1. ________________ last night as two more days of wind and rain were forecast. In the 2. ________________, gusts had been recorded of 94 mph in Aberporth, southwest 3. ________________. 82 mph in the Cairngorms in

4. ________________ and 78 mph in Camborne, Cornwall. The Clarence Esplanade at Southsea, Hampshire, was 5. ________________ due to fears that walkers could be swept over 6. ________________.

Indicate whether the following statements are true or not by writing

T for a statement which is true;

F for a statement which is false;

? if there is insufficient information.

7. Police in London had warned people not to travel unless their journey was essential.
8. 3 000 houses were blown down.
9. A 33 000 volt cable was damaged because of the gales.
10. Engineers battled to restore electricity supplies to 3 000 customers in Scotland.

Listening Activity No.9

You will hear a dialogue between two friends. As you listen, fill the missing words in the notes below.

There was a lot of traffic in Chase Village 1. ________________ years ago. People drove too fast. Richard had a very serious 2. ________________ on Newland Street. He was afraid to drive there so he always tries to 3. ________________ that road when he visits his sister. But now things are 4. ________________. People put on their brakes and 5. ________________ on Newland Street because they can see a 6. ________________ there.

Indicate whether the following statements are true or not by writing

T for a statement which is true;

F for a statement which is false;

? if there is insufficient information.

7. Now some people still take a risk when the police officer is away on Newland Street.
8. The police officer there doesn't get any pay for the work.
9. Officer Springirth is a real man and he is a volunteer there.
10. Officer Springirth helps the police to reduce the crime rate in Chase Village.
11. The police department will put more mannequins on other roads.

Listening Activity No. 10

You will hear some advice from a British programme adviser. As you listen, fill in the gaps with the relevant words in the notes below.

When you first arrive in Britain you will be given the name and telephone extension number of the 1. ________________ who will be administering your programme. It will be 2. ______________ if you make a note in your diary of this 3. ______________ and also if you make an appointment 4. ______________ by telephone whenever you want to see your programme officer.

If your base is to be outside London, you will be given 5. ______________ about reaching your destination. Please follow these carefully and, again, keep a note of them in your 6. ______________.

Indicate whether the following statements are true or not by writing

T for a statement which is true;
F for a statement which is false;
? if there is insufficient information.

7. If you bring money to Britain you'd better carry large sums of cash on your person.
8. Your money will be more secure if you convert it into traveller's cheques.
9. It's not safe to deposit your money with hotels or hostels.
10. It's wise to put your purchases in your shopping bag.
11. You should never put anything into your own pockets or bag until it has been paid for.
12. All shops provide a receipt for you.

Listening Activity No. 11

You will hear an interview between a reporter and an officer from the British Council. As you listen, fill in the gaps below.

The Student Union Welfare Office will put overseas students in touch with overseas students' societies and organizations, which are often run by overseas students. The 1. ______________ which will have been put in the student's passport by the 2. ______________ officer indicates whether or not they are required to 3. ______________ with the police. If you are from a 4. ______________ Community or Commonwealth country, you should 5. ______________ register with the police. If you are required to register with the police you must do so 6. ______________ of arrival in Britain.

Indicate whether the following statements are true or not by writing

- **T** **for a statement which is true;**
- **F** **for a statement which is false;**
- **?** **if there is insufficient information.**

7. All overseas students are required to register with the police as soon as they arrive in Britain.
8. Working in Britain without acquiring the relevant permission is illegal.
9. If overseas students are to get a job in the UK, they need to get forms OW1 and OW5 at the job centres.
10. Overseas students have to get forms OW21 and OW22 from job centres if they are looking for work experience.
11. Overseas students can only take part-time work.
12. It is free of charge to register with the police when you arrive in the UK.

Listening Activity No. 12

You are going to listen to a talk about the Student Union. As you listen, fill in the gaps in the notes below.

All 1. ______________ students automatically belong to the Student Union and have full 2. ______________ and membership rights. Part-time students also have 3. ______________ to what the Union has to offer. Further details of this are available from the Student Union offices. The Union is 4. ______________ to the NUS, which represents students on a 5. ______________ level. Students can take advantage of 6. ______________ travel facilities and a wide range of reductions on 7. ______________ goods, through the Student 8. ______________ Card.

Indicate whether the following statements are true or not by writing

T **for a statement which is true;**

F **for a statement which is false;**

? **if there is insufficient information.**

9. The talk gives an introduction to the Student Union.
10. The Social Committee is responsible for entertainment on campus.
11. The Student Union finances all the clubs and societies at college.

Listening Activity No. 13

You are going to hear a conversion that took place at an accommodation agency. As you listen, fill in the gaps in the notes below.

I'll start with self-contained flats. The flats are 1. ______________ but you will find you have your 2. ______________ to do what you want. With bedsitters, you would have your 3. ______________ although you will have to 4. ______________ the kitchen and bathroom. Lodgings are more expensive than 5. ________________ as you receive a meal.

Indicate whether the following statements are true or not by writing

T for a statement which is true;

F for a statement which is false;

? if there is insufficient information.

6. Hostels are more expensive than lodgings.
7. The agent suggests that the best option is to look through the local papers for accommodation.
8. The accommodation office in the university will offer students a list of cheap accommodation in the area.

Listening Activity No. 14

You are going to listen to a talk about Cambridge. As you listen, fill in the gaps in the notes below.

The university town of Cambridge, just one hour 1. ________________ of London, has been one of the world's most important centres of learning for 2. ________________ years. Its academic vitality and beauty create the perfect 3. ________________ in which to study. Like other students here, you will enjoy 4. ________________ unique to the Cambridge way of 5. ________________. During your free time you might like to 6. ________________ along the "Backs", or try your 7. ________________ at "punting" on the river.

Indicate whether the following statements are true or not by writing

T for a statement which is true;

F for a statement which is false;

? if there is insufficient information.

8. Cambridge is home to some famous museums.
9. The city has extensive sporting facilities.

10. Many fine performing actors and musicians are originally from Cambridge.
11. The university has many excellent restaurants.

Listening Activity No. 15

You will hear a talk about Skunks. As you listen, fill in the gaps in the notes below.

Some animals which people hate and fear are gaining new 1. ________________. People have begun to 2. ________________ their ideas about skunks. Cherry Briggs, an animal researcher, said that skunks are very 3. ________________ animals because they catch 4. ________________ and beetles. They are great for 5. ________________ control.

Indicate whether the following statements are true or not by writing

T **for a statement which is true;**
F **for a statement which is false;**
? **if there is insufficient information.**

6. People fear the skunks because of their awful smell.
7. Skunks always warn you after they spray.
8. Skunks are easily recognized by their color.
9. One of the skunk's warning signs is to raise its feet.
10. Skunks will move away when they hear loud rap music.
11. Skunks love all kinds of milk products.
12. Skunks are wanted to be back because they are great for pest control.

Listening Activity No. 16

You will hear a conversation between Gladys and Jack. As you listen, fill in the gaps in the notes below.

The lecture was interesting. The new student really 1. ________________ it.

The student enrolled in the M.A. teaching programme 2. ______________ .
He'd like to know something about 3. ______________. He asked the lady about the assessment and the exams for this particular programme. He is nervous about 4. ______________ because he hasn't had an exam for a 5. ______________.

Indicate whether the following statements are true or not by writing

T for a statement which is true;

F for a statement which is false;

? if there is insufficient information.

6. Five essays are required before the finals.
7. The lecturer and the student are good friends.
8. The lady lived on the campus while she was studying in the university.

Listening Activity No. 17

You are going to listen to a doctor's talk. As you listen, complete the notes below.

In Western countries, many people have 1. ______________ deposits on the inside wall of their arteries. These deposits build up over 2. ______________ of years, narrowing the arteries. Sometimes the deposits can 3. ______________ the formation of blood clots. If a clot breaks free, it can enter the 4. ______________ and sooner or later it will become trapped and block off a blood vessel, possibly causing a 5. ______________ attack or a stroke.

Indicate whether the following statements are true or not by writing

T for a statement which is true;

F for a statement which is false;

? if there is insufficient information.

6. Too much saturated oil in your diet can result in developing cancer.
7. What people eat may determine the cholesterol level in their blood.

8. Saturated fat will help to lower blood cholesterol level.
9. People are suggested to eat more saturated fat.
10. Fatty acids are essential for people's health.
11. The human body can make a lot of fatty acids.
12. Some nuts, seeds and fish contain a high proportion of polyunsaturated fats.

Listening Activity No. 18

You are going to listen to a talk about the city of Pompeii. As you listen, fill in the gaps in the notes below.

Over 2,000 years ago, many rich Romans spent 1. ________________ in the city of Pompeii which was located on the Bay of Naples. Pliny saw the eruption of 2. ________________, Vesuvius. It was a 3. ________________ sight. Rock and ash flew through the air. The city of Pompeii was 4. ________________ of Mt. Vesuvius. When the volcano first erupted, many people were able 5. ________________ the city. Unfortunately, there was 6. ________________ time for everyone to escape. More than 7. ________________ people died. They were buried alive under the volcanic ash. The eruption lasted for about 3 days.

Indicate whether the following statements are true or not by writing

T **for a statement which is true;**
F **for a statement which is false;**
? **if there is insufficient information.**

8. Pompeii was buried under 20 feet of volcanic rock and ash.
9. The city of Pompeii could never be forgotten.
10. An Italian farmer found a part of a wall of the ancient city of Pompeii on his farm.
11. Today the whole of the ancient city of Pompeii was uncovered.
12. Now, tourists come to see the ruins of the famous city of Pompeii.

Listening Activity No. 19

You will hear a dialogue about accommodation in the UK. As you listen, fill in the gaps in the notes below.

If you pay your rent weekly, you have to pay it in 1. ________________ on a fixed day of the week. If you want to leave, you have to give 2. ________________ notice. If you pay 3. ________________, it's one month's notice. But if you have 4. ________________ accommodation or no meals are provided, then 5. ________________ you have to give a month's notice, even if you're 6. ________________ weekly. It's therefore important to have a definite 7. ________________ with your landlady at the beginning of your 8. ________________.

Indicate whether the following statements are true or not by writing

T for a statement which is true;

F for a statement which is false;

? if there is insufficient information.

9. The landlady doesn't have to give you any notice if she wants you to leave.
10. If you don't return the key at the end of your tenancy, you may lose your deposit.
11. The rent book provides a record of payment.
12. The house regulations in the rent book are legally binding.
13. The landlady may evict you if you try to share a single room.
14. You're more likely to have to sign an agreement if you live in lodgings.

Listening Activity No. 20

You are going to listen to a conversation between two students. As you listen, complete the following notes.

If you are living in 1. ______________ you should find out when meals are served and be 2. ______________ for them. You should also find about when it's most 3. ______________ for guests to visit you or to have a 4. ______________. If you know that you will be 5. ______________ you should let her know, so she can 6. ______________ your dinner or give you a 7. ______________.

Indicate whether the following statements are true or not by writing

T **for a statement which is true;**
F **for a statement which is false;**
? **if there is insufficient information.**

8. The landlady would appreciate your help in keeping the house clean.
9. In lodgings, gas and electricity are usually included in the rent.
10. All private houses have central heating.
11. The landlady will provide enough blankets to keep you warm for the winter.
12. Before using your own electrical apparatus, make sure they work on the voltage of the house.

Unit Six

Summary

——Practising Taking Notes

本单元共有20个练习。内容以在英国生活和学习的场景为主，同时还有一些有关美国、爱尔兰等国家情况的介绍。这些内容提供了大量的西方文化背景知识，如英国的超市、酒吧、如何到英国人家做客、英国的警察、美国人的特点、美国的总统、爱尔兰的历史和音乐等。

本单元的练习形式主要以摘要填空题（Summary or Notes Completion）为主。这种练习是根据所听文章内容或部分段落内容给出一段或多段留有空格的内容概要，要求考生根据所听内容填空，以测试其对所听文章的理解概括能力。答案常可从所听内容中直接找出。

本单元的听力材料都比较长，其目的是通过大量的、长段的练习，培养考生在听英语讲座和报告中，捕捉重要信息的能力以及边听边读边记笔记的综合能力。

建议考生在听之前要把题或摘要读一遍，并根据上下文推断要填的是什么词，这样才能在听的过程中有针对性地去寻找所需要的关键词。

Listening Activity No. 1

You are going to hear a talk about security in the UK. Listen to the talk and complete the statements below by writing no more than three words in the spaces provided.

1. Don't carry ___________ cash than you need for daily expenses.
2. When you stay at a hotel, ask the manager to keep your valuables in ___________.
3. Don't keep a note of ___________ together with your traveler's cheques.
4. You should carry wallets and purses in an inside ___________.
5. Your passport, travel tickets and other important documents should be taken ___________.
6. You can leave your heavy luggage in a ___________ at most large stations and pick it up later.
7. It's necessary to keep ___________ and check the opening hours when you leave your luggage at the station.
8. The Lost Property Office can be found at both ___________ and ___________.

Listening Activity No. 2

You are going to hear a lecture on some useful information for your travelling around Britain. Listen to the first part of the lecture and complete the notes below by writing no more than three words in the spaces provided.

You will find Tourist Information Centres at major 1. ___________, airports, stations, 2. ___________ and towns and holiday centres. You will see two kinds of public telephones in operation. One is 3. ___________ and the other is card-phones. For the latter ones, you can buy at 4. ___________, news kiosks, station bars and 5. ___________. Banks are normally open from 6. ___________ Monday to Friday but at London's two 7. ___________ there are 24-hour banks. Trafalgar Square Office opens from 8. ___________ weekdays and Saturdays. On Sunday, it opens from 10:00 to 17:00. The Bureau de Change services are available to 9. __________. You can also change money at Bureau de Change, large hotels, 10. __________ and travel agents.

Listening Activity No. 3

Listen to the second part of the lecture. As you listen, complete the notes below by writing no more than three words in the spaces provided.

In Britain shops usually open at 9:00 and close at 17:30, but in many cities, they have a 1. __________ once a week. They stay open 2. __________ about 20:00. British voltage is 3. __________ V AC, 50 HZ. Many hotels will be able to supply 4. __________ for electric shavers. Stamps can be bought at 5. __________. Most hotel bills include a service charge, usually 6. __________, but in some larger hotels it's 15%. People often leave 7. __________% for the waiter in the restaurants, and give 8. __________ per suitcase for porters, 9. __________% of the fare for taxis and 10. __________ for hairdressers and 50p to the assistant who 11. __________ your hair. You must remember it is the rule to drive on the 12. __________ and overtake on the 13. __________. Driver as well as front-seat passengers must wear 14. __________.

Listening Activity No.4

You are going to hear a dialogue between two students talking about how parliament makes new laws. As you listen, complete the notes below by writing no more than three words in the spaces provided.

New laws can start in either the House of Lords or the House of Commons. They are usually proposed by 1. __________. A law which is being proposed is called 2. __________ until it is passed. Then, it becomes 3. __________ of Parliament.

The bill goes through its 4. __________ which means that the title of the bill is set to be discussed, then it goes through its Second Reading which is the 5. ___________ stage. If the bill is passed it will go on to the 6. ___________ stage where a small group of members meet and discuss it in detail. The Report stage will be the stage in which 7. ___________ can be made. After the Report stage, the bill is taken for its 8. ___________ where a vote is taken. If the bill is passed, it will go to the 9. ___________. When both Houses pass the bill, it goes to the 10. ___________ for the Royal Assent. When the Queen gives her assent the bill becomes an act.

Listening Activity No.5

You are going to hear a talk about the English policeman. As you listen, complete the notes below by writing no more than three words in the spaces provided.

A "copper" is one of 1. ___________'s nicknames. It comes from the verb "cop" which means to 2. ___________. "Bobby" comes from the 3. ___________ name of Sir Robert Peel who was the founder of 4. ___________. "Peeler" used to be an 5. ___________ nickname for the policeman but this one has 6. ___________.

The British bobby is a very 7. ___________ sort of character. They are very busy 8. ___________visitors about the city. British bobby has some very distinctive features. For example, he doesn't carry 9. ___________. An English policeman can be seen from a distance because of his height and 10. ___________. The police are aware that they are the country's 11. ___________ and not its 12. ___________.

Listening Activity No.6

You are going to hear a short talk about the banks in Britain. As you listen, complete the statements below by writing no more than three words in the spaces provided.

1. The safest place to keep your money is ___________.

2. A __________ account is the most useful type of account offered by the banks for students in Britain.
3. There will be an __________ if you overdraw on your account.
4. You should open __________ account if you have more money than you need for month-to-month expenses.
5. You do __________ tax on the interest if you are not normally resident in Britain.
6. A check card can be used as a check guarantee card. With this card, you can draw up to __________ cash from almost any bank in Britain. A Euro-check card can be used to draw cash from most banks in __________.
7. Many shops will not accept a check unless a __________ backs it.
8. Many banks provide a cash card, which can be used to draw cash from __________.
9. Most banks provide dispensing machines which are set __________ of the bank outside.
10. When the bank is closed, a cash card allows you to draw up to __________ a day.

Listening Activity No. 7

You are going to hear a talk about some British customs. Listen carefully and complete the notes below by writing no more than three words in the spaces provided.

In Britain, there is a common saying, "An Englishman ' s home is 1. __________." It ' s important to act thoughtfully if you are living in a 2. __________ or are visiting a British home. There are a few British 3. __________. You should be 4. __________ for meals . Make you own bed and keep you room 5. __________. When you stay with a British family for several days you should give 6. __________ when you leave. British people normally wait until 7. __________ has got their food before they start eating. You ' d better use 8. __________ and title if you are unsure how to call them. At a formal meal, the host 9. __________ expect guests to help with household chores.

Listening Activity No. 8

You are going to hear a series of lectures on Irish culture. Listen to the first part of the lecture. As you listen, complete the notes below by writing no more than three words in the spaces provided.

Riverdance is based on a culture which had its 1. ___________ from the 6th to the 9th century. Before that period, 2. ___________ was oral and based on a love of complicated stories and 3. ___________. In the 6th century, missionaries introduced 4. ___________. Since then the culture of Ireland began to develop and had 5. ___________ in northern Europe. In the 9th century this golden age 6. ___________ because of the invasions and there never was real recovery. At the end of the 7. ___________ Irish Nationalism began to influence 8. ___________ in English to write in a way that was 9. ___________ from English writers of the period. A distinct style of writing in English called 10. ___________ literature came out. There are many 11. ___________ writers, for example William Butler Yeats, Geoge Bernard Shaw and Samuel Beckett. All of them have received 12. ___________ for Literature. Irish music was 13. ___________ as people move to the cities. Some efforts were made to make it 14. ___________ to city people but without success. Since 1980's this has begun to change. Modern Ireland has been 15. ___________ more than just a revival of traditional music. There are 16. ___________ people employed in Ireland in the music industry.

Listening Activity No.9

Listen to the second part of the lecture. As you listen, complete the notes below by writing no more than three words in the spaces provided.

In 1849 Irish people were largely 1. ___________ and living in the countryside. There was a 2. ___________ in the agricultural system. All crops were grown to pay the rent of the land and all that was grown to eat was 3. __________. A great famine struck the Irish people. From 1845 to 1848 the crops failed so 4. __________ people died or left the country by 5. __________. The population continued to 6. __________ until 1961. The people left their homes and went to England, 7. __________ or Australia. Ireland has the highest 8. __________ rate of any country in Europe for the 9. __________ centuries. Almost every family in Ireland has 10. __________ abroad.

Listening Activity No. 10

Listen to the last part of the lecture. As you listen, complete the notes below by writing no more than three words in the spaces provided.

The emigrants experienced a lot of 1. __________ in their new countries. In England, there used to be signs for 2. __________ which read "Irish need not apply". The emigrants often experienced 3. __________ so they formed many organizations to 4. __________ their own fellow emigrants. In America, the Irish chose 5. __________ and some significant cities were controlled by 6. __________. President 7. __________'s grandparents came from Ireland and his election had a significant impact in 8. __________, helping the process of recovery of 9. __________, which they have today. Today there are 10. __________ people of Irish descent living 11. __________ Ireland. In America there are 12. __________ who have 100% Irish background. Many emigrants who came back to live in Ireland often found it 13. __________ to fit into Irish society, but they have always had 14. __________ in the old country.

Listening Activity No. 11

You are going to hear a talk about universities and colleges in Britain. As you listen to the talk, complete the notes below by writing no more than three words in the spaces provided.

There are 1. __________ universities and 2. __________ polytechnics in the UK. In 1973-1974, there were over 3. __________ full-time students in universities. 10% of them were from 4. __________. University first degree courses usually last three or four years. The academic year normally has 5. __________ terms, beginning from 6. __________. You should apply to a university at least 7. __________ months before the proposed date of admission. When you have filled in your application form you must send it to 8. __________. If you want to enter Oxford or Cambridge University, you should remember to return your application by the closing date, in 9. __________. The usual minimum qualifications for entry to a first degree course in a university are good passes in the 10. __________ or an 11. __________ examination. All enquiries should be accompanied by a copy of the 12. __________ certificate and where appropriate an approved translation.

Listening Activity No. 12

You are going to hear a talk on Canada. As you listen to the talk, complete the notes below by writing no more than three words in the spaces provided.

Canada is located in the northern half of the continent of 1. __________. The most northern parts of Canada are called the land of 2. __________ because at certain times of the year the sun 3. __________. This northern part of Canada is cold and mostly 4. __________ with snow all year round. The original people in the northern part of Canada are called 5. "__________". They are also called the "First Nation". The populations in the Atlantic provinces of Nova Scotia, Newfoundland, New Brunswick and Prince Edward Island are 6. __________. The land there is not very fertile so their main industries are forestry, 7. __________ and mining. The province of British Columbia is in the 8. __________ of Canada and is an attractive place for 9. __________ because of its mild climate, mountains, seacoast and 10. __________. The original settlers came from 11. __________. In the 16th century, the first Europeans arrived in 12. __________ Canada. They came from 13. __________. By the end of the 14. __________ all of Canada was under British rule. In this century, Canada has had an influence of settlers from all 15. __________.

Listening Activity No. 13

You are going to hear a conversation between two students. They are talking about the English bars. As you listen, complete the notes below by writing no more than three words in the spaces provided.

Bar is the place where 1. __________ are kept. At the bar, people don't wait for someone to take 2. __________, instead, they go to the bar directly to 3. __________ their drinks. They pay as soon as they 4. __________. It's not the custom to give 5. __________. When you want to have another drink you ought to take your 6. __________ back to the bar for refill. You can get 7. __________ alcoholic and non-alcoholic drinks in the bar. Alcoholic drinks include beer and wine. Cider is made from 8. __________, port is a type of 9. __________ wine from Portugal, and sherry is a type of wine from 10. __________. Spirtis are a kind of 11. __________ drinks. Non-alcoholic drinks include all kinds of fruit juices, such as orange and 12. __________. Soft drinks are sweet drinks made with 13. __________. Cordials are strong and sweet drinks tasting of 14. __________. VAT stands for 15. __________ Tax. VAT can be 16. __________ to you if you take the goods with you when you leave Britain.

Listening Activity No. 14

You are going to hear a talk about the English pubs. As you listen, complete the notes below by writing no more than three words in the spaces provided.

There are 1. __________ different methods of serving beer in Britain. Some beer is 2. __________ and draught beer is a kind of beer that comes from

3. ___________. There are two different methods of serving draught beer. Keg beer is served with modern method which uses 4. ___________ and traditional draught uses 5. ___________ to pull the beer up the pipe and out of the tap. Keg beer is sold almost 6. ___________ in Britain, and you can always have exactly 7. ___________ in any pub. Traditional beer is not served 8. ___________ but allows you to taste 9. ___________. Lager is served cold and available in 10. ___________. Guinness is a thick, almost black, bitter tasting 11. ___________ beer. Pale ale is less strong and 12. ___________ than bitter. The pub's opening times are regulated by 13. ___________ and usually a pub is open from 14. ___________ and from 5:30 to 11:00. 15. ___________ is forbidden in pubs. Children are 16. ___________ to enter pubs according to the law.

Listening Activity No. 15

You are going to hear a talk about the Tall Ships Race in Britain. As you listen, complete the notes below by writing no more than three words in the spaces provided.

In July 1956, a fleet of 21 sailing ships from 1. ___________ countries raced each other from Torbay in Devon to 2. ___________. The purpose of the gathering was to mark the passing of the 3. ___________. They raced again 4. ___________. Since then the title "the Tall Ships" was given to them. As race succeeded race, 5. ___________ ships began to be built and young people from all 6. ___________ wanted to participate. The race ship has to satisfy 7. ___________ requirements. First of all, it has to have a minimum 8. ___________ of 9.09 metres, then half its crew must be between the ages of 9. ___________, and its principal means of propulsion must be a sail. The race has 10. ___________ huge crowds of spectators. In 1984 more than 11. ___________ people watched the fleet set off in the River Mersey in 12. ___________, and in 1986 two million spectators with 13. ___________ watched the parade at Newcastle-upon-Tyne. The Ship Race started from London in 14. ___________. A grand fleet of up to 100 vessels gathered on the River Thames near 15. ___________. All of their crews were 16. ___________ and few were expert sailors. The ships were berthed on 17. __________ side of Tower Bridge. Many of the large ships were open to 18. __________. It was an amazing and historic spectacle as the ships sailed slowly up the River Thames.

Listening Activity No. 16

You are going to hear a conversation about using recorded delivery and registered post. As you listen, complete the notes below by writing no more than three words in the spaces provided.

You can use the recorded delivery to send all kinds of 1. __________ postal packets except parcels and airway and railway letters. You can get a Certificate of 2. __________ from the container in the post office. The certifficate 3. __________ your record of posting. You can obtain confirmation of delivery by completing an 4. __________ form. This form will be signed by the post office official, not by the 5. __________. The compensation is very limited and 6. __________ paid for loss or damage, but will not be paid for 7. __________ or any other inadmissible item. Registered post is a 8. __________ service. All registered mail receives special security treatment. Packing is very 9. __________. You will get the compensation if you send your articles in one of the 10. __________ envelopes sold by the post office since these envelopes are already stamped for 11. __________ postage and have the 12. __________ registration fee. The registered mail is signed by 13. __________ on delivery. The post office delivers registered mail to the 14. __________. You can obtain confirmation of delivery by paying an 15. __________ and completing an Advice of Delivery form either at the time of posting or later. The Advice of Delivery fee is lower if the form is handed in 16. __________ of posting.

Listening Activity No. 17

You are going to hear the first part of a lecture on American culture and American customs. As you listen, complete the notes below by writing no more than three words in the spaces provided.

The population of the USA:		260 million
The population of White:	1.	______
African American:		12%
Hispanic:	2.	______
Asian or Pacific Islanders:	3.	______
American Indian or Eskimo:		1%

Americans value individualism, independence, 4. ______, directness, 5. ______, achievement and 6. ______. Individualism is the most highly 7. ______ value in American culture and an important 8. ______ to understanding American behavior. If a group of friends go to a restaurant everyone wants to pay 9. ______. If you do too many favors, this may create an 10. ______ situation for the American. Americans are direct. They are quick to get 11. ______ and do not spend much time on 12. ______ amenities. They think it gives an indication of 13. ______ to look at the person if they speak to him or her. It is considered better to refuse graciously than to 14. ______ an invitation and not go. Punctuality is an important 15. ______ in the U.S. You should be 16. ______ for school or business appointments at the 17. ______ agreed upon. In social appointments you can arrive 18. ______ minutes after the agreed-upon time without giving offense. But, if you are more than 15 minutes late for an 19. ______, you need to offer an 20. ______ and an explanation.

Listening Activity No. 18

Listen to the second part of the lecture. As you listen, complete the notes below by writing no more than three words in the spaces provided.

Americans are often 1. ______ but they also have a good sense of 2. ______ and cooperate with others to achieve a goal. They are friendly, but in their 3. ______. Friendships among Americans tend to be 4. ______ and more casual than friendships among people from

5. ___________. Americans are not comfortable with 6. ___________. They are open and usually eager to 7. ___________. When you accidentally bump someone you should say 8. "___________". Men don't hold hands or link arms 9. ___________ with other men. This is acceptable between women and it is quite 10. ___________ between men and women. For your safety, don't walk alone 11. ___________. Don't carry too much cash or wear 12. ___________ of great value. Don't 13. ___________ when you travel. You should give up your 14. ___________ and observe as much as possible about 15. ___________ to tell the police when you are threatened by one. Don't judge what you see as 16. ___________, but make it a challenge to try to 17. ___________ the variety of American behaviors. You do not have to 18. ___________ in something you disagree with, but you can try to understand it.

Listening Activity No. 19

You are going to hear a talk on two famous American presidents. As you listen, fill in the gaps in the notes below. Write no more than three words for each answer.

John F. Kennedy and Abraham Lincoln lived in different times. Kennedy was born in 1. ___________, whereas Lincoln was born more than 2. ___________ earlier. As for their family backgrounds, Kennedy came from a rich family. He was able to attend expensive private schools. He graduated from 3. ___________ University. Lincoln had only one year of formal schooling. In spite of his lack of 4. ___________, he became a well-known lawyer. He was 5. ___________ man.

In spite of these differences in Kennedy and Lincoln's backgrounds, some interesting 6. ___________ between the two men are evident. For example, take their political careers. Both of them began their political career as a 7. ___________. They went to the Congress just 8. ___________ apart. Another interesting coincidence is that each man was elected president of the United States in a year ending with the number 9. ___________. Furthermore, both men were President during years of civil 10. ___________ in the country. Both of them died by 11. ___________ while in office. Both presidents were shot while they were sitting next to 12. ___________.

Listening Activity No. 20

You are going to listen to a lecture on American history. As you listen, fill in the gaps in the notes below.

The American Civil War was 1. ____________ over 140 years ago. It lasted 2. ____________ years. The American Civil War resulted in the death of 3. ____________ Americans. What caused this terrible civil war between the North and the South? There were many causes of the war. One of the important causes of the war was the 4. ____________ between the North and the South over the 5. ____________ of slavery. The southern way of life and the southern economy 6. ____________ on the use of slave labor. Many Northerners were opposed to slavery and they wanted to 7 ____________ slavery. The growth of industry in the North resulted in increased population and money. It also made the Southerners fear northern political and economic 8. ____________. So many Southerners wanted to leave 9. ____________ and form their own country. By June of 1861, 10. ____________ southern states had seceded and established a new country. The North went to war in order to 11. ____________ the United States one country. 12. ____________ won the war because of its economic and industrial strength and power. The Civil War had two important results for the United States:

(1) The Civil War preserved the United States as 13. ____________.

(2) It ended 14. ____________ in the United States.

Unit Seven

Practice Tests

本单元提供了四套不同形式的 IELTS 听力考试摸拟试题，是根据英国使馆提供的不同时期的 IELTS 练习题编写而成。目的是帮助考生了解和熟悉 IELTS 听力考试题型，提高应试能力。

Test 1

Section 1 Questions 1-10

Questions 1-4

Decide which of the pictures best fits what you hear on the tape, and circle the letter under that picture.

1. Where does the conversation take place?

A

B

C

D

2. Which office helps overseas students with their particular problems?

SPORTS CLUB
A

UNION SOCIETIES
B

ACCOMMODATION OFFICE
C

WELFARE OFFICE
D

3. What kind of sport doesn't the student mention?

A

B

C

D

4. Where can the Filipino student find his compatriots at the school?

TRAINING SESSIONS	FILIPINO SOCIETY
A	B
BADMINTON COURT	BASKETBALL TEAM
C	D

Questions 5-10

Fill in the gaps numbered 5-10.

Name		Caesar
Surname	5.	______________
City	6.	______________
Subject	7.	______________
Length of the course	8.	______________
Job in the future	9.	______________
Reason for choosing this university	10.	______________

Section 2 Questions 11-20

Questions 11-16

Answer the questions by writing a word or a phrase.

11. When does the student have to move out of his present accommodation?

____

12. For how long did the college offer him a temporary room?

____

13. Circle the problems that the student has now.

A. No friends. B. No money.

C. No place to live in. D. Homesick.

14. Circle the help that the Welfare Office can give.
    A. To provide long-term accommodation for him.
    B. To contact the accommodation service.
    C. To subsidize his rent payments.
    D. To offer him a grant.
15. Where could the student get money?
    A. From a bank.
    B. From a landlord.
    C. From the British Council.
    D. From the Student Union.
16. How much could the student get as an emergency loan?
    A. Up to £200.
    B. About £250.
    C. £220.
    D. £2000.

Questions 17-20

Write a word or a number in the spaces provided.

17. Would the Union be able to provide a long-term emergency accommodation? ________________
18. How much money does the student have left? ________________
19. Will the student apply for an emergency loan? ________________
20. How does the student feel after talking with the welfare officer? ________________

Section 3 Questions 21-30

Questions 21-25

Complete the statements below. Use up to three words.

21. The Student Union is run by four ________________.
22. The president is responsible for the day-to-day running of the Union according to established policies ________________.
23. A new vice-presidential post has been created to focus on ____________.

24. One way to improve communications within the college will be
   A. with regular meetings of the Student Union.
   B. with the regular publication of the Student Union magazine.
   C. with regular elections.
   D. with regular visits by journalists.
25. One possible way to see the president is
   A. to fix a time with the office assistant, Pat.
   B. to call the president directly.
   C. to leave a notice for the president.
   D. to drop in the president's office.

Questions 26-30

Indicate whether the following statements are accurate or not by writing

A for an accurate statement;
I for an inaccurate statement;
N if the information is not given.

26. The president advises students not to waste time on relaxation and enjoyment.
27. The Student Union is a very helpful organization.
28. Central London is only 20 minutes away by tube from Ealing.
29. The Student Union is an organization run by the college.
30. The president is a third-year student at Ealing College.

Section 4 Questions 31-38

Questions 31-35

Fill in the gaps numbered 31-35 in the notes below.

A Vice-president Finance 31. __________ the spending of the Union's grant to ensure that all areas of Student Union activity run smoothly without any 32. __________. There are 33. __________ members on the finance team. We are all here to help you 34. __________ as we can. Although I administer the Union's finances, in the end, it is you who have the 35. __________ in expenditure policy, either directly or through the Executive Finance Committee.

Questions 36-38

Indicate whether the following statements are true or not by writing

T **for a statement which is true;**

F **for a statement which is false;**

? **if there is insufficient information.**

36. The speech is a vice-president's introduction.
37. The speech is an election speech.
38. The vice-president is increasing the number of hours that the Finance Office is open.

Test 2

Section 1 Questions 1-8

Listen to the interview and fill the missing information in the form. If a student's experience in the first homestay is positive or very good, make two ticks (√√). If it's Ok, make one tick (√). If it's not good and negative, make a cross (×).

Name	Country	Impression of first homestay	Experience of first homestay	Time in Canada
Fumi	Japan	They give me freedom. *Example*: *I feel safe.*		*Example*: 3 *months*
Linda	1. ________	They are very nice but the food is 2. ________.	3. ________	4. ________
Ali	5. ________	The room is terrible and the meal is 6. ________.	7. ________	8. ________

Section 2 Questions 9-20

Questions 9-15

You are going to listen to a conversation. As you listen, complete the notes below, using NO MORE THAN THREE WORDS in each space.

Napoleon was born in 9. _________ on the island of Corsica. When he was ten, his father sent him to a 10. _________ school. Napoleon was not a brilliant student but he excelled in 11. _________ and military science. When he was 16 years old he joined the French army. His military 12. _________ brought him fame, power and riches. He became a 13. _________ when he was only 24 and a few years later he became 14. _________ of France. His coronation ceremony was at Notre Dame on 15. _________. Napoleon won many military victories because his soldiers were ready to die for him. He was a great military leader.

Questions 16-20

Indicate whether the following statements are true or not by writing

T for a statement which is true;
F for a statement which is false;
N if the information is not given.

16. Napoleon controlled all of Europe at one time.
17. Austria and Russia fought fiercely against Napoleon, but England did not.
18. Napoleon lost most of his soldiers when he attacked England.
19. Napoleon died before he reached the age of fifty-two.
20. He was married when he was very young.

Section 3 Questions 21-30

Questions 21-23

You will hear a talk on ocean spills. As you listen to the talk, circle the appropriate letter for questions 21-23.

21. The plastic toys were washed off the ship

A. in Alaska.
B. in the Pacific Ocean.
C. in the Arctic Ocean.
D. in the Bering Sea.

22. How long did it take the first ducks to arrive at the beach?

A. About two weeks.
B. About two months.
C. About ten months.
D. About twelve months.

23. Who were most excited by the plastic toys?

A. The reporters.
B. The tourists.
C. The children.
D. The oceanographers.

Questions 24-30

Complete the notes below by writing NO MORE THAN THREE WORDS in the spaces provided.

24. The floating toys made it possible to study ocean ___________ and winds.
25. Some toys floated ___________ the North Pacific, while others headed for the North Atlantic.
26. Many of the toys were ___________ northeast by the wind and were expected to cross the North Pole.
27. In 1990, a ship from Korea to the west coast of ___________ was caught in a storm.
28. There were ___________ pairs of Nike shoes spilt into the water.
29. People set up ___________ to find matches for their shoes since they arrived one at a time.
30. Many pairs of running shoes are still on their ___________ around the world.

Section 4 Questions 31-40

Questions 31-38

Complete the notes below by writing NO MORE THAN THREE WORDS in the spaces provided.

Julia feels guilty. She knows that most chocolate has 31. ___________ but she can't stop eating it because she is 32. ___________ it. Chocolate is a

33. __________ food for the people all over the world. They spend over 34. $________ on it for Valentine's Day. The idea of 35. __________ chocolate started in the 19th century. Before that, the Aztecs drank bowls of chocolate to 36. __________. When chocolate was brought to Spain people thought it was 37. __________ because it tasted bitter. Soon people discovered that 38. __________ chocolate with sugar made a wonderful drink.

Questions 39-40

Circle the appropriate letter.

39. No one in Spain could talk about chocolate
    A. because it tasted bitter.
    B. because the king loved it.
    C. because the king put out an order.
    D. because the druggists made it into drinks.
40. People who eat chocolate are healthier
    A. because it became a popular drink in Europe.
    B. because it tasted good with milk.
    C. because it doesnt have much fat or sugar.
    D. because feeling pleasure can protect against illness.

Test 3

Section 1 Questions 1-9

Questions 1-4

Listen to a conversation between a foreign student and the accommodation secretary of a college, and complete the accommodation table.

College Accommodation

Types of room	Names of shared rooms	What is not provided
Example: *a single bedroom* 1. ______________	*Example*: *a bathroom* 2. ______________ 3. ______________	4. ______________

Questions 5-9

Write NO MORE THAN THREE WORDS for each answer.

5. What kind of washing machines are there in the launderettes?

____

6. How often are the rooms cleaned in the college accommodation?

____

7. Where can the students watch TV?

____

8. What kind of accommodation provide breakfast and dinner?

____

9. What kind of accommodation does the student sign up for?

____

Section 2 Questions 10-20

Questions 10-14

Fill in the gaps numbered 10-14.

Full name	10. ______________	
Nationality	11. ______________	
Home address	12. ______________	, Bonne
Age	13. ______________	
Programme	14. ______________	

Qestions 15-17

Circle the correct answer.

15. What dietary requirements does the student have?
    A. German food. B. British food.
    C. Vegetarian. D. No requirement.
16. What kind of sports does the student like very much?
    A. Football. B. Basketball.
    C. Skiing. D. Swimming.
17. What kind of family does the student want to live with?
    A. A large family.
    B. A family with children around his age.
    C. A family with young children.
    D. A family with two boys.

Questions 18-20

Tick (√) if the information is correct or write in the changes.

		Answer
Example:		
Name of the family is Roberts.		√
Mr. Roberts is a clerk.		*a bank manager*
Mrs. Roberts is a full-time teacher.	18.	________
They have two children.	19.	________
The student will stay in the boy's room.	20.	________

Section 3 Questions 21-32

Questions 21-27

Complete the table showing the time, name of the programme and place in a social activity programme.

A Social Activity Programme

Day	Time	Name of Programme	Place
Example: *Monday*	20:00 21:00	*Singing with Guitar* 21.	*Gibson Hall* 22.
Tuesday	23.	*Tennis*	24.
25.	26.	27.	

Questions 28-32

Listen to the second part of the conversation and complete the table.

	Trip to Stratford-on-Avon
Day	28.
Price	29.
Where to sign up	30.
When to sign up	31.
Bus departure time	32.

Section 4 Questions 33-40

Questions 33-34

Charles and Belinda are meeting at a hotel for an anniversary conference. Look at questions 33-34 below. Tick (√) the relevant boxes in the table.

	33. How did Belinda come to the conference?	34. How did Charles come to the conference?
By plane		
By coach		
By bus		
By train		
By taxi		

Question 35

Tick the relevant boxes in the table.

	35. Advantages of the train mentioned by Charles
Very quick	
Comfortable	
Regular service	
Cheap	
Nice view	
Nice lunch	

Questions 36-40

Write NO MORE THAN THREE WORDS for each answer.

36. Why did Charles come by coach last time? ____________
37. When did he leave home? ____________
38. How long did the journey take? ____________
39. How many coaches are there during the day? ____________
40. What will Belinda try next time? ____________

Test 4

Section 1 Questions 1-9

Questions 1-6

Listen to a conversation between two students talking about markets in London and complete the market list.

Market List

Address	Open hours	Days	Tube Station
East Street SE17	8 am-5 pm	Sat. Tue.	Castle
Leather Lane WC1	lunch times	1.	Chancery Lane
2. _____ Lane E1	9 am-12 noon	Sunday mornings	3.
Walthamstow E17	4.	Mon.-Sat. except Wed. Sun.	Central Line
Brixton SW9	9 am-6 pm	Mon.-Sun. half day on Wed.	5.
Camden High St. NW1	8 am-5 pm	6.	Chalk Farm, Camden Town

Questions 7-9

Write NO MORE THAN THREE WORDS for each answer.

7. Who is Barbara going to shop with? ____________________
8. How is Barbara travelling to the shops tomorrow? ____________________
9. What time are they going to meet? ____________________

Section 2 Questions 10-20

Questions 10-14

Listen to a talk about the women's Conference and circle the correct answer.

10. How many meetings are going to be held from August to September in Beijing?

A. 2 B. 3

C. 4 D. 5

11. When will the Non-government Organization Forum on Women be held?

A. From August 13 to September 8, 1995.

B. From August 30 to September 8, 1995.

C. From September 4 to September 15, 1995.

D. From September 4 to September 16, 1995.

12. Where was the Third World Conference on Women held?

A. In Beijing. B. In Mexico City.

C. In Copenhagen. D. In Nairobi.

13. How many people are expected to attend the Fourth World Coference on Women?

A. 30000. B. 184.

C. About 6000. D. About 60000.

14. How many years has it taken to prepare for the Fourth World Conference in Beijing?

A. 13 years. B. 10 years.

C. 5 years. D. 3 years.

Questions 15-17

Listen to the directions and match the places in questions 15-17 to the appropriate letters A-G on the campus map.

Example: The campus branch bank ____*C*____

15. Students' Library ________
16. Student Union ________
17. Bookstore ________

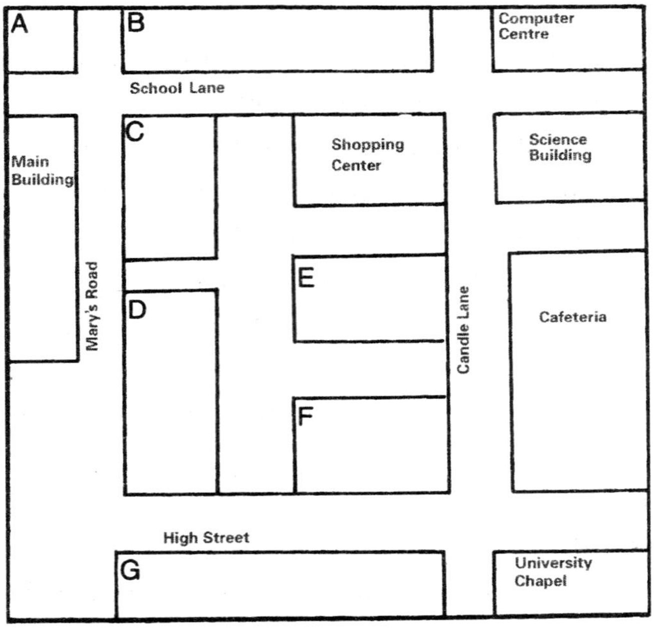

Questions 18-20

Look at this note. Tick (√) if the information is correct or write in the necessary changes.

Note

Example:		Answer
The director is Mr. Cole.		*Mr. Smith*
There will be a reception after the tour.		√
The reception starts at 5:00.	18.	________
is on the 1st floor.	19.	________
is in Room 304.	20.	________

Section 3 Questions 21-32

Questions 21-24

You are going to hear a conversation between Maria and Jack. Listen to the conversation and write down their opinions about some of these things. Complete the table showing the weather, the rooms, their roommates and food.

Things / Name	Weather	Room	Roommate	Food
Jack	*Example*: *fine and sunny*	21.	*intelligent*, *friendly*	24.
Maria	*Example*: *raining*	22.	23.	*disgusting*, *has no taste*

Questions 25-32

Complete the table showing the number of points, 1, 2, 3 or 4, scored to the university facilities.

	Lecture Rooms	Car Parks	Computer Centre	Periodical Room	Photocopying Room
Robert	*Example*: *3*	25.	27.	29.	31.
Mary	2	26.	28.	30.	32.

Section 4 Questions 33-40

Listen to a talk and complete the statements below.

33. One of the crucial problems we face now is the __________ problem.
34. People say we live in a __________ society.
35. Recycling and reuse can stop the __________ of waste and can also help save energy.
36. To stop using __________ can help to save wildlife and habitats.
37. It's suggested to buy __________ goods for the kitchen and bathroom.
38. Don't use __________ that contain chemicals that do harm to the environment.
39. __________ is a good way to save energy.
40. Using public transportation can avoid __________ problems.

Teacher's Book

Tapescript

Unit One

Listening Activity No. 1

Telephone Conversations

1. Is that 4013745?
   Yes. Can I help you?
   I'd like to speak to Miss Jones, please.

2. Hi. Is that 2016453?
   Yes. Who do you want to speak to?
   Helen Parker, please.

3. Hello. Is that 7849253?
   Who do you wish to speak to?
   Dr. Robinson, please.

4. Good morning. Is that 5066423?
   Yes. Can I help you?
   I'd like to speak to Mr. Egge, please.

5. I'm sorry to disturb you, but is that 5094287?
   Who do you want to speak to?
   Jane Casting, please.

Listening Activity No. 2

Addresses

1. My new address is
   23A Smithfield Road
   Ealing W5
   London
   My telephone number is 71 8402146.

2. My sister lives at
27 Greenford Avenue
Nottingham
Her telephone number is 602 5795942.

3. My friend Alan lives in London. His address is
25 Saint Mary's Road
Ealing, London W5 5RF
His telephone number is 71 5795076.

4. My brother Larry's address is
3 Gresik Road
Birmingham
His telephone number is 21 9920221.

5. My parents live at
64 Manor Drive
Edinburgh
Their telephone number is 31 3246738.

6. My uncle George lives at
30 King's Road
Leeds
His telephone number is 532 8375029.

7. Mrs. Harper lives at
17 Green Street
Liverpool
Her number is 51 3627884.

8. Mr. Johnson lives at
48 Church Street
Brighton
His telephone number is 273 843065.

Listening Activity No. 3

1. EF Language School
EF House
1 Farman Street

Hove, Brighton
Sussex BN3 1AL
Tel: 723651
Telex: 877743

2. EF International School of English
221 Hills Road
Cambridge
CB2 2RW
Tel: 240040
Telex: 817713

3 EF International School of English
1-2 Sussex Road
Brighton
Sussex BN2 1FJ
Tel: 571780
Telex: 94012032

4. EF International School of English
74/80 Warrior Square
Hastings
East Sussex TN3 6BP
Tel: 423998
Telex: 957005

Listening Activity No.4

(*Alison and Alan are in London talking about telephones.*)

Alison: I've got to make a phone call. There is a phone-box over there.

Alan: Now it is 5:30 already. Why don't you make a call later? It is cheaper after 6 pm.

Alison: Is it? Oh, good. I thought it cost the same. I'll wait till I get home then. Where can you find out how much phone calls cost?

Alan: You can find out at the front of any telephone directory.

Alison: Ah, I must have a good look. Does it give any other information?

Alan: Yes, you will get any information you need, such as the weather forecast, gardening information, etc.

Alison: Good. I'll have a look. How can I arrange an alarm call? My brother's arriving from Paris early tomorrow and I must get to the airport very early in the morning.

Alan: Well, you'd better book before 10:30 pm the previous evening.

Alison: That seems simple enough. Actually I think I'll phone my brother this afternoon. I've got the phone number of his hotel but what if he isn't in when I phone? It could be expensive and I can't afford to keep phoning all afternoon.

Alan: Well, you could make a personal call. You can tell the operator your brother's name, then your message can be left for your brother and you would not pay any money until you talk to him.

Alison: Perfect. I'll do that. Thank you, Alan.

Listening Activity No.5

1. My name is Barbara Cooper. I'll spell it for you. Barbara, B-A-R-B-A-R-A, Cooper, C-0-0-P-E-R. Did you get it? I'm Barbara Cooper.

2. Do you need my full name? My first name's John, J-O-H-N. Yes, J-O-H-N. And my surname's Murphy, M-U-R-P-H-Y.

3. A: My Christian name is Stephen.
   B: Now, there are different ways of spelling that, aren't there?
   A: Yes. Mine's P-H.
   B: Pardon?
   A: You spell it S-T-E-P-H-E-N.
   B: Thank you.

4. A: Place of birth, please madam.
   B: Adelaide. A-D-E-L-A-I-D-E. Would you like me to spell it again? A-D-E-L-A-I-D-E.

5. Hello, I'd like to order a book by Martha Hunt. Hello? It's not a very good line, is it? Martha Hunt, M-A-R-T-H-A H-U-N-T. That's it. The title of the book is *Slight*.

6. Hello, er... I have a reservation. The name's James, James Black.

7. A: Where do you live?
   B: A suburb of London called Greenwich.
   A: Gren.
   B: No, no. G-R-double E-N-W-I-C-H, Greenwich.

8. A: Hello, I have an appointment with Miss Parker.
   B: Your name, please?
   A: Terry Fisher. That's T-E-R-R-Y, Terry. F-I-S-H-E-R, Fisher.
   B: Thank you.

Listening Activity No.6

Operator: Long distance. May I help you?
Caller: Yes. I want to make a person-to-person call to Leeds, please.
Operator: What is the name of the person, please?
Caller: David Barker.
Operator: How do you spell that?
Caller: It's B-A-R-K-E-R.
Operator: And what is the number?
Caller: It's 5027745, but I don't have the area code.
Operator: Just a minute, please.

Listening Activity No. 7

Operator: Directory Enquiries. What city please?
Enquirer: Manchester. I'd like to have the telephone number of Mr. John Abel, please.
Operator: Yes, ma'am. How do you spell his last name?
Enquirer: It's A-B-E-L, Abel.
Operator: Thank you. And could you tell me his address?
Enquirer: It's 2418 Grestone Road.
Operator: The number is 3659783.
Enquirer: 3659783. Thank you very much.
Operator: You're welcome. Have a good day.

Listening Activity No. 8

Operator: Directory Enquiries. What city please?
Enquirer: Edinburgh. I want to have the telephone number of Mrs. Diana Paxton, please.
Operator: Yes, ma'am. Could you spell her last name, please?
Enquirer: Yes. It's P-A-X-T-O-N, Paxton.
Operator: Thank you. And her address?
Enquirer: 932 Beach Road.
Operator: The number is 4023685.
Enquirer: 4023685. Thank you very much.
Operator: You're welcome.

Listening Activity No.9

Secretary: Good morning. Can I help you?
Student: Yes. I'd like to enrol for the course.
Secretary: Certainly. What's your surname please?
Student: Williams.
Secretary: Could you spell that for me?
Student: Yes. It's W-I-L-L-I-A-M-S.
Secretary: Thank you. What's your first name?
Student: Peter. That's spelled P-E-T-E-R.
Secretary: Thanks. Where are you from, Mr. Williams?
Student: Canada.
Secretary: I see. Where do you live now?
Student: I live at 9 Crew Street RC4 and my telephone number is 2342965.
Secretary: Your number is 2342965.
Student: Yes, that's right.
Secretary: Thank you. How old are you?
Student: 25.
Secretary: Thanks.

Listening Activity No. 10

Secretary: Good morning. Can I help you?
Student: Yes. I'd like to enrol for the course.
Secretary: Certainly. What's your surname please?
Student: Turnball.
Secretary: Could you spell that for me?
Student: Yes. It's T-U-R-N-B-A-L-L.
Secretary: Thank you... and what's your first name?
Student: Gill. That's spelled G-I-L-L.
Secretary: Thanks. Where do you come from, Miss Turnball?
Student: I come from Australia.
Secretary: I see. Where do you live now?
Student: Now I live with my sister. Her address is 32 Broadway SE23. The telephone number is 2073346.
Secretary: Thank you. And how old are you?
Student: 23.
Secretary: Thank you.

Listening Activity No. 11

Secretary: Good afternoon. Can I help you?
Student: Yes. I'd like to enrol for the English short training course.
Secretary: Certainly. What's your surname please?
Student: Potters.
Secretary: Could you spell that for me?
Student: Yes. It's P-O-T-T-E-R-S.
Secretary: Thank you... and what's your first name?
Student: Mike. That's spelled M-I-K-E.
Secretary: Thank you. Where are you from?
Student: The United States.
Secretary: I see. How old are you?
Student: 27.
Secretary: Good. Where do you live now?
Student: I live at 45 Hardcourt Lane E24.
Secretary: I see... and do you have a telephone number?
Student: Yes, 3653241.
Secretary: Thanks.

Listening Activity No. 12A

1. A: Excuse me. Can you tell me the time, please.
   B: Yes. It's a quarter to three.
2. A: Do you have the right time, please?
   B: I think it's twenty past five.
3. A: Do you know what time the next bus is, please?
   B: Yes. It's half past seven.
4. A: What time do you finish your work today?
   B: Twenty past six.
5. A: When do the shops open, please?
   B: At eight o'clock.
6. A: What time does the London train leave, please?
   B: Twelve thirty.
7. A: What's the next train to Birmingham, please?
   B: Eleven five.
8. A: Excuse me, please. What time does the Liverpool train arrive?
   B: Seventeen forty.
9. A: When does the Paris flight leave, please?
   B: Twenty-two fifty.
10. A: What time's the next flight to Amsterdam, please?
    B: Fifteen thirty.

Listening Activity No. 12B

A: Have you got your timetable?

B: Yes, I have.

A: When do we have Dr. Kent's lecture?

B: Monday morning at nine thirty and then at eleven thirty, erm... also Friday morning at ten thirty.

A: How long do they last?

B: An hour.

A: Which rooms are they in?

B: The Monday morning lectures take place in Room 50. The Friday morning one is in Room 15.

Listening Activity No. 13

1. The train now standing at Platform 4 is the 13:30 to Cambridge.
2. The express train to Birmingham is now due in on Platform 2 at 14:20.
3. The next train to arrive at Platform 3 is the 16:40 to Liverpool.
4. The next train to London will depart from Platform 1 at 7:30.
5. British Rail apologises for the delay to Leeds. It will now depart at 9:10 from Platform 5.
6. The next train to Oxford will depart from Platform 2 at 10:30.
7. The train now standing at Platform 5 is the 11:05 to Leeds.
8. British Rail apologises for the delay to the Manchester train. It will now depart at 11:30 from Platform 3.
9. British Airways announces the departure of Flight BA207 at 8:30 to Paris.
10. Olympic Airways Flight OA535 for Athens will depart at 12:05.
11. British Airways next flight to Belfast is Flight BA965 at 12:00.
12. SAS Flight SK506 to Stockholm will depart at 17:15.
13. British Airways announces the departure of Flight BA205 at 9:30 to Dublin.
14. British Airways next flight to Paris is Flight BA305 at 11:30.
15. Olympic Airways next flight to Athens is Flight OA593 at 14:40.
16. British Airways Flight BA707 for Edinburgh will depart at 15:05.

Listening Activity No. 14

The population density of the UK is about 234 inhabitants per square kilometre, which is well above the European Community average of 143 per square kilometre. England is the most densely populated member of EC with 364 people per square kilometre (with Greater London having a density according to the latest figures of 4263 people per square kilometre) and Scotland the least densely populated with 56 people per square kilometre, while Wales and Northern Ireland have 138 and 112 people per square kilometre respectively. Now let's turn to the figures for some of Britain's largest urban areas.

Greater London, the first city in the list, has an area of 1580 square kilometres. It also has a large population of 6735. 4 thousand in 1988. Birmingham in the English Midlands is 264 square kilometres in area with a population of 993. 7 thousand. Leeds, the largest city in the north of England, is 562 square kilometres with a population of 709. 6 thousand. The industrial Scottish town of Glasgow, with an area of 198 square kilometres, has a surprisingly high population of 703. 2 thousand. Edinburgh, Scotland's capital, with an area of 261 square kilometres has a population of 433. 5 thousand. Manchester is 116 square kilometres with a population of 445. 9 thousand. Bristol on the southwest of England is 110 square kilometres with a population of 377. 7 thousand. In the Midlands, Coventry is the smallest city in this list. It's 97 square kilometres with a population of only 306. 2 thousand.

Listening Activity No. 15

In 1985, there were 6261 full-time undergraduate students with 3472 men and 2742 women at the university. The distribution of these students was as follows.

1 Beginning with the field of science, we find high domination of the field by men, with 1137 men and 616 women enrolling in science.

2 Next, in the field of social science, we again find domination by men, the figures being 484 for men, 401 for women.

3. In the field of engineering, the difference is even greater. The number for men is 509 while only 56 women are enrolled in engineering.

4. In the field of arts, the number for men is 593 and for women it is 943. This is the first field we find dominated by women.

5. In medicine there are 306 men and somewhat more women at 336. This is a second field in which women lead.

6. Turning to dentistry, as you might expect, the field is dominated by men. The number for men is 139 and for women it is 107.

7. In law and in veterinary science, we are happy to see there isn't much difference between men and women in these two fields. In law men number 182 and women 171. In veterinary science the figure for men is 110 while for women it is 104.

Listening Activity No. 16

From 1975 to 1985, the percentage of households with one car decreased slightly from 46.4% in 1975 to 45.2% in 1985. However, the percentage of households with two or more cars rose during this period. It is perhaps surprising that more households had a television than a washing machine. In fact, the percentage of households with a television was over 90% throughout the ten years. There was a steady rise in the percentage of homes with central heating from 30% in 1975 to 60% in 1985. The percentage of households with a telephone showed a steep increase from 51.9% in 1975 to 80.5% in 1985. The number of UK households with home computers showed a large jump, from only 2.5% in 1975 to 12.6% in 1985. One of the most noticeable features of this report is the addition of figures for video recorders. 30% of British homes had video recorders in 1985. It seems likely that both video recorders and home computers will become more common in homes in the UK in the future.

Listening Activity No. 17

Good morning. I'd like this morning to continue our discussion about British trade, and I have brought a couple of pie charts that I'd like you to look at. They give information about British trade by geographical distribution in 1987.

The left pie chart is for exports and the right one is for imports. Now let's look first at the left pie chart, the exports pie chart. You can see the European Community accounted for 49% of Britain's exports trade in 1987, and the other developed countries accounted for respectively, North America at 16%, the rest of Western Europe outside the European Community at 10%, and the other developed countries accounted for 5%. These shaded areas represent the developing countries' portion. The larger one is for other developing countries except the oil-exporting countries, which accounts for 11%. And the smaller, which is for the oil-exporting countries, received 7% of Britain's exports in 1987. The last and smallest was Britain's rather minor exports to former centrally planned economies and this figure was only 2% in 1987.

Now let's take a look at the right pie chart which is for imports. The distribution here is roughly similar. The European Community accounted for 53% of Britain's imports in 1987, and the other developed countries accounted for... again... a large portion. The rest of Western Europe imported 40%... oh pardon me, 14% of Britain's imports in 1987. North America accounted for 11%, and other developed countries represent 8% of Britain's imports in 1987. Turning to other developing countries once again, the largest of the two shaded areas is for developing countries other than oil-exporting countries. And these accounted for about 10% of Britain's imports in 1987 and the remaining shaded area which is for oil-exporting countries accounted for only 2% of Britain's import in 1987. 2% also is the figure for Britain's imports from centrally planned economies, as you can see from the lined area in the figures.

Listening Activity No. 18

Researchers have done some investigation into what young people believe is a woman's place in society. Here is a report on some of their findings.

The Chinese are consistent supporters of sex equality with only 12% of young people believing that a woman's place is in the home. 93% are enthusiastic about sharing the housework and 85% of them believe that women should be paid the same for doing the same job. 80% think that nursing is a woman's job and 90% of them believe that mining is only men' s work. 13% of Chinese, an extremely low percentage, believe cooking is solely a woman's job and 7%, even fewer, think that only she should do the washing.

For a more traditional view of a woman's place, turn to the Japanese. 52% think women belong in the home. 89% of young people believe that a couple should share the housework and get equal pay for doing the same job. 65% of them believe nursing is a good job for women and 90% believe that mining is solely men's work. 75% of them believe a woman should do the washing and 82% of them think she should do the cooking at home.

80% of Koreans believe men and women should get the same pay for the same job. 39% believe a woman's place is in the home. 75% of them believe that housework should be shared between men and women if both work, but there's almost a complete reversal when it comes to doing the washing and cooking. Here, very few believe in sharing the work. 62% and 65% respectively believe that women should do both. 85% of Koreans believe nursing is a woman's job and 87% think mining is a man's job.

Turning to Thailand, we find a country that's not over enthusiastic about equality: 45% of young people believe that a woman should stay at home. However, there's an interesting 20% gap between whether cooking and washing are soly women's jobs. 67% vote for women doing the washing, while only 47% feel the same way about cooking and 86% of Thais believe that housework should be shared between men and women. 87% of young people believe that men and women should be paid the same for the same job. 92% think nursing is women's work and 95% of them believe mining should be done by men.

Listening Activity No. 19

1. A: When's Lincoln's birthday?
   B: It's February the 12th.
2. A: Do you know Valentine's Day ?
   B: Yes, it's February 15th, oh sorry, 14th.
3. A: When's Washington's birthday?

B: It's the 21st of February.

4. A: Do you know when April Fool's Day is?

   B: Yes, of course. It is April the 1st.

5. A: When's Easter?

   B: It is the 3rd of April.

6. A: When's Mother's Day?

   B: It's May the 8th.

7. A: What date is Memorial Day?

   B: It's May 30th.

8. A: Do you know when Father's Day is?

   B: Yes, it's the 19th of June.

9. A: Do you know when Independence Day is?

   B: It's July the 4th.

10. A: Is there a Friendship Day?

    B: Yes. It's on August 7th.

11. A: When's Halloween?

    B: It's on October the 31st.

12. A: When's Thanksgiving Day?

    B: It's the 24th of November.

Listening Activity No. 20

The British are a nation of newspaper readers. Many of them even have a daily paper delivered to their homes in time of breakfast. British newspapers can be divided into two groups: quality and popular. Quality newspapers are more serious and cover home and foreign news thoughtfully while popular newspapers like shocking, personal stories as well as some news. These two groups of papers can be distinguished easily because quality newspapers are twice the size of popular newspapers.

Now you are going to hear the circulation of some of these two groups of newspapers in 2003, and when they were founded.

First, quality daily newspapers:

The Daily Telegraph was founded in 1855 and its circulation was 990,000 in 2003. The circulation of *The Times* was 690,000, and it was founded in 1785. *The Guardian* was founded in 1821 and its circulation was 410,000 in 2003. *The Financial Times* was founded in 1888 and its circulation was 450,000.

Now come to quality Sunday newspapers:

The Sunday Times was established in 1822 and its circulation was145,000 and the circulation of *The Observer* was 480,000. *The Observer* was founded in 1791. *The Sunday Telegraph* was established in 1961 and its circulation was 830,000 in 2003.

Now let us look at the circulation for popular daily newspapers in 2003.

The Daily Express was founded in 1900 and its circulation was 1,000,000 and *The Sun* was founded in 1964 and its circulation was 3,730,000. *The Mirror* was established in 1903 and its circulation was 2,130,000. The circulation of *Daily Mail* was 2,470,000 and it was founded in 1896.

Now look at the popular Sunday newspapers.

News of the World was founded in 1843 and the circulation of it was 4,100,000. *Sunday Mirror* was founded in 1963 and the circulation was 1,880,000. *The People* was founded in 1881 and its circulation was 1,390,000. *The Mail on Sunday* was founded in 1982, and the circulation was 710, 000. *Sunday Express* was founded in 1918 and the circulation was 850,000.

Unit Two

Listening Activity No. 1

A: If you wouldn't mind answering just a few more questions, your family name is Riley, isn't it?

B: That's right.

A: How do you spell it, please?

B: R-I-L-E-Y.

A: Thank you. And could you let me have your first name, as well?

B: Certainly. Peter.

A: Could you tell me how long you've been studying English, Mr. Riley?

B: Six years.

A: And what examinations have you passed?

B: The IELTS test and my overall band is 6.

A: Thank you, Mr. Riley. Now I have to ask you to try and assess your English in relation to your special subject needs. Let's start with reading. How much help do you need as regards reading?

B: I read quite a lot in my special subject. None, really.

A: What about listening? Do you need any help with that?

B: Yes, I think so. I need a lot of help there.

A: And what about writing?

B: Erm... some help, I think. My main problem in that area is time.

A: And speaking?

B: A lot of help there. That's certainly my biggest worry.

Listening Activity No. 2

A: Good morning. I' m Peter Smith from Indian.

B: Good morning. My name is Li Ying from China.

A: Ah, have you registered for the courses yet?

B: Yes, I have.

A: Good. So, what subject did you put first?

B: Computer Science.

A: I see. And what subject did you put last then?

B: Oh, Arts.

A: That's interesting. Could you give any reasons for your choice? I mean why did you put Computer first, for example?

B: Well, now in my country, computers are very popular and it will be easier to find a job after graduation and also computer-related jobs are well paid. I suppose that makes a difference. Besides, information technology does have a very big effect on our lives, doesn't it?

A: Yes, I agree. It allows us to store very large amounts of information, transmit a lot of information quickly and process a lot of information as soon as we receive it.

B: Yes. With developments in information technology we can use computers in so many different ways, such as sending messages directly and receiving TV programmes from one country to another and processing all kinds of information.

A: Yes, it is more commonly used in my country too. And why did you put Arts last ?

B: Oh, yes, that's simple. I've nothing against Arts. It's quite interesting and creative but I really don't have talent in that area. So I put it last.

A: I see. What about the other subjects? What order did you put those in?

B: Medicine second, Dentistry third and Engineering fourth.

Listening Activity No. 3

Conversation 1

Mary 4217845

Peter: Hello. May I speak to Mary?

Mary: Speaking.

Peter: Mary, Freda and I were wondering if you and David would like to have a night out with us sometime.

Mary: All right, we'd like that very much. What did you have in mind?

Peter: Well, perhaps we could go and see a film, and then have something to eat afterwards.

Mary: That would be great. When?

Peter: We were thinking of Friday.

Mary: That should be OK. I'll have to check with David, but I don't think we are doing anything.

Peter: All right. Perhaps you could let me know tomorrow?

Mary: OK. Or I'll phone later. See you then! And thanks for the invitation.

Conversation 2

Peter: Hello, 2045789.

Mary: Hello, Peter?

Peter: Yes. Is that Mary?

Mary: Yes. How are you?

Peter: Fine. Have you spoken to David?

Mary: Yes. I'm afraid we're busy on Friday. We're going to a party, apparently. What are you doing on Saturday?

Peter: Freda's parents are coming over.

Mary: Oh, that's a pity. Some other time then.

Peter: Yes. See you tomorrow then.

Mary: Yes, see you.

Listening Activity No.4

And now the weather forecast by BBC's Rob McElnee. Rob.

Here's the weather forecast for the next twenty-four hours for the whole of England, Wales, and Scotland. Well, in South England and Midlands it'll be mainly cloudy with showers or longer spells of rain, and there will be quite a cold wind coming from the west creating temperatures around 3-5 degrees celsius. I don't think you'll see much of the sun: cloudy all day with showers, I'm afraid.

And in Wales and Northern Ireland, there will be a mixture of sunny spells in the morning and in the afternoon there will be quite a strong northeastly wind causing the temperature to be lower than yesterday, around 2-4 degrees. You can expect some rain in the evening.

The east coast of England will see the best of today's weather. It will be warmer than yesterday, no winds, and sunshine, so quite warm for the time of the week.

In Scotland and Northern Ireland, however, there'll be heavy rain and snow over the highest ground. The temperature will drop to below freezing, −3 or −5 and on the highest spots −10. It will be very cold and very windy everywhere with gales in places and severe gales in parts of the north. Again very cold below freezing and very windy. And that's all from me.

Listening Activity No.5

A: Good morning. May I help you?

B: Yes. I'm looking for a flat. I'd like one with two bedrooms.

A: All right. Have a seat, please. Let me ask you a few questions. First of all, may I have your name, please?

B: My name's Perry Pratley.

A: How do you spell your last name, Mr. Pratley?

B: It's P-R-A-T-L-E-Y.

A: P-R-A-T-L-E-Y. First name: Perry. And what's your present address, Mr. Pratley?

B: It's 14 Twyford Avenue.

A: How do you spell Twyford?

B: T-W-Y-F-O-R-D.

A: Twyford. That's in West Ealing, isn't it?

B: Yes, it is.

A: Do you have a phone number?

B: Yes. It's 5638995.

A: 5638995. And could you tell me your occupation, please?

B: I'm a clerk.

A: I see. And the name of your employer?

B: I work for Barclays Bank in West Ealing.

A: Barclays Bank, fine. And you're looking for a two bedroom flat.

B: That's right.

A: Could you wait just a minute, please? I'll take a look in our files.

Listening Activity No.6

Landlord: Hello. Can I help you?

Tenant: Yes. I saw an advert in the local paper for a room to rent. Is it still available?

Landlord: Yes, it is. Would you like to see it?

Tenant: Thank you.

Landlord: Here is the room. As you can see, it is large and has plenty of space. There is a single bed and a settee in the corner. The kitchen, toilet and bathroom are on the first floor.

Tenant: I see. Would I share them with anyone else?

Landlord: Yes, you would share them with four other people who have rooms here. Is that alright for you?

Tenant: Yes, that's fine. May I ask you a few questions about the accommodation?

Landlord: Certainly. Go ahead.

Tenant: Is there a phone in the house I can use?

Landlord: I am sorry there isn't, but you can receive calls here and you can make calls from the phone box down the road.

Tenant: I see. Will I have to pay any bills?

Landlord: No, your rent covers all the bills.

Tenant: That's very good. The rent is £200 per month, isn't it? When is it due?

Landlord: The rent is due on the first day of the month. Is there anything else you would like to know?

Tenant: No. I think you've told me all that I need to know. Can I think about the room and call you before 6 pm with my decision?

Landlord: Certainly, if you decide to take the room you will have to pay £200 plus £150 deposit which is refundable when you leave, providing you haven't damaged anything. If you break anything, though, I can't refund all your deposit.

Tenant: I understand. Would you please tell me your telephone number?

Landlord: Yes. 4093378.

Tenant: 4093378. Thank you very much. I will speak to you later on today.

Landlord: Fine, but you'd better phone back as soon as you can if you want it because I may rent it out to someone else in an hour or two.

Listening Activity No. 7

Officer: Next, please. Good morning, Sir. May I have your disembarkation card?

Student: What?

Officer: Your landing card. Do you have one?

Student: No, I have no card.

Officer: I see. Well, I'm afraid you need one. Here, let me help you. First of all, could I have your surname, please?

Student: My name?

Officer: Yes, your last name. You know, your family name.

Student: Ah, Yes. Anthony Butcher.

Officer: I beg your pardon?

Student: Anthony Butcher.

Officer: Could you spell that for me, please?

Student: B-U-T-C-H-E-R, Butcher.

Officer: B-U-T-C-H-E-R. And your first name?

Student: Anthony.

Officer: I'm sorry, but I'm afraid you're going to have to spell that one too.

Student: A-N-T-H-O-N-Y.

Officer: All right. And what's your occupation, Mr. Butcher? What do you do?

Student: My job?

Officer: Yes.

Student: I'm a student. I don't have a job right now.

Officer: And when were you born? Uh, what's your birthday?

Student: 14 April, 1966.

Officer: April 14, 1966. And your nationality?

Student: Sorry?

Officer: What country do you come from?

Student: My country?... Italy.

Officer: So you're an Italian. And what's the reason for your trip? Why have you come to the UK?

Student: Why? To study English.

Officer: Fine. And where will you be staying?

Student: With my brother.

Officer: All right. What's his address, please?

Student: Address?

Officer: Yes, your brother's address. Where does he live?

Student: 35 Halefield Road, Tottenham, London.

Officer: 35 Halefield Road, Tottenham. OK, that's it. Have a nice stay. Next, please.

Listening Activity No. 8

A: Excuse me, please. I seem to have lost my handbag.

B: Oh, I see. Well, I'll have to fill out this lost property report for you. It was a handbag you say?

A: That's right.

B: What sort of a handbag?

A: Well, it was oval shaped and made of leather.

B: I see. And what colour was it?

A: It was a black and white checked one.

B: And what would it be worth?

A: Well, it was quite an expensive one. I bought it last month and I paid fifty pounds for it.

B: What was in your bag?

A: A purse with two hundred pounds cash, my car keys and my driving licence as well.

B: And where did you leave it?

A: I'm sure I left it in the coffee shop on the sixth floor.

B: And when was that?

A: About 2:30 I think.
B: Where did you go when you left the coffee shop?
A: To the record department. I wanted to buy some magazines there, but I found I'd lost my handbag so I came here.
B: I'm sure it will turn up. Now could you tell me your name?
A: Thomas. Janet Thomas.
B: And your address, Mrs. Thomas?
A: 25 King Street.
B: Your telephone number please?
A: 4237689.
B: All right, Mrs. Thomas. We will let you know as soon as we find it.
A: Thank you very much.

Listening Activity No.9

A: I wonder if you'd mind telling me your full name please, Miss Sutton.
B: Shirley Sutton.
A: How do you spell Sutton?
B: S-U-T-T-O-N.
A: Thank you. Now let me see. Uhmm, you studied English at college, didn't you?
B: Yes, that's right. I was at Leeds University.
A: When was that?
B: In 1990.
A: So you graduated about 4 years ago.
B: That's right.
A: And could you tell me what kind of work experience you've had?
B: My last position was as a teacher at Smithfield Secondary School in Leeds.
A: When was that exactly?
B: From 1992 to 1993.
A: Uhuh.
B: Before that I worked for K Mart as a shop assistant. That was from 1990 to 1992. And I've been doing freelance work for the last few months.
A: Well, Ms. Sutton, your qualifications for the job are excellent. Could you tell me what kind of salary you are expecting?
B: Well, in my last job I was making five hundred pounds a month. I understand that this position has a starting salary of around six hundred a month.
A: That's right.
B: That would be fine with me.
A: And is there anything you'd like to ask about the job?
B: Yes. I'd like to know if the company provides opportunities for further education.
A: Yes. Our employees are allowed to take up to four hours a week at full pay to attend col-

lege courses.

B: That's very generous.

A: Is there anything you'd like to know?

B: No, not at this time.

A: Well, I've enjoyed meeting and talking with you. We'll call you within the week.

B: Thank you. I appreciate the time you've given me. Bye.

A: Goodbye.

Listening Activity No. 10

Message 1

John Hello, 562261.

Mary Oh, hallo. Er... could I speak to Bill?

John Ah, afraid he's not here at the moment. Could I take a message for him?

Mary Um, yes... er... um yeah, would you ask him to phone me tonight before 10:00, if he gets back before then—I go to bed at 10... yes? Er... or tomorrow morning... er... before I leave for work. I... I leave the house at about 8:30. OK?

John: Right, yeah.

Mary: My number is 235669.

John: Right and you, oh... what's your name?

Mary: Oh, oh, sorry. Mary... Mary Roberts.

John: Mary Roberts.

Mary: Right. Thank you. Thank you very much.

John: Fine. I'll give him the message. Goodbye.

Mary: Bye.

Message 2

Linda: Hello, 237561.

Henry: Oh, Henry Grey here. Can I speak to Tom, please?

Linda: Ah, I'm afraid Tom's not in. Can I take a message for him?

Henry: Oh... um... yes... look... look, I've... I've arranged to meet him tomorrow morning in my office.

Linda: Yeah.

Henry: At half past nine. Um... look, I can't make it at that... as early as that now. Can you give him a... a... message?

Linda: Er... yes.

Henry: I want to... want to change the time of the meeting to 10:30 please, instead of 9:30.

Linda: Yeah.

Henry: All right? Now, look, if ... if this isn't possible, can you get Tom to phone back at any time this afternoon before 5:30?

Linda: Yes. What... what's your number?
Henry: Er... my number is 488992.
Linda: 488992, 10:30 tomorrow morning in your office. What's your name again?
Henry: Henry Grey.
Linda: Fine. I'll leave him the message.
Henry: Thanks so much. Bye-bye.
Linda: Goodbye.

Message 3

John: Hello, 345714.
Anne: Oh... um... is... is Linda there?
John: Er... no, I'm afraid she's out at the moment.
Anne: Oh, Lord... um... well, look... um... this is Anne Bridge speaking... um... my...
John: Oh, hang on. I haven't got a pencil. Hang on just a second... right. Anne Bridge, yeah.
Anne: Would you please tell Linda that the film will be shown at 8:00 this evening instead of 8:30.
John: Yeah.
Anne: So I think we'd better meet at 7:30 in front of the school gate.
John: Right, so you are coming to meet her at 7:30 in front of the school gate.
Anne: Could you get Linda to call me at lunch time?
John: Yeah.
Anne: Thanks.
John: Oh... what's your... what's your number?
Anne: Um... 444...
John: Yeah.
Anne: 0456.
John: 0456.
Anne: Yeah.
John: Right. I'll give her the message as soon as I see her.
Anne: Oh, thanks a lot. Sorry to trouble you. Bye.
John: That's all right. Bye-bye.

Message 4

John: Hello, 409267.
Debbie: Hello... hallo. Do you think I could speak to Linda?
John: Er... afraid she's out at the moment. Can I take a message for her?
Debbie: Ah, now, it's about the arrangements for Sunday.
John: Yes.

Debbie Saturday, no? Um... this is awfully difficult. Now, well, perhaps you could tell her that I've heard the weather forecast this evening. It's going to rain tomorrow, so we have to use the school hall for our stalls in stead of the playing-ground.

John Just a minute. Let me get a pencil and write them down. Yes. Use the school hall instead of playing-ground.

Debbie Would you please tell her to come earlier tomorrow morning? Let's say at 8:30, yeah, 8:30 at the school hall, so we will have plenty of time to rearrange our stalls. Could you say that? She should be there at 8:30.

John: Yeah. Who actually are you?

Debbie: I... Debbie Harris.

John: Yeah. Has she got your number?

Debbie: She has. Thank you so much.

John: Fine. Do you want to give it to me just in case?

Debbie: No. It's all right, I think. It's perfectly all right.

John: Fine. I'll give her the message, then. Goodbye.

Debbie: Goodbye to you.

Listening Activity No. 11

Interviewer: Excuse me, my name is Kendra Hammer. I'm doing a survey on transportation in the city. Are you college students?

Mike: Yes, we are. I'm Mike. He is Tom and she is Liz. They are my classmates.

Interviewer: Hi. It's nice to meet you. Can I ask you some questions?

Mike: Uh... OK, if it's quick.

Interviewer: Sure. Mike, how do you usually get to work?

Mike: By bus.

Interviewer: And Liz, how about you?

Liz: I drive to school.

Interviewer: I see. Do you drive too, Tom?

Tom: No. I ride a bicycle to school.

Interviewer: How far is your school from your home?

Tom: Not very far, only about a few blocks.

Interviewer: How long does it usually take you to get to school?

Tom: Oh, about fifteen minutes by bike.

Interviewer: How far is it from your home, Mike?

Mike: About five miles.

Interviewer: How many minutes does it take you to get to school?

Mike: About 15 minutes or twenty minutes.

Interviewer: How about you, Liz? How far is your school from your home?

Liz: Twenty miles. But some days it seems like a hundred.

Interviewer: How long does it usually take you to get to school?

Liz: It depends. In good weather, it takes about one hour. In bad weather, on rainy days like today, ninety minutes.

Interviewer: Uh ... are you ever late to school because of transportation problems?

Liz: Well, no. If there is a car accident, it slows me down a lot, but when it rains, I just leave earlier.

Interviewer: How about you, Mike? Are you ever late for school?

Mike: Well, yes. Sometimes the bus is late.

Tom: I'm lucky. I don't have that problem.

Interviewer: Do you think that transportation is a serious problem in this city?

Mike: Yes, it is a problem. We need more buses.

Liz: Yes, definitely. We need a better subway system.

Interviewer: Well, that's all. Thank you very much.

Mike: You are welcome.

Listening Activity No. 12

Operator: Good morning. Pan Am.

Penny: Yes. I'm phoning about the job advertised in this morning's paper.

Operator: Oh, yes. I'll put you through to the personnel manager Mr. Bradshaw. Could I have your name, please?

Penny: Yes. It's Penny Jacobs.

Operator: All right, just a second.

Bradshaw: Hello, Bradshaw speaking.

Penny: Er... Mr. Bradshaw. My name is Penny Jacobs. I'm phoning about your advertisement for an air stewardess.

Bradshaw: Oh, yes. Um... are you a graduate?

Penny: Yes. I graduated from college last year.

Bradshaw: Which college did you graduate from?

Penny: UEA. The University of East Anglia.

Bradshaw: I see. And what did you study there?

Penny: I did sociology and foreign languages.

Bradshaw: Foreign languages? How many languages can you speak?

Penny: I can speak French and Italian.

Bradshaw: What kind of work experience have you had?

Penny: Well, I worked at K Mart in West Road for three months, then I began to work for Jade Travel Agency. I've been working for this agency for about six months.

Bradshaw: I see. And... er... you want to be a stewardess?

Penny: Yes, very much. When I was a child I dreamt of being an air stewardess. You see, I really like travelling and meeting people.

Bradshaw: OK, Miss Jacobs, well... um. Could you come in for an interview... say 9:30 on Friday morning?

Penny: Yes, that would be fine.

Bradshaw: Good. We're on the sixth floor of the ABB Building in Oxford Street. And could you bring your degree certificate and your birth certificate with you?

Penny: Yes, of course.

Bradshaw: Good. Miss Jacobs, see you on Friday morning then.

Penny: Thank you. Goodbye.

Listening Activity No. 13

A: I'm from the local newspaper. May I ask you some questions?

B: Yes, of course.

A: What's your name?

B: I'm Caroline Wood from England.

A: How long have you been an airline stewardess, Miss Wood?

B: Just over four years.

A: And you've never had any other job?

B: No. I've worked as a stewardess for Singapore Airlines ever since I left university.

A: University? What subject did you do?

B: Mathematics.

A: You didn't finish your degree then?

B: Oh, I got a degree all right, and quite a good one too.

A: But then,... why?

B: People are always asking me that question. The answer's quite simple. I'm doing what I want to do.

A: Yes, but you don't make any use of your education that way.

B: Well, most people who have degrees don't either, except to make money or to get on in the world. Well, I don't especially want to get on. I like to travel and love meeting people. In my work as a stewardess I meet all kinds of people and travel from one country to another. I really enjoy this work. Besides, I make money too, enough to live on.

A: But in effect, you've thrown away a very expensive education.

B: Do you think so?

A: Hm.

B: Actually I make very good use of it.

A: Hm.

B: You see. When I finish work I don't take any problems home with me. I have time to read and I have time to learn foreign languages and then to practise them.

A: How many languages can you speak?

B: I can speak Spanish, French and a little Chinese.

A: Chinese?

B: Yes. My boyfriend is Chinese and lives in Singapore. I lived there for one year with my father. He was an engineer.

A: I see. Well, thank you for your time, Miss Wood.

Listening Activity No. 14

Clerk: Can I help you?

Customer: Yes. I'd like to transfer some money to a bank account in New York.

Clerk: Er... um, do you have all the details?

Customer: Yes.

Clerk: OK. We can fix that up for you right now. Do you have the name of the bank?

Customer: Yes. It's Great Western Bank in New York.

Clerk: And who is the money to go to?

Customer: Mrs. Ellen Robbins.

Clerk: Mm... Right. And her address?

Customer: 3021 Sagebrush Drive in New York.

Clerk: Sorry, could you say that again please?

Customer: 3021 Sagebrush Drive, S-A-G-E-B-R-U-S-H Drive, New York.

Clerk: Thank you. And her name is Robbins?

Customer: Yes, that's right.

Clerk: Good. And the money is to be forwarded to her account at Great Western Bank?

Customer: Yes. Her account number is V0233779.

Clerk: V0233779. Right. And the amount?

Customer: Three hundred pounds.

Clerk: Three hundred pounds. Mm. OK. Now let's see, the exchange rate today is... er... ah yes. 1.5 dollars to the pound. So three hundred pounds comes to four hundred fifty American dollars. And your name?

Customer: Elton John.

Clerk: Elton John.

Customer: Right.

Clerk: Mm... and your address?

Customer: 8 Grange Park, Ealing Broadway.

Clerk: 8 Grange Park, Ealing Broadway. Right. Well, now, there's a transfer fee. It's three pounds for a payment order and six pounds if we telegraph it through.

Customer: What's the difference?

Clerk: Well, with a telegraphic transfer it will get there in 3 days. The other way will take about two weeks.

Customer: Oh, it's fairly urgent, so I think we'd better telegraph it.

Clerk: All right. Well, I'll hand this on to the teller and she'll call out your name in a few minutes.

Customer: Thank you.

Listening Activity No. 15

Tom: Hello. I'd like to open a bank account.

Clerk: What type of account do you want?

Tom: Well, I'm going to London University in October and I need somewhere to deposit my grant.

Clerk: Well, who pays your grant?

Tom: The British Council.

Clerk: You could open a student account with us.

Tom: What does it offer?

Clerk: Oh, normally, you'd receive a cheque book which saves you having to carry a lot of cash around. You would also get a connect card which you can use twenty-four hours a day in our machine at any branches and in the machines of Lloyds, Bank of Scotland and the Royal Bank of Scotland. You can obtain up to two hundred per day and night by using your connect card. The connect card can also be used for a cheque guarantee card.

Tom: Sorry, what is that?

Clerk: A cheque guarantee card enables you to cash up to fifty pounds without prior arrangement at most banks in the UK. And you'll need it to pay shops, garages, hotels, etc. because it guarantees that your cheque will be honoured.

Tom: I see. Will I get interest on the money in my student account?

Clerk: Yes, you will get a small amount of interest, i. e., up to five hundred, interest is four percent. Five hundred and more, the interest goes up to six percent.

Tom: What other advantages do student accounts have?

Clerk: Well, we offer a two-hundred-fifty overdraft limit at our lower rate of interest.

Tom: Can I open a student account then? What do I need?

Clerk: You need a letter to prove that you are getting a grant from some authority and identification such as your passport. Then, you need to fill in some simple forms about your course and the duration of your stay in the UK, your address and your signature.

Tom: OK, I will bring them in later. Thank you for your time.

Clerk: You are welcome. Goodbye.

Listening Activity No. 16

Jane: Look at this picture. This is a party my sister had two years ago for her wedding I think it was.

John: Who's that? I mean the woman on the very left?

Jane: Oh, that's Aunt Elme. She's my mother's sister. She got married very young and has two grown-up children, now who have all left home. She's great fun and she and I get on really well. She says she's old-fashioned and doesn't know anything about the world 'cause she's always been a housewife, but in fact she is really very broadminded about most things. The lady she's talking to is my aunt, Louise, but on my father's side. She is a music teacher in London University. She married someone really odd but it didn't work out and they ended up in the divorce courts after two years.

John: And who's that man?

Jane: The one with his back to the camera?

John: Yes, in the middle of the two other men.

Jane: Oh, that's my uncle, Tom. He is humorous. He's a freelance designer and works in Paris. We see him at Christmas time every year. I like him very much. The man he is talking to is his friend, Lewis. They used to work together. Now he lives in London. Now, let's see.... Who else is there? The man in the middle of the group on the right is my cousin, Roger. He's a sales manager and he's really pompous and full of himself. Thank goodness he lives up in Scotland. And do you see that chap with the long hair and the beard over to the right? He's wearing glasses.

John: Oh, yes.

Jane: Well, he's another cousin, Mark. He's a student in Oxford University. He is one of the clever ones in the family. He is talking to his girlfriend. I can't remember her name.

Listening Activity No. 17

Landlord: Hello. 6593427.

Julia: Hello. I saw your advertisement on the college accommodation board for a room.

Landlord: Oh, oh, yeah. That's right.

Julia: I wonder if you could give me some more information?

Landlord: Yeah. Well, well, what would you like to know?

Julia: Well, I was wondering... er... what's the rent?

Landlord: Fifty pounds per week.

Julia: And what does that include?

Landlord: The room, obviously. It's your own room—a single one—so you don't have to share. But you share the bathroom and you can use the kitchen, but there are no meals included.

Julia: Right. Uhm... and what about heating and cooking arrangements?

Landlord: No, no, you don't have to pay for that. There's central heating in all the rooms, so there's nothing extra to pay there. The cooker is electric.

Julia: Oh, lovely. And do you want the rent weekly? Is there a deposit?

Landlord: You have to pay weekly. And there's a one-month deposit, payable in advance.

Julia: Right, that sounds fair enough. Are there any particular house rules, you know, that I've got to keep to?

Landlord: What do you mean?

Julia: Well, like what about guests and hours?

Landlord: Oh, yes. Well, you can come and go as you want, of course, but you must pay a deposit for the front door key. That's separate from the other deposit, I'm afraid.

Julia: I see.

Landlord: As for guests, they should be out by eleven o'clock. We don't like to say that, but we've had a bit too much trouble, so we have to.

Julia: Right. Is it quite near public transport?

Landlord: Oh, yes. Five minutes to the tube station, and the bus stop is just round the corner with buses into town every ten minutes or so.

Julia: Lovely. It sounds just the thing. Do you think I could come and have a look at it tomorrow afternoon?

Landlord: Yes, of course. I'll give you the address. Now it's 46 West Avenue, Acton, just opposite the post office.

Julia: West Avenue, yes, I know it. If I come about 4:30, is that all right?

Landlord: That's fine. By the way, your name is...?

Julia: Julia Smith.

Landlord: Right, Julia, I'll see you at 4:30 tomorrow afternoon then. Goodbye.

Julia: Bye-bye.

Listening Activity No. 18

A: Good morning, nurse. You're early.

B: Really? I don't think so—it's just gone nine.

A: Oh—so it has.

B: There's been an accident, then.

A: Yes. Ten minutes ago. A young woman saw it and telephoned us.

B: OK. We'd better get this form filled out. Did you get her name?

A: Yes. It's Julia Smith.

B: And what's her address?

A: 32 Westminster Road, Watford.

B: Now let's turn to the lady who had the accident. Is the injury bad?

A: No, I don't think so. Cuts, bruises, and shock.

B: Oh, not too serious at all.

A: No, she shouldn't be in for long.

B: Who is she?

A: A housewife.

B: What's her name?

A: Susan Thomas.

B: Thomas, OK. Where does she live?

A: 37 Merton Road, Harrow.

B. 37 Merton Road, Harrow. OK, what happened?

A: A boy ran in front of her car. She swerved to miss him and the car hit the kerb, and the lady hit the windscreen.

B: What about the boy?

A: The boy is all right, but the lady is in shock. The casualty officer is sending her to the Windsor Ward.

B: Have you got her things?

A: Yes. These things were in her bag. There's a purse with some money, and her driving licence.

B: Anything else?

A: Yes. There were some things in the car.

B: Could you call them out while I write a list?

A: Sure.

B: Oh, is it the 7th of March today?

A: No, the 2nd.

B: Right. What have we got, then?

A: OK. One Medical Card.

B: Oh, good. What else?

A: A sort of shopping list, a couple of pictures of her kids, I think.

B: Oh, dear. Has the family been notified?

A: Yes. I told the police, and they told her husband.

B: What else is there?

A: A dentist's appointment card, some tickets for a film.
B: Oh, dear, for tonight. What bad luck. Is that all?
A: That's the lot. OK, see you later, nurse. I hope the lady will be all right.

Listening Activity No. 19

The eruption of Mt. Vesuvius was probably the most famous eruption in history. However, the eruption of Mt. Vesuvius did not kill the most people of any volcanic eruption. Let's compare Mt. Vesuvius with some other famous volcanoes. Here is a chart with the names of six volcanoes. The chart tells you the name of the volcanic mountain, where it is located, the date of an eruption, and the approximate number of people who died in the eruption. Look at Mt. Vesuvius on the chart. It is located in Italy. It erupted in 79 A.D. Approximately 2,000 people died in the eruption. Write the number 2,000 in the correct place. Let's fill in the missing information on the chart for the other volcanic mountains. Are you ready to write in the information and complete the chart? OK. Let's begin with the next mountain on the chart—Cotopaxi. It's C-O-T-O-P-A-X-I. It is located in Ecuador. It erupted in 1877, and about 1,000 people died. Now look at Krakatoa. It is located in Indonesia. It erupted in 1883 and killed about 36,000 people. Write the year 1883 in the correct place. Now let's complete the information for Mount Pelee. It's P-E-L-E-E. Mount Pelee is located in Martinique. It erupted in 1902, killing 38,000 people. Did you write 38,000 in the correct space? OK. Next, fill in the blank for Mount St. Helens in Washington State in the United States. It erupted in 1980 and 60 people were killed. Finally, let's complete the chart for Mount Tambora in Indonesia. It erupted in 1815, killing 12,000 people. 12,000 people died in 1815. Now your chart should be complete.

Listening Activity No. 20

Landlord: Hello, 6438186.
Gretta: Hello, I'm ringing about the room you have advertised.
Landlord: Oh, yes...
Gretta: Is it still available?
Landlord: Yes, yes, it is.
Gretta: I wonder if you could tell me something about it?
Landlord: Yes. Well, what would you like to know?
Gretta: Well, I was wondering... er... how much is the rent?
Landlord: It's forty pounds a week.
Gretta: And what does that include?

Landlord: The room, of course. It's a single room. So you don't have to share. But you do have to share the bathroom and the kitchen.

Gretta: Are any meals included?

Landlord: No, no meals. You have to cook for yourself.

Gretta: Right,... and what about heating?

Landlord: There is a coin metre in the room. You can turn the heating on any time just by putting some coins in. So the heating is exclusive of the rent.

Gretta: Oh, I see. Is the cooker gas or electric?

Landlord: Electric. As I said, you share the kitchen with the other tenants.

Gretta: OK, and do you want the rent weekly or monthly?

Landlord: You have to pay weekly, on Monday.

Gretta: And do I have to pay a deposit?

Landlord: Yes, I'd like a deposit of one month's rent.

Gretta: Right. That sounds fair enough. Are there any particular rules that I have to keep to?

Landlord: Well, guests should be out by eleven o'clock. We don't really like to say that, but well, we've had a lot of trouble, so we have to.

Gretta: Uhuh. Is it quite near public transport?

Landlord: Oh yes. Five minutes to the tube station, and the bus stop is just round the corner—the buses into town run every ten minutes or so.

Gretta: Lovely. It sounds great. When is the room available?

Landlord: It'll be available from the 2nd of April.

Gretta: That will be next week then, good. ... Er... do you think I could come and have a look at it this evening?

Landlord: Yes, of course. Do you have the address?

Gretta: No, I don't. Could you tell me where it is ?

Landlord: All right. It's 34 Church Road, Highgate. How'll you be coming?

Gretta: By tube.

Landlord: Good. It is very close to Highgate tube station. It's near the post office, opposite the school.

Gretta: I see. I think I know it now. Can I come about six this evening?

Landlord: Well, I might not be back at six. So let's say eight. Is that OK?

Gretta: Fine.

Landlord: Oh, could you tell me your name?

Gretta: Gretta Faulkner.

Landlord: Sorry, the line is not good. Could you say it again?

Gretta: Gretta.

Landlord: Gretta, I'll see you around eight then. Goodbye.

Gretta: Bye-bye.

Unit Three

Listening Activity No. 1

A: Mr. Wang, would you like some tea?

B: Yes, please.

A: Here you are.

B: Thanks. Oh, it tastes different from Chinese tea.

A: Do you like it?

B: Yes. It's not too bad. How do you make English-style tea?

A: It's easy. Put some water in a kettle and boil the water. Then you should warm the pot.

B: Warm the pot? How do you do this?

A: Just by putting a little hot water into the teapot and swilling it round—you know, to make the very best tea, the water must be as hot as possible.

B: Uhuh, so what do you do then?

A: So then, you put some tea into the teapot, about two to three teaspoons, and then you pour the boiling water over the tea.

B: And then is it ready to drink?

A: No, you should let the tea stand for a few minutes to let it brew properly—it has to be quite strong—and then pour a little milk into a cup.

B: Some milk?

A: Yes, if you like tea with milk, which most English people do. Pour the tea into the cup and it's ready to drink, or if you want you can add some sugar to the tea, maybe one or two teaspoons.

B: That's it?

A: Yes, that's it.

B: I may give it a go next time, then.

Listening Activity No. 2

(Jack is staying with his sister Mary in England. He wants to have a shower but he doesn't know how to use it. So he phones Mary.)

Mary: 563721, EBC Company.

Jack: Good morning. Can I speak to Mary? It's her brother here.

Mary: Oh, Hi, Jack. This is Mary. When did you come? I thought you were coming this afternoon.

Jack: Yes. Well, I planned to. But my friend bought a ticket for this morning instead, so...

Mary: I see. Well, I'm sorry I'm very busy now so I can't really leave. Well, you can have a rest and take a shower...

Jack: That's just it. I'm going to take a shower but I don't know how to use your hot water tank.

Mary: Oh, OK... well..., don't plug in the electricity—the hot water tank, until you're absolutely sure you've filled it with water.

Jack: Don't plug in the hot water tank? Sorry?

Mary: Don't plug it into the mains.

Jack: Oh.

Mary: Yep?

Jack: I see... before it's full of water... Oh. I'm with you.

Mary: Um... because at the moment, er... it's drained off for the winter, you see.

Jack: I get you. Yeh.

Mary: Now the tank... it's got two taps underneath it.

Jack: Yes.

Mary: One's red. One's black.

Jack: Right.

Mary: You are all right?

Jack: Uhuh.

Mary: Now here... you've got to... you've got to close the red one first.

Jack: Close the red first, yes.

Mary: That's the drainage tap.

Jack: Yeah.

Mary: Then you've got to open the black one...

Jack: Open the black one.

Mary: ... which is the supply tap...

Jack: Yes... um, well, yes... open the black one, right.

Mary: And it'll take about five minutes probably to fill up.

Jack: Umhmn...

Mary: And then you can plug it into the mains.

Jack: Good. And then I get...?

Mary: And... about half an hour later you should have some hot water with any luck.

Jack: About a half hour?
Mary: Um.
Jack: Fine... so I've got electricity and water.
Mary: Yes.
Jack: Great... well... (*laughs*) sounds like...
Mary: You should be all right.
Jack: OK. Thanks. See you soon.

Listening Activity No. 3

Police are searching for a man who is wanted for questioning about a string of burglaries in the London area. In the incidents, a man tied a woman in her own house in the early hours of the morning and escaped with goods valued at around five thousand pounds. They included items of jewellery, a stereo, a video recorder and a colour TV set. The woman managed to free herself unhurt after the man fled. She described the man as follows.

He is about thirty years old and of medium build. He has a long angular face and a pointed nose. He has a small moustache and short black hair. His eyes are small and he wears glasses. He also has a faint scar on his left cheek.

I'll repeat that description. A man of medium build with a long angular face, a pointed nose and small eyes. He has a small moustache, short black hair and he was wearing glasses. He has a faint scar on his left cheek. As I said, please contact your nearest police station if you think you can offer any assistance.

Listening Activity No.4

Last night, a man broke into a factory in Leeds area and got away with cash of around six thousand pounds. He is about forty years old and very short, about 155 cm. He is almost completely bald and has got a little hair at the sides above each ear. But he does have big brown beard. He was later seen driving away from the scene in an old blue Escort car. Police warn that this man could be armed and therefore dangerous. If anyone has any information as to his whereabouts, please contact your nearest police station.

I'll repeat that description. A man about forty years old, 155cm tall, almost bald with a little hair above each ear. He has big brown beard. If anyone sees him, please contact your nearest police station.

Listening Activity No.5

A: Hello, 2345786.

B: Hello. Could I speak to Jim Schaefer, please?

A: Speaking.

B: Oh, hi, Jim. This is Kathy. I'm sorry to bother you so late. I just want to ask you a little favour.

A: Oh, sure. I'd like to help out, just anything you want.

B: Look. My sister Diana is coming to visit our campus. We're supposed to meet at the front of the main building at 9:00 am tomorrow.

A: Yes.

B: Unfortunately, I forgot that I've got a doctor's appointment tomorrow morning so I can't go and meet her. Could you possibly meet her for me?

A: Yes, I could do, but I've never seen your sister before.

B: Well, she is sort of average height and quite slim. She's twenty-one years old with short curly hair and she has an attractive face and usually looks pretty cheerful. It's easy to recognize her. She usually wears a jumper and trousers with flat shoes.

A: OK. Let me write that down... average height and slim... about twenty-one years old, with short curly hair and an attractive face. She will probably be wearing a jumper and trousers. Is that right?

B: Yes.

A: OK. I think I should be able to recognize her.

B: Thank you very much.

Listening Activity No.6

Woman: Officer, officer.

Officer: Yes, ma'am.

Woman: Somebody just took my purse. My money, my credit cards and everything's gone.

Officer: All right, just calm down a minute... OK. Now, what did the person look like?

Woman: He was kind of tall and thin.

Officer: About how tall ?

Woman: Around 1.70, something like that.

Officer: Around 1.70, and how old was he?

Woman: I'm not sure. Oh... he was fairly young... er in his teens, I think... seventeen or eighteen.

Officer: And what colour was his hair?
Woman: Blond, and it was long and frizzy.
Officer: Eyes?
Woman: I don't know. It all happened so fast.
Officer: Yes, of course. What was he wearing?
Woman: He was wearing old jeans and a T-shirt, and boots. Oh yes, he was wearing glasses.
Officer: Fine, and now tell me about your purse. What did it look like?
Woman: Well, it was red and it had a shoulder strap.
Officer: What was it made of?
Woman: Leather.
Officer: OK. Now I'll need your name and address.

Listening Activity No. 7

A: Clifton Police Station. Can I help you?
B: Yes. It's about my daughter, Mary. She went to school this morning and she hasn't arrived yet, and it's 11 o'clock.
A: Just a moment, Mrs. . . . ?
B: Mrs. Joe Smith, 34 Bath Road.
A: Thank you. Now Mrs. Smith, what exactly is the matter?
B: Well, Mary left home this morning at about 9:00, then her teacher telephoned me about an hour ago and asked if Mary was ill. I said: "No. Why?" and then she said. . .
A: I see. Now, let's have a few details. How old is Mary?
B: She is six.
A: And what does she look like?
B: Well, she is slim and has long dark hair tied in a pigtail with a ribbon in it.
A: Yes, slim, long dark hair tied in a pigtail with a ribbon in it. And what colour is the ribbon?
B: It's pink.
A: Pink, OK. What does she wear?
B: She is wearing a white short-sleeved blouse and a pink and white striped skirt, long stockings and black shoes.
A: Just a minute, let me write them down. A white short-sleeved blouse and a pink and white striped skirt, with long socks and black shoes. Is that right?
B: Yes, exactly.
A: All right, Mrs. Smith, we'll help you find out your daughter. We'll give you a call as soon as we get the information about your daughter.
B: Thank you very much.

Listening Activity No. 8

A: Uh, excuse me. I'm looking for a bank. Is there one around here?

B: A bank? Let's see now. Oh, OK, the road we're in now is the Broadway, so you need to go down this street to the intersection, turn left and go one block until you come to Beach Road, turn right onto Beach Road and then it's on the right side of the street, just past the Chemist's. You can't miss it.

A: I see. Down to the intersection, turn left, go to the end of the block, and then turn right.

B: That's it.

A: Thanks a lot.

B: You're welcome.

Listening Activity No.9

A: Excuse me. Could you tell me where the university library is, please?

B: The university library? Oh, yes. Well, when you leave the bus station, you should turn right. And if you walk a little way down the road, you'll come to a crossroads. Turn right here, and about...

A: Er... what's the name of the street?

B: Oh, it's First Avenue. So you walk along this street, and about two hundred yards further down, there's another crossroads, and this time you turn left into Hill Road.

A: So that's right at the first crossroads and left at the second?

B. Uhuh... then as you walk up Hill Road, you'll see the post office on your left, and next to it a large supermarket. The library's just across the road from it, on your right.

A: OK, Hill Road, opposite the supermarket.

B: It's a fairly distinctive building, easy to spot, next to a big hotel.

A: That's great. Opposite the supermarket and next to the big hotel. Actually, I could do with finding a good bookshop. Are there any nearby?

B: Hmm... there are a couple, one on Second Avenue and another on First. I think the one on First Avenue is probably the best.

A: How do I get there?

B: Well, instead of turning left up Hill Road at the second crossroads, just carry straight on. You'll see a pub on the corner. Then it's not the next building, but the one after that.

A: So it's pretty near the library, then?

B: Yeah. The one on Second Avenue is nearer actually, but, as I said, this one's bigger.

A: Wonderful. Oh, hang on. Before I go to the bookshop, I should get some money first. Is there a Lloyds Bank in town?

B: Er... Lloyds Bank? Yes... now... it's... well, if you go straight across the first crossroads when coming out of the bus station, you'll eventually get to a junction with Second Avenue. And I think Lloyds is on the corner there, opposite a small hairdresser's.

A: OK. I think I can remember all those directions. Thank you ever so much. You've been very kind.

B: Not at all. I hope you find all the places OK.

Listening Activity No. 10

1. You've just come out of the bus station. Turn right and walk to the junction of Elm Avenue and Hanover Road. Turn left and walk up Hanover Road. Cross Woodlawn Lane. and continue up Hanover Road, you will see a big building on your right.
   What is the building on your left?
2. You've just come out of the bus station. Turn right and walk to the junction of Elm Avenue and Hanover Road. Turn left and walk up Hanover Road. Pass the Bank of Asia on you left and a small park just opposite. Cross Woodlawn Lane. Keep straight on until you see the zebra crossing, turn right, walk along Street Lane till the end of this road.
   What is the building on your right?
3. You've just come out of the bus station. Turn left. Walk straight on. Take the first turning on the right. Go along the Street Lane. Take the second turning on the left.
   What is the building on your right?

Listening Activity No. 11

1. *(Mr. Smith has just come out of the station and is asking the driver the way.)*

Smith: Excuse me. Could you tell me where the bookshop is?

Driver: When you leave the station, turn left, then cross Station Road at the junction, and walk up North Street. Take the first turning on the right, and the bookshop is the first building on the right.

Smith: Thank you.

2. *(Miss Actin has just come out of the station and is asking the driver where a coffee bar is.)*

Actin: Excuse me. Could you tell me where the coffee bar is?

Driver: Go straight along Station Road, pass the zebra crossing until you reach a crossroads with Market Street. The coffee bar is facing you on the right corner.

Actin: Thank you very much.

3. (*Miss Abby has just come out of the station and wants to do some shopping*)

Abby: Excuse me. Can you tell me where the nearest chemist's is?

Driver: A chemist's? Oh, yes. There's one on West Street. When you leave the station, turn left, and go along North Street until you get to some traffic lights. Take the right turning there, and walk straight on until just before a left hand turning called South Street. The chemist's is on the left, on the corner of these two streets.

Abby: Thank you very much.

4. (*Mr. Robert Smith wants to find a hotel.*)

Robert: Excuse me. Could you tell me where I can find a hotel?

Driver: A hotel? Yes, there is one on the corner of West Street and Market Street next to the bookshop.

Robert: The corner of West Street and Market Street, next to the bookshop. Is that right?

Driver: Yes, that's right.

Robert: Thank you very much. Goodbye.

Driver: Goodbye and have a nice day.

5. (*Mary and Jack want to visit the art museum. They don't know where it is.*)

Mary: Excuse me. Could you tell us where the art museum is?

Driver: Yes. It's on Market Street, opposite the hotel.

Mary: Thank you very much.

Driver: That's OK.

Listening Activity No. 12

Conversation 1

A: Excuse me. Could you tell me how to get to the post office from here?

B: The post office? Let me think for a minute. The post office, ah, yes. It's on Victoria Road. Go straight along High Street until you get to the park, turn right at this junction into Church Road and then take the second turning on your left. That's Victoria Road. The post office is in the middle of the block on your left, opposite the church.

Conversation 2

A: Excuse me. I'm trying to find the bank. Do you know where it is?

B: The bank? Let me see now. We are on Lake Street so you go down this road until you come to Victoria Road. Turn left, and the bank is on you right. It takes up the whole block between Lake Street and Church Road. You can't miss it.

Conversation 3

A: Excuse me please. Could you tell me how to get to the Windsor Hotel?

B: Yes. I think it's on Oxford Road. When you come out of the church, turn left and walk to the junction with Church Road, where you turn right. Go up Church Road, pass the coffee shop on you left and the Windsor Hotel is on your right, just pass the coffee shop.

Conversation 4

A: Excuse me. I'm trying to find a Chinese restaurant. Do you know where it is?

B: A Chinese restaurant? Yes, there is one on High Street. When you come out of the church, go straight up Church Road until you reach High Street, turn left, and it's the second building on you right.

A: I see. Thank you very much.

B: You're welcome.

Conversation 5

A: Excuse me. Could you tell me if there's a newsagent's somewhere around here?

B: Er... yeah. Now then, if when you come out of the park, you go straight on Church Road, you'll come to a crossroads. Turn right here and there's a newsagent's on your right, at the end of that road, on the corner of Lake Street.

A: Thanks a lot.

Conversation 6

A: Excuse me. I'm looking for a grocer's shop. Is there one nearby?

B: Yeah. So, just walk along Victoria Road, you will see a coffee shop on your left and turn left at the junction into Church Road. Carry on down this road, past another crossroads, you will see a building on the right, pass the building on your right, the grocer's shop is standing at the corner of Church Road and High Street, opposite the park.

A: At the corner of Church Road and High Street, opposite the park. That's great. Thanks a lot.

Listening Activity No. 13

Allan: Hello, Janet. I'm glad to see you back. Did you have a nice holiday?

Janet: Yes, it wasn't bad.

Allan: What did you do? Tell me all about it.

Janet: All right, if you're really that interested. We arrived at our hotel at five o'clock on Saturday afternoon and didn't really do anything much until the next morning, when my father hired a small family car and we all went to Safari Park, which is not far from London. It was a very interesting park full of lovely wild animals. We motored through the monkeys' compound first and that was an experience. They climbed all over our car and we had a wonderful view of the monkeys. Then we continued into the lions' compartment and we had to lock ourselves in, because the lions could come very close.

Allan: Yeah, it must have been terrifying. Did they come to you?

Janet: Oh, no. We saw them sleeping under trees, quite far away from us. We were unlucky and didn't see them clearly. Anyway, we had a good time there.

Allan: Oh, it sounds interesting—it is the kind of park I like.

Janet: On Monday we all went off to Oxford and spent a whole day there. On the way to Oxford we stopped at Stonehenge.

Allan: Stonehenge. It reminds me of my own experience when I was a student at Oxford.

Janet: Oh, yeah.

Allan: I thought it would be rather a romantic thing to do to drive off in the early hours of the morning and watch the sun rise behind the stone. So...

Janet: That was a good idea. Did you do it?

Allan: Yes. I went there with some of my classmates. When we got there it was still dark. It was very cold and wet. We stayed in the car and waited for the sun to come up.

Janet: Well, did you see it?

Allan: No. When it began to get a little bit light we couldn't see anything at all because there was so much fog around.

Janet: Oh, no, I'm sorry to hear that. But it was a beautiful day when we got there. We took lots of photographs there.

Allan: You were lucky. Well, did you do any sightseeing in London?

Janet: Yes. The next two days we stayed in London. On Tuesday we joined a sightseeing tour run by London Regional Transport, an excellent introduction to all London's principal sights. We visited Trafalgar Square, Westminster Abby, the Houses of Parliament and about 11:30 we were at Buckingham Palace and saw the changing of the guard there.

Allan: Yes. The changing of the guard always takes places at 11:30 at Buckingham Palace from May to July every day. During winter it is on alternate days.

Janet: We also went to Tower Bridge and the Tower of London. Anyway, we were pretty tired so we went to bed very early. The next day we went to Greenwich by boat from Westminster Pier.

Allan: Oh, it sounds wonderful. A unique way of seeing some of London's most famous landmarks is to take a trip on one of the passenger boats which follows the river Thames through the heart of London.

Janet: Yes, that is my favourite part of a holiday, just relaxing. And the day after that we went shopping for presents and souvenirs. I've brought some really lovely things back. You should see some of them. And then in the evening we went to the cinema and saw a really great film.

Allan: What was it?

Janet It was called *Star Wars*. It was really exciting. You'll have to go and see it.

Allan: Oh, yes. I've heard it's good. I should go. Well, I'm thinking of going to London for my next holiday actually.

Janet: Oh, you should. And then the last day, Friday, unfortunately it rained all day, so we stayed in the hotel. But we had quite a good time playing table tennis. Then the next morning we got up pretty early and left the hotel at ten, to give us plenty of time to get back.

Allan: Yeah, it's a long journey. You must have been tired.

Janet: Yes, we were, but then we had Sunday to recover before I started work again.

Listening Activity No. 14

A: Hello, Mary. Did you go to the university for registration yesterday?

B: Yes. That day was a bit hectic. I was really tired.

A: Why, what happened?

B: Oh, I went to the West Building to register first, then on the way to the library to apply for my library card. I had to go to the South Building to see my tutor there. After the library, I had to go to the Student Union's Office to book a ticket for the Oxford trip next week.

A: Yes, you did a lot of things.

B: Yes, but that wasn't the end of it. I was pretty tired after all that. Anyway I went to the bar for lunch and I met Kathy there.

A: Kathy? Is it the girl you were talking about before?

B: Yes, she is my old schoolmate. She studies computing at my university. She now lives in the YMCA very close to the bar. She wanted to show me the computer centre, but it was closed. So she took me to the shopping centre in Ealing Broadway instead. We came back at 6:00 pm.

A: No wonder you were looking so tired.

Listening Activity No. 15

Over half a million children under five are taken to hospital each year after an accident at home. Tragically, about two hundred die. Most of these accidents need never have happened.

Think how your adult-size home looks through a young child's eyes. Think how quickly your child is growing and changing. "Out of reach" may be much higher than it was not long ago. So think ahead, their safety is in your hands.

Things look different from where children are. They can see lots of things to grab hold of or poke into: pan handles, the lead on the kettle, a hot drink, or the iron. If they grab something hot, it could burn or scald them. Even a cupful is dangerous.

When they're moving around they don't always look ahead. They don't see: panes of glass in doors and screens, things left on the floor, like toys, or spills in the kitchen, drawers or cupboard doors left open.

They can trip and fall over things, fall through panes of glass, or bump into things which stick out. Children like to explore and soon learn to open things. They can find lots of things you thought were hidden away, like in a kitchen cupboard or under the stairs. They can find: medicines and household cleaners—all these can harm them, matches, lighters, knives, and other sharp tools, plastic bags and things they could choke on like peanuts.

Children don't know which things are dangerous. For instance, they can't tell the difference between lemonade and turps. As children grow and explore they see new things they want to reach and play with. They can: climb the stairs on their own but then they don't know how to get down again safely; climb on a chair to reach a window, then they could fall out of it; climb inside things, like cupboards and freezers; reach switches and knobs and turn them on and off. They could be anywhere. If you can't hear them playing, please go and look for them.

Keeping a constant eye on them as they move around is very difficult. You can't be everywhere at once, and anyway it's important for them to learn about the world around them. But you can help keep them safe by planning ahead and making the right arrangements. You can: store all medicines and household chemicals out of reach of children, make sure they are not left lying around; make it more difficult for them to touch or grab hot things, for instance, turn pan handles away from the front of the cooker; use a short or curly lead on an electric kettle. Make sure all fires and heaters are guarded; use barriers on stairs and in doorway until they have learned to move around safely; fit safety glass at low level; make sure things are not left around on the floor or the stairs—this is safer for you as well as for them. Teach them about safety. Show them how to do things safely, like going up and down the stairs. Tell them about how hot things could hurt them.

Listening Activity No. 16

Well, my room is L-shaped. There's a round dining table and four chairs opposite the kitchen door. So I can look out onto the garden when I eat. My record-player is in the corner, between the kitchen door and the small window. There are bookcases on both sides of the fireplace, and a rectangular coffee table in front of the fire. My bed is against the long wall, under the large window. I use it as a sofa during the day, so there are some big, striped cushions on it. Opposite the bed, against the kitchen wall, there's a desk, and between the bed and the desk there's a large armchair. I like sitting and reading in front of the fire with my feet up on the coffee table. In the empty space in front of the door, there's an oval carpet on the floor. And the piano's against the wall between the door and my bed.

Listening Activity No. 17

Richard: Good morning. 5723490.

Sally: Good morning, Richard. This is Sally.

Richard: Hello, Sally. How are you?

Sally: Fine, thanks. Listen, are you free this weekend?

Richard: Yes. Why?

Sally: You know, I've just brought a new house in the countryside.

Richard: Oh, have you? Congratulations.

Sally: Thank you. I would like to invite you to have dinner with my family this weekend.

Richard: That's very kind of you. I'd love to. You'd better tell me how to get there. Where is your new house?

Sally: In Greenwich. How will you be coming?

Richard: By car, of course.

Sally: All right. So you'll be coming from Andover. You need to take the road to Grand Town...

Richard: Take the road... yeh. Hang on a moment, hang on a minute...

Sally: from Grand Town...

Richard: 'Cause I'm... I'm writing this down, 'cause I... Grand Town, that's Gra...

Sally: That's G-R-A-N-D, T-O-W-N. That's right. Now, you'll approach the village from the north.

Richard: Coming from the north. Uhuh.

Sally: The house is about two miles outside the village, by the way.

Richard: House is two... Uhuh.

Sally: Mmhmm. So now you get... you... you come into the centre of the village and you'll arrive at the main square...

Richard: Come into centre...

Sally: On the far side...

Richard: Yeh, I... I can't get lost there, can I?

Sally: No, you can't miss it.

Richard: Mm.

Sally: ... far side of the square you'll see the Town Hall, "Le Mairie"...
Richard: Far side... hang on, far side... see Town Hall...
Sally: Right.
Richard: Yah.
Sally: Now, you need to go past the Town Hall, leaving it on your left...
Richard: Past... leave it on my left... yeh.
Sally: And cross the bridge over the river...
Richard: Bridge... over... river. OK.
Sally: Now, the thing I, when you get across the bridge...
Richard: Mm.
Sally: There's a junction but there aren't any signposts.
Richard: Oh, that's helpful.
Sally: Well... you know how it is. So you turn right...
Richard: I cross the bridge... hang on. There's a junction... yeh... and then I have to go right at the junction?
Sally: That's right. You turn right immediately after the bridge.
Richard: Mmhmm.
Sally: And... basically you keep on that road. The road bears round to the left...
Richard: Oh, that doesn't sound too bad... yeh.
Sally: First of all... um... after about half a mile, there's a chateau on your right.
Richard: Is that your place?
Sally: Mm... 'fraid not. Couldn't afford it.
Richard: Chateau... on... on the right, yehm?
Sally: And there's a road going off opposite that... but ignore that road.
Richard: Oh?
Sally: Keep straight on... you keep straight on right.
Richard: Yeh.
Sally: Past the chateau.
Richard: Keep straight on... yes?
Sally: The next thing you come to is a farm at a place called Villac...
Richard: Farm... and then... Villac. That's V-I-L-L...?
Sally: A-C.
Richard: A-C?
Sally: That's it.
Richard: Uhuh?
Sally: And just after that the valley narrows and the road comes much closer to the river.
Richard: Yes.
Sally: So you run along the river...
Richard: Uhuh.
Sally: For a little... few hundred metres really. The house is in the next group of buildings.

Richard: Ah.

Sally: You've got a mill... opposite the house.

Richard: Ah... it sounds beautiful.

Sally: Well... it's got... er... I think... I think you'll like it when you get there.

Richard: So... hang on a minute, the mill is opposite...

Sally: Yeh, you've got the river on your right.

Richard: Yeh.

Sally: You come to the mill... which is on your right and three...

Richard: Yes?

Sally: Three houses on the left opposite the mill... and the house is the middle one.

Richard: House is the middle... one. OK.

Sally: Right? So do you think you'll find it?

Richard: Well... well, with my sense of direction I'm not sure, but now... I... I think I've got everything down.

Sally: Fine. I'm sure you will. Dinner will start at six.

Richard: Do I need to bring something?

Sally: No, just bring yourself.

Richard: OK. I'll be there by six.

Sally: Goodbye.

Listening Activity No. 18

Conversation 1

A: Can I help you, madam?

B: Yes. Could I have a second class return ticket to Nottingham to arrive by ten?

A: That is forty-one pounds please.

B: Here you are. Could you tell me which train I could take?

A: Let me see. It is 7:00 now, Friday. Yes, you can take the 7:30 train to get there.

B: Thank you very much.

Conversation 2

A: Excuse me, Sir.

B: Yes, madam. What can I do for you?

A: Could you tell me the time of trains to Nottingham, please?

B: What sort of time do you want to go?

A: You see, I would like to go to Nottingham to visit my daughter. She will meet me at the station at 6:30 this Saturday. Which train should I take?

B: Take the 16:30 train and you will get there at 18:24. Is that all right?

A: That's fine. Thanks a lot. Oh, by the way, how much does a weekend return ticket to London cost, please?

B. It costs forty-one pounds.

A. Thank you.

Conversation 3

A: Excuse me, Sir.

B: Yes, madam. May I help you ?

A: Could you tell me which trains I can take if I buy a saver ticket to Nottingham?

B: Let me see. Oh, yes, you can take any train except 7:30 and 8:30 morning trains, and any trains after 17:30. Generally speaking, a saver ticket can be used on most trains except on a few peak-hour trains. Here is a timetable. You can check it by yourself.

A: Lovely. That will be very helpful.

Conversation 4

A: May I help you, young lady ?

B: Yes. I have to get to Nottingham by 10:30 this Saturday morning. Could you tell me which train I should take to get there on time?

A: The 8:30 train will do.

B: I see. Could you tell me which platform the train leaves from?

A: Platform 4.

B: Thank you.

Conversation 5

A: Can I help you, madam?

B: Yes. I would like to get to Nottingham on Friday by seven o'clock. Which train should I take?

A: The 17:05 train.

B: How much for a return saver ticket to Nottingham?

A: Twenty pounds, but I am afraid you can't use a saver ticket on that train.

B: Can't I ? How much is standard fare?

A: Forty-one pounds, please.

B: Well, I think I should take standard fare. Here is forty-five.

A: Thanks. Here is your ticket and change.

B: Thank you very much.

Listening Activity No. 19

The graph shows the number of visitors to London Zoo, Kew Gardens and Regent's Park from 1978 to 1987. Apart from the period from 1980 to 1983, London Zoo has been the most popular attraction. In 1978 almost 60000 people visited the Zoo. Although this number decreased slowly during the next 3 years, it then rose gradually until 1985. In this year a children's zoo was opened, resulting in a sharp rise from 70000 to 95000 within one year. In contrast, in 1979 to 1981, the number of visitors to Kew Gardens increased after a restaurant had been opened in 1979, from 48000 to 64000, but then it dropped steadily to approximately 45000 in 1986. The least popular attraction was Regent's Park, with only 26000 visitors in 1978. This number rose only slightly in 1981, but in 1983 boating was introduced on the lake and the number of visitors rose quite suddenly, from almost 30000 to 40000 within one year. Unfortunately, however, the number levelled off in 1984 and has remained steady since then.

Listening Activity No. 20

Exhibition Centre is the most popular attraction. In 1978, almost 40000 people visited the Exhibition Centre although this number dropped slowly during the next 5 years. In 1983, the number of visitors was a little over 35000. It then increased suddenly until 1984. In this year a restaurant was opened, resulting in a sharp rise from 37000 to almost 50000 within two years.

The number of visitors to the Museum was about 25000. This was better than the number to the Art Gallery. which was only 15000 in 1978. It then decreased steadily until 1982. The number was the same as the number of visitors to the Art Gallery. That was about 18000. In 1983, a building extension was open and the number of visitors to the Museum began to level off at 17000 visitors each year.

The least popular attraction was the Art Gallery. In 1979 the number dropped slowly from 15000 to less than 12000. But in 1980 free admission was carried out so the number of visitors increased suddenly from 12000 to 25000. It then levelled off since then. There is a slight rise every year.

Unit Four

Listening Activity No. 1

You are going to hear a telephone conversation. As you Listen, indicate whether the statements are true or false.

Operator: Operator. Can I help you?

Tom: I'm calling from a pay phone in Ealing Shopping Centre. I've been trying to get through to a number for the past 15 minutes, but I keep getting a funny noise.

Operator: Are you sure it's the right number, Sir?

Tom: Yes. I've checked in the telephone book. Are the lines busy?

Operator: What kind of sound are you getting?

Tom: A continuous humming sound.

Operator: Did you put in enough money?

Tom: Yes. I put in the correct amount.

Operator: What number are you calling, Sir?

Tom: 567 0802

Operator: I'm sorry, Sir. Could you repeat that once more slowly, please?

Tom: 567 0802

Operator: Ah, that explains it then. We've been having a lot of trouble with that area because of crossed lines. One moment, and I'll try and get the number for you...
I'm just trying to connect you, Sir.
... (*ringing of the telephone*)
Your number's ringing now, Sir. Put in 20p, please.

Tom: Thank you very much.

Operator: Go ahead, please.

Listening Activity No. 2

You are going to hear some announcements. As you listen, answer the questions below.

Ladies and gentlemen, if I could have your attention for a moment, please. I have the final notices for this final session of the conference. Now, first of all I'd like to mention that the cross cultural session has been very popular, so we're moving the final discussion to Room 203. That's Room 203, which means that the grammar session will be changed from Room 203 to Room 302. That's the grammar session in Room 302. I hope everybody's got that.

Now, I have a notice here that you must return your keys to the reception desk before you leave. Thank you.

Turning now to your discussion records, I would like to see you return them to the session chairpeople by four o'clock this afternoon. That's 16:00 hours. Thank you.

Regarding coaches for the airport ... er ... they will be gathering outside the main building at 3:30. That's ... er ... 15:30 hours. And there will be another one a little later than that at 16 hou ... that's 17:15. That's 5:15. I'd like to ask you all to be there, ready for the buses, at least five minutes before the departure times, so we can all leave promptly and everybody will get home on time. Thank you.

I have particular messages for ... er, Professor Hurst and Professor Cole and Professor Malnachurk. I'd like to ask you three—are you here? Professor Hurst, Professor Cole? Yes. And Professor Malnachurk? I'd like to ask you to collect your reprints from the conference desk before you leave. Thank you.

Finally, I have a reminder from Professor Olsen of Leeds University, that the Sixth Annual Convention of EFL will be held in Bangkok October ... er, 2006. I think you'll all be ... er interested in marking that date on your calendar. That's the Sixth Annual Convention of EFL October, 2006. And I'd like anybody that's interested in that conference to leave your name at the conference desk. Thank you very much.

Ladies and gentlemen, I know it has been a very happy event for me, this conference, and I hope that you, too, have found it a happy and productive time. Thank you all for coming.

Listening Activity No. 3

You are going to hear a conversation between Jane and her parents. Listen to the conversation carefully and answer the questions.

Jane: There's a letter here for you, mum.

Mum: Thanks, Jane. Oh, no, not another telephone bill. I hope it is not as much as last time.

Jane: How much is it ?

Mum: £130.94 for three months. How can it be so much? Your father and I hardly make any calls. You must have been using the phone all the time.

Jane: Only to speak to my friends.

Mum: Jane, I don't think you realise just how much it costs when you telephone your school friends, and you speak to them for so long, especially during the day. Why can't you call them after 6 pm when it is cheaper. Your father is going to be upset when he finds out.

Jane: I'm sorry.

Mum: Well, being sorry just isn't good enough. I've told you often enough not to use the telephone so much. If you had to pay the bill, you wouldn't be so irresponsible with the telephone. You see your friends every day. Why do you need to phone them up as well?

Dad: Hello.

Mum: Hello. Look at this bill for the telephone. Jane has been phoning all her friends again.

Dad: £130.94 for three months. Jane, this has got to stop. We both told you the last time to be more responsible when phoning your friends and not to take so long speaking to them. It costs too much. You'll have to pay half of this bill out of your wages from your Saturday job.

Jane: But Dad, that's not fair.

Dad: To teach you that the phone costs a lot of money you will have to pay half of this bill. You are lucky I'm not going to make you use the phone box down the road to make your calls.

Jane: OK. But it'll take me weeks to pay your half of £130.94.

Mum: We may have to get one of those phone locks and I'll keep the key, then you won't be able to make any calls.

Listening Activity No.4

You are going to hear a talk about undeground tickets in London. Look at questions 1-8. Now listen to the talk and answer questions 1-8.

Underground tickets are available at all underground stations. Ticket prices for the underground vary according to the distance you travel. The network is divided into five zones, a central zone and four outer zones. Generally, your fare will increase, the more zones you travel through. You must buy your ticket before you start your journey, from a ticket office or machine. Keep your ticket for inspection and collection at your destination.

The easiest and most economical way to travel around London is with a travelcard. This gives you the freedom of London's trains, tubes and buses in whichever zones you choose. It's perfect for the visitor because one ticket combines travel on the trains of Network Southeast with the underground, Dockland Light railway and most of London buses. It's more convenient than buying separate tickets for each journey. Travelcards are available from any train or tube station.

A one-day travelcard is ideal for a day's shopping, sightseeing, and all tourist trips in London. You can travel anywhere you like within the vast 650 square mile travelcard area. No need to keep queuing for tickets or carry a pocketful of change for ticket machines, just use whatever form of transport suits you best for any combination of trips. One-day travelcards can be bought from staffed train or tube stations after 9:30 am at weekdays and any time at weekends.

Travelcard season tickets include 7-day, monthly and annual tickets. This is the modern, convenient and flexible ticket for your daily journey to work. For travelcard season tickets, please bring a passport-size photograph with you. Smoking is not allowed anywhere on the underground. Smoking is permitted, however, on the back of the upper deck of buses.

Listening Activity No.5

You are going to hear a talk about looking for a job. Look at questions 1-8. Now listen to the talk and answer questions 1-8.

Ann: Look. Here's one that might interest you.

Philip: What is it? Are you sure? The last one you sent me off to was a disaster.

Ann: Yes. Look. It says they want a junior sales manager, and it looks like it's a big international company. That'd be good. You might get to travel.

Philip: What kind of company is it, though?

Ann: Um, let's see. Yes, it's a textile company that seems to import from abroad. That's odd, isn't it? What else? ... They say the salary is really good. They operate a system of paying you a basic salary and then offering a sales commission on top of that. They say it's high. And, oh look! They give you a car to travel round in. Gosh! That's not bad, is it?

Philip: Um... do they say anything about experience?

Ann: Um... let's see. No, they want someone young with ambition and enthusiasm. Oh yes, they want graduates, so that's OK. You've been to university. Now what else? Let's see.

Philip: There must be some catch.

Ann: No. The only thing is you have to travel, but then that's what the company car's for. Oh, and you have to be able to get on well with other people 'cause it says you have to be good on a team.

Philip: Um, perhaps I'll have a closer look at that one.

Listening Activity No.6

You will listen to a conversation between two friends. As you listen, answer the questions below.

Tom: Hello, Mike. What's up with you?
Mike: Oh, Tom. It's my landlady again.
Tom: You're always in trouble. What is it this time?
Mike: You see, she left a note for me. Just read it.
Tom: Well, did you leave the front door open?
Mike: I honestly don't remember. I got back late from a party. Anyway, what does it matter? It's all complaints in that house. first noise, then the bathroom.
Tom: Well, in that case, why don't you look around for another place?
Mike: I've already started. I looked in the paper this morning, plenty of advertisements as usual, but most of the places are too far from school.
Tom: Look, why don't you come and share with us?
Mike: But surely there are four of you in the flat already, aren't there?
Tom: Yes, but, you know, Jane is leaving at the end of the month. She's got a job down south. There will be a spare room. It's rather small, but you can sleep there for the moment till you find a nice one.
Mike: That's a good idea. How many rooms do you have?
Tom: We have four bedrooms and a big living room.
Mike: What are the arrangements?
Tom: Oh, we share all expenses, of course, rent, light, and heating.
Mike: What about food?
Tom: Oh, we each buy our own. It works out fine that way. And you can do anything you like in your own room, but there is one thing...
Mike: What's that?
Tom: Don't leave the front door open. Strange people may wander in.
Mike: All right. I promise that won't happen again. By the way, when is Jane leaving?
Tom: Let me see... yes, this time next week.
Mike: Today is the 22nd, Tuesday, so she's leaving on the 29th. Well, I will move in one day after she leaves.
Tom: Yes, no problem. We will get ready by then.
Mike: Thanks a lot.
Tom: You're welcome.

Listening Activity No. 7

You will hear a dialogue between a researcher and a chief librarian. Listen to the dialogiue and answer

the following questions.

Librarian: Good morning, Julia.
Researcher: Good morning, Peter.
Librarian: Do come in. You've brought the results with you, I see.
Researcher: Yes, in fact, I completed the survey last week.
Librarian: So, I can hear the criticisms now, then?
Researcher: That's right. And perhaps you'll be able to tell me what can be done about them.
Librarian: I'll certainly do my best. Well, what would you like to start with?
Researcher: The catalogues. I'm afraid many of the Science students complain that they're incomplete and out of date. They think they're really bad. Is there anything you can do to improve things there?
Librarian: Oh yes. We can either check all the cards and reprint them where necessary, or we can change to a computer system.
Researcher: How much would it cost to do the first?
Librarian: About six thousand pounds.
Researcher: And how long would it take?
Librarian: Oh, maybe three months.
Researcher: And how much would it cost to do the second?
Librarian: Change to a computer system? Yes, oh, about sixty thousand pounds.
Researcher: And how long would that take?
Librarian: Oh, nine months, I'd say. About nine months.
Researcher: Thank you. Now... next I'd like to move on to the borrowing facilities. The Social Science students described these as rather disappointing. They complained that they were only allowed to borrow three books. Most of them felt they ought to be able to borrow more books, perhaps five or six for undergraduates and up to ten for graduates.
Librarian: That may be possible.
Researcher: Also, they'd like to keep the books for a longer period, say three weeks instead of the present two.
Librarian: That also sounds reasonable. I'll see what I can do.

Listening Activity No. 8

You are going to hear a conversation between a student and a counsellor. Listen to the conversation and answer the questions.

Counsellor: Good morning. Sit down, please.
Student: Good morning.
Counsellor: What can I do for you?

Student: I've come for some advice. My name is Sophie Cole and I'm Italian. I came to this country about six months ago.

Counsellor: Yes?

Student: And I don't know if I can use my ... qualifications here. Maybe I need to do another course. And then I'm worried about my English. You see, I'm worried about not understanding... er... people very well.

Counsellor: I see. Mm... Well, I need to get a bit more information about you. What are you doing at the moment?

Student: Now I'm studying English because my English is very poor.

Counsellor: How many hours a week?

Student: Twelve hours a week.

Counsellor: Yes, but how many ... well, never mind. What sort of job do you see yourself doing in this country?

Student: Well, in this country... er... well, it seems that it's very difficult for me to get a job. They want experience in this country and I have not got any. My qualifications may not be accepted here and with... all the unemployment and everything I'm... I'm really worried.

Counsellor: Yes, but... what kind of work do you want to do?

Student: I'm a civil engineer, but that's not the problem. If I have a degree, I can work for myself.

Counsellor: Do you have any engineering qualifications?

Student: Yes. I studied civil engineering at the university in Rome.

Counsellor: Oh, when was that?

Student: About three years ago.

Counsellor: Mmhmm. And then, what did you do? I mean did you have any work experience in your own country?

Counsellor: Oh, yes. I worked for a big company for about two years after the university. Now, I would like to get ... a Master degree in this country. But first I need to study more English.

Counsellor: Yes. I think you are quite right. First you need to improve your English, then you could start looking for a university and apply for the degree in engineering for next year. Have you enrolled in our intensive English courses?

Student: Yes.

Counsellor: I suggest you study English for another six months, then take the IELTS test. This test will check how well your English is and the score will be accepted by all the universities in the UK. Here is the IELTS test booklet. You can get more detail about this test.

Student: That's a great help. Thank you very much.

Counsellor: You are welcome.

Listening Activity No.9

You are going to hear a talk about the services in Ealing College. Look at questions 1-10. Now listen to the first part of the talk and answer questions 1-10.

Welcome to Ealing College of Higher Education. Today I'll talk about student services at the college.

All student services are to be found in the North Building. Social life and some of the welfare services are run by the Student Union, of which all students are automatically members. After enrolment, take your receipt to the Student Union and they will give you your student card. Your student card also entitles you to membership in the Student and Staff Club.

The Student Union will give you a handbook which gives more details on all the services offered plus more information on the health service, accommodation and so on.

Let's talk about medical services first. ECHE has a student health centre. The centre is open from 9:30 to 8:45 Monday to Thursday and from 9:30 to 5 on Fridays during term time. The college doctor, Dr. B. Kearns, holds a surgery in the Medical Centre four days a week: Monday and Tuesday mornings, Thursday afternoons and either Wednesday or Friday afternoons. The Nurse will tell you which on any particular week. Appointments for these are made through the nurses and are usually for the following day. Outside of these times Dr. Kearns can be found at her surgery which is located at No. 2 Ascott Avenue, W5 (very close to college). During your stay in England you must register with a local doctor and if you live in the London Borough of Ealing you can register with Dr. Kearns.

Listening Activity No. 10

You will hear the last part of the talk about the services in the college. Look at questions 1-10. Now listen to the rest of the talk and answer questions 1-10

Last time I talked about the student services in the college. Today I'd like to talk about the Counselling Services.

The College Counselling Service is located in the North Building. The Counsellors are Ms. Penny Rawson and Ms. Ann David. I have asked Ms. Rawson to join us today to discuss their role. Ms. Rawson...

Ms. Rawson: Thank you. Both Ann and I are full-time counsellors. Students either come to us on their own or are referred to us by a tutor. We see students individually, run group therapy sessions and courses of sessions as we think necessary. We are here to help with any problems, no matter how great or small, such as homesickness, relationship difficulties, death and separation, sexual problems, undue stress due to work and so on. You will not be the first to be homesick, find college life stressful, or decisions problematic. So please don't hesitate to come and have a chat if there is anything bothering you.

This is a confidential service but we are willing to arrange with your course directors, your tutors, Student Union officers, career department or doctors. We can also put you in touch with outside counselling services. As a part of the university, all counselling is free of charge for full-time students. I know some of you may feel that seeing a counsellor has a stigma attached to it, but let me assure you even the best balanced individuals encounter situations where they need someone to talk with. So please don't hesitate.

You're welcome to make use of this service. We hope you will enjoy your studies at the university. Thank you.

Listening Activity No. 11

Susan came to a Barclays Bank and talks to a bank clerk. Listen to their conversation.

Clerk: Good morning. What can I do for you?
Susan: Good morning. I'd like to open a bank account.
Clerk: What kind of account do you want?
Susan: I'm not quite sure. I'll be a college student. I simply require a safe place to keep my money and easy access to it. Can you recommend an account for me?
Clerk: All right. Do you get a grant?
Susan: No. I will be supporting myself.
Clerk: I see. You could open an Instant Account.
Susan: What's an Instant Account?
Clerk: Basically, it's an interest account. It has all the usual current account facilities such as a cashcard and a deposit book, except a chequebook, and pays competitive interest on your account when it's in credit. There are two levels of interest for this account. If your balance is up to five hundred pounds, the interest is five point two-five per cent. If your balance is five hundred or over, it attracts an even higher rate of interest which goes up to seven point two-five per cent. You will receive a cashcard for our machines, so you can withdraw money with the card from any machines at any Barclays branches when the bank is closed.
Susan: Oh, I see. How can I withdraw money if I have no chequebook?
Clerk: Well, you have to withdraw money either using your card or visiting your branch.
Susan: I see. How can I find out how much money I have in my account?
Clerk: You can ask your branch and tell them how often you would like to receive your statement, which provides you with a permanent record of income and expenditure. It will show every transaction on your account and the balance remaining at the end of each day. You also can use your cashcard to check your balance.
Susan: That's fine. I think I'll open an Instant Account.

Listening Activity No. 12

You will hear a job interview. As you listen, answer questions 1-10.

Smith: Please sit down, Mr. Wilson. My name's Jane Smith and I'm the personnel manager.

Peter: Hello. How do you do?

Smith: Now, this is just a short preliminary interview. I'd like to talk about your present job and what you've done up till now.

Peter: Yes, of course.

Smith: Well, could you tell me how long you've had your present position in *Evening News*. It is *Evening News*, isn't it?

Peter: Yes, that's right. Um, I'm not sure. Let's see. I left university in 2002 ... is that right? — Yes, 2002. Then I was unemployed for about two months, and then I travelled round Britain for a few weeks, so it must be more than three years now in fact.

Smith: Um... yes. And have you any particular reason for wanting to change job? I mean why do you want to move?

Peter: Well, I actually like my present job and still find it interesting. The salary's OK so it's nothing to do with money, though you can always do with more. I suppose the thing is that I'm really very ambitious and keen to get promoted, so that's the real reason.

Smith: You say you like your job. Can you tell me what aspect you like most?

Peter: Oh, dear. That's difficult. There are so many things. My colleagues are quite nice to go along with so there's a good cooperative atmosphere. And compared to other press the working conditions are great. I mean the office itself is good.

Smith: Um, yes.

Peter: And then there's the fact that as a journalist I regularly write articles about what is happening at home or in the world so I have to make decisions. I must be responsible for what I have written. You know, that is what I really like most about the job. They give me lots of room for initiative.

Smith: Yes. Well, we are looking for someone who isn't a clock-watcher and who isn't too concerned about working fairly long hours.

Peter: Oh, I don't mind that. I'm used to it. I often work irregular hours. I was very often made to work at night. Some sort of job that would come up ... that was very important and they said it had to be finished ... er ... it's got to go into the newspaper the next day. There was a lot more pressure in writing an article for the newspaper.

Smith: And what about your education? You went to Leeds University, didn't you?

Peter: Yes. After leaving school I started a diploma course in design at the University but I decided to change courses and did a postgraduate diploma in Social and Public Policy instead.

Smith: Good, and have you done any courses since?...

Listening Activity No. 13

You'll hear a dialogue between a foreign student and a Student Union officer. As you listen, answer the following questions.

Officer: Good morning. Can I help you?

Student: Yes. I' d like to know something about the British Medical Scheme.

Officer: Yes. What's your question?

Student: Can I use British doctors if I fall ill?

Officer: That will depend on how long your course of study is. If it is six months or more, then you are entitled to treatment from the British Medical Scheme called the National Health Service—NHS, as if you were a British citizen. With the NHS, consultations with doctors are free, but you will be asked to pay something towards the cost of medicines. In 1987, this is two pounds forty for each item of medicine. You are also entitled to free treatment in British hospitals. Always make sure the doctor knows you want treatment from the NHS, as doctors also take private patients, who pay the full cost of all their treatment.

Student: How do I make sure I can be treated by the NHS?

Officer: If you are eligible for treatment, that is, you are registered on a course of six months or longer, then the first thing you should do is to register with a doctor. You should register with any doctor close to where you live—local post offices have lists. All you need to do is visit the doctor or the doctor's receptionist during consulting hours and ask to be included on the doctor's list of patients. If the doctor decides to accept you, you will then be sent a medical card by post which will carry your National Health Service number. Take great care not to lose this. If the doctor cannot accept you, try elsewhere or contact the local Family Practitioner Committee. You can get the address from the post office or any doctor. Find out your doctor's consulting hours from the doctor or the receptionist and ask whether or not you need to make an appointment before seeing the doctor. Remember to be on time for any appointment you make. You can see him or her during those hours, unless you are seriously ill. If you are seriously ill the doctor can be called out to see you. Once you have registered you should tell your warden, landlord, landlady or a friend the name, address and telephone number of your doctor, so that if you are suddenly taken ill, the doctor can be called out to see you.

Student: I see. Could you tell me something about British hospitals?

Officer: Yes. Hospitals provide specialist treatments, or treatment for which any kind of extended stay is required. Your doctor will recommend you to go if it is necessary.

Casualty or emergency treatment following accidents is free for everyone. As not all hospitals provide such services, you should find out which local hospitals do in case you ever need treatment.

Student: How about dental care in Britain?

Officer: You can find lists of dentists who give National Health Service treatment at local main post offices. You do not register with a dentist, but you should ask whether they are willing to give you NHS treatment, as dentists are free to accept or refuse patients and to provide private treatment only. If you are accepted, you should give the dentist the NHS number which is on your medical card. There is a charge for all dental treatment. For basic treatment this could be up to seventeen pounds. More extensive dental treatment will cost more if you are not registered with a doctor. You will have to pay the full cost of dental treatment as a private patient. You will have to make an appointment to see your dentist and should give notice if you are unable to attend an appointment, or you will be charged for loss of time. You should try to have your teeth checked at least once per year by the dentist. From the NHS you are entitled to a free 6-monthly check-up.

Student: Thank you very much. This helps me a lot.

Listening Activity No. 14

You are going to listen to the director of a college talking about his school. Listen to the talk and answer the questions.

Many of you already have a reasonably firm idea of the general subject area you wish to study. Others are more open and searching for ideas. Whatever your situation, I hope you find that we have a course that meets your needs.

Our firm aim is to be a student-centred institution with a special emphasis on *flexibility*. This begins with our attitude to access. We judge people on their motivation and commitment to study as much as, if not more than, formal qualifications. This is reflected in the vitality and diversity of our student population.

Some of our students come direct from sixth form or college; others are coming into higher education after a short or long gap from formal education. Some are seeking a specific set of skills with a particular job or profession in mind; others are re-training or studying to give their careers a new direction or dimension. Some are learning about the very latest scientific, technological and commercial knowledge; others are stretching their mind on sensitive environmental, social and cultural issues. Even a casual observation of the mix of our student body indicates that we are close to our aim of being a polytechnic for the *whole* community.

To meet our students' needs we have 500 academic and a further 500 support staff committed to good quality teaching, high standards and sensitive and sympathetic student care. We have probably the longest experience of understanding and dealing with the differing needs of a diverse student population.

I hope you will find a suitable course at the polytechnic college. If you want to come to the college and we consider you suitable, we will do our best to find you a place. And when you are here we will work hard to make your experience enjoyable, stimulating and educationally rewarding.

Listening Activity No. 15

You are going to hear a talk about Bell College. As you listen, answer questions 1-10.

Welcome to Bell College. The aims of the College is to foster the growth of international understanding through the provision of high standard educational courses. Second, the College is based in a residential setting for adult students from abroad. And last is to make a positive contribution to the development of teaching English as a foreign language. Bell College is one of a group of schools run by the Bell Educational Trust, a non-profit-making educational foundation.

The College offers an attractive environment for study and leisure for students aged 18 or over. A hundred and sixty students live in comfortable single and twin study bedrooms on the campus, and a further seventy or eighty with carefully selected local families. The excellent common room facilities in the College are matched by the extensive gardens and sports fields.

Superb academic facilities including a modern learning centre and library and sophisticated computer networks are available for students' use in class hours and in the evenings and at weekends.

A wide range of courses is offered in three areas: the Main English Programme, Teacher Training and English for Specific Purposes. The teaching staff are highly qualified native speakers with wide experience of working in schools, colleges and universities in many parts of the world.

Living in an international community of thirty or more nationalities is an important part of the Bell College experience. Great stress is laid on pastoral care and the College has its own medical centre.

A busy and interesting programme of sporting, cultural and social activities is provided in the evenings and at weekends with excursions to many parts of Britain.

Listening Activity No. 16

Anna receives a phone call from her friend Peter. You will hear an extract from their conversation. As you listen to the conversation, answer questions 1-10.

Anna: Hello.
Peter: Hi, Anna. Look, I'm sorry to bother you so late. I just wanted to ask you a little fa-

vour.

Anna: Oh, sure. Well, I'd like to help out. Anything you want.

Peter: Look, I'm ... erm ... I'm going to London for a week.

Anna: Oh, how wonderful. Oh, I wish I could get away on holiday.

Peter: Look, I got a problem though, I ... you know, I got some cats and ... er I ... I need a home for them.

Anna: Oh, er ... well, the only thing is, how many of them are there?

Peter: Well, there're only two.

Anna: Oh, well, that's okay then. I think I still have a box. But it's pretty worn out and a bit dirty, not too nice, you know.

Peter: Well... erm, I think that'll be all right. I... I'm sure it'll be fine as long as you clean it up. I mean you will have to clean it up because... er... er... well, I didn't... didn't want to mention this earlier, perhaps, but ... er ... one of them is pregnant, you see. One of the cats is pregnant and she's going to be delivering... er... pretty soon.

Anna: Oh, no. I'm a little nervous about it now. I mean... er... I don't know if I can cope with that.

Peter: Of course you can. Look, I mean, they're okay. She looks after her babies. She had six the last time. You'll love them.

Anna: Six? Wow, that's just a little too many. I mean, oh, I... I don't think I could cope with that, I mean. And... and how do I tell when they are due, you know, when... when they're going to be delivered?

Peter: Very simple. You see, the mother starts spending more time in her box and starts meowing a lot. You will know that she's ready to have the babies.

Anna: Well, what kind of food do I have to give them?

Peter: Very simple. They don't need anything and the mother nurses them for about five to six weeks. You just give the mother cat food and milk.

Anna: Well, does it have to be hot?

Peter: No, just fresh milk.

Anna: Anyway, why do you keep them? I mean, don't they cause you an awful lot of work and trouble?

Peter: Oh, no. Ther're so sweet. They are so beautiful. You're going to just love them when you see them. They're so nice. Er... look, the mother also needs some fresh milk every day.

Anna: Well, how often do I have to give her milk?

Peter: Just two or three times a day.

Anna: Well, here's an idea. Why don't you bring what they need, then I'll just have—then I won't have to worry about it.

Peter: Okay, I could do that. I'll bring a big bottle of fresh milk and a large box of cat food, then that should be okay.

Anna: A large box? How long did you say you were going to be away?

Peter: Now look, don't start worrying too much. She may not produce these little cats this week at all.

Anna: Well, I sincerely hope not. I mean, I'm not used to this sort of thing, you know.

Listening Activity No. 17

You are going to listen to a talk about the food we eat. Look at questions 1-10. Now listen to the talk and answer questions 1-10.

Welcome to *the Food We Eat*, sponsored by Safeway. Increasingly, we know more about the effects of our eating habits and lifestyles on our health. While new information can change old ideas, the new stories can often be confusing. At Safeway we try to help customers not only in the range and types of food offered, but also by providing up-to-date reliable information in areas we know are of interest and which relate to the diet we eat. Today we are going to talk about *sugar*. Recently, doctors have been advising us to eat less sugar.

The health recommendation to use less sugar is for two reasons. Firstly, for the sake of our teeth: since the amount and frequency of sugar consumption links to decay. Secondly, as sugar is a good source of calories, it can easily be a problem if we tend to be overweight.

The dental risk is because bacteria which occur naturally in our mouth feed on carbohydrates—sugar and starch—to form plaque and acid. Plaque is a sticky coating that prevents the bacteria from being removed by saliva. The acid attacks the tooth itself.

This takes time, however, so the trick is to avoid sticky foods like sweets which stay around in crevices feeding the bacteria. Regular brushing, preferrably with a fluoride toothpaste, helps remove particles and resist acid. The worst thing you can do is nibble sweet things between meals—it puts your teeth under constant attack.

A sweet tooth develops gradually... and you might be surprised at how you can steadily "unlearn" the taste, taking in fewer calories, and saving your teeth. Here's some ways:

A. Gradually cut down the sugar in tea and coffee till you can stop altogether, or switch to sweeteners.

B. Choose snacks with a lower sugar content—fresh fruit, raw vegetables, crackers, milk or low-fat, natural yogurt. Remember some fruits, like raisins, have lots of sugar.

C. Look for reduced sugar alternatives: there are more and more around, from diet drinks to yogurts, even jams and sauces.

D. Try gradually to cut back on the sugar you use in cooking—especially in baking.

Listening Activity No. 18

You are going to listen to a talk about au pairs in the UK. Look at questions 1-10. Now listen to the talk and answer questions 1-10.

What is an au pair? An au pair is a single girl without any dependants who comes to the UK to learn English and to live as part of an English speaking family. She is not a domestic servant but may help in the house for up to 5 hours a day for pocket money. Suitable tasks would be light housework and taking care of children. She should have one day each week completely free and she should be free to attend language classes and religious services if she wishes. Pocket money should be between 15 and 20 pounds per week and she should have her own room.

Before she arrives she should have as much information as possible about the home she is going to and what she will be expected to do. She will find it helpful to have a letter from her hostess explaining the arrangements to show the immigration officer when she arrives.

An au pair must be a single girl aged at least 17 and no older than 27 when she first becomes an au pair. She must be a national of a Western European country, which includes Malta, Cyprus and Turkey. The longest a girl may stay in the UK as an au pair is two years. A girl who has been in the UK before as an au pair will be allowed to come to the UK again as an au pair only if the total period is not more than two years.

An au pair is not allowed to take a job in this country—the light household duties which are part of the au pair arrangement are not regarded as employment.

An au pair who is a national of a country which is not in the Commonwealth or European Community (EC) and who is admitted for longer than 6 months will normally have to register with the police. This will be shown in her passport. She must take her passport and two passport-size photographs to a police station. She will have to pay a fee, about 25 pounds.

If an au pair wishes to stay longer than the time stamped in her passport she may apply either by post to Lunar House, Croydon, or in person at one of the Public Enquiry Offices. If she applies by post, it is a good idea to send any valuable documents by recorded delivery post. She should apply before the time limit on her permitted stay runs out. She must show that the arrangements are still those of an au pair. She may change host families during her time in the UK, providing that the new arrangements are also those of an au pair.

Listening Activity No. 19

You are going to hear a travel agent discussing a holiday booking with two customers. Listen to their conversation and answer questions 1-10.

Agent: Good morning. Can I help you?

Customer 1: Yes, good morning. We'd like to book a holiday for July, please.

Agent: Certainly. Where did you have in mind?

Customer 1: Oh, well, we haven't thought a lot about it, really. We'd just like to go somewhere hot, you know, and it must be in July.

Agent: I see. Well, let's get the dates cleared up first, then we can see about availability. What part of July were you thinking of?

Customer 2: Oh, well, you see, we have slightly different holidays. I've got the whole month except for the last five days, so I could go from the first to the twenty-sixth, but my friend here doesn't start until the seventh, so I suppose it will have to be the middle two weeks really.

Customer 1: Yes, but I've got to be back before the twenty-third.

Agent: Ok. Now, let's find a destination. Any preferences... France... Italy...?

Customer 1: Oh, not France. We went there last year and it was absolutely packed with teenagers making noise and getting drunk all the time.

Customer 2: Yes, it was terrible. We definitely want somewhere quieter this year.

Agent: Well, of course it depends more on the resort rather than the country. There are resorts in every country which cater for the family or the slightly older person. They're usually a shade more expensive, though, as you might expect...

Customer 1: Oh, well, we don't mind paying a bit more if it means more peace and quiet, do we?

Customer 2: Definitely not. It'll be well worth it.

Agent: All right. Let's have a look at what we've got on the computer. ... July... was it ten or fourteen nights you wanted?

Customer 1: Oh, the fortnight, please.

Agent: Right. Well, let's start with Italy. Umm, we've got fourteen nights bed and breakfast in Sorrento for three hundred and forty-five pounds, from Manchester, on the fourteenth, or we've got...

Customer 1: No, wait a minute, that's no good for me. We wouldn't get back till the twenty-eighth, and I've got to be back at work before that.

Agent: Oh, yes. Umm... how about Sweden, two weeks, half-board...

Customer 2: How much would that be?

Agent: That would be five hundred and forty pounds, from Manchester again.

Customer 1: Well, five hundred and forty... er... that seems too much.

Agent: Well, madam, there's a surcharge for the airport, and it is a five-star hotel.

Customer 2: Oh, well, it's a bit over our budget, really...

Agent: All right. Let's try somewhere else. How about Portugal?

Customer 2: Oh, that sounds great. We've never been there before, have we?

Agent: Let's see now. We've got fourteen nights in Albufira, half-board, from Gatwick, for three hundred and eighty-five pounds.

Customer 1: Albufeira? Oh, wait a minute. Did you say the flight was from London?

Agent: That's right, from Gatwick.

Customer 1: Oh, well, really, we'd prefer a flight from the north somewhere, Manchester perhaps, or even Glasgow...

Listening Activity No. 20

You are going to listen to a talk about tea in the UK. As you listen, answer questions 1-15.

During the 1930s there was a popular song which had the title "Everything Stops for Tea" and to millions of British people a restful "cuppa" is still an ideal way to relax for a few minutes from the rigours of the day.

The English custom of drinking tea has its roots in the seventeenth and eighteenth centuries. When first imported to Britain, the exotic "tcha", "chai" or "chaa" (as the Chinese tea was variously called) was considered a man's drink to be enjoyed with colleagues at London coffee shops. These were popular meeting places for many walks of life— politicians, lawyers, poets, actors and writers. Many London clubs began in this manner and the famous Lloyd's insurance underwriters stared out as Lloyds Coffee House.

In 1706 the first coffee house that offered tea was Tom's Coffee House owned by Thomas Twining. He realised that he needed to introduce an added attraction to compete with the many other coffee houses in London and tea was rare, exotic and extremely expensive. With these credentials tea became an exclusive drink and enabled Twining to open a tea shop under the sign of the Golden Lion in the Strand.

By the eighteenth century the ladies of the more affluent classes were going "China Mad", using tea as an excuse for displaying their extravagant purchases of Chinese porcelain and Dresden tea-sets. A comprehensive tea-tray would consist of a teapot and stand, teacups and saucers, a sugar bowl, a milk jug and a basin (for discarded tea and tea-leaves). Tea was still expensive and kept in locked "tea-caddies". Skilled craftsmen fashioned "caddies" of carved, inlaid woods fitted with crystal and precious metals. To ensure the servants weren't tempted by this priceless commodity, the "Caddy" was kept locked and only the mistress of the house held the key and prepared tea when guests came to visit. No well-brought-up young Englishwoman could consider herself socially acceptable unless she knew how to brew a proper cup of tea.

As the eighteenth century progressed changes in commerce and working hours resulted in the main meal of the day being taken much later in the evening. The prospect of lasting from breakfast until evening did not appeal to the Duchess of Bedford, who was usually credited with being the first to alleviate late-afternoon hunger pangs by introducing a small four o'clock meal served with tea. With time, the light, wafer-thin toast or delicate white bread gave way to exotic fillings like tomato and egg, cucumber, chicken or potted shrimps followed by buttered scones, crumpets or elegant pastries.

The popularity of tea continued to spread but it was not until 1839 that the first shipment of Assam Indian tea was landed in Britain. A healthy trade with India was soon established and tea clippers (like the Cutty Sark, now a museum in a dry dock at Greenwich) were reaching the peak of their sailing days. In 1879 the first limited shipments of Ceylon tea began to arrive and by 1880 this had been firmly established alongside Indian and China teas, giving the broad range of teas that are available today.

There have been few changes in three centuries of tea trading. London is still the centre and indeed Twining still has a shop on the site of the original Tom's Coffee House at 216 Strand. The name Twining has been linked with tea for over 280 years. Indeed it was Richard Twining, in his capacity as Chairman of the Dealers of Tea, who in 1784 persuaded Prime Minister William Pitt to reduce the high tax on tea, making the beverage more accessible to the general public.

Unit Five

Listening Activity No. 1

If you're a student in full-time education or a sixth former aged sixteen or over, you can get a Student Coach Card for only £3.90. It will save you 33% off standard fares throughout Britain on National Express and Scottish Citylink services. You even get this discount on Mid-week Returns. It also entitles you to 10% off some continental services and to discounts on some Oxford Citylink and Invictaway services. A Student Coach Card lasts for a full twelve months with no restrictions. You can get your Student Coach Card at Student Travel Offices, many National Express and Scottish Citylink agents by post simply by completing the attached coupon

Listening Activity No. 2

Alarm calls, to wake you up in the morning, should be booked before 10:30 pm the previous evening. Transferred charge calls are those where the people you want to speak to agree to pay for your call to them. Transferred charge calls can also be made to many countries abroad. Personal calls are those where you tell the operator the name of the person you wish to speak to. You are not connected if that person cannot be found, though a message can be left for him or her to ring the operator later. This service is normally available for international calls as well

For emergency calls, if you want the police, fire or ambulance services in an emergency, dial 999. Tell the operator the service you want, give your exchange and number or all figure number as appropriate. Wait until the emergency authority answers. Then give them the full address where help is needed and other necessary information. 999 calls are free.

Listening Activity No. 3

Good morning. I'm James Austin, an animal researcher. Today I'd like to talk about the bats. Many people are terrified of the black creatures that hang upside down and fly in the dark. Lately bats have become more popular. The reason is that the last few summers have been unusually warm with more mosquitoes than usual. Bats eat mosquitoes, sometimes up to 600 in an hour. Bats are an environmentally friendly way to get rid of mosquitoes. So some people who didn't like bats now actually want them to come back.

In preparation for more hot summers, people are building bat houses in their basements or garages. The problem is that most people don't know what bats really like. I guess that about 40 percent of the bat houses will remain empty. Bats like hot places so bat houses should be of a dark color to hold the heat inside. They should be 12 to 15 feet off the ground, but not in a tree where they will cool off too quickly when the sun sets. People like the idea of getting rid of mosquitoes without using harmful chemicals.

Listening Activity No.4

(*Patricia bought a videocassette recorder two weeks ago and she has some problems with it now. She is phoning the shop.*)

Salesman: Hello, can I help you?

Patricia: Yeah, I hope so. I've got a problem with a Sony videocassette recorder that I bought from your shop.

Salesman: A VCR?

Patricia: Yeah.

Salesman: Programmable, isn't it?

Patricia: Beg your pardon?

Salesman: Programmable.

Patricia: What do you mean by "programmable"?

Salesman: You can programme the VCR to record TV shows while you're away.

Patricia: Yes, that's what it is—what it ought to do . Yes, but I'm afraid it's not doing that. It won't record when I set the timer.

Salesman: How long have you had it?

Patricia: Only two weeks. I think it's got a one-year guarantee, hasn't it?

Salesman: Yes, I believe it does.

Patricia: Yeah, the problem is that I can't find the guarantee certificate.

Salesman: You've got your receipt?

Patricia: Yes, I've got the sales receipt. Yes, now.

Salesman: Yes.

Patricia: Uh, can I bring it in to you?

Salesman: Yes, I'd suggest you bring it back.

Patricia: Yeah.

Salesman: I'll take your name, just let me get a piece of paper, right, your name is...?

Patricia: OK. My name is Patricia Hedge.

Salesman: Yes, Miss Hedge, and the address?

Patricia: It's 27 Greenford Avenue.

Salesman: Greenford Avenue. I know where that is.

Patricia: OK.

Salesman: Well, if you bring it in, with your receipt.
Patricia: Yeah, I will.
Salesman: I'll now talk to my manager about it and...
Patricia: Yeah.
Salesman: Um, you've had it two weeks?
Patricia: Yes, two weeks.
Salesman: Two weeks. All right.
Patricia: All right. Thank you very much for your help.
Salesman: I'll put it down in a book, so that if I'm not here, somebody will know about it. All right?
Patricia: OK. Thanks a lot.
Salesman: Oh, sorry. How much did you say you pay for it?
Patricia: 100 pounds.
Salesman: I see. All right. I've got the particulars. Thank you then.
Patricia: OK. Thank you. Bye.

Listening Activity No.5

(Mr. Smith wants to open a bank account. He comes to a Barclays Bank and talks to one of the staff there.)

Clerk: Good afternoon. What can I do for you, Sir?
Smith: Good afternoon. I have just come to London for a visit. I need to open an account, but I don't know what type of account I could open.
Clerk: All right. How long will you stay in London?
Smith: A couple of months, then I will go back to my country.
Clerk: And how much money would you like to put in the bank?
Smith: About two thousand pounds.
Clerk: Well, you could open a Higher Rate Deposit Account. It requires five hundred pounds to open the account.
Smith: What is the advantage of this account?
Clerk: As the name implies, the main feature of this option is that interest is nine per cent on net and eleven point five on gross. If you are a non-resident, you could get interest on gross. And another bonus point to note is that interest is calculated daily and paid quarterly. In other words, the interest earned over a quarter, you are getting interest on your interest.
Smith: Oh, I understand. How can I withdraw money? Do I get a cheque book?
Clerk: I'm afraid the only access to it is to come to your branch.
Smith: I see. What happens to the account if the balance goes below five hundred pounds?
Clerk: The rate of interest will be reduced and goes down to five point five-two per cent. You can go below five hundred pounds, but you can't overdraw on this account.

Smith: What should I do if I want to close the account?

Clerk: One day's notice is needed. You should go to your branch and give notice that you would like to close the account, then, come in the following day, take your money out. That's it.

Smith: Thank you very much for your help. Now I would like to open a Higher Rate Deposit Account.

Clerk: That's lovely. Please fill in this form.

Listening Activity No.6

I'd like to welcome you all here today and to say how pleased we are with the interest you have shown in our PGCE training course at Sussex. We hope this morning to provide you with a brief introduction to the course, and take you around the department to meet some of the present trainees. Please don't hesitate to raise with me any questions that may come up.

Firstly, let me say something about our approach to teacher training. There is a variety of opinions about the proper balance that should exist within initial teacher education between working in schools and the study of the disciplines of education. Our strong conviction that beginning teachers need to confront and reflect on ideas about the aims and methods of education shows the weight we give to the latter. But we believe even more strongly that the craft of teaching is best learnt in school, working with practising teachers. This is why teachers in school are our partners in providing the course, and why there is a major stress on the school experience. Finally, we believe that learning should be an enjoyable activity, conducted in co-operation rather than competition with others, and we hope that the university and school settings and the structure of the course enable it to be so. In the university, most of the teaching takes place in small group seminars and workshops, and the Sussex interdisciplinary ideal is maintained by many tutors who are engaged in teaching and research in Arts, Social Studies or Science, as well as in Education.

Most applicants are interviewed before places are offered. This not only helps us with the selection process, but gives you the opportunity to decide whether our course is for you. You'll generally know a couple of weeks after the interviews whether your application has been successful or not. Well, if there are no questions, let me hand over to Mrs. Jean Brodie, who'll tell you a bit about the actual course content.

Listening Activity No. 7

Ladies and gentlemen, if I could have your attention for a moment, please. We're arriving at Cambridge now, and there are a few important things I need to say.

First of all, please remove all valuables from the coach, because we can't guarantee their safety. That's all cameras, bags of value, etc. Thank you. Now, it would be a good idea to make a note of the number on the front of the coach, so that you can recognize it in the coach park.

Turning to the tour, I'd like to ask you all to stay with your own group. Please don't wander off as the town is quite large and you can get lost easily, so please keep with your group. Thank you.

Regarding photographs—these can only be taken at certain points in the town, so please obey your guide's instructions. That's photographs—please watch the restrictions.

Finally, ladies and gentlemen, the coach will leave the coach park at 18:15 — that's 6:15 — so please be on time. Have an enjoyable tour. Thank you.

Listening Activity No. 8

Debby: Hello, do you mind if I sit here?

Man: No, please do.

Debby: This is horrifying, isn't it? Have you read the news about the gales? It says that gales reaching 90 mph swept Britain last night and two more days of wind and rain are forecast.

Man: Oh, no.

Debby: It says that in the early evening, gusts had been recorded of 94 mph in Aberporth, Southwest Wales, 82 mph in the Cairngorms in Scotland and 78 mph in Camborne, Cornwall.

Man: Oh, yes. The Clarence Esplanade at Southsea, Hampshire, was closed due to fears that walkers might be swept away over seawalls.

Debby: Police in London had warned people not to travel unless their journey was essential.

Man: Oh, look at the report for Wales. It was very serious. The roofs were blown off houses and trees were blown down. Engineers battled to restore electricity supplies to 3000 customers in Anglesery after a 33000 volt cable was damaged.

Debby: Yes. Oh, it says 1000 homes in Gwynedd also lost their electricity supply. These were the worst gales of this year.

Man: Yes, I think so. It's really unusual weather this year and...

Listening Activity No.9

Richard: Hi, Linda, did you have a nice holiday?

Linda: Yes. I went to visit my aunt Cathy in Chase Village for a week.

Richard: Oh, you went to Chase Village? I know the place. My sister lives there. How is the traffic there?

Linda: Not too bad. Why do you ask about the traffic?

Richard: You know, I went to the village 3 years ago. There was a lot of traffic in Chase Village. People drove too fast. I had a very serious accident on Newland Street. I was afraid to drive there, so I always try to avoid that road when I visit my sister.

Linda: Things are changing now. You know, people put on their brakes and slow down on Newland Street because they can see a police car there with a police officer in it.

Richard: Oh, it's good to have a policeman there because there were many accidents that happened on that road. But the police officer wouldn't be there all the time so some people wouldn't be too careful about the police. Sometimes they just took a risk.

Linda: You know, the police officer has been working on that road 24 hours a day seven days a week for about two and a half years now.

Richard: Oh, how can a policeman do this without any break?

Linda: No break at all.

Richard: How much does he get paid for the overtime work?

Linda: In fact he doesn't get any pay at all.

Richard: What is his name? He must be a volunteer there but I can't believe it.

Linda: His name is Officer Springirth. The police department put him to work there.

Richard: What do you mean? Why did the police department put him there?

Linda: In fact, he isn't a real man. He is a mannequin. Before he was put there people broke into 16 cars in two months in the village. When the police department put Officer Springirth on that road there were no more break-ins in that area.

Richard: I'm glad to hear it. I think the police department should put more mannequins on other roads which often cause accidents.

Linda: It's a good idea. You know, the crime rate in Chase Village is very low compared to the neighboring village.

Richard: So the most important effect Officer Springirth has is reducing the crime rate.

Linda: Exactly.

Richard: I will go to visit my sister next month so I will try that road again.

Linda: Yes, please do. You will see the changes.

Listening Activity No. 10

When you first arrive in Britain you will be given the name and telephone extension number of the officer who will be administering your programme. It will be helpful if you make a note in your diary of this information and also if you make an appointment in advance by telephone whenever you want to see your programme officer.

If your base is to be outside London, you will be given instructions about reaching your destination. Please follow these carefully and, again, keep a note of them in your diary.

You should never carry large sums of cash, of whatever currency, on your person. If you bring money to Britain you should deposit it in a bank at the earliest opportunity or have it converted into traveller's cheques and put any other valuables in a safe place. Be on the look-out for pickpockets, especially in crowded streets and at underground stations. Carry valuables in an inside pocket or a firmly closed handbag. Never leave a jacket, bag or case lying about unattended in public places such as shops, restaurants, buses or trains.

Hotels and hostels usually display a notice disclaiming responsibility for the loss of money and valuables that are left in rooms. It is in your interest to leave valuables and large amounts of currency with the hotel or hostel management and obtain a receipt for deposited items.

As in many other countries, there are various systems of shopping and for your own peace of mind, you should be quite sure you understand the system of payment when making your purchases. The following notes may be helpful:

If the shop provides baskets or trolleys, put your purchases in them, never in your own pockets or shopping bag. They will be taken out of the basket by the cashier at the pay point and once you have paid for them, they can go into your own shopping bag. It is always wise to use the shopping basket even if you are buying only a few items. Baskets and trolleys are likely to be found in the larger food shops. This system is less likely to apply if you are buying clothing and in this case you may have to take your purchases or to ask a shop assistant, but you should still never put anything into your own pockets or bag until it has been paid for.

Always try to obtain a receipt for your purchases. Some shops do not provide these as a matter of course, but it does no harm to insist.

Listening Activity No. 11

Sally: In recent years, more and more foreign students have been coming to the UK to study. But when they first arrive many students are unsure of the formalities they have to follow and even where to go for help. So we have Alan McLean from the British Council here today to offer some advice. Alan, first of all, where do overseas students get help when they have problems at college?

Allan: Well, the Welfare Office of the Student Union can provide students with information and advice on all aspects of college life and living in the UK. The college will also have a counsellor for overseas students who will specifically look after the interest of foreign students. They can also put you in touch with overseas students' societies and organizations, which are often run by overseas students. So, as you can see, there's quite an extensive support service for the students, and new arrivals shouldn't feel they have to tackle problems alone.

Sally: Indeed. So what formalities should students coming from abroad complete upon first arriving?

Allan: One important thing is to register with the police. The stamp which will have been put in the student's passport by the immigration officer indicates whether or not they are required to register with the police. If you are from the European Community or the Commonwealth, or if you intend to stay in the United Kingdom for less than six months, you should not have to register with the police.

Sally: So not all overseas students have to register with the police, but if you are not from an

EEC or Commonwealth country, presumably you must register.

Allan: That's right. If you are required to register with the police you must do so within seven days of arrival in Britain. You must also inform the police every time you change your address while you are in the United Kingdom.

Sally: And what do you have to bring for registration?

Allan: You will need to take your passport, of course, and two passport-sized photographs of yourself. If you are living in London you should go to 10 Lambs Conduit Street, London WC1. It opens 9 am to 4:45 pm Monday to Friday. In other parts of the country you should go to the nearest police station for advice on where to register. There is a charge of twenty five pounds for registration.

Sally: I see. So, your passport, two passport-sized photos and twenty five pounds.

Allan: Uhuh. Another important thing is that holders of student visas aren't usually entitled to claim state benefit or to work. Attempting to do so may affect your right to stay in the UK. You might be prosecuted and fined about five hundred pounds. It will say on your visa whether you are entitled to get a job in the UK or not.

Sally: So that's something non-resident students should be aware of. Working in Britain without permission is a criminal offence. But if they are entitled to get a job in the UK, how do they go about finding one?

Allan: If you are allowed to work, you will need to get forms OW1 and OW5. These can be picked up at any job centre, where work permits for overseas students can now be issued. The OW1 form is filled out by your prospective employer and returned to the job centre along with your passport and a letter from your college indicating that the employment will not interfere with your studies. If you are looking for work experience or practical learning you must get forms OW21 and OW22 from the Work Experience section of the Department of Employment. You will be asked for proof of the purpose and intended length of stay here and that you are going to return to your native country.

Sally: Well, I hope that will answer a few questions for overseas students. Thank you very much for coming in, Allan.

Listening Activity No. 12

... Now, I'd like to tell you a little bit about the Student Union in this college. All full-time students automatically belong to the Student Union and have voting and membership rights, which means you can vote in Union meetings and in election for the student officers. Part-time students also have access to what the Union has to offer. Further details of this are available from the Student Union offices.

The Union is affiliated to the National Union of Students (NUS), which represents students on a nationwide level. Through the Student Union and its parent body students can take advantage of reduced price travel facilities, Endsleigh insurance, the main student insurance company, and a wide range of reductions on consumer goods through the Student Discount

Card.

The Social Committee of the Student Union organizes dances and other entertainments, including the Folk Club, Womb Cinema, and the Third Eye, which caters for a more developed taste in music, theatre, art and poetry.

The Student Union also finances over twenty clubs and societies for a wide range of interests. You can get details of these from the Student Union offices.

Listening Activity No. 13

(Janet has just come down to London for the day. In September, she will be studying at university and she needs to find somewhere to live. Janet goes to an accommodation agency which she knows is offering free advice.)

Man: Hello, can I help you?

Janet: Yes. I'm soon to be studying here in London and I need to find somewhere to live.

Man: OK, have a seat and I will look through some places with you. What type of accommodation are you looking for?

Janet: Well, obviously, I need somewhere quite cheap, but I don't really know much about the kind of places which are available. Perhaps you can tell me about some.

Man: Right, I'll start with self-contained flats. Now, these are the most expensive option out of the list I have here. You will usually have to sign a tenancy agreement of some sort and pay a deposit and one month's advance rent. Although the flats are expensive, you'll find you have your freedom to do what you want.

Janet: Are there any other kinds of place?

Man: Well, let's see. If you still want your freedom you could try bedsitters. With this, you would have to share the kitchen and bathroom.

Janet: Aren't there any places where I could get meals?

Man: There are lodgings. Here you will receive breakfast and sometimes half board, that is, breakfast and evening meal. You would usually pay your rent weekly to a landlord who lives on the premises. Lodgings are usually more expensive than bedsitters as you receive a meal. There are also hostels, which are very similar in price to lodgings.

Janet: Would I have my own kitchen facilities then?

Man: No, you usually have to share. You could try looking through the local paper for a flat or house share, or why don't you try the accommodation office in your university?

Janet: I didn't know there was one.

Man: Yes, and they might get you a room in the halls of residence with other students. You share a kitchen and washing facilities with the other students. Also they may be able to offer you a list of other cheap accommodation in the area. That is your best option.

Janet: Thank you for your help.

Listening Activity No. 14

Just one hour north of London lies the university city of Cambridge, which, for seven hundred years, has been one of the world's most important centres of learning. The academic vitality of the city and its sheer physical beauty combine to produce the perfect atmosphere in which to study. Like the other students here, you will enjoy privileges which are unique to the Cambridge way of life.

During your free time, you might like to wander along the "Backs" —the lawns which slope gently down to the River Cam—or try your hand at "punting" on the river itself. Equally relaxing is a cycle ride through the town centre: here you can practise your English in the charming old market place, meet other students in a traditional English pub or pay a visit to one of the city's world-renowned museums. Afterwards, if you are still feeling energetic, there are facilities for every kind of sport.

Although London is only a short journey away, Cambridge will tempt you with entertainments of its own. You can watch Britain's finest actors and musicians in performance, see the latest films, or dine in one of Cambridge's excellent restaurants. In addition, the university social functions provide the perfect chance to make new friends and improve your English at the same time.

Listening Activity No. 15

If you ask people which animals they hate or fear the most, chances are you will hear the following: skunks, bats, snakes and rats. But some of these animals are gaining new respect.

Most people fear the skunks because of their awful smell, for example. But recently people have begun to rethink their ideas about skunks. "Skunks are very useful animals", says animal researcher Cherry Briggs, "they catch rats and mice and beetles. They are great for pest control".

Skunks are very fair. They always warn you before they spray. They raise their tails and stamp their front feet. It's also good to know that you can spot a skunk before it sees you. We recognize the skunk by its white stripe. But skunks are very nearsighted and can't see more than three feet ahead. So if you pay attention to the skunk's warning signs and move away, you probably won't get sprayed.

Most people would not be too pleased if a skunk moved in under their house, and here is some advice on how to get rid of the creatures. First of all, skunks hate rap music, so if you play loud rap music, skunks generally will move away from your house after a few hours. Also, they love cheese, especially cheddar, so you can just put some cheese a few feet away from your house. When the skunk leaves to get the cheese, block the holes so it can't get back in. But mostly, skunks just want to be left alone to do their work, which is pest control. Some people who got rid of skunks now actually want them back.

Listening Activity No. 16

Jack: The lecture was interesting. I really enjoyed it.

Gladys: Yes, indeed I agree, but I wonder, are you new here?

Jack: Actually yes. I'm a new student. I enrolled in the M. A. teaching programme last week.

Gladys: Oh, really. Well, I don't want to boast but I was in this programme only two years ago after my degree. I joined the staff of London University.

Jack: I see. Well, then you couldn't tell me something about this programme, could you?

Gladys: I'd be only too glad to. What do you want to know?

Jack: Well, what kind of assessment is there for this particular programme? It's just that I haven't taken an exam for quite a long time, so I'm nervous about the course.

Gladys: Oh, take it easy. There's no need to worry at all. I was nervous too when I first came here until I found that the course assessment emphasises essays and seminar papers. This helped me to gain confidence in my academic work before the final examinations.

Jack: How many papers are required before the finals?

Gladys: Five essays and about six short papers, something like that.

Jack: I see. That doesn't seem too bad. Did you enjoy the course?

Gladys: Yes, very much. I greatly appreciate the year that I studied here. At first I thought the course would be very theoretical, but in fact it was very practical and relevant to the actual teaching. It proved to be of a great assistance to me in my education career.

Jack: What about the teachers here?

Gladys: Oh, they're very helpful. Throughout my time as a student the academic staff here were always approachable, encouraging and supportive.

Jack: Well, that makes me feel much better.

Gladys: I'm sure you'll like studying here. You know, all my time spent in this university was a very happy one. I made many good friends and thoroughly enjoyed the student life on campus. The lecturer today is one of my good friends here.

Jack: Oh, is she? Well, sorry but I have got to leave now. I enjoyed talking with you. Thanks for your help.

Gladys: It's been nice talking with you too. Good luck.

Listening Activity No. 17

In Western countries, many people have fatty deposits on the inside wall of their arteries. These deposits build up over a number of years, narrowing the arteries. Sometimes the deposits can stimulate the formation of blood clots. If a clot breaks free, it can enter the circulation and sooner or later it will become trapped and block off a blood vessel, possibly causing a heart attack or a stroke.

When researchers looked at the fatty deposits they found they contained huge amounts of a substance called cholesterol. Everyone has cholesterol in their blood although often the amounts detected in heart disease victims are much greater. So what is the link between what you eat and the cholesterol in your blood? The answer seems to be that the amount and type of fat in your diet are crucial in determining the cholesterol level in your blood.

Food contains two main types of fats. They are called saturated and unsaturated fats. Saturated fats are the baddies, raising blood cholesterol level, while unsaturated fats, called polyunsaturated, will help to lower it.

Polyunsaturated fats also contain lots of essential fatty acids like linoleic acid. As their name suggests, essential fatty acids are vital for health and cannot be made by the body. We should try to reduce the amount of saturated fats we eat and partially replace it with polyunsaturated fats. Polyunsaturated fats are naturally found in some nuts and seeds like sunflower seeds, and in oily fish like mackerel. Margarine and oils which contain a high proportion of polyunsaturated fats are clearly labelled as such. Products which are high in polyunsaturated are also low in saturated fats.

Listening Activity No. 18

Today many people who live in large metropolitan areas such as Paris and New York City leave the city in the summer. They go to the mountains or to the seashore to escape the city noise and heat. Over 2,000 years ago, many rich Romans did the same thing. They left the city of Rome in the summer. Many of these wealthy Romans spent their summers in the city of Pompeii. Pompeii was a beautiful city. It was located on the ocean, on the Bay of Naples.

In the year 79 A.D., a young Roman boy who later became a very famous Roman historian was visiting his uncle in Pompeii. The boy's name was Pliny the Younger. One day Pliny was looking up at the sky when he saw a frightening sight. It was a very large dark cloud. This black cloud rose high into the sky. Rock and ash flew through the air. What Pliny saw was the eruption—the explosion—of the volcano, Vesuvius. The city of Pompeii was at the foot of Mt. Vesuvius.

When the volcano first erupted, many people were able to flee the city and to escape death. In fact, 18,000 people escaped the terrible disaster. Unfortunately, there was not enough time for everyone to escape. More than 2,000 people died. These unlucky people were buried alive under the volcanic ash. The eruption lasted for about 3 days. When the eruption was over, Pompeii was buried under 20 feet of volcanic rock and ash. The city of Pompeii was buried and forgotten for 1,700 years.

In the year 1748, an Italian farmer was digging on his farm. As he was digging, he uncovered a part of a wall of the ancient city of Pompeii. Soon, archaeologists began to excavate—to dig—in the area. As time went by, much of the ancient city of Pompeii was uncovered. Today tourists come from all over the world to see the ruins of the famous city of Pompeii.

Listening Activity No. 19

(Terry who is from Australia, is talking to his friend, Mary, who came to study history at Leeds University two years ago. He is asking her about accommodation.)

Terry: ... so, do you have to pay the rent weekly or monthly?

Mary: Well, usually monthly, but sometimes weekly. If it's weekly, then you have to pay it in advance on a fixed day of the week; then if you want to leave you have to tell your landlady or landlord one week in advance on the day of the week on which you pay your rent.

Terry: Oh, right, so that's one week's notice. What about monthly payment?

Mary: Er... if you pay your rent monthly you usually have to give one month's notice. But if you have furnished accommodation, or you don't get any meals, then legally you have to give one month's, even if you're paying weekly. So it is really important to have a definite arrangement with your landlady at the beginning of your tenancy so you know the exact amount of notice you have to give. The same applies to the landlady if she wants you to leave. She has to give you either a week or a month's notice, whatever she decides. You usually have to pay a deposit too. If you do, you should make sure that you know exactly what it is for.

Terry: So I have to pay a deposit whenever I move to a new place then.

Mary: Yeah, most landladies ask for a deposit against damage, or in lieu of notice.

Terry: What do you mean?

Mary: You know, if you have to leave without giving the required amount of warning, or sometimes the deposit's on the key which is returnable when you give it back when you come to leave.

Terry: That sounds fair enough.

Mary: You should really get a receipt for any deposit you pay, because it'll probably say what it's for. Oh, and you should also make sure that you have a rent book or some sort of receipt for your rent. If your landlady doesn't give you one, get one yourself and make sure that she signs it when you pay.

Terry: Why's that?

Mary: Well, you know, some students have had some trouble with paying their rent. Sometimes the landlady may say that you didn't pay or something so it is good to have a rent book to have proof.

Terry: OK, so that's pretty important.

Mary: Yes, and quite often there are "house regulations" written in the back of the rent book or sometimes displayed somewhere in the house. They may well be a part of your contract of tenancy, so make sure you check them.

Terry: What happens if I want to share a room with a friend? Will that be allowed?

Mary: Well, if you have a single room, it should only be used by one person. If you want to share, you have to ask your landlady's permission, so it really depends on her.

Terry: Do I have to sign any contract or agreement with the landlady?

Mary: Yeah, sometimes, especially if you're living in self-contained accommodation. Make sure you read it really carefully, as it' ll be legally binding and you' ll have to pay rent for as long as the agreement says. You can get legal advice if you're not sure about anything. Oh, and get a copy of it too.

Terry: Ok, thanks for your help. It'll be really useful, I' m sure.

Listening Activity No. 20

Terry: I hear you live in lodgings—how do you get on with your landlady?

Mary: Oh, really well actually.

Terry: Yeah. I'm thinking of taking lodgings. Have you got any tips on living with a landlady or landlord?

Mary: Well, basically I just try to fit in with the customs of household, so right at the beginning you should find out when meals are served and be punctual for them. British people seem to get quite annoyed if you are late for the dinner table.

Terry: What about having friends round?

Mary: Yeah, it's a good idea to ask your landlady when the most convenient times are, and also for things like having a bath, or receiving telephone calls. If you know you're going to be late for a meal, or late home at night, you should let her know so she can save your dinner or give you a key.

Terry: Do I have to do any housework?

Mary: No, no, you don't have to at all, but I' m sure your landlady would be really glad if you kept your part of the house clean and tidy, and made your own bed, things like that. Of course, if you live in your own flat, you'll have to do the housework yourself.

Terry: What about gas or electricity? Is that included in the rent?

Mary: Sometimes, but usually it's an extra charge in lodgings. There' ll be a meter which you have to put coins into.

Terry: Oh, I've never seen one before. How do you use it?

Mary: Well, they vary quite a bit. You' ll have to ask about how exactly it works. You may have to use some extra blankets. Not all places have central heating and bedrooms can get pretty cold in the winter.

Terry: Oh no, I can't stand the cold.

Mary: Oh, it's not too bad. If it's really cold, you can buy a hot water bottle to warm the bed up before you get in. It would be very expensive to heat your bedroom throughout the night.

Terry: Good idea. I' ll get myself a hot water bottle for winter.

Mary: Yeah, gas and electric heaters shouldn't really be left on all night anyway unless you have good ventilation. If there is a gas fire in your room, you should be really careful about turning the gas tap off before you go to bed.

Terry: Oh yes, I always check the gas before I go to bed or go out.

Mary: You mustn't blow out the flame on the gas fire, or turn on the gas without lighting it immediately.

Terry: Yeah, you have to be really careful with gas.

Mary: Also, the voltage in the UK is 240 volts, so you should make sure that if you use any electrical appliances, it's the right voltage. I used my hairdryer without checking when I first arrived and fused all the lights.

Terry: I'll check all my stuff before I leave then. Thank's for the advice.

Unit Six

Listening Activity No. 1

In large cities, for instance, London, and crowded places such as airports and stations, there is the risk of theft. We do not want you to suffer the distress of losing important documents and valuables as soon as you step onto British soil, so here are some important do's and don'ts:

Don't carry more cash than you need for daily expenses. If you stay at a hotel, do ask the manager to keep large sums of cash, documents and valuables in the hotel safe and give you a receipt for them. This is a free service. If cash is stolen, it is very unlikely to be recovered. Do keep separately a note of the serial numbers on your traveler's cheques, so if they are lost you can inform your bank. Do take particular care of bank and credit cards.

Do carry wallets and purses in an inside pocket or a handbag. Don't ever leave a bag unattended and make sure it is securely fastened when you are carrying it. Do carry jewelry and valuable such as cameras, radios, and typewriters on you or with you and keep a note of any serial numbers.

Do take special care of your passport, travel tickets and other important documents; documents are at risk particularly at airports and stations where it is obvious that most people will be carrying them. Do make a note and keep it in a safe place of the number of your passport, and its date and place of issue. This makes replacement easier if you are unlucky enough to lose it.

If you don't want to carry heavy luggage around with you, you can leave it in a luggage office at most large stations and pick it up later. Keep the receipt so that you can reclaim your luggage. Check the opening hours, or you may find your luggage locked away when you need it again.

If you lose any of your luggage in transit, take this up immediately with the officials of the airline or shipping line, but don't worry too much: ninety-eight per cent is found within three days. If you lose anything, go first to the Lost Property Office at the airport or station, as it may have been found and handed in. If your lose your luggage in the street, or suspect it has been stolen rather than gone astray, find the nearest policeman who will advise you what to do.

Listening Activity No. 2

Good afternoon and welcome to the session on Britain. This afternoon, I would like to provide some useful information for you about travelling around Britain.

Britain has over 700 Tourist Information Centres. You will find them at major ports, airports, stations, historic landmarks and towns and holiday centres, so just look out for this sign that says Tourist Information. The staff will be able to answer your holiday queries, as well as provide essential maps, guides and brochures. Tourist Information Centres at major ports and airports in London and addresses of British tourist authority European offices are all listed on the Tourist Information Centres.

Now, let's talk about the telephone in Britain. You know, Britain is well supplied with public telephones. Street kiosks take 10p coins. In city centres, mainline railway stations, airports and central London Underground stations, payphones and cardphones are in operation. For the latter, small plastic phonecards are used and these come in 10, 20, 40, 100 and 200 units and can be bought at post offices, news kiosks, station bars and shops where the green and white Cardphone sign is displayed. When using the different public telephone systems, make sure you read the dialing instructions carefully.

Now, Let's see the banks in Britain. There are 24-hour banks at London's two main airports. One is Heathrow and the other is Gatwick. Otherwise, banks are normally open from 9:00 to 15:30 hours Monday to Friday. Barclays Bank and National Westminster Bank offer a Saturday morning service at some of their branches. National Girobanks has forty-two Bureaux de Change located in post offices throughout the country in main tourist areas. Opening hours are 9:00 to 17:30 weekdays, 9:00 to 12:30 Saturday mornings. One exception to this is the Trafalgar Square office whose opening hours are 8:00 to 20:00 weekdays and Saturdays, and 10:00 to 17:00 on Sundays.

The Bureau de Change services are available to overseas visitors. Visitors can change their money there. You can also change money at Bureaux de Change, large hotels, department stores and travel agents. Be sure to check in advance the rate of exchange and the commission charged, as these vary considerably.

Wherever possible you are advised to use a bank or Bureau de Change, which conforms to the BTA Code of Conduct. In most cases this is indicated by display of the code.

Listening Activity No. 3

Now let's turn to shopping which may interest you more.

In general, shops open at 9:00 in the morning and close at 5:30 in the afternoon. In country towns and quieter suburbs, smaller shops close for an hour at lunchtime, and once a week there tends to be an early closing day when most shops shut during the afternoon. Many cities have a late night once a week when shops stay open until approximately 8:00 in the evening.

You should ensure that anything you bring into the country, such as travelling irons, heated rollers, hairdryers and electric shavers, can be used on the standard British voltage which is 240V AC, 50HZ. Many hotels will, on request, be able to supply adapters for electric shavers.

When you travel you may want to send postcards home. Stamps can be bought at post offices throughout Britain. They are open from 9:00 am to 5:30 pm Monday to Friday, and until 12:30 pm on Saturday. Stamps can also he bought at Postal Centre stamp dispensers at large stores and major tourist attractions. For posting letters, you don't have to go far before finding a red-painted letterbox. Alternatively, use the letterboxes at post offices.

You may ask how much to tip in hotels and how much is for a taxi.

There are no fixed rules or tariffs about this, and the following is intended only as a guide to customary practice. Most hotel bills include a service charge, usually 10-12 per cent, but in some larger hotels, 15 per cent. Where a service charge is not included, it is customary to divide 10-15 per cent of the bill among the staff who have given good service. In restaurants, if a service charge is not included in the bill, then 10-15 per cent is usually left for the waiter. For porters we usually give 30p to 50p per suitcase. For taxis 10 to 15 per cent of the fare. Hairdressers, 2 pounds according to how much work they have done, plus 50p to the assistant who washed your hair.

If you drive in Britain, you should remember to drive on the left and overtake on the right. The wearing of seat belts is compulsory for the driver and front-seat passengers. Now let's talk about the full details of Britan's road regulations. A copy of the Highway Code can be obtained from offices of the Automobile Association (AA) or Royal Automobile Club (RAC) at most ports of entry. These two motoring organizations can also provide plenty of helpful information to all motorists. Contact AA—telephone is 01-854 7373, 24-hour service. RAC telphone is 0304 204256, 24-hour service.

For something more serious, telephone operators will give you the telephone number and address of a local doctor's surgery. Alternatively, you can go to the casualty department of any general hospital or, in the case of severe emergency, dial 999. 999 is free. Remember, unless you belong to a European Community country, or one with which the UK has reciprocal health arrangements, you will be charged for the full cost of medical treatment in Britain, except in the case of accidents or emergencies requiring out-patients treatment only. It would therefore be wise to take out full medical insurance before leaving home.

Listening Activity No.4

Chris: Hi there, Alison. How are you getting on with your tutorial paper?

Alison: Oh, I haven't finished yet. Chris, could you tell me how Parliament makes new laws? This may help for my tutorial next week.

Chris: OK. I'd be glad to help. You know, new laws can start in either the House of

Lords or the House of Commons. They are usually proposed by the Government although they may be proposed by ordinary members. A law which is being proposed is called a "bill" until it is passed; then it becomes an "act" of Parliament.

Alison: I see. What is the procedure that a "bill" has to go through?

Chris: The bill first of all goes through its First Reading as we call it. This just means that the title of the bill is announced and a time is set for it to be discussed.

Alison: Yes, and then what is the next stage?

Chris: And the bill will go through the Second Reading which is really the Debate stage. The bill may be rejected at this stage. If it is an important bill this may cause the Government to resign. On the other hand, it may be passed, or there may be no vote.

Alison: If the bill is passed, what will happen?

Chris: If the bill is passed, it goes on to the Committee stage where a small group of members meet and discuss it in detail.

Alison: Do all the members have to attend the meeting?

Chris: It depends. For certain important bills the whole House can turn itself into a committee which means that the detailed discussion is carried on by all the members. When the committee has finished its work it reports the bill with all the changes that have been made to the House. The bill is discussed again at this stage and more changes can be made. This is called the Report stage.

Alison: And then the bill becomes an "act" of Parliament?

Chris: No, the Report stage is not the last stage. The bill is taken for its Third Reading which is a debate, just like the Second Reading. A vote is taken and the bill is either passed or rejected. If it is passed, it goes to the other House, not the one it was started in. So if the bill started in the House of Commons, it would go at this point to the House of Lords.

Alison: I see. The bill has to pass by both Houses no matter which House proposes the bill.

Chris: Yes. When both Houses have passed the bill, it goes to the Queen for the Royal Assent. A bill may not become law until the Royal Assent has been given, but this does not mean that the Queen decides on what will become law and what will not. It is understood that the Queen will always accept bills which both Houses have passed. When the Queen gives her assent, the bill becomes an act, and everyone that it affects must obey the new law.

Alison: I see. Thank you for all that information.

Listening Activity No.5

The English policeman has several nicknames but the most frequently used are "copper" and "bobby". The first name comes from the verb "cop" which is also slang, meaning "to take" or "to capture", and the second comes from the first name of Sir Robert Peel, the nineteenth-century politician, who was the founder of the police force as we know it today. An early nickname for the policeman was "peeler", but this one has died out.

Whatever we may call them, the general opinion of the police seems to be a favorable one: except, of course, among the criminal part of the community where the police are given more derogatory nicknames which originated in America, such as "fuzz" or "pig". Visitors to England seem nearly always to be very impressed by the English police. It has, in fact, become a standing joke that the visitor to Britain, when asked for his views of the country, will always say, at some point or other, "I think your policemen are wonderful."

Well, the British bobby may not always be wonderful but he is usually a very friendly and helpful sort of character. A music hall song of some years ago was called, "If You Want to Know the Time Ask a Policeman." Nowadays, most people own watches but they still seem to find plenty of other questions to ask the policemen. In London, the policemen spend so much of their time directing visitors about the city that one wonders how they ever find time to do anything else.

Two things are immediately noticeable to the stranger when he sees an English policeman for the first time. The first is that he does not carry a pistol and the second is that he wears a very distinctive type of headgear, the policeman's helmet. His helmet together with his height enables an English policeman to be seen from a considerable distance, a fact that is not without its usefulness. From time to time it is suggested that the policeman should be given a pistol and that his helmet should be taken from him, but both these suggestions are resisted by the majority of the public and the police themselves. However, the police have not resisted all changes: radios, police-cars and evern helicopters give them greater mobility now.

The policeman's lot is not an enviable one, even in a country which prides itself on being reasonably law-abiding. But, on the whole, the English policeman fulfils his often thankless task with courtesy and good humor, and with an understanding of the fundamental fact that the police are the country's servants and not its masters.

Listening Activity No.6

Good afternoon, everyone. Thanks for turning up today to this short talk I'm going to give on student banking. Many of you are unfamiliar with the way banks work in this country and today's talk should just give you a few starting points. Well, as you probably know you'll need to open a bank account while you are here. The safest place to keep your money is a bank; choose one that is near where you study.

All the major banks in Britain offer special facilities for students and will be only too happy to explain how to open an account. The most useful type of account is a current account. You can pay in money received in any form and then draw it out when you need it by using your checkbook. Writing out checks in their name can make payments to other people. If you want to draw out cash for yourself, make the check payable in your own name or "To Cash". A check crossed with two parallel lines is even safer as it must be paid into a bank account.

Payment by a crossed check has the added advantage that when the person to whom you have given the check presents it at a bank, it will eventually come back to your bank and provide proof of payment. Most people now ask their bank to supply only ready-crossed checks.

Most banks don't make charges if you keep more than a certain amount of money in your account. However, you shouldn't overdraw on your account (i.e. withdraw more money than you have in) without the bank's permission. If you borrow money from the bank there will be an interest charge. You will also have to pay a small charge to convert foreign currency paid into your bank into sterling.

If you have more money than you need for month-to-month expenses, it is a good idea to open a deposit account for some of it, where it can earn interest. This interest is taxable, but if your bank knows that you are not normally resident in Britain then you do not pay tax on it. You can't pay by check on a deposit account and to withdraw money you should give the bank seven days' notice or you'll lose seven days' interest.

When you have established yourself as a satisfactory customer with the bank, they can issue you a check card. This is really an identity card, which guarantees that correctly written checks up to the value of £50 will be honored by the bank. A check card can be very useful, as many shops and enterprises, particularly in London and the cities, will not accept a check unless a check guarantee card backs it. You can also use it with your checkbook to draw up to £50 cash from almost any bank in Britain. If you also ask for a Eurocheque card this can be used in the same way to draw cash from most banks in Europe.

Many banks provide dispensing machines, generally set in the wall of the bank outside, where you can draw cash when the bank is crowded or closed. Provided you are a satisfactory customer, the bank can issue you a cash card which allows you to draw up to £100 a day.

Listening Activity No. 7

Good morning. My name is Marcia Smith, a counselor here at the Student Services Section of the university and this morning I'd like to talk to you about visiting a British home. This may help you to cope well with your study and social life in Britain.

There is a commonly quoted saying in Britain, "An Englishman's home is his castle", which sums up the importance we give to our own bit of private territory. If you are living in a British home or are invited to visit or stay with someone, it is important to act thoughtfully. For example, be punctual for meals and, if you know you have to miss one, let your host know as soon as possible. Check whether it is convenient for the others in the house when you wish to take a bath or wash and dry laundry. And unless your host employs someone to do housework, you are expected to make you own bed and keep your room clean and tidy yourself. if you don't have a door key, remember to make arrangements if you intend to be out late and keep your hosts informed of your whereabouts so they don't worry. These suggestions apply whether you are a guest or a lodger and will help the household to run smoothly.

If you're staying as the guest of a British family or even visiting for one meal, it is customary to make a small gift of flowers, chocolates or something to drink. Don't spend too much as this could embarrass your hosts. If you're staying for several days as a guest, it is usual to give a small present when you leave.

Usually you will get on to first name terms with people you meet quite naturally and quickly. If you're unsure, continue to use their family name (surname) and title until they ask you to use their first name. Older people and those with whom you have a more formal relationship may prefer to stick to surnames (for example, Dr. Smith or Mrs. Smith).

If you're going to eat with British people or to stay with a British family, you may want to know if there are things that they normally do (or don't do) at the table. Rather than worry too much about rules, you may like to watch other people and copy what they do. It also helps to understand a few customs first. Both at home and in restaurants people normally wait until everyone has got their food before they start eating. However, they will start before this if someone says, "Please don't wait" or "Don't let it get cold". When people have started they keep their cutlery (knives, forks and spoons) on the plate when they are not using them and leave them on the plate when they've finished the course. For each course different cutlery is used. You may also notice that people don't usually spend much time at the table talking, drinking and smoking. In fact, after dinner at home, it's fairly common for everyone to leave the table together and have coffee in the living room.

If you are staying with a family or visiting informally, it's usual to offer to help with household chores, for example clearing the table and washing up the dishes after a meal. Even men are expected to offer, though you may not be accepted. At a more formal meal, however, the host won't normally expect guests to help.

Listening Activity No. 8

Riverdance is an expression of modern Irish culture, but it is based on a culture, which had its golden era from the 6th to the 9th century. Before that period, Irish culture was oral and based on a love of complicated stories and poetic styles. But in the 6th century something wonderful happened — writing was introduced by missionaries. From then on, the culture of Ireland began to develop in ways impossible before and had considerable influence in northern Europe in the period up till the 9th century.

With the invasions which began in the 9th century this golden age collapsed and there never was any real recovery. There were no wealthy kings to sponsor the poets and scholars so the traditions survived only in a form which the peasants liked. The love of story and song did not die but no real attempt was made to find a distinctive Irish style until the end of the 19th century when Irish Nationalism began to influence writers, in English called Anglo-Irish literature. There are many famous writers from that period.

There is also William Butler Yeats, George Bernard Shaw, and Samuel Beckett, all of whom have received the Nobel Prize for Literature. In all, Ireland has received the Nobel Literature Prize four times. When you consider we have only a population half the size of Beijing you see how unusual that is.

Now, let me talk about the music.

The Irish love of music has succeeded in surviving the change from Irish, the native language, to the language of the invader and has once more begun to blossom and become influential outside the country.

Irish music was reduced to being the language of the country people and was dying out as people moved to the cities. Young city people did not want to listen to "peasant music" although we were all told it was important. Some efforts were made to make it attractive to city people, but largely without success. More recently, this has begun to change and since the 1980's has taken off. But modern Ireland has been looking for more than just a revival of traditional music. Many of the most famous popular singers in the world are Irish — U2, Enya, the Cranberries, and many others. There are 10,000 people employed in Ireland in the music industry. Riverdance is an expression of that new interest in the old and that ability to understand the new.

Listening Activity No.9

Riverdance is not just an expression of self-confidence, a kind of culturally interesting pop song. It tells the story of a people through song and dance. It tells the story of the people whose spirit was broken by an event which occurred in the middle of the last century but continued to affect the society until 1961, the Great Famine.

What is a famine?

In 1840 the official population of Ireland was 8,000,000. They were largely poor, and living in the countryside. They were beginning to have an interest in independence and perhaps had things been different Ireland might have been independent much earlier, but there was a serious problem in the agricultural system. All crops were grown to pay the rent of the land, and all that was grown to eat was the potato. This was fine until the potato crop failed as it did from 1845 to 1848. The stories of what happened in those times live on in the popular culture of Ireland and I won't tell them here but the result was that 2 million people died or left the country by 1851. When you realize that the population continued to go down until 1961 you can realize what a disastrous effect this famine had on the people.

Compared with China, imagine if the famine of 1960 reduced the population by 1/4 and it kept falling to less than half of its pre-famine figure.

Anybody with ideas left and went to England, America or Australia. The people left behind were broken by their experiences and, in effect, the famine and its consequences put an end to all serious development in the country until well into this century. The Irish in Ireland lost all hope and self-confidence and much of our modern culture is about the sadness of that time and the sorrow of saying goodbye to those who left and left well into this century. Ireland has the highest emigration rate of any country in Europe for the last two centuries. We even have an expression for this saying goodbye. It is called the "American Wake". It means the ceremony, like that of a funeral for someone going to America, because you will never see him or her again.

Do you know why there is Irish music on the film *Titanic*? It is because most of the people killed were Irish.

The leaving continued until the 1970's because Independence in 1921 was followed by a civil war and an economic depression. Almost every family in Ireland has relatives abroad, and up to the 60's in some places, of a class of 30 graduating from high school all left. Along the west cost, closed-up houses from that time falling into ruins are still common.

Listening Activity No. 10

Last time I said that a lot of Irish people left the country and went to England, America and many other foreign countries. Today, I'd like to talk about the emigration.

The effects of the emigration were not all bad. The emigrants experienced a lot of hardship in their new countries. There is a famous story about a park in Shanghai where "Chinese and dogs were not allowed". Well, in England, until into the 1950's, signs for jobs sometimes read, "Irish need not apply". The emigrants often experienced discrimination but they formed many organizations to look after their fellow emigrants. Many of these organizations later became very important. In America, the Irish chose politics as the way forward and significant cities were controlled by Irish politicians. This movement reached its peak with the election of John F. Kennedy in 1960. His grandparents came from Ireland and his election had a significant impact in Ireland, helping the process of recovery of self-confidence which we have today. Today there are 70 million people of Irish descent living outside Ireland. In America alone there are 40 million people, and 10 million of these people have 100% Irish background. They carried the culture of their home country with them and adapted it to their new home. They made changes which would be unthinkable in the home country and we often laughed at the Yankees' Irishness. In fact any emigrant who came back to live in Ireland, often after many years, found it very difficult to fit into Irish society again. They had been changed by the experience.

These emigrants have always had an interest in the "old country". "The American letter" was a letter containing dollars sent back to one's family. More recently, President Clinton has been very influential in bringing peace to the North of Ireland. Riverdance itself was the idea of a dancer who was American who applied American methods to traditional dancing, and the fusion was immediately popular.

Modern Ireland has been able to use the disaster of the last century to learn modern marketing techniques and apply them, without at the same time loosing what is distinctive about itself. Riverdance is a demonstration of that distinctiveness.

Listening Activity No. 11

Every year thousands of young people want to study in Great Britain. They come from a range of backgrounds and have varying expectations of what their study in the country will be like and how to apply to the university. Today I'd like to talk on universities and colleges in Britain. There are 45 universities, 30 polytechnics and about 1,000 major technical, commercial, education and art colleges in the UK. In 1973-1974 there were over 251,200 full-time students in universities, of whom almost 10% were from overseas, a total of nearly 276, 350 students attending full-time courses in estabishments of further education, and about 130, 270 in colleges of education.

University first degree courses in arts and sciences are normally of three or four years' duration and, with very few exceptions, students are not admitted for any shorter period of study. The academic year normally extends from October to June and is divided into three terms. Information about courses and entrance requirements should be obtained by writing direct to the university at least twelve months before the proposed date of admision. All applications for admission are dealt with by the Universities Central Council on Admissions (the UCCA) to which all candidates seeking admission to a full-time internal first degree course or a first diploma course of more than one year's duration must apply. Full details of the admission procedure are to be found in the UCCA handbook *How to Apply for Admission to a University*. A copy of this handbook and the standard application form should be obtained from the UCCA at PO Box 28, Cheltenham, and Gloucestershire GL501HY. The application form must be returned to the UCCA by a stated closing date, usually in December (October for Oxford and Cambridge). The UCCA will continue to send application forms to universities for consideration at their discretion for a limited period after 15 December, but candidates are strongly advised to ensure that their application forms reach the UCCA by the stated closing date to help their chances of selection. Candidates who fail to obtain a place in the initial selection period are automatically put into the "Clearing House Scheme" in June/July when these candidates' application forms are again sent to those universities which still have vacancies.

Student from the following countries should send their application forms to the UCCA via the Overseas Student Office of their own country in London: Bahamas, Brunei, Cyprus, Ghana, Guyana, India, Luxembourg, Singapore, Tanzania, Thailand and Uganda.

Graduates of a university in Britain or overseas who wish to take another first degree course should approach the university concerned to enquire whether it wishes them to apply direct or through the central UCCA scheme.

Now let's turn to transfer. It is very rare for a student who has begun a first degree course at one university in Britain to transfer to another British university with a view to completing it there, and there is no provision for the automatic granting of "credit" for university studies already undertaken. Students who have already completed some university level study should make enquiries directly with the individual university.

To be considered for admission, a candidate must show that his earlier education has qualified him to enter the course and that he speaks, writes and understands English sufficiently well. The usual minimum qualifications for entry to a first degree course in a university are good passes in the General Gertificate of Education, the British school-leaving examination—either three passes at ordinary level and two advanced level or one at ordinary level and three at advanced level. A certificate which gives admission to a university in the candidate's own country will be taken into consideration for admission to a British university, but a university may still require passes in some subjects of the GCE or an equivalent examination. It should be noted that possession of the minimum entrance requirements does not guarantee admission. Selection is competitive and each application is judged on its merits. The British Council offices overseas and the Schools Council, 160 Great Portland Street, London WIN 6LL, are prepared to offer advice on the acceptability of specific overseas qualifications in place of the British General Certificate of Education. A copy of the original certificate and where appropriate an approved translation should accompany all enquiries.

Listening Activity No. 12

Good morning and welcome to this talk on Canada. Many people think of Canada as a land of ice and snow. They think of it as a young country with few inhabitants, a country of English-speaking white people. While some of this is true, it is also an inaccurate description of the country we call Canada.

Canada lies in the northern half of the continent of North America. The most northern parts of Canada are sometimes called "the land of the midnight sun", because at certain times of the year the sun never sets and is still shining faintly at midnight. This northern part of Canada is cold and mostly snow-covered all year round.

Most of the people who live in this northern part of Canada are called Inuit or Dene—they were once called "Eskimos". They are the original people of this land and are part of what are called the "First Nation". As we move to the more southern parts of Canada the land changes and so does the people. Moving from east to west in southern Canada we travel from the Atlantic provinces of Nova Scotia, Newfoundland, New Brunswick and Prince Edward Island. These small provinces, with small populations, border on the Atlantic Ocean. The land in these provinces is not very fertile so fishing, forestry and mining are the main industries, although in some small areas agriculture is also important. If we travel west from the Atlantic Provinces we come to central Canada composed of the large provinces of Quebec and Ontario. Both provinces are rich in natural resources, have fertile land and are the centers of industry for Canada's largest cities; Toronto and Montreal are found in these provinces.

The province of Quebec is the center of French language and culture in Canada. In fact, Montreal is the second largest French-speaking city in the world after Paris. Finally, in the far west of Canada we come to the province of British Columbia. This province is separated from the prairies by the Rocky Mountains and is bounded on the west by the Pacific Ocean. British Columbia is often called simply "the West Coast". British Columbia is an attractive place for tourists because of its mild climate, spectacular mountains, seacoast and beautiful forests.

Agriculture, forestry, shipping and fishing are major industries in British Columbia.

The people of this land of Canada are as varied as its lanscape. The original settlers, those we call the people of the first nations, came from Asia by crossing the Baring Strait from Siberia to Alaska. In their new environment they developed many new languages and cultures. In the 16th century the first Europeans arrived in eastern Canada. They came from Britain and France. By making treaties with the original inhabitants they gradually established colonies in eastern and central Canada. After a war with France, Britain took over the French colonies in Quebec and eastern Canada. by the end of the 18th century all of Canada was under British rule. From this time until the present century most of the immigrants to Canada were British, Scottish and Irish. In this century, however, Canada has had an influence of settlers from all over the world. There are now hundreds of thousands of people from Asia, Africa and South America who now call Canada their home.

Listening Activity No. 13

Tom: Kevin, could you tell me something about the bars? I have never been to a bar. You see, Steve, my classmate, has invited me to go to a bar tonight.

Kevin: I see. You know, the word "bar" means a room in a pub. We say the bar when we mean the part of that room where drinks are kept. Soon after you go into the pub, you'll realize that nobody comes to the tables to take orders or, money, instead, customers go to the bar to buy their drinks.

Tom: I see. People will go to the bar directly to get their drinks and don't wait for someone to come to take their orders.

Kevin: That's right. People don't queue at the bar, but they do wait till it's their turn.

Tom: Oh, how do I pay? I mean do I pay directly after I get the drink or do I have to wait till I am ready to leave like I do in a restaurant?

Kevin: It's not the custom to pay for all your drinks when you're ready to leave, instead, you pay at the bar each time you get drinks. It helps if you're ready to pay as soon as you're served, and you'll notice that many people wait with their money in their hands.

Tom: I see. Do I have to give a tip?

Kevin: No, it's not the custom to give a tip. It's very common for friends to buy their drinks together in rounds. This means that each person takes a turn to buy drinks for everybody in the group. It's faster and easier, both for you and for the person serving if drinks are bought in this way. Naturally you don't have to have a drink in each round if you don't want one.

Tom: That's interesting.

Kevin: When you're looking for somewhere to sit, remember that people have to leave their seats to get drinks, etc., so an empty seat may not in fact be available to use. If you're not sure whether a seat is free, ask someone sitting near it. When it's time for another drink, people usually take their glasses back to the bar to be filled again. If you're leaving, the friendly thing to do is to take your glasses back to the bar, thank the persom who's been serving you, and say "goodbye" or "goodnight".

Tom: Thank you, Kevin. This helps me a lot. By the way, what kind of drinks are available in pubs?

Kevin: Well, you can get both alcoholic and non-alcoholic. Beside alcoholic drinks such as beer and wine, there is cider, which is made from apples, usually sold in bottles, port—a type of thick, sweet wine from Portugal, sherry, which is a type of wine from Spain, and spirits—these are a kind of strong alcoholic drinks such as whisky and brandy.

Tom: What about non-alcoholic? I don't drink alcohol.

Kevin: Well, they offer all kinds of fruit juices, such as orange and tomato. These drinks are usually sold in small bottles. And soft drinks, we often call sweet drinks, like Coke and Fanta. They are normally sold in small bottles or cans. And lemonade, which is a clear and sweet drink made with carbonated water. They also serve cordials.

Tom: What are cordials?

Kevin: Cordials are strong and sweet drinks tasting of fruit, such as lime cordial, black-currant cordial. They are often added to other drinks or drunk with water.

Tom: I don't like sweet drinks. Are there any other non-alcoholic drinks?

Kevin: Yes, mineral water, but it's not available in all pubs.

Tom: Kevin, one more question. What is VAT? I saw this on most goods in Britain.

Kevin: Well, VAT stands for Value Added Tax. The price shown on most goods in Britain includes a tax of 15%. If you use the Retail Export Scheme this tax can be returned to you if you take the goods with you when you leave Britain. You may have to spend a certain sum of money before you qualify for the scheme, and you'll have to show your passport. Ask in the shop if they operate the Retail Export Scheme. If they do, the shop assistant will explain how you can get the tax back and fill in a form with you. VAT is also charged on hotel and restaurant bills, theatre and cinema tickets and car hire.

Tom: Are these refundable?

Kevin: No, it's not refundable in these cases.

Tom: Thank you very much. I really learned a lot.

Listening Activity No. 14

In English pubs, the food is usually plain but of good quality; in fact, to taste good, traditional English food, you would do well to visit a reputable pub. Many businessmen habitually have lunch in a pub near their office. In the country, the pub is often part of an inn where you can put up for the night.

The Englishman's favorite drink is beer. There are three different methods of serving beer in Britain. As you'd expect, some beer is served in bottles. Beer that comes from a tap is called draught beer, and there are two different methods of serving it: Keg beer is served with modern method, which uses a gas called carbon dioxide, and traditional draught has no gas in it and a pump is used to pull the beer up the pipe and out of the tap. Keg beer is served colder than traditional draught. It's easy to look after, and some keg beers are sold almost everywhere in Britain. This means that you can always have exactly the same drink in any pub that sells a particular keg beer.

Traditional British beer is probably quite different from the beer in your country. It has no gas in it and it's not served very cold, but this is not a mistake. Traditional beer drinkers will tell you that this allows you to taste the beer better. Traditional draught is not always looked after as well as it should be, but in a good pub — a traditional draught beer drinker will tell you — there can be no better drink.

There are a lot of different breweries (companies that make beer) in Britain, but they make the same types of beer and you can see them in the list below: Lager is the kind of beer that is common in many countries. Normally keg is served cold. Strong lager is often available in bottles. Bitter is the most popular kind of British beer. It tastes slightly bitter and can be keg or traditional draught. Most pubs have more than one kind. Guinness is a thick, almost black, bitter tasting Irish beer.

Pale ale is less strong and a bit sweeter than bitter, and often is keg. Mild is a fairly sweet beer, often dark, not as strong as bitter. It can be keg or traditional. It can not be found everywhere. Bottled beers are sometimes served cold. There are several kinds available, for example, light ale like pale ale. Brown ale is a brown, often rather sweet beer. Stout is a very dark beer.

Law regulates the pub's opening times. Local variations are possible but usually a pub is open from half past eleven to three o'clock and from half past five to half past ten or eleven o'colck. Betting is forbidden in pubs. Children are not allowed on licensed premises, which may mean that father and mother cannot have a quiet drink together, if children are with them. In the old days when people drank too much and pubs were often rowdy, the law against children entering pubs was a wise one. Today, drunkenness is much less frequent than it was, say fifty years ago. It would be quite wrong to consider the average English pub as anything other than a respectable, friendly place that provides good drink, good food and a pleasant social atmosphere. Far too often the foreigner has read accounts of sordid nineteenth century drinking places, haunted by people whose one desire was to drink as much as they could afford as quickly as possible.

Listening Activity No. 15

In July 1956 a fleet of 21 sailing ships from 11 countries raced each other from Torbay in Devon to Lisbon. The ships had been converted from cargo-carrying to sail-training ships.

However, their future seemed uncertain and the purpose of the gathering was to mark the passing of the age of the sail.

What happened instead was that the sailing ships refused to say goodbye and two years later they raced again and the fleet was even larger. It was then that the title "the Tall Ships" was given to them and the name remains today. The original organizers (the Sail-Training Ship International Race Committee, now called "the Sail-Training Association") saw that a new international movement had begun — adventure training under sail.

As race succeeded race, it became clear that the events had more to do with bringing adventure and widening the horizons of young people than of commemorating the passing of sail. Now sail-training ships began to be specially built and young people from all walks of life wanted to participate. Now, to compete, a vessel has to satisfy just three requirements. It has to have a minimum waterline length of 9.09 meters, half its crew must be between the ages of 16 and 25, and its principal means of propulsion must be a sail.

Since 1972 the race has been sponsored by Cutty Sark Scots Whisky, and it has started to attract huge crowds of spectators. In 1984 more than 250,000 people lined the River Mersey in Liverpool to watch the fleet set off and in 1986 two million spectators joined Her Majesty Queen Elizabeth at Newcastle-upon-Tyne to watch the parade.

1989 was the year that the spectacular Cutty Sark Tall Ships' Race started from London. A grand fleet of up to 100 vessels gathered on the River Thames near Tower Bridge on Tuesday, the 4th of July. The only thing that the racing yachts (ancient and modern) had in common was their young crews. Few were expert sailors, and the majorities were strangers to the sea and to each other. Between Tuesday, the 4th of July when the fleet began to assemble and Saturday, the 8th of July when the ships took part in a grand parade of sail down the River Thames, vessels were berthed on either side of Tower Bridge. Some were moored in the Pool of London, opposite the Tower of London, while others were moored to the east of Tower Bridge. Smaller vessels were accommodated in St. Katharine's Dock. Many of the larger ships were open to the public.

It was an amazing and historic spectacle as the ships sailed slowly up the River Thames.

Listening Activity No. 16

Susan: Tom, where are you going?

Tom: To the post office. I am going to send some packets to Leeds. Do you know the best way to send them?

Susan: Well, if your need is for a record of posting and delivery rather than compensation for loss, recorded delivery is particularly suitable for sending documents and papers of little or no monetary value.

Tom: Well, what can we send for recorded delivery?

Susan: All kinds of inland postal packets except parcels, airway and railway letters and parcels. The service does not apply to mail for the Irish Republic.

Tom: I see. How do I post them?

Susan: You should get a Certificate of Posting form from the container in the post office and follow the instructions shown on the reverse. The certificate will be your record of posting.

Tom: Can I send anything in the post?

Susan: No, you can't. You must not send bank notes, currency notes, and some valuable things because there is no special handling in the post. Recorded delivery mail is carried with the ordinary unregistered post. And there is no special security treatment.

Tom: How do we use recorded delivery?

Susan: Well, when your letter or packet is delivered it is signed for by the recipient and a record is kept by the post office. The post office does not undertake to deliver recorded delivery or any other mail, to the addressee in person, but to the address shown. You can obtain confirmation of delivery by completing an Advice of Delivery form either at the time of posting or later. This form will be signed by a post office offcial, not by the addressee or the recipient. A fee is payable, which is lower if the form is handed in at the time of posting.

Tom: Is there any compensation for loss?

Susan: Well, compensation is limited. Compensation may be paid for loss or damage, but will not be paid for money or any other inadmissible item. If you want a speedy service for articles of value with extra security of handling en route, and wish to have compensation in the event of loss or damage you should use registered post.

Tom: What can we send if we use registered post?

Susan: Any first-class letter or packet except airway letters and railway letters.

Tom: How do we post? I mean what we should do?

Susan: Well, you should make sure that the packet is made up in a strong cover and then, it is fastened with wax, gum or other adhesive substance. Hand the packet to the post office counter clerk together with the cost of postage and the registration fee. Do not post it in the posting box. Make sure that the fee paid is adequate to cover the value of the content. The counter clerk will give you a certificate of posting which he has initiated with the date stamped.

Tom: Is there any special security for the registered post?

Susan: Yes. All registered mail receives special security treatment. Packing is very important because registration is not in itself a safeguard against damage. The contents of registered packets must be adequately packed.

Tom: How do we pack then? Do we have to use special envelopes?

Susan: Yes, you have to send the articles in one of the registered letter envelopes sold by the post office. These envelopes are already stamped for first-class postage and have the minimum registration fee.

Tom: What about the compensation?

Susan: Compensation will not be paid for the following articles, such as bank notes, currency notes, trading stamps, coupons and some valuable things unless they are enclosed in one of the registered letter envelopes sold by the post office.

Tom: I see. How does it deliver?

Susan: The recipient on delivery signs for your registered mail. The post office does not undertake to deliver registered or any other mail to the addressee in person, but to the address shown. You can obtain confirmation of delivery by paying an additional fee, and completing an Advice of Delivery form either at the time of posting or later. If you require the recipient's signature on the Advice of Delivery, the form must be handed in at the time of posting, otherwise a post office official will sign the certificate. The Advice of Delivery fee is lower if the form is handed in at the time of posting.

Tom: Thank you very much for all this useful information.

Listening Activity No. 17

Well, last week we talked about American education and today I'm going to discuss American values, characteristics, personal habits and courtesies. Keep in mind as you are listening to this lecture that your goal is to understand, not to emulate or judge. Just briefly, I'd like to mention that there is remarkable ethnic diversity in the United States. The population of the USA is about 260 million, 73% of the American population is White, 12% is African American, 8% Hispanic, 3% Asian or Pacific Islanders, and less than 1% American Indian or Eskimo. Many Americans resent generalizations being made about them because Americans see themselves as very unique and individualistic. On the other hand, Americans tend to lump foreigners together into one lot and condescendingly view foreigners as people who are not as intelligent or sensible as Americans. Despite Americans' dislike of generalizations and their ethnocentric point of view, it becomes evident that they are indeed "American". Americans value individualism, independence, informality, directness, punctuality, achievement and competition.

Individualism is probably the most highly esteemed value in the American culture and an important key to understanding American behavior. In the historical development of the country, individuality was crucial for survival. If you asked Americans to characterize the ideal person, they would probably use adjectives such as "autonomous", "independent" and "self-reliant". Persons tend to be viewed as individuals rather than as representatives of a family or a group. Here are some examples of how this value affects behaviors:

1. If a group of friends go to a restaurant, everyone "wants to pay their own way". In other words they want to have separate checks and not be someone's guest.

2. In friendships, which seem to initially develop more quickly in the U.S. than in other cultures, the Americans may feel uncomfortable if you give them more help than they need. This is a tendency to draw back and see dependency as weakness.

In some says the stress on the individual rather than the family or group has led to a more informal society. Sometimes this lack of formality is viewed by members of other cultures as a sign of lack of respect, but that is not the intention in the American value system. This informality is even more predominant on the university campus than in other segments of society. Some ways in which you might see this value expressed in behaviors are:

1. You will generally be on a first name basis with other students, in spite of any age differences.

2. Dress is very informal on campus.

3. Language is informal and sometimes confusing. Phrases like "See you later" and "Drop by any time" are not meant literally. They are informal ways of saying goodbye.

Americans are direct — honesty and frankness are more important to Americans than "saving face". They may bring up impolite conversation topics which you may find embarrassing, too controversial or even offensive. Americans are quick to get to the point and do not spend much time on formal social amenities. This directness encourages Americans to talk over disagreements and to try to patch up misunderstandings themselves rather than ask a third party to mediate disputes.

It is particularly interesting to see what behaviors have culturally become associated with straightforwardness:

1. A firm handshake somehow has come to be interpreted as a sign of sincerity.

2. Looking at a person when you speak to him or her gives an indication of honesty.

3. In a question of honesty versus politeness, honesty wins. It is considered better to refuse graciously than to accept an invitation and not go.

4. You will be taken at your word. If you refuse food the first time it is offered (to be polite), it may not be offered again. An American will not know that your initial refusal is politeness.

Great value is attached to time in the U.S. Punctuality is considered an important attribute. As with all values, there are different rules of acceptability in different cultures. In the U.S. you should be present for school or business appointments at the exact time agreed upon. In social appointments you can arrive 10-15 minutes after the agreed-upon time without giving offense. If you are invited somewhere for dinner and are more than 15 minutes late, you will need to offer an apology and an explanation. A phone call explaining you have been detained and will be late will save face for you and patience for the other person.

Americans also value achievement and competition. The American style of friendly joking or banter of "getting the last word in" and the quick and witty reply are subtle forms of competition. Although such behavior is natural to Americans, you may find it overbearing or disagreeable. Americans are obsessed with records of achievement in sports, and sports awards are often displayed in their homes. Also, sometimes books and movies are judged not so much on quality but on how many copies are sold or on how many dollars of profit are realized.

Listening Activity No. 18

Many typically "American" characteristics—individualism, self-reliance, informality, punctuality and directness—are a result of those values mentioned earlier. Other "national traits" could also be identified, however.

1. Americans cooperate—Although often competitive, Americans also have a good sense of "teamwork" and cooperate with others to achieve a goal.

2. Americans are friendly, but in their own way. In general, friendships among Americans tend to be shorter and more casual than friendships among people from other cultures. This has something to do with American mobility and the fact that Americans do not like to be dependent on other people. Americans also tend to compartmentalize friendships—having friends at work, family friends, friends on the softball team, etc.

3. Americans ask a lot of questions, some of which may to you seem pointless, uninformed or elementary. Someone you have just met may ask you very personal questions. No impertinence is intended; the questions usually grow out of a genuine interest.

4. Americans tend to be internationally naive—Many Americans are not very knowledgeable about international geography or world affairs. They may ask uninformed questions about current events and may display ignorance of world geography. Because the U.S. is not surrounded by many other nations, some Americans tend to ignore the world.

5. Silence makes Americans nervous. Americans are not comfortable with silence. They would rather talk about the weather than deal with silence in a conversation.

6. Americans are open and usually eager to explain. If you do not understand certain behavior or want to know "what makes Americans tick," do not hesitate to ask questions.

Just as values and traits differ somewhat from one culture to another, so do the personal habits associated with good manners and courtesy. While very often there does not seem to be any particular reason why a particular way of doing something is considered good manners, observing these cultural rules will make Americans more comfortable with you and therefore you with them. It is, of course, impossible to cover all the possibilities here. If you are unsure in a situation, just ask—Americans like to be helpful.

1. Queuing up or lining up is essential. Courtesy requires that you do not push from behind, stand next to the person being helped or cut into a line. If you should accidentally bump someone, you should say, "Excuse me."

2. Americans blow their noses into a tissue. Spitting, clearing phlegm or sniffing as from a cold are considered rude.

3. It is considered poor manners to slurp, chew noisily or open your mouth while chewing.

4. Questions are seen as a good way of getting acquainted, but questions about a person's age, financial affairs, cost of clothing or personal belongings, religious affiliations and sex life are considered too personal for questioning except between very close friends.

5. Men generally do not hold hands or link arms in public with other men. This is somewhat more acceptable between women and quite common between men and women.

Now, a few words about personal safety. Unforunately, in the U.S. one must be aware of crimes. It is wise to be especially careful until you are familiar with the community in which you live. Remember that good judgment and common sense can significantly reduce chances of having an unpleasant and perhaps harmful experience. Basic safety rules include the following:

1. Do not walk alone at night.

2. When you leave your room, apartment, or automobile, make sure that all doors are locked and all windows are secured.

3. Do not carry too much cash or wear jewelry of great value.

4. Never accept a ride from a stranger. Do not hitchhike and do not pick up hitchhikers.

5. Be careful of purses and wallets, especially in crowded metropolitan areas, where there may be purse-snatchers and pickpockets.

6. If a robber threatens you, at home or on the street, try not to resist unless you feel that your life is in danger and you must fight or run away. Give up your valuables as calmly as you can and observe as much as possible about the robber to tell the police when you report the crime.

A final note: Keep an open mind. Don't judge what you see as right or wrong, but make it a challenge to try to understand the variety of American behaviors which you may observe. You certainly do not have to participate in something you disagree with, but you can try to understand it. This will help you build an attitude of intelligent and liberated respect for cultures, both your own and others'.

Listening Activity No. 19

John F. Kennedy and Abraham Lincoln lived in different times and had very different family and educational backgrounds. Kennedy lived in the 20th century, while Lincoln lived in the 19th century. Kennedy was born in 1917, whereas Lincoln was born more than 100 years earlier, in 1809. As for their family backgrounds, Kennedy came from a rich family, but Lincoln's family was not wealthy. Because Kennedy came from a wealthy family, he was able to attend expensive private schools. He graduated from Harvard University. Lincoln, on the other hand, had only one year of formal schooling. In spite of his lack of normal schooling, he became a well-known lawyer. He taught himself law by reading law books. Lincoln was, in other words, a self-educated man.

In spite of these differences in Kennedy and Lincoln's backgrounds, some interesting similarities between the two men are evident. In fact, many books have been written about the strange coincidences in the lives of these two men. For example, take their political careers. Lincoln began his political career as a U.S. congressman. Sililarly, Kennedy also began his political career as a congressman. Lincoln was elected to the U.S. House of Representatives in 1847; Kennedy was elected to the House in 1947. They went to the Congress just 100 years apart. Another interesting coincidence is that each man was elected president of the United States in a year ending with the number 60. Lincoln was elected President in 1860, and Kennedy was elected in 1960. Furthermore, both men were President during years of civil unrest in the country. Lincoln was President during the American Civil war. During Kennedy's term of office civil unrest took the form of civil rights demonstrations.

Another striking similarity between the two men was that, as you probably know, neither lived to complete his term in office. Lincoln and Kennedy were both assassinated while in office. Kennedy was assassinated in Dallas, Texas, after only 1,000 days in office. Lincoln was assassinated in 1865, a few days after the end of the American Civil War. It is rather curious to note that both presidents were shot while they were sitting next to their wives.

These are only a few examples of the uncanny and unusual similarities between the destinies of these two American men who hnd a tremendous impact on the social and political life of the United States and the imagination of the American people.

Listening Activity No. 20

The American Civil War was fought over 140 years ago. It began in 1861 and lasted until 1865. The American Civil War resulted in the death of 800,000 Americans. What caused this terrible civil war between the North and the South?

Well, historians believe that there were many causes of the war. One of the important causes of the war was the friction between the North and the South over the issue of slavery. The southern way of life and the southern economy were based on the use of slave labor. For almost 250 years before the Civil War, the economy of the South depended on the use of black slaves. The slaves were used to plant and pick cotton and tobacco. Cotton and tobacco were the main crops grown in the South. Most Southerners did not think it was wrong to own, buy, or sell black slaves like farm animals. Slavery was, in fact, the foundation of the entire economy and way of life in the South. This was not the situation in the North. The northeren economy did not depend on the use of slave labor. Why not?

Well, in the South, there were many large cotton plantations that used hundreds of black slaves. In the North, however, there were smaller farms. The northern farmers planted many different kinds of crops, not just cotton or tobacco. The Northerners did not need slaves since their farms were smaller than most of the southern plantations. In fact, many Northerners were so opposed to slavery that they wanted to end slavery completely. The northern attitude against slavery made the Southerners angry. So, for many years before the war there was constant friction between the North and the South over this issue. This friction eventually led to war.

There was other friction, too, as I said before, between the North and the South. There were, in other words, other causes of conflict between the North and the South. One involved the growth of industry in the North. While the South remained an agricultural area, the North became more and more industrialized. As industry increased in the North, it brought more people and greater wealth to the northern states. As a result, many Southerners began to fear northern political and economic domination. Because of this fear, many Southerners believed that the South should leave the Union and that they should form their own country.

In 1860, the Southerners decided it was time to leave the Union when Abraham Lincoln became President of the United States. Lincoln, as you may know, was against slavery. The people of the South were afraid that their way of life and their economic system were in danger with Lincoln in the presidency.

Consequently, the southern states decided to secede from the Union. In other words, they wanted to break away from the North and form a separate country. In 1861, South Carolina seceded, and by June of 1861 eleven southern states had seceded and established a new country. They called the new country the Confederate States of America. The war between the North and the South began when the southern states seceded from the Union. The main reason that the North went to war against the South was to bring the southern states back into the Union. In other words, the North went to war to keep the United States one country.

After 4 years of terrible fighting, the North won the war against the South, and the United States remained one country. The North won the war mainly because of its economic and industrial strength and power.

The Civil War had two important results for the United States: (1) the Civil War preserved the United States as one country; and (2) it ended slavery in the United States. Many Americans wonder what the United States would be like today if the South had won the Civil War. The history of the United States would have been very different if the South had won the war between the States.

Unit Seven

Test 1

Instruction:

You will hear a number of different recordings and you will have to answer questions on what you hear. There will be time for you to read the instructions and questions, and you will have a chance to check your work. All the recordings will be played once only. The test is in 4 sections. Write all your answers in the listening question booklet. At the end of the real test you will be given 10 minutes to transfer your answers to an answer sheet.

Now turn to Section 1.

Section 1

Look at questions 1-4. For each of the questions, decide which picture, A, B, C or D is the best answer and circle the letter in your book. First have another look at questions 1-4.

Now you will hear the recording. Listen carefully and circle the appropriate letter for each question.

A: Hello. I am a new student here.

B: Hello. What can I do for you?

A: Can you tell me what the Student Union does?

B: Well, we're part of the National Union of students, who represents students' interests across the country. We provide services for all students at this college.

A: What kind of services?

B: There are advisors and welfare staff, entertainments, sports clubs, union societies, meetings, campaigns, and special interest groups. We offer everything from ballroom dancing to karate, jazz, and political debates.

A: Sounds great. How can you help overseas students?

B: As I've said, we have welfare officers who are used to the sort of problems overseas students may have. They know where to get advice on a particular situation, or basically, give whatever help is asked for.

A: I am from the Philippines and I hope I can meet other Filipino students who are here. I play chess and many sports, especially badminton, basketball and wrestling. Please can you tell me how to find out about these things?

B: There is a Filipino society at the college. Regular meetings take place and lots of social activities are organized, such as meals, plays and dances. The Society is made up of Filipino students and other students who have an interest in the Philippines.

A: And what about the sports? Does the Union offer the ones I' m interested in?

B: Yes, we do. There are basketball and wrestling teams. If you want to play in one of the college teams, you have to go along to training sessions and compete for a place. For badminton, you can either go to the badminton club or book a court to play with friends.

A: Is there also a chess club or team?

B: No, I'm afraid not. It may be best for you to put a notice on our notice board to find other players.

A: Will that cost me anything?

B: No. It's a free service available to all students, but you have to give your notice to a Union officer first, so that it's fair for everyone who wants to use the notice board.

A: I only have a room for one month at the moment. I need to find a house or a flat to live in near the college. Are you able to help me with any accommodation problems?

B: There are always rooms available in shared flats or houses on our notice board. The college has some of its own accommodation and you can also apply for these. If you have any problems at all you should talk to one of the Student Union's welfare officers, who can give specialist advice on accommodation.

A: Thank you for your help.

B: You are welcome. Now would you mind helping us? We're conducting a survey to learn more about the students who visit our Union office, so that we can improve our services. Would you mind if I asked you a few questions?

A: Not at all.

Now look at questions 5-10. As you listen to the student's conversation with the Union officer, fill in spaces 5-10 on the form. First you have some time to look at the form.

Now listen carefully and fill in gaps 5-10.

Officer: Now would you mind helping us? We're conducting a survey to learn more about the students who visit our Union office, so that we can improve our services. Would you mind if I asked you a few questions?

Caesar: Not at all.

Officer: First of all, what is your name?

Caesar: My name is Caesar Bautisto.

Officer: How do you spell your last name?

Caesar: B-A-U-T-I-S-T-O.

Officer: Thank you. And what are you studying?

Caesar: Development Economics.

Officer: I see. And how long is the course for?

Caesar: One year. It's a post-graduate diploma.

Officer: What would you like to do at the end of it? Have you made your mind up yet?
Caesar: Yes. I'd like to be a United Nations project adviser.
Officer: Oh, would you? That sounds interesting. Tell me, though, why have you chosen this university?
Caesar: It's got a good reputation in the field of economics.
Officer: And you say you come from the Philippines.
Caesar: Yes, that's right.
Officer: And which city do you come from?
Caesar: Manila.
Officer: Oh, that's the city I've always wanted to go to. What do you do in your spare time?
Caesar: I go to play games. I love sports.
Officer: Ah, yes. You mentioned that. Basketball, badminton, and wrestling, wasn't it?
Caesar: Yes, that's right.
Officer: OK, that's it. I' ll add your name to our mailing list. We appreciate your help with this survey. If you have any suggestions, be sure to give us a call or drop by at any time.
Caesar: All right, I will. Thank you. Bye.
Officer: Bye.

That is the end of Section 1. Now you will have 30 seconds to check your answers.

That's the end of Section 1. Now turn to Section 2.

Section 2

The next day Caesar goes to the Welfare Office. You will hear a conversation between Caesar and a welfare officer. As you listen, answer questions 11-20. First you have some time to look at questions 11-20.

Now, listen carefully to the conversation between Caesar and a welfare officer and answer questions 11-20.

Caesar: Good afternoon. My name's Caesar Bautisto.
Wendy: Hello. I'm Wendy—one of the welfare officers. Can I help you?
Caesar: Yes. I have to move out of my accommodation in two weeks and I can't find anywhere else to live.
Wendy: Okay. I' ll need to know some details about your current situation.
Caesar: I'm an overseas student, from the Philippines. The college gave me a temporary room for one month. I can' t find anywhere else and I have no money.
Wendy: Have you told the college about your position or asked them to let you stay longer in your accommodation?

Caesar: No, not yet. I didn't think that would be possible.

Wendy: Well, we can contact the accommodation service on your behalf to see if they'll let you stay a little longer, until you find an alternative.

Caesar: Thank you. But I'm not sure that I can find another place, as they all ask for money before moving in and I don't have any.

Wendy: Yes, it is usual in this country for landlords to ask for up to a month's rent in advance. Don't you have any money at all?

Caesar: Hardly any. I'm waiting for my grant cheque to be sent from the Philippines at the moment. It should have been here for me to collect when I arrived in Britain, but it seems to have been lost.

Wendy: You can apply for an emergency loan from the Union if you want. The loan can be for up to £200, and we ask for a post-dated cheque for the same amount to be given to us so that we can recover the money once you receive your grant cheque.

Caesar: That would be very good. I'll apply, but I'm still worried about how to find new accommodation.

Wendy: As I said earlier, we can ask the college to extend the time you are allowed to stay in your present accommodation. They may refuse, of course.

Caesar: Then what will happen?

Wendy: If the worst comes to the worst, the Union may be able to provide some very short-term emergency accommodation. If you want me to, I'll contact one or two of the addresses on the notice-board and arrange for you to visit them.

Caesar: But what if they ask me for the rent in advance? I only have £90 left and I need that for food and books.

Wendy: It'll be all right. By the time they actually need the money, we'll have your emergency loan ready. Just fill in this application form and write me a cheque for £200 please, payable to the Student Union.

Caesar: Right. I'll do that. Thank you very much for your help. I'm feeling more optimistic now.

That is the end of Section 2. You will have 30 seconds to check your answers.

That's the end of Section 2. Now turn to Section 3.

Section 3

You will hear a Student Union officer's speech. First, you have some time to look at questions 21-30.

Now, as you listen, answer questions 21-30.

Hi, there!

May I wish you a very warm welcome to Ealing College and, more especially, to the

Student Union. The Student Union is run by four sabbatical officers, of which I am one. As the president, I am charged with the overall day-to-day running of the Union itself, according to established policies within the Constitution. We also have a brilliant staff team who help us and you'll meet them when you have five minutes to drop in and see us.

The last year has seen the Student Union grow from incorporating a bar and a few officers with a small shop into being a thriving concern, which controls, to its credit, two bars, a café-bar or restaurant, a shop, a comprehensive welfare department and numerous offices.

All this has been achieved by sheer hard work and dedication on the part of last year's sabbatical team and staff, who overcame many obstacles and teething problems, but won through in the end. This year, our aims as a team will be to consolidate on what has already been achieved and to secure the future of the Union.

With the new post of Vice-president Social and Communications, our main emphasis will be on communications within the College, which has always proved a problem in the past, but one which we hope to improve upon this year. One way will be with the regular publication of a Student Union magazine, so all you budding journalists, come on down.

We are very aware that a lot of you have never had any contact with Student Unions before and don't know what they are or what they can do for you. So basically, here's a quick run down. If you have any problems at all, either when you start college or throughout your time here, don't hesitate to drop in the SU office in the North Building and see Pat, our office assistant. She will be able to help you with most of your day-to-day general enquiries, or if she can't, she will direct you to one of our staff who can.

Myself and the other three vice presidents are here every day, and if you need to see us, just fix a time with Pat and we'll be only too happy to help you. By the way, queries or problems can range from a late grant cheque, finding a place to live and academic matters, right through to the best places to eat, directions to the bar, or somebody blocking you in the car park. We'll give any thing our best shot.

Please remember while you're at Ealing that going to college is not just about education. Make sure you enjoy yourself as well because, believe me, time will fly once you're here.

Ealing is a really good place to live as there is lots to see and do, and don't forget the Metropolis of Central London is only twenty minutes away by tube. Finally, the Student Union is an organization run by students for students, so if there is anything you don't agree with or you have any new ideas, please come along to the Union General Meetings and don't be afraid to speak up. Or you could give up a little of your time and stand for the Executive Committee, which is made up of students who help us out with lots of interesting things.

I would like to take this opportunity to thank all the sabbaticals of the last two years who have worked so hard. My very special thanks goes to Winston, Martin and Peter and all the staff who not only did a great job, but have been my good friends as well.

Lots of luck and success for your year at Ealing. Work hard, but play hard as well.

That is the end of Section 3. Now You will have 30 seconds to check your answers.

That's the end of Section 3. Now turn to Section 4.

Section 4

You will hear a speech by the Student Union vice president for finance. As you listen to the speech, fill in the gaps numbered 31-35 and answer questions 36-38 by writing a T if the information is true, an F if the information is false or a question mark if the information is insufficient. First you will have some time to look at questions 31-35 as well as questions 36-38.

Now you will hear the speech.

Hello. As VP Finance, my job is to oversee the spending of our grant to ensure that all areas of Student Union activity run efficiently and smoothly, without any financial headaches.

I have a thoroughly efficient finance team—Ursula, Ella and Henryk. We are all here to help you as best as we can. Remember that even though I administer the Union's finances, it is ultimately you who have the final say in expenditure policy either directly, through the democratic process of the General Meetings, or by voicing your opinions through the Executive Finance Committee. I would like to take this opportunity to thank last year's VP Finance, Martin Currie, for his excellent work in improving the financial running of the Union to what it is today.

Finally, remember to enjoy yourself and to use the Union facilities and services to the full. And if you're still not satisfied, come and let us know why. Extra note: In order to maximise my time as VP Finance and to give a more efficient service to students, the Finance Office will only be open to students from 11:00 am to 1:00 pm and 2:00 pm to 3:00 pm. The Cashiers Office will be open from 12:00 noon to 2:00 pm daily.

That is the end of Section 4 and you will have 30 seconds to check your answers.

That is the end of Section 4 and of the listening test.

Test 2

Instruction:
You will hear a number of different recordings and you will have to answer questions on what you hear. There will be time for you to read the instructions and questions, and you will have a chance to check your work. All the recordings will be played once only. The test is in 4 sections. Write all your answers in the listening question booklet. At the end of the real test you will be given 10 minutes to transfer your answers to an answer sheet.

Now turn to Section 1.

Section 1

In Section 1 you will listen to an interview about the homestay programme between a coordinator and three students. As you listen, fill in the missing information in the chart. If a student's experience in the first homestay is positive and very good, make two ticks. If it's Ok, make one tick. If it's not good and there are negative feelings, make a cross. Look at the example and questions 1-8.

Now you will hear the interview for Section 1 and fill in the form as you listen because you will hear the recording once only. First, have another look at questions 1-8.

Now you will hear the interview. Listen carefully and fill in the form.

John: Hi, Fumi. Come in. How are things?

Fumi: Ok.

John: Hi, Linda and Ali. How are you?

Ali: Fine, thanks.

John: Well, as I explained on the telephone, I'm a coordinator of the Homestay Programme here, at the Student Services Section of the University and I'm doing a survey on host families to help me draw up a guide for new students. So I'd be grateful if you could tell me about your own experience on the Homestay Programme.

Fumi: Right.

Ali: Good idea.

John: Now, Fumi, let's start with you, OK? How long have you been staying with your host family?

Fumi: It's about three months now since I came from Japan.

John: What do you like about your host family?

Fumi: Oh, they are very nice to me and give me freedom to do what I want. I feel quite safe there, just like at home.

John: Do you like the food there?

Fumi: Yes, I love Canadian food. I always want to try new things.

John: It sounds good. Is your experience a positive one for the Homestay Programme?

Fumi: Yes, I think this homestay programme is very good and it really provides an opportunity for cultural exchange between Canadians and International students.

John: Thank you, Fumi. We will come back to you in a minute. Linda, I'd like to ask you some questions. You have been here for about a year and a half. Is that right?

Linda: Actually it's about two years since I left Beijing in 2003.

John: What do you think about the programme?

Linda: The Homestay Programme? The programme itself is quite good. But, it really depends on the individual host family. My first host family was quite a nice family, especially the first two weeks. They took me to the bank, shopping center and did many things for me, but I had a problem later.

John What was the problem?

Linda My biggest problem was the food. It was awful. They provided me with sandwiches for breakfast and lunch, and they liked to eat raw vegetables and not fully cooked meat for supper. I was not used to their food and sometimes I felt sick. I had stomach problems for quite a long time.

John I see. I'm sorry to hear that.

Linda: So after 3 months I moved out and now I live with two other students in a student house.

John: Well, Linda, if the food was changed to what you like, would you stay in that family?

Linda: Sure, I would.

John: I see. What about you, Ali? You come from Japan?

Ali: No. I come from Korea.

John: I'm sorry. Ali, how long have you been in Canada?

Ali: About eight months.

john: Do you enjoy staying here?

Ali: Yes. It's a nice place and a very good college.

John: What do you think about the Homeastay Programme?

Ali: I quite agree with Linda. The programme is good. The host family is different. And if you are lucky, you may get a good one. But the first one I stayed with was really terrible.

John: Ah, I'm sorry to hear that. Could you tell me a little more about it?

Ali: Yes. My first host parents seemed very busy. They usually came back home at about 10 in the evening so I would be hungry until they came back.

John: Did they leave some food for you when they came back late?

Ali: No, never, they didn't. They didn't allow me to cook in the kitchen, which was a house rule.

John: That's odd. What about your room? Was it comfortable?

Ali: No, it wasn't. I'd say it was awful. Their dogs often slept in my bed. I complained quite a bit about the dogs. But they were not sorry that the dogs were in my room because my room used to be their dog's room.

John: I'm very sorry to hear that. Did you tell this to anyone in the office?

Ali: Yes, I did. So I was moved out and changed to the host family where I stay now.

John: Are you happy with the new host family now?

Ali: Yes, I'm very happy now. They are nice and very considerate and often help me with my homework.

John: How about the food?

Ali: It's good and often served on time.

John: Good for you. Thank you very much.

That's the end of Section 1. You will have 30 seconds to check your answers.

Now turn to Section 2.

Section 2

In this section you will hear a conversation between two students. As you listen to the conversation, fill in the gaps numbered 9-15, and answer questions 16-20 by writing a T if the information is true, an F if the information is false, and an N if the information is not given. First look at questions 9-20.

Now listen to the conversion and do questions 9-20.

Tom: Hi, Marti. What did you think of the lecture?

Marti: It was really good. I enjoyed it very much. By the way, how are you doing with your European studies tutorial paper?

Tom: Oh, good. I have just finished it actually. I need to do something different tonight. What are you doing tonight? would you like to go out with me?

Marti: Oh, I'm sorry I can't. I have to work late tonight.

Tom: What for?

Marti: Well, I have to finish my paper and prepare my presentation for tomorrow.

Tom: Ah, I see. What's your presentation topic?

Marti: Well, after some consideration I decided to talk about Napoleon.

Tom: Oh, that's an interesting topic. Napoleon is one of my favorite characters too. Have you got time for a cup of coffee? You can tell me about it as a sort of practice.

Marti: That would be great.

Tom: Now, tell me about Napoleon. I know he used to be a French soldier and very quickly he became emperor of France. Do you know when he was born?

Marti: Yes. He was born in 1769 on the island of Corsica. And when he was only ten years old, his father sent him to a military school in France.

Tom: Was he a brilliant student at school?

Marti: No, he wasn't, but he excelled in mathematics and military science. And then, when he was sixteen years old, he joined the French army.

Tom: Oh, I didn't know he joined the army that young.

Marti: His military career brought him fame, power and riches, but, finally, defeat. Napoleon became a general in the French army at the age of twenty-four. Several years later he became emperor of the French Empire.

Tom: Do you know when he became an emperor?

Marti: Yes. On May 18, 1804 he became emperor of France and the coronation ceremony was held at Notre Dame on the 2nd of December. He was only 35 that year. He was really many things. But he was, first of all, a brilliant military leader. His soldiers were ready to die for him.

Tom: Yes, he was really short too. Of course, Napoleon had so many military victories so his size wasn't an issue.

Marti: You are right. At one time he controlled most of Europe.

Tom: Yes, but at that time many countries, including England, Russia, and Austria, fought fiercely against Napoleon.

Marti: Right. His defeat came when he decided to attack Russia. In this military campaign into Russia, he lost most of his army. Shortly after his defeat, his abdication followed at waterloo, and then he tried to escape to America but he failed. He finally surrendered to the British government and then they exiled him to St. Helena Island.

Tom: I know his last years were spent there with a few chosen comrades. Do you know how old he was when he died?

Marti: He lived there until he died. He died in 1821 when he was only fifty-one years old. he died alone, deserted by his family and his friends.

Tom: Well, that's a pretty sad way to end the life. Well, Marti, I'm sure your presentation will be really good. You know, you could also give the chronological order of his life and this may help your classmates to follow your presentation.

Marti: Yes, that's a good suggestion. Thank you, Tom.

Tom: You are welcome. I have to go now. I have another lecture to attend. Good luck.

Marti: Thank you. You have been really great help. I'm sorry that I can't come out with you this evening, but have a nice time. Bye.

Tom: Bye.

That's the end of Section 2. You will have 30 seconds to check your answers.

Now turn to Section 3.

Section 3

In Section 3 you will hear a talk on ocean spills. As you listen to the talk, circle the appropriate letter for questions 21-23 and complete the statements numbered 24-30 by writing no more than three words in the spaces provided. First, you'll have some time to look at questions 21-30.

Now listen to the talk and do questions 21-30.

Good morning, everyone. Today I will talk about unusual ocean spills that have occurred in the world's oceans.

In November of 1992, people at beaches in Canada and Alaska noticed something strange: blue turtles, red beavers, green frogs, and yellow ducks came bobbing toward them. They soon found out where the strange creatures were coming from.

A ship from Hong Kong was on its way to Tacoma, Washington, when it was hit by a severe storm in the middle of the Pacific Ocean. During the storm, huge waves washed 12 containers overboard. Inside the containers were 29,000 plastic bath toys. One of the containers opened, and thousands of plastic bath toys spilled out and began to float across the Pacific

Ocean. Ten months later, the first yellow ducks arrived on the North American shore. Beachcombers along the shore began to find the toys and reported them to local newspapers. But the people who were most excited by the plastic toys were the oceanographers. It gave them an opportunity to study ocean currents and winds; oceanographers drop bottles into the ocean to study these things. But it would be too expensive to drop 29,000 bottles into the ocean at once. Image the value of studying the plastic ducks and frogs. These give some interesting information for the oceanographers.

The first toys were picked up in Sitka, Alaska, ten months after they were washed off the ship. Some headed back into the North Pacific, while others drifted around the Arctic Ocean and headed for the North Atlantic. Many of the toys were swept northeast by the wind and were frozen in the ice of the Bering Sea. They are expected to cross the North Pole and float on down to the British Isles.

This reminds me of another unusual ocean spill. In 1990, a ship traveling to the West Coast of the United States from Korea was caught in a severe storm. The waves swept 21 containers of Nike shoes into the water. Scientists estimate that about 80,000 running, jogging, and hiking shoes, 40,000 pairs of shoes to you and me hit the water at once. The shoes were for men, women, and children.

About six months later, people at beaches from Oregon to British Columbia began to find running shoes washed ashore. By the end of the year, Washington newspapers reported people finding hundreds of shoes. In Seattle, thousands of shoes floated to shore. Since the shoes were not attached, they arrived one at a time. The shoes were dirty, but after they were washed they were still in good condition. People set up exchanges to find matches for their shoes.

Oceanographers studied the information to learn more about the ocean. Some Nike shoes reached Hawaii. Others went to the Philippines and Japan. According to the scientists, some of the shoes are on a trip around the world and should end up back in Washington and Origon. Can you believe it? Many pairs of running shoes as well as plastic ducks and frogs are still on their ocean journey. So if you go to a beach anywhere in the world, don't be surprised if you see a green plastic frog or a woman's size 7 jogging shoe bobbing toward you. So keep your eyes out so you may find free bath toys and even a new pair of shoes. Thank you for attending my lecture.

That's the end of Section 3. You will have 30 seconds to check your answers.

Now turn to Section 4.

Section 4

In this section you will hear a talk about chocolate. As you listen complete the notes below by writing no more than three words in the spaces numbered 31-38 and circle the appropriate letter for questions 39-40. First, you will have 30 seconds to look at this section.

Now listen to the talk and do questions 31-40.

Good morning, everyone. Today my talk is going to be about chocolate. I'm going to talk a little bit about the history of chocolate. But first I'm going to tell you a story about Julia Procter.

She eats her favorite food; she feels guilty. She knows that chocolate has a lot of fat and sugar. But Julia says she is addicted to chocolate. And once she starts eating it, she can't stop. Julia isn't the only one who is addicted to chocolate. It is a favorite food for people all over the world. And in a survey of 16 different countries, people preferred chocolate to ice-cream, cakes, and cookies. In the United States, chocolate is a £10 billion industry. For Valentine's Day, for example, people spend over £400 million on chocolate. The idea of eating chocolate didn't begin until the 19th century. Before that, people drank chocolate. The custom began in Central America, where the Aztecs drank bowls of chocolate to stay alert. When the liquid chocolate was brought to Spain in the 1500s, people thought it was medicine because it tasted bitter, like other medicines. In fact, the people who made chocolate into drinks were either druggists or doctors. Then people discovered that mixing chocolate with sugar made a wonderful drink. King Fedinand of Spain loved this drink so much that he put out an order: Anyone who talked about chocolate outside the court would be killed. So for about 100 years, chocolate was a secret in Spain.

But finally, people found out about chocolate, and it became a popular drink throughout Europe. In the 1800s, a British chocolate maker discovered a way to make chocolate smooth and velvety, then the Swiss added milk to the chocolate. Today, most Americans prefer milk chocolate, while most Europeans prefer dark chocolate.

Now research shows that chocolate is actually good for us because chocolate has a variety of vitamins and minerals. And it has more than 300 different chemicals. One chemical works on the part of the brain that feels pleasure. People who feel good when they eat chocolate are actually healthier, because feeling pleasure is important for health and can protect against illness. Good chocolate doesn't have much fat or sugar. You can enyoy it if you "eat a little at a time". So thinking about Julia Procter who I mentioned at the beginning, if you just eat a little at a time, that isn't a big problem. That's the end of my talk today on chocolate.

That's the end of Section 4. You will have 30 seconds to check your answers.

That's the end of the listening test.

Test 3

Instruction:

You will hear a number of different recordings and you will have to answer questions on what you hear. There will be time for you to read the instructions and questions, and you will have a chance to check your work. All the recordings will be played once only. The test is in 4 sections. Write all your answers in the listening question booklet. At the end of the real test you will be given 10 minutes to transfer your answers to an answer sheet.

Now turn to Section 1.

Section 1

You will hear a conversation between a foreign student and the accommodation secretary of the college at which he has enrolled. Listen to the conversation between the student and the accommodation secretary, and complete the accommodation table. Write no more than three words or numbers for each answer.

Look at questions 1-9 now. You will see that there is an example which has been done for you on the accommodation table. The conversation relating to this will be played first.

Now we shall begin. You should answer the questions as you listen because you will not hear the recording a second time. First, you have another chance to look at questions 1-9.

Now listen carefully and answer questions 1-9.

Student: Excuse me, is this the accommodation office?

Secretary: Yes, it is.

Student: Hi. My name is... um... Wolfgang. I... I'm a new student here. I'm wondering if you can tell me some information about the housing arrangements at this college?

Secretary: Yes, certainly. Well, I mean... basically there are two types of ... um... accommodation. The most popular is... um, the college accommodation... um... but also we offer accommodation with local families.

Student: You mean a kind of homestay?

Secretary: Yes, that's right.

Student: Well, let me.. can I... do you mind if I ask you a few questions about both of them? Let me start with the college accommodation. Um... what kind of rooms are they?

Secretary: Well, there are basically two types of room, either a single or a twin study bedroom. So that's...

Student: I'd have a roommate, then?

Secretary: That's right, yes. So it's two people sharing a room.

Student: Do all of the rooms have their own bathrooms?

Secretary: Erm... they don't. You... you... have to share... um, a bathroom and a toilet... and showers with a group of rooms. So it's with about six to eight other students.

Student: I see. Well, is it... can I wash my hands and so on, in the room or...?

Secretary: Er... yes, there is a washbasin in the rooms.

Student: But if I want to use the toilet or take a shower I have to go down the hall?

Secretary: That's right, yes.

Student: Oh, I see. Well, well... that sounds fine. What about bedding? Is er... is that provided by the college or...?

Secretary: Yes, yes, it is. Um... so all the bed linen is supplied...

Student: And the towels?

Secretary: No. So you have to bring your own towels with you.

Student: Oh... uhuh. Well, if I... then... to wash my towels, is there a place where I can go to do that or...?

Secretary: Yes, yes. So... um... there are two accommodation buildings in the college and both of these have launderettes.

Student: I'm sorry, they have a what?

Secretary: They have launderettes. So these are places... um... where you can take your washing and there are washing machines...

Student: Oh, is... is it free or...?

Secretary: Er, no. They're coin-operated washing machines...

Student: Oh. So I use the coins to make the machine work.

Secretary: Uhuh, yes, that's right.

Student: Oh, OK. That sounds fine.

Secretary: And the... the... rooms are actually cleaned... um... every week and the bed-linen is changed, also at the same time.

Student: Oh, that's wonderful. That sounds fine. Um... if I... if I do decide to stay in the... in the dormitory, I'm going to want to... er... have a chance to watch television. I want to use TV to practise my English. Is there a TV in the room?

Secretary: Well, no, there isn't a TV in every room... um... but there is a common room which has... um... a colour TV in it, and some kind of sitting areas so students can meet together and they can watch TV.

Student: Oh, well, that sounds fine.

Secretary: Uhuh... and, oh, but actually there's also a large hall for films and discos, and kind of parties and other social occasions.

Student: Oh, well, that sounds very good. That sounds interesting. I may want to do that, but before I decide for sure, let me ask about the other possibility. I think you said there's a kind of homestay programme, is that right?

Secretary: Yes, that's right. So we select local families who... um... want to have students staying with them for short periods.

Student: Hmm... well, that sounds interesting. How do I... er... how does that work? Do I eat there every day and... and sleep there as well, and so on?

Secretary: Oh, well, basically there're... there're two kinds... um... of accommodation available here... so... um... The first one is half board so this is where... um... you just eat breakfast and evening dinner with the family.

Student: Oh, and then lunch I would have on campus?

Secretary: That's right, yes. So that's... that's during the week, but at weekends you'll have all your meals...

Student: All the meals there...?

Secretary: ... With the... yeah... with the family. Um... so that's...

Student: The other one was...

Secretary: Uhuh. So that was half board. The... the other one is bed and breakfast. So this is where you just have breakfast with the family, seven days a week. So that includes weekends.

Student: And then I would have the lunch and dinner on campus. Is that how it'd work?

Secretary: That's right, yes. So it's just breakfast.

Student: Well, now that I think about it, I wonder if maybe that might not... not be the better option for me. That way I would have a chance to be practising my English with the British family. I... yes, I think I'll sign up for that. I'm pretty much sure that's what I want to do right now. Is it OK to go ahead and sign up immediately?

Secretary: OK, yes, yes, that's fine. Right, let me just see if I can find the forms.

That's the end of Section 1. You'll have 30 seconds to check your answers.

Now turn to Section 2.

Sections 2

You'll hear the second part of the conversation between the foreign student and the secretary. Fill in the form as you listen. Now look at questions 10-20.

As the talk continues, fill in the form as you listen and answer questions 10-20.

Student: I think I'll sign up for that. I'm pretty much sure that's what I want to do right now. Is it OK to go ahead and sign up immediately?

Secretary: OK, yes, yes, that's fine. Right, let me just see if I can find the forms. OK, right... so your name is...?

Student: My name is Wolfgang Schmidt. That's Wolfgang...

Secretary: Wolfgang? OK, how do you spell that?

Student: W-O-L-F-G-A-N-G.
Secretary: OK... G-A-N-G... uhuh.
Student: And my last name is Schmidt.
Secretary: Schmidt, ahah...
Student: S-C-H-M-I-D-T.
Secretary: S-C-H-M-I-D-T. And your address?
Student: You mean in Germany?
Secretary: Yes... yes, your home address.
Student: Ah... it's Franz Dieter Strausse.
Secretary: Oh, how do you spell that?
Student: That's F-R-A-N-Z...
Secretary: F-R-A-N-Z... we say "Zed" in Britain.
Student: Oh. I'm sorry—zed, yes, F-R-A-N-Z, and the next word is Dieter. That's D-I-E-T-E-R.
Secretary: Uhuh... and...
Student: And the last word is Strausse.
Secretary: Strausse, so that's S-T...
Student: S-T-R-A-U-S-S-E.
Secretary: ... S-S-E.
Student: Franz Dieter Strausse, number five.
Secretary: Number five... uhuh...
Student: In Bonne...
Secretary: Right, and that's Germany, obviously.
Student: Germany, uhuh.
Secretary: And your age?
Student: I'm 20... I'm sorry... no... I just turned 21 yesterday.
Secretary: Oh, really? Happy birthday.
Student: Thank you.
Secretary: Uhuh... OK... and the programme that you're in?
Student: I'm on the four-month programme, so I'll be staying here until the end of December.
Secretary: Right. And so you have any special dietary requirements?
Student: I'm sorry, I'm not sure what you mean...
Secretary: Ah, is... is there any kind of special food that you... you need or that you don't eat?
Student: Oh, no. I like to eat most anything ... um...
Secretary: Oh, that's just as well with British food.
Student: I don't think so. I'm looking forward to... er... trying some British dishes.
Secretary: Really? Well... OK... um... we like to... to ask you something about yourself... your personal interests and things, so that we can match you with a... an appropriate family, so...
Student: Oh, OK...

Secretary: So, do... have you got any personal interests or hobbies?

Student: Well, I... I like to do sports... um... I specially like football. If it's possible I'd like to be with a family maybe where there's somebody I could practise football with.

Secretary: Right... football... um... and have you got any special requirements as to the family that you are going to stay with... um...

Student: Oh, well... you know, I come from a large family back in Germany, so maybe, if it's possible, you could put me with a family where there might be... er... another young person or two, perhaps—would be good...

Secretary: Right, so someone about your own age, perhaps...

Student: Mmm, maybe someone I could play football with... yeah.

Secretary: Right. Well, actually I interviewed a family yesterday who seem just right for you...

Student: Oh.

Secretary: Um... their name is Roberts... so it's the Roberts family. Um... Mr. Roberts is a bank manager.

Student: Oh really? My father is a bank manager.

Secretary: Oh, well, and...

Student: That sounds very good.

Secretary: So his... his wife is a part-time nursery school teacher, so she just works in the morning.

Student: Oh, OK...

Secretary: And they have two children... the girl is eighteen, but she's actually just gone away to college, so this is why they have a room vacant.

Student: Oh, so I would... I would stay in her room then?

Secretary: That's right, uhuh.

Student: Oh, that sounds fine.

Secretary: And their son is sixteen years old and he likes football very much.

Student: Well, that sounds very good. I think I... I'd like to meet this family. Is that possible to... to do that?

Secretary: Yes, it is. Um... what I'll do is... I'll give Mrs. Roberts a ring now. In fact, she should be... should be home at this time. So I'll give her a ring.

Student: OK, thank you.

That is the end of Section 2. You will now have half a minute to check your answers.

Now turn to Section 3.

Section 3

In this section you will hear a conversation between Wolfgang and his new friend Mary who has

already been at the college for a few months. In the first part of the conversation they are talking about a social activity programme at college. First look at questions 21-27. Note the examples that have been done for you.

Now listen to the first part of the discussion and answer questions 21-27.

Mary: Hi, Wolfgang.

Wolfgang: Ah, Mary. How are you?

Mary: Oh, fine. How's it going? Have you just had a class?

Wolfgang: Yes. I just finished my listening class. It was... er... a little bit difficult.

Mary: Yeah, yeah, it's always difficult when you first arrive somewhere. I found it quite hard when I first arrived. Mnn... but you know, what really made a difference was going on these social activities that the... the college arranges for you. It kinda... gives you a chance to practise your English and...

Wolfgang: Hmm... I've heard that the college is pretty good about organizing those kinds of things. How... how do I find out about it?

Mary: Well, I've just picked up a schedule today. Let's ... let's have a look at it. Here it is...

Wolfgang: What is it? A schedule for... for this week or...?

Mary: Yeah, yeah. Let's have a look.

Wolfgang: Oh, OK... yeah... maybe we can do some things together... in fact.

Mary: Yeah, that'd be great, so...

Wolfgang: Let's see. What are they doing tonight? Monday night...

Mary: Well, they've... so... oh. They've got Singing with Guitar. So I went to this last week. It's...

Wolfgang: Oh, really?

Mary: Yes, it's quite good fun.

Wolfgang: Is it pretty good?

Mary: Yeah, yeah.

Wolfgang: What do they do? Do they have a concert or...?

Mary: It's... they teach you... um... modern and traditional songs.

Wolfgang: Mm... well... I'm not much of a singer, but... er...

Mary: Oh, come on. You should go. It's really good fun.

Wolfgang: Well, I suppose it'd be a good way to practise my English.

Mary: Yeah, 'cause you learn kinda British folk songs and things. It's... yeah... it's really interesting.

Wolfgang: Oh, but look at that. That starts at eight. But I notice at nine o'clock there's a... er... late night coach to Cambridge for a film. I think I'd want to go to try that... er... what time does this singing thing finish? Do you know?

Mary: Oh, well, usually it... it kinda lasts about two hours, but I mean, we can always leave earlier—they don't mind, do...

Wolfgang: Oh, OK. So we can do both then?

Mary: Yeah, so...

Wolfgang: Right. So that's at nine o'clock... yea... yeah...

Mary: What movie is it? Let me see...

Wolfgang: Er... Oh. It's *Rocky*. Have you seen it?

Mary: *Rocky*... *Rocky*? Oh, that's... that's... er... the one with Richard Dreyfuss, isn't it?

Wolfgang: Richard Dreyfuss? No, it's Slvester Stallone.

Mary: Oh, yes. I remember now... American movie... yes, I haven't seen that. I wanna see that. Good, let's go to that.

Wolfgang: All right, OK. Oh, did you see on Tuesday that there's a tennis tournament?

Mary: Tennis? Mm... what time is that?

Wolfgang: Well, that's at four o'clock in the afternoon.

Mary: Where is it? Is it on campus or...?

Wolfgang: No... no. It's at Wembley, so that's in London.

Mary: Oh, oh, so that... it's pretty far away then. What time will it be coming back?

Wolfgang: Um... so it... the coach gets back at midnight.

Mary: Oh, midnight? Well, hmm... tell you what, I think maybe I'd better cancel on that because I've got a class Wednesday morning, and I'm afraid... at about eight thirty... I'm afraid if I came back that late I probably would... er... I'd be very tired in class, and actually I... I'm more into football myself, anyway.

Wolfgang: Oh, football? Well, did you see there's a football match on Wednesday?

Mary: Oh yeah? Well, who's... who's playing? Let's see...

Wolfgang: Oh. It's England and Brazil.

Mary: Oh, I really want to see that. Would you like to go together?

Wolfgang: Yeah, sure. What time is it?

Mary: Let me see... It says fifteen thirty, so that would be three thirty.

Wolfgang: Three thirty? Huh...

Mary: Now, I've got a... I have a lecture... er... right after lunch on Wednesday, at one thirty.

Wolfgang: Uhuh, what lecture is that?

Mary: Oh, well, there's a journalist coming from the BBC. He's going to talk about his experiences as a foreign correspondent.

Wolfgang: Huh, that sounds interesting.

Mary: Would you... would you like to go?

Wolfgang: Yeah. What time did you say it was?

Mary: Er... right after lunch, around one thirty.

Wolfgang: Oh, one thirty? I have a class then. What a sh... yeah...

Mary: Oh, that's too bad. Well, what time does your class finish?

Wolfgang: Well, it finishes... it's an hour long... so it finishes at two thirty.

Mary: Oh, well, I shouldn't imagine... the lecture shouldn't go much later than that either, so after your class and after my lecture we can get together to go to the football game.

Wolfgang: OK... so we can meet...

Mary: Let's see, maybe three o'clock or... or maybe three fifteen?

Wolfgang: Yeah, I think three fifteen would be all right.

Mary: OK. Where should we meet?

Wolfgang: Well, usually these... on these kind of trips, the coach leaves from in front of the dining hall, so maybe we could meet there.

Mary: OK, so in front of the dining hall at three fifteen. That sounds fine.

Wolfgang: Yeah, right. On Thursday there's International Evening in the school hall.

Mary: Yeah, all songs and dances, performance by students from all over the world. That's very interesting. Would you like to go and see?

Wolfgang: Yes. When is that?

Mary: It will start at eight. Shall we meet at seven fifty in front of the school hall?

Wolfgang: Fine, seven fifty in front of the school hall.

Now listen to the second part of the conversation and answer questions 28-32.

Mary: Oh. And another thing I definitely want to do this weekend... er... is to go to see... er... they're going to have a trip to Stratford-on-Avon. I think it's on... let me see, what day is that? Friday, I think my roommate told me.

Wolfgang: Oh, Friday?

Mary: Would you like to go to that?

Wolfgang: Yeah, but are you sure it's Friday?

Mary: I thought that's what she said, but I might've been mistaken.

Wolfgang: Well, usually these things are on weekends.

Mary: Right.

Wolfgang: Let's see here. Oh, you're right, yeah... Saturday morning, eight thirty.

Mary: Ahah. Right, Friday's the disco.

Wolfgang: Oh, disco.

Mary: Yeah. So, actually I've arranged to go with some of my friends. So if you'd like to come along with us...

Wolfgang: Oh, that would be very nice, yeah.

Mary: Yeah, you can meet some more students.

Wolfgang: Oh, well, what time... what time shall we go to that then?

Mary: Well, it starts at... what time...? Eight thirty, but we don't want to go too early, so let's say nine or nine thirty. Let's say nine thirty.

Wolfgang: OK, yeah... we can meet there. Um... but we'd better not stay too late, because the Stratford thing is... er... pretty early in the morning. The bus will be leaving at eight thirty.

Mary: Oh, yeah, right. So we want to make sure we get up for that.

Wolfgang: Yeah. Say, by the way, this trip... um... since... it's... er... quite a way away, do we have to pay anything extra for that or is it free?

Mary: Mmm... well, usually most of the trips are free, but, yeah... for these ones which are quite a distance away, then we usually have to pay a ... a little bit extra.

Wolfgang: Is it a lot or... ?

Mary: No, it's usually about twenty-five pounds, something like that.

Wolfgang: Oh, well, do we have to tell them ahead of time that we're going to go?

Mary: Yeah, usually you have to sign up a couple of days in advance, so...

Wolfgang: Oh, where... where do we do that?

Mary: Um... well, you do that at the Student Services Office. So you have to go and see one of the Social Activities Officers.

Wolfgang: Oh, so I just tell them that I want to go and I pay my money and then sign my name. Well, I think I'll go ahead and do that today. Actually, I've got some free time right now. Do you know where I go to do that?

Mary: Um... yeah, yeah. It's... the... the Student Services Office. It's just across the road from here.

Wolfgang: Oh, OK.

Mary: Um... well, across the kind of...

Wolfgang: You mean the green building over there?

Mary: Yeah, yeah. So it's on the second floor.

Wolfgang: Oh, OK. Well, tell you what... um... Are you going to the Shakespeare thing?

Mary: Er... yeah, yeah, sure.

Wolfgang: Would you like me to go ahead and sign you up as well?

Mary: Oh, yes, yeah. That'd be great, but... well, I haven't got any money on me at the moment.

Wolfgang: Ah, don't worry about the money. That's fine. You can pay me back this evening. I'll go and sign us now, and then when I meet you tonight at the singing, you can... er... give me the money then.

Mary: Oh, well, if... if you are sure, that'd be great.

Wolfgang: No, it's no problem.

Mary: OK. Oh, is that the time? I'd better go. I've got a class. I'll be late.

Wolfgang: OK, sorry. I'll see you later then.

Mary: All right. See you tonight.

Wolfgang: Bye.

Mary: Bye.

That is the end of Section 3. You will now have half a minute to check your answers.

Now turn to Section 4.

Section 4

In Section 4 you will hear a conversation and answer questions 33-40. First you have some time to look at questions 33-40.

Now listen carefully and answer questions 33-40.

(*Charles and Belinda are meeting in the hotel. They came for the anniversary conference.*)

Belinda: Ah, that's much better.

Charles: Ah, that's yours, Belinda. How are you?

Belinda: Fine, thank you very much, Charles.

Charles: Right. You have a good journey then, Belinda?

Belinda: Yes, I did, I did. I must say the plane was marvellous.

Charles: Do you want a drink?

Belinda: Yes, please. You know, the plane journey was terrifically quick... it got in at ... er ... 10:30 and we left Gatwick at 9:15.

Charles: What time did you have to start though in the morning?

Belinda: Well, that was ... er ... that was a different story, because I had to go to Victoria... um... at ... you know, to get to Gatwick and it's... from Victoria to Gatwick's three quarters of an hour. Then I had to leave home at 7:30 am and get up at 6:20.

Charles: Oh, gracious me.

Belinda: So I'm not sure if you save much really.

Charles: Jet travel, my goodness me. It was worth the experience, though?

Belinda: Oh, I mean, you know, I've never flown across the South of England and it really looked absolutely fantastic, especially as we proach... approached Plymouth, you know, with this sunshine and it looked really marvellous... marvellous.

Charles: Well, when you come up next time, would you be coming the same way?

Belinda: Oh, I don't think so. I don't... to be honest...

Charles: Well, why not?

Belinda: Well, to be honest it was a bit of a luxury because it was a really expensive flight and of course there are only three planes a day. Did you have a good journey?

Charles: Yes, I had a lovely time. I came by train.

Belinda: What time did you start then?

Charles: Oh, about half past ten, I think. Got here about half past one. So it's only... what... three hours. Very quick.

Belinda: Very good.

Charles: Well, this was... er... this was a nice train, you know, very modern and comfortable. And of course lots of trains... about every hour, I think.

Belinda: Oh, great. Did you get something to eat on the train?

Charles: Yes. Had a nice lunch. Oh, it's wonderful. You can sit there drinking your soup and watching the view go by. I like it . . .

Belinda: I bet it's a hell of a lot cheaper than the plane.

Charles: Well, actually, I thought it was quite expensive . . . um. . . unless you've got a student card or something.

Belinda: Oh, those days are long gone.

Charles: But it was quite crowded. I was. . . I was glad I'd booked a seat, you know.

Belinda: Yes. How did you come for the conference last time?

Charles: On the coach.

Belinda: Good lord.

Charles: And it was really cheap. I thought I'd try it because I hadn't got much money at that time.

Belinda: You didn't have to start the night before, did you?

Charles: No, no. I set off at about twenty past eight and I got here at round about two o'clock.

Belinda: Good.

Charles: And it was really comfortable as well.

Belinda: A lot of motorway travel, then?

Charles: Well, there was a lot of motorway travel. Because there was a lot of motorway travel I was able to read. . . to sit and read my book. And it was a really smooth journey, I remember.

Belinda: Didn't you get travel sick?

Charles: No, I didn't feel sick at all.

Belinda: I think they were really hot, those coaches.

Charles: Well, it was air-conditioned, actually, and it was really nice.

Belinda: Well, you had nearly six hours in the coach. Wasn't that very tiring?

Charles: Yes, I suppose, about five and a half hours, but I mean once I started looking at my book, you know, I didn't notice the time at all. It just flew by. It's incredible.

Belinda: What was the service like, then? I mean, were there a lot of coaches?

Charles: I think it is pretty good. . . er. . . there are about five coaches in the day and there's one overnight coach as well, I believe. So it's really nice.

Belinda: Splendid. Well. . . I think I'll try next time.

Charles: Another drink?

Belinda: Oh, no, thanks. I really think. . .

That is the end of Section 4. Now you have half a minute to check your answers.

That is the end of the listening test.

Test 4

Instruction:

You will hear a number of different recordings and you will have to answer questions on what you hear. There will be time for you to read the instructions and questions, and you will have a chance to check your work. All the recordings will be played once only. The test is in 4 sections. Write all your answers in the listening question booklet. At the end of the real test you will be given 10 minutes to transfer your answers to an answer sheet.

Now turn to Section 1.

Section 1

Tom and Barbara are talking about markets in London. Barbara has a market list and she wants to find out more details about them. Listen to the conversation and complete the market list. Write no more than three words for each answer. Look at questions 1-6 on the market list now.

Now listen and complete the market list.

Tom: Hi, Barbara. What will you do this weekend?

Barbara: Well, I'd like to do some shopping, but I have no idea where to go. I've only been here a few days. I was told London is an expensive place to live.

Tom: Yes, but that's not completely true. London can be an expensive place to live, but if you shop in the right places, you can live relatively cheaply.

Barbara: Is that true? Could you tell me something about the shops?

Tom: All right. You know, food tends to be cheapest in the big supermarkets like Sainsburys and Tescos. Most of them have quite a good variety of food and household items. You can buy your fruit and vegetables on the street. You will find these street markets in almost every part of London. You can also buy clothes, shoes and household items in these markets for a real bargain. Have you got a market list provided by the Student Union?

Barbara: Yes. Here you are.

Tom: This might give you some ideas. Let me see. East Street SE17. This market sells cheap food, clothes and hardware. It's open from 8 am to 5 pm.

Barbara: Yes, but how can I get there?

Tom: You can take the underground. We call it the tube. You see, there is a tube station on the list.

Barbara: Let me see. Yes, it's Castle Station.

Tom: Right. You can get off at the Castle.

Barbara: Good. Look at Leather Lane WC1.

Tom: Yes, that's a good central London market for clothes, food and hardware. It opens at lunch times from Monday to Friday. It's near Chancery Lane Station.

Barbara: Well. What about the one in Petticoat Lane?

Tom: Oh, Petticoat Lane E1. It sells clothes, shoes and household goods. It opens only on Sunday mornings from 9 am to 12 noon.

Barbara: Yes, we can get off at Aldgate Station. OK. What about the one in Walthamstow E17?

Tom: Oh, that's a big market for clothes and food. It's open between 9 am and 4 pm on Mondays to Saturdays, except Wednesdays and Sundays.

Barbara: Let me see... yes, we can get there on the Central Line. What about Brixton?

Tom: That's Brixton SW9. It's an indoor and outdoor market with a lively atmosphere. It sells vegetables from all over the world. It opens 9 am to 6 pm Mondays to Sundays and half day on Wednesdays.

Barbara: Oh, it's close to Brixton Station, very near my place. Great. It's very convenient. Tell me more detail about Camden Lock.

Tom: Yes, there are several markets on Camden High Street and plenty of shops. They sell fashion clothes, jewellery, recorders and pottery. It's good for buying presents, very close to Chalk Farm and Camden Town Station.

Barbara: I see. It says that it opens on Sundays only from 8 am to 5 pm. Well, I think these markets might help to keep my costs down.

Tom: Well, if you need to buy new electrical goods or large household items, you can wait until the January sales when almost all the shops sell goods at discount prices.

Barbara: Thank you very much for your help. Tom, shall we go to Brixton together this weekend?

Tom: I'd love to.

Barbara: Oh, I'm afraid I've got to go to a lecture. I will ring you tonight. Bye.

Tom: OK. Bye.

Barbara is phoning Tom about shopping. Look at Questions 7-9.

Now listen to their telephone conversation and answer questions 7-9. Write no more than three words for each answer.

(*Telephone rings.*)

Tom: 4010625?

Barbara: Hello. Is that you, Tom?

Tom: Hi, Barbara. Have you decided where to go tomorrow?

Barbara: Yes, that's right. I want to go to Camden Town to shop. Would you like to go there with me?

Tom: Yes, I'd love to. That's a good market. Mary is here with me now. She wants to go there too. Shall we meet at Camden Town Station?

Barbara: OK. How are you going there?

Tom: We will go there by bus. It's only three stops from my place. Well, we might walk there if the whether is fine. How will you get there?

Barbara: I think I will have to take the underground. I'm at Bond Street and I'll take the Central Line first and get off at Tottenham Court Road.

Tom: That's it. Take the Central Line and get off at Tottenham Court Road. Then You want the Northern Line to Camden Town. It's only about four stops. Make sure you get a northbound train though. You want northbound Camden Town. OK?

Barbara: OK. I think I can find the way. I have an underground map with me now. What time shall we meet there tomorrow?

Tom: How about ten thirty?

Barbara: Well, I think that's a bit too late. It might be crowed by that time.

Tom: How about one hour earlier, say nine thirty?

Barbara: Fine. That will be all right. See you tomorrow.

Tom: Bye.

That's the end of Section 1. You now have half a minute to check your answers.

Now turn to Section 2.

Section 2

You are going to hear a talk about the Women's Conference. First look at questions 10-14.

As you listen to part of the talk, answer questions 10-14.

There will be two meetings held in Beijing, and they will overlap. One—the NGO (Non-governmental Organization) Forum on Women will be held in Beijing from August 30 to September 8, 1995. The other one—the Fourth World Conference on Women (FWCW) of the United Nations will be held in Beijing from September 4 to 15, 1995.

Why is the UN (United Nations) holding these meetings? The UN has noticed that discrimination against women has been increasing. The UN definition of discriminations—any distinction, exclusion or restriction made on the basis of sex, which has the purpose of deciding or not allowing the full recognition of a woman on a basis of equality between male and female, human rights, freedom in political, economic, social, cultural or other fields.

Women are discriminated against in every country of the world. The UN has issued policies to deal with the discrimination. The UN has also placed the improvement of women's status position high on the global agenda.

The world is getting smaller. We are becoming a global family that shares problems and difficulties. We can learn from one another, help one another and share ideas and information.

There have been three previous world conferences on women. First in Mexico City in 1975, second in Copenhagen in 1980 and third was in Nairobi in 1985. During the first conference held in Mexico City in 1975, which was during the "International Women's Year", one outcome was the declaration by the UN General Assembly for "Decade for Women" (1976-1985).

In Copenhagen in 1980 the participants adopted a "Program of Action" for the second half of the UN Decade for Women. The 1985 Nairobi Conference was held at the end of the UN Decade for Women and the results were published in a book called the *Forward Looking Strategies*, which provided a framework for action at the international, national and regional levels of government and groups to promote greater equality and opportunities for women.

The slogan for the UN Decade for Women was equality, development and peace. This year from the end of August until the middle of September, Beijing will hold two conferences. They are separate conferences but related. The NGO Forum '95 from August 30 to September 8 about 30000 participants, both women and men, are expected to attend. It will be about women, their lives and their perspectives. This will provide women around the world with an opportunity to discuss and develop ideas, perspectives, plans and strategies and share information, to celebrate women's achievement and contributions in society, and to draw attention to and develop solutions to the discrimination facing women worldwide.

Who can participate in the NGO Forum '95? Any individuals or groups who fill in an application form and send 50 USD to NGO Forum, New York, by April 30, 1995.

Who will attend the Fourth World Conference? Each member state of the UN will send an official delegation. There are 184 member states in the UN. Also any person that represents an organization which has received accreditation. This had to be done by January 13, 1995. Six thousand people are expected to attend this Conference.

There has been over three years of preparations for this Conference in Beijing, at the international, national and regional levels in all the participating countries.

The Preparation Committee has organized all the issues into ten categories. The Conference in Beijing will discuss all these issues. At the end of the Conference the UN will issue a "Platform for Action". The Platform for Action will address the following critical areas of concern...

Now look at questions 15-20.

Listen to the following directions and answer questions 15-20.

Ladies and gentlemen,

You are all welcome to this afternoon's tour of the campus. I'll be your guide for the duration. Before we start, could I please ask you to look at your campus map? That's the one you just got when you came in. Because the university buildings are not quite spread out, the tour will be on foot. Now, let's start where we are, the Main Building. As you come out of the Main Building, you will see two other big buildings opposite you. One is the campus branch of the Midland Bank on your left, the other one is the Post Office. Then we will follow Mary's Road until we come to the School Lane. Here, on the opposite side of the road, you will see a huge white building directly on your left hand corner. That would be the Students' Library. The Student Union is next to it, opposite the bank. Then we turn right and get into Candle Lane. There is a big shopping centre directly on the corner and the Science Building is on the left hand side.

As we go down Candle Lane, past the shopping centre, we come to the school bookstore which has a good reputation. All necessary course books can be bought there, not the one next to the shopping centre, but the one after that, on the High Street. Opposite the bookstore, there is the Sports Centre which takes up the whole block between Mary's Road and Candle Lane on the High Street. Finally we circle back to the Main Building. The tour will last about an hour and a half. I hope you will enjoy this afternoon's tour.

Oh, one more important note from Mr. Smith, your director. Please be back to this Main Building after the tour. There will be a reception at five thirty in Room 204, on the first floor, in the lecture hall. You will meet your teachers and staff there. All of you are welcome.

That is the end of Section 2. You will now have half a minute to check your answers.

Now turn to Section 3.

Section 3

In this section you will hear a discussion between two students, Maria and Jack. In the first part of the discussion they're talking about their opinions about some of the things in their universities. First look at questions 21-24. Note the examples that have been done for you. Complete the table showing the weather, the rooms, their roommates and food.

Now listen to their talk and answer questions 21-24.

Jack: 2414331.

Maria: Good afternoon. May I speak to Jack Robert, please ?

Jack: Speaking, please.

Maria: Hi, Jack, this is Maria.

Jack: Hello, Maria. How are you getting on there?

Maria: Fine. I arrived in Nottingham yesterday. I've just settled down and I live on the campus of Nottingham University.

Jack: Oh, that's good. Do you like the campus?

Maria: Yes, it's beautiful. What do you think of yours?

Jack: Edinburgh University? It's marvellous. It's on a hill and very close to the sea. I like it very much.

Maria: It sounds beautiful. Jack, what's the weather like there?

Jack: Oh, it's fine and sunny. It's said that the weather here is very nice in summer, but awful in winter. What's the weather like in Nottingham?

Maria: Well, it's a bit depressing. It's been raining since yesterday. I can't go out so I have to stay in my room.

Jack: What about your room? Is it a nice one?

Maria: Yes, it's small and elegant. How about yours?

Jack: Mine is an ordinary one. It's a twin study room. I share it with one of my classmates. He's intelligent and very friendly. We are getting on quite well. How's your roommate?

Maria: She's very nice but a little bit quiet. She likes reading and seldom speaks. By the way, do you like the Scottish food there?

Jack: Oh, I like it. It's very delicious.

Maria: Oh, really? I don't like the food here. It's disgusting. It has no taste. I have to cook for myself in my room.

Jack: Well, Maria, as the saying goes "When in Rome do as the Romans do." Come on. Don't be too choosy. Oh, someone's at the door. I have to answer it. Maria, I'll call you this evening. Bye.

Maria: Bye.

Ellan, a Student Union officer, is conducting a survey about the university facilities. She is asking two students about their opinions. Look at questions 25-32.

As you listen to the discussion, complete the table showing the number of points, 1, 2, 3 or 4, awarded to the university facilities by two students. One has been done as an example. Now answer questions 25-32.

Officer: I'm Ellan and I work for the Student Union. Now I'd like to hear your opinions about a few things in the university. We've asked for some volunteers to help us conduct this survey into how satisfied students are with the university facilities. First of all let's take the lecture rooms. We could score them. For instance, 1 is excellent, 2 satisfactory, 3 rather poor and 4 really bad. Robert, you first please. What do you think about the lecture rooms here?

Robert: Not so good, I'm afraid. I would score 3. They are too small for one thing. Sometimes we can hardly find a seat.

Maria: Yes, but that doesn't happen very often. Personally I think they are all right. They 're comfortable and the acoustics are quite reasonable. It doesn't matter where you sit you can always hear the lecture. I would give 2 for them.

Officer: How do you feel about the car parking facilities? Are they adequate?

Robert: You must be joking. I can never find a car parking space when I need one, and when I finally do, it's a very long walk to the university's teaching building. I'd give it a 4.

Maria: I'm afraid I also agree. We need more car parks urgently. This is perhaps one of the major shortcomings of this campus. It gets a 4 from me as well. I come to the university 20 minutes early just so I can drive around looking for a parking space.

Officer: What about the Computer Centre then?

Robert: I think it's first class. The software base contains a large selection of learning programmes, language games and word-processing facilities. I would give a score of 1.

Maria: I quite agree with you. It's very modern and also under the supervision of qualified staff who can offer help to us while we work, should we need them.

Officer: Oh, good. Well, what do you think of the library facilities? Let's say the periodical room first?

Robert: Well, I've scored that 3. I'm sorry to have to say, but... er... I think the room has poor lighting and I'm disappointed about that.

Maria: I've given it a score of 1. As far as I'm concerned, it's excellent and well-stocked.

Officer: Thank you, Robert and Mary. Now let's turn to the photocopying facilities.

Robert: Mmm, I would give it a score of 2. Personally I think it's all right and it's very helpful.

Maria: Uh, I would score 3. I think it's too expensive for photocopying and there are not enough machines. Sometimes we have to stand in a line.

Officer: OK. Now let's talk about the...

That is the end of Section 3. You will now have half a minute to check your answers.

Now turn to Section 4.

Section 4

In Section 4 you will hear a talk and answer questions 33-40. First you have some time to look at questions 33-40.

Now listen carefully and answer questions 33-40.

Ladies and gentlemen:

At Safeway we are committed to working for a better environment. We have been actively looking for environmentally responsible solutions over the last 20 years, and it has never been more important than it is today to continue with that initiative. We believe our actions are helping to solve some of the problems, but just as importantly, we are looking ahead too, with new ideas to help protect our environment for the future.

Action for the environment goes beyond the Safeway store and into your home. What can you do? Here are some practical things you can do when you get back home to help the environment.

Sort out your waste at home so that you can take the different types to be recycled. Recycle all you can, such as glass bottles and jars, plastic bottles, textiles, newspapers and plastic bags—these are among the many things that can be recycled today.

Your recyclable material can be taken to your local Safeway store's recycling centre or to your local Council recycling centre. Use recycled paper at home and at the office if possible. Recycle for the garden too. Food scraps, such as decayed vegetables and fruit, but not meat, and some garden waste such as leaves, dried grass, these can be used to make compost. It's useful in the garden and helps conserve the countryside. Compost is a good alternative to peat; peat digging damages wild peatlands.

Reuse as well as recycle. The back of once-used paper can be used again for rough work, old plastic bottles can be cut in half to be used as cloches for seedlings, and yoghurt pots and plastic film canisters are ideal for storing small things like screws and seeds. Don't forget plastic carrier bags can often be used again. We can all take action for a better environment if we start now. We can make a difference and enjoy a cleaner and brighter future.

The environmental problem is one of the crucial problems we face now. Energy efficiency cuts down the increase of carbon dioxide in the atmosphere, which is the main cause of global warming. People say we live in a throwaway society, in other words, waste is building up. We really need to find a way to solve this. Recycling and reuse can stop the build-up of waste, and can help save energy. Using CFC-free alternatives or pump-action aerosols is one way everyone can help. Every grower, from a farmer to a gardener, can help to save wildlife and habitats by avoiding the use of artificial chemicals which can poison plants and animals and pollute the land, air and water.

There are plenty of environmental problems facing the world. Small but consistent environmental actions by everyone can help to make sure they do not become overwhelming. It's remarkable how the different environmental actions work together to prevent a variety of problems.

You can buy 100% recycled paper goods for the kitchen and bathroom as well as recycled bin bags. Buy environmentally responsible products—try to use products that do not contain chemicals that can do harm to the environment, such as phosphates, chlorine and solvents. Regular purchases will begin to make a difference.

To save energy—when it is convenient, walk or cycle. It is good for the environment, your health and for your pocket too. In the home, cleaning jobs can be carried out with a thought for the future—use the washing machine on low temperature cycles. Use public transport when you can. Get a timetable—you may find a convenient alternative to the car and you will avoid the problem of where to park. Share a car—a sociable way to go to work or the shops. Two sharing a car only uses half as much fuel as if they had driven alone. Use unleaded petrol if you can.

We are all responsible to make the world a healthier, safer place for all of us in the future.

That is the end of Section 4. Now you have half a minute to check your answers.

That is the end of the listening test.

Answer Key

Unit One

Listening Activity No. 1

1. 4013745; Miss Jones
2. 2016453; Helen Parker
3. 7849253; Dr. Robinson
4. 5066423; Mr. Egge
5. 5094287; Jane Casting

Listening Activity No. 2

1. 71 3402146
2. 27 Greenford; 602 5795942
3. 25 St. Mary's; 71 5795076
4. 3 Gresik Road; Birmingham; 21 9920221
5. 64 Manor Drive; Edinburgh; 31 3246738
6. 30 King's Road; Leeds; 532 8375029
7. 17 Green Street; Liverpool; 51 3627884
8. 48 Church Street; Brighton; 273 843065

Listening Activity No. 3

1. EF Language School

EF House	√
1 Farman Street	√
Hove, Brighton	√
Sussex BN3 1AW	1AL
Tel: 723651	√
Telex: 77843	877743

2. EF International School of English

21 Hills Road	221
Cambridge	√
CB2 2RL	2RW
Tel: 240020	240040
Telex: 817713	√

3. EF International School of English

1-2 Sussex Road	√
Brighton	√
Sussex BN2 1FJ	√
Tel: 571802	571780
Telex: 957005	94012032

4. EF International School of English

64/80 Warrior Square	74/80
Hastings	√
East Sussex TN7 6BP	TN3
Tel: 432898	423998
Telex: 957005	√

Listening Activity No. 4

Alison wants to make a phone call.	√
It's cheaper to make a call before 6 pm	after 6 pm
Telephone directory provides gardening information.	√
Arrange an alarm call before 10:30 pm	√
Tuesday evening.	previous evening
You would pay until you talk to the right person.	not pay
Alison will make a personal call.	√

Listening Activity No. 5

1. Barbara Cooper 2. John Murphy 3. Stephen 4. Adelaide
5. Martha Hunt 6. James Black 7. Greenwich 8. Terry Fisher

Listening Activity No. 6

1. make a person-to-person call to Leeds 2. David Barker 3. 5027745

Listening Activity No. 7

1. Manchester 2. John Abel 3. 2418 Grestone Road 4. 3659783

Listening Activity No. 8

1. Edinburgh 2. Diana Paxton 3. 932 Beach Road 4. 4023685

Listening Activity No. 9

1. WILLIAMS 2. Peter 3. Canada
4. 25 5. 9 Crew Street RC4 6. 2342965

Listening Activity No. 10

1. TURNBALL 2. Gill 3. Australia
4. 23 5. 32 Broadway SE23 6. 2073346

Listening Activity No. 11

1. POTTERS 2. Mike 3. The United States
4. 27 5. 45 Hardcourt Lane E24 6. 3653241

Listening Activity No. 12A

1. 2:45 2. 5:20 3. 7:30 4. 6:20 5. 8:00
6. 12:30 7. 11:05 8. 17:40 9. 22:50 10. 15:30

Listening Activity No. 12B

1. 9:30; 11:30   2. 50   3. 10:30   4. 15   5. an hour

Listening Activity No. 13

Trains

	Platform No.	Time	Destination
1.	4	13:30	Cambridge
2.	2	14:20	Birmingham
3.	3	16:40	Liverpool
4.	1	7:30	London
5.	5	9:10	Leeds
6.	2	10:30	Oxford
7.	5	11:05	Leeds
8.	3	11:30	Manchester

Planes

	Flight No.	Time	Destination
9.	BA207	8:30	Paris
10.	OA535	12:05	Athens
11.	BA965	12:00	Belfast
12.	SK506	17:15	Stockholm
13.	BA205	9:30	Dublin
14.	BA305	11:30	Paris
15.	OA593	14:40	Athens
16.	BA707	15:05	Edinburgh

Listening Activity No. 14

Table 1

Area	People /sq km
UK	234
European Community	143
England	364
Greater London	4263
Scotland	56
Wales	138
Northern Ireland	112

Table 2

City	Area (sq kms)	Population (thousand)
Greater London	1580	6735. 4
Birmingham	264	993. 7
Leeds	562	709. 6
Glasgow	198	703. 2
Edinburgh	261	433. 5
Manchester	116	445. 9
Bristol	110	377. 7
Coventry	97	306. 2

Listening Activity No. 15

Undergraduate Students at the University

	Men	Women
Total	3472	2742
Science	1137	616
Social Science	484	401
Engineering	509	56
Arts	593	943
Medicine	306	336
Dentistry	139	107
Law	182	171
Veterinary Science	110	104

Listening Activity No. 16

1. 46.4%　2. 45.2%　3. 30%　4. 60%　5. 51.9%
6. 80.5%　7. 2.5%　8. 12.6%　9. 30%

Listening Activity No. 17

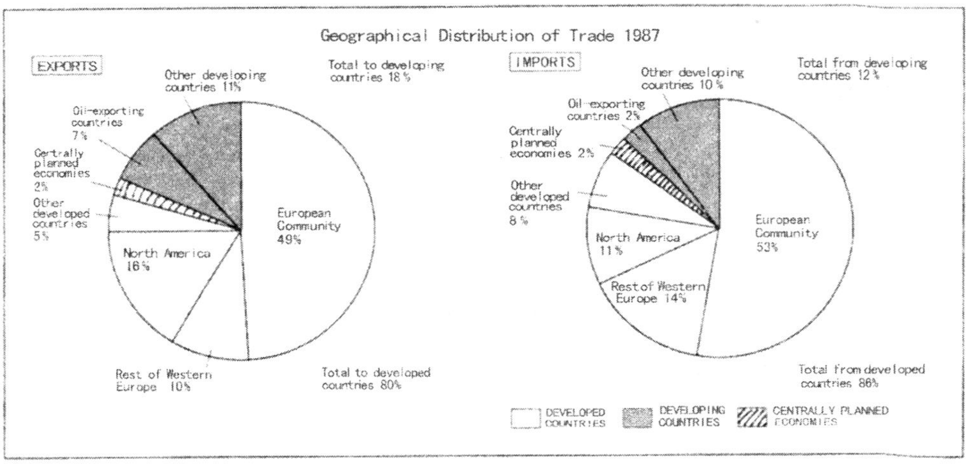

Listening Activity No. 18

1. 93%　2. 85%　3. 80%　4. 13%　5. 7%　6. 52%
7. 89%　8. 89%　9. 65%　10. 90%　11. 75%　12. 39%
13. 75%　14. 80%　15. 85%　16. 87%　17. 65%　18. 62%

19. 45%　20. 86%　21. 87%　22. 92%　23. 95%　24. 47%
25. 67%

Listening Activity No. 19

1. A　2. B　3. B　4. A　5. A　6. B
7. B　8. A　9. B　10. B　11. B　12. B

Listening Activity No. 20

	When founded	**Circulation in 2003**
Quality Daily Newspapers:		
The Daily Telegraph	1855	990,000
The Times	1785	690,000
The Guardian	1821	410,000
The Financial Times	1888	450,000
Quality Sunday Newspapers:		
The Sunday Times	1822	145,000
The Observer	1791	480,000
The Sunday Telegraph	1961	830,000
Popular Daily Newspapers:		
The Daily Express	1900	1,000,000
The Sun	1964	3,730,000
The Mirror	1903	2,130,000
Daily Mail	1896	2,470,000
Popular Sunday Newspapers:		
News of the World	1843	4,100,000
Sunday Mirror	1963	1,880,000
The People	1881	1,390,000
The Mail on Sunday	1982	710,000
Sunday Express	1918	850,000

Unit Two

Listening Activity No. 1

1. Riley 2. Peter 3. 6 years 4. IELTS
5. 6 6. listening, writing, speaking 7. speaking

Listening Activity No. 2

1. Computer Science
2. It's very popular, easier to find a job, well-paid, has a big effect on our lives
3. Medicine 4. Dentistry 5. Engineering
6. Arts 7. Don't have talent in that area

Listening Activity No. 3

Conversation 1
1. 4217845 2. Mary 3. To have a night out/invitation
4. See a film, eat out 5. Friday

Conversation 2
1. 2045789 2. Mary 3. Peter
4. David and Mary are going to a party. 5. Freda's parents are coming over.

Listening Activity No. 4

Places	Weather	Temperature
S. England and Midlands	cloudy, showers, cold, westerly wind	3-5
Wales and Northern Ireland	sunny spells, strong winds, rain	2-4
East Coast of England	warmer, sunshine, no winds	
Scotland and Northern Ireland	very cold, windy with gales, heavy rain and snow	-3- -10

Listening Activity No. 5

1. Perry Pratley
2. 14 Twyford
3. 5638995
4. a bank clerk
5. Barclays Bank

Listening Activity No. 6

1. Yes
2. one
3. kitchen, toilet and bathroom
4. four
5. Yes
6. No
7. £200
8. the first day of the month
9. £350
10. 4093378

Listening Activity No. 7

1. Butcher
2. Anthony
3. male
4. 14 April, 1966
5. Italian
6. a student
7. to study English
8. 35 Halefield Road, Tottenham, London

Listening Activity No. 8

1. handbag
2. £250
3. oval shaped, leather, black and white checked
4. 2:30 pm
5. coffee shop, 6th floor
6. Janet Thomas
7. 25 King Street
8. 4237689

Listening Activity No. 9

1. Shirley Sutton
2. Leeds University
3. English
4. 1990
5. a secondary school teacher
6. 1992-1993
7. £500 a month
8. sales woman
9. 1990-1992
10. £600 a month
11. four hours per week at full pay to attend college courses

Listening Activity No. 10

Message 1

1. Mary Roberts
2. Bill
3. phone tonight before 10 pm or before 8:30 am tomorrow
4. 235669

Message 2

1. 237561
2. Henry Grey
3. Tom
4. meeting time changed to 10:30 tomorrow, not 9:30; phone back before 5:30 this afternoon.
5. 488992

Message 3

1. 345714 2. Anne Bridge 3. Linda
4. Film starts at 8, not 8:30; meeting her at 7:30 in front of the school gate. Please call (her) at lunch time.
5. 4440456

Message 4

1. 409267 2. Debbie Harris 3. Linda
4. Because of rain tomorrow, have to use the school hall (instead of the playing-ground); come to the school hall at 8:30.

Listening Activity No. 11

1. By car 2. By bike 3. 5 miles
4. 20 miles 5. A few blocks 6. 15-20 minutes
7. 15 minutes 8. Yes 9. No
10. No 11. Need more buses 12. (Need a) better subway system

Listening Activity No. 12

1. job application 2. Mr. Bradshaw
3. Penny Jacobs 4. University of East Anglia
5. Sociology and foreign languages
6. K Mart (3 months), Jade Travel Agency (6 months)
7. French, Italian
8. 6th floor, ABB Building in Oxford Street
9. 9:30 am, Friday
10. degree and birth certificates

Listening Activity No. 13

1. Wood 2. Caroline 3. England
4. Single 5. B. Sc. Mathematics 6. air stewardess
7. over 4 years 8. 4 (incl. English) 9. travel, reading and languages
10. none

Listening Activity No. 14

1. New York 2. Great Western Bank 3. Ellen Robbins
4. 3021 Sagebrush Drive 5. VO233779 6. £300
7. $450 8. Elton John
9. 8 Grange Park, Ealing Broadway
10. Telegraphic transfer 11. Telegraphic transfer

Listening Activity No. 15

1. √	2. √	3. a connect card	4. √
5. a cheque guarantee card	6. 4%	7. £250	8. √
9. passport	10. √	11. duration of your stay	12. √

Listening Activity No. 16

1. √	2. a music teacher	3. √	4. a freelance designer
5. London	6. cousin	7. √	8. √
9. girlfriend			

Listening Activity No. 17

1. Julia Smith
2. 46 West Avenue, Acton
3. 6593427
4. £50 per week
5. single
6. B, C
7. one month's rent in advance
8. deposit for front door key; Guests must leave by 11 pm.
9. yes
10. 4:30 pm tomorrow

Listening Activity No. 18

ACCIDENT REPORT FORM

Name of casualty: Susan Thomas Age: ____ Sex: F__
Address: 37 Merton Road, Harrow
Occupation: housewife
Details of accident: Date 2nd March Time 8:50
Category of accident: Road √Domestic __Sporting __Other __
Injuries sustained: cuts, bruises, shock
Witness's name: Julia Smith
Address: 32 Westminster Road, Watford
Action: Police notified √ Ward: Windsor
Family notified√
Employer notified Casualty officer: __________

Listening Activity No. 19

Name of the Place	Location	Date of Eruption	Number of People Who Died
Vesuvius	Italy	79 A. D.	2,000
Cotopaxi	Ecuador	1877	1,000
Krakatoa	Indonesia	1883	36,000
Mount Pelee	Martinique	1902	38,000
Mount St. Helens	Washington State	1980	60
Mount Tambora	Indonesia	1815	12,000

Listening Activity No. 20

1. 5438186
2. 34 Church Road, Highgate
3. single
4. £40 a week
5. bathroom, kitchen
6. Monday
7. £160
8. Guests should be out by 11 pm.
9. the tube, buses
10. 2nd of April
11. Highgate
12. 8 pm

Unit Three

Listening Activity No. 1

Task 1

1. some
2. Boil
3. Warm
4. some tea; the teapot
5. the boiling water
6. stand; a few minutes
7. milk into
8. the tea; the
9. sugar

Task 2

1. I 2. D 3. C 4. G 5. B 6. E 7. H 8. F 9. A

Listening Activity No. 2

Task 1

A. electricity/hot water tank/the mains

B. red C. five D. supply E. half an hour; some hot

Task 2

1. B 2. D 3. C 4. A 5. E

Listening Activity No. 3

Task 1 C

Task 2

1. questioning 2. £5000 3. a video recorder; a colour TV set
4. a woman 5. long angular; pointed 6. glasses
7. faint scar 8. police station

Listening Activity No. 4

Task 1 A

Task 2

1. In Leeds area. 2. £6000. 3. In an old blue Escort car.
4. He could be armed. 5. Contact the nearest police station.

Listening Activity No. 5

Task 1 B

Task 2

1. At the front of the main building. 2. At 9 am tomorrow.
3. She has a doctor's appointment. 4. No.
5. 21. 6. A jumper, trousers with flat shoes.

Listening Activity No. 6

Task 1 B

Task 2

1. √ 2. √ 3. in his teens 4. blond
5. jeans, T-shirt and boots, glasses 6. red 7. √

Listening Activity No. 7

Task 1 A

Task 2

1. √ 2. 34 Bath Road 3. lost / missing 4. 6
5. √ 6. short-sleeved 7. √ 8. black shoes

Listening Activity No. 8

A

Listening Activity No. 9

the university library	5
the supermarket	4
the hotel	6
the best bookshop	8
the Lloyds Bank	1

Listening Activity No. 10

1. K Mart   2. Post Office   3. Church

Listening Activity No. 11

1. D   2. I   3. C   4. E   5. F

Listening Activity No. 12

1. J   2. L   3. H   4. A   5. C   6. E

Listening Activity No. 13

Sat	Arrived at hotel at 5 pm.
Sun	Hired a small car. Went to Safari Park and saw monkeys and lions.
Mon	Went to Oxford and Stonehenge. Took photographs.
Tues	Joined a sightseeing tour. Visited Trafalgar Square, Westminster Abby, the Houses of Parliament and saw the changing of the guard. Also went to Tower Bridge and the Tower of London.
Wed	Went to Greenwich by boat.
Thurs	Went shopping for presents and souvenirs. Went to see a film called *Star Wars* in the evening.
Fri	Rained all day. Stayed in hotel. Played table tennis.
Sat	Left hotel at 10 am.

Listening Activity No. 14

Task 1

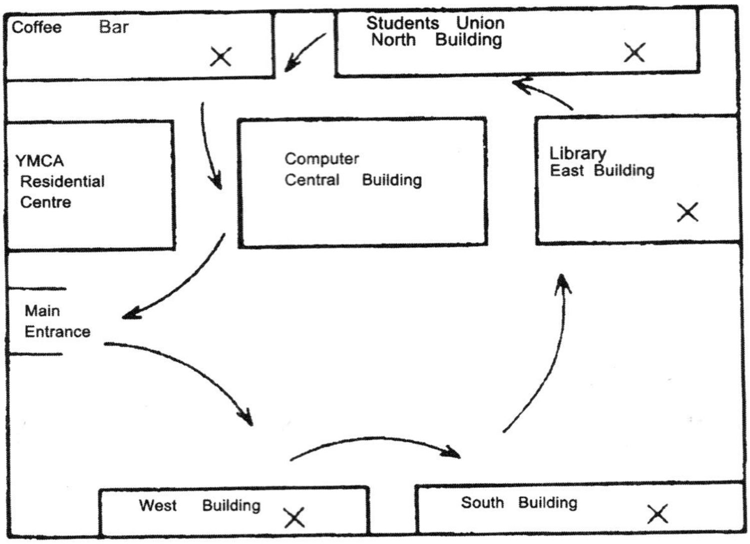

Task 2

Place	Reason
1. South Building	to see the tutor
2. the library	to apply for the library card
3. the Student Union's Office	to book a ticket for the Oxford trip
4. the bar	for lunch

Listening Activity No. 15

Keeping Children Safe in the Home

	What children can see	What children can't see	What children can find	What children can do
At home	pan handles, lead on the kettle, hot drink, iron	panes of glass in doors or screens, things left on the floor like toys or spills, drawers or cupboard doors left open	medicines, household cleaners, matches, lighters, knives, other sharp tools, plastic bags, things they could choke on like peanuts	climb the stairs and don't know how to get down, climb on a chair to reach a window, climb inside things, reach switches and knobs and turn them on and off
The dangers	burn or scald them	trip and fall over things, fall through panes of glass or bump into things which stick out	can't tell the difference between lemonade and turps.	They can do anything which are dangerous and can be anywhere.

What can you do:

1. ahead; arrangements
2. store; touch
3. pan handles
4. guard
5. barriers; up and down

Listening Activity No. 16

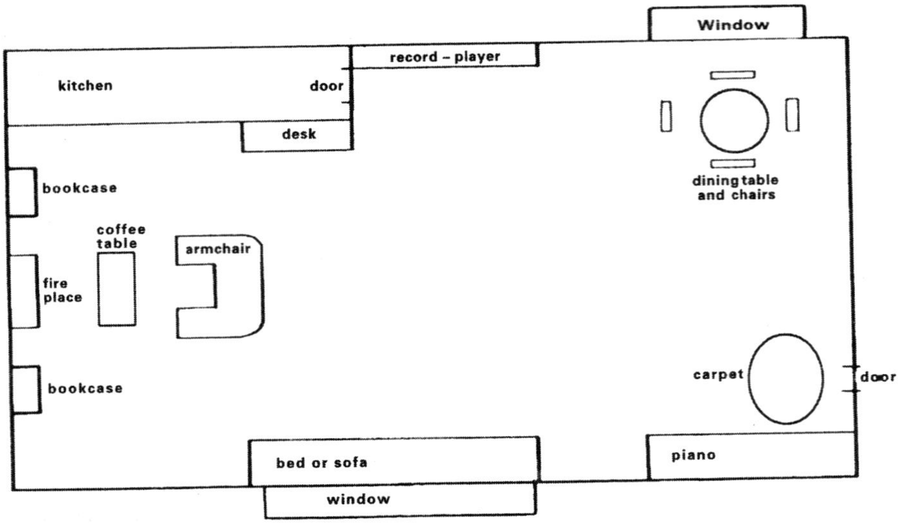

Listening Activity No. 17

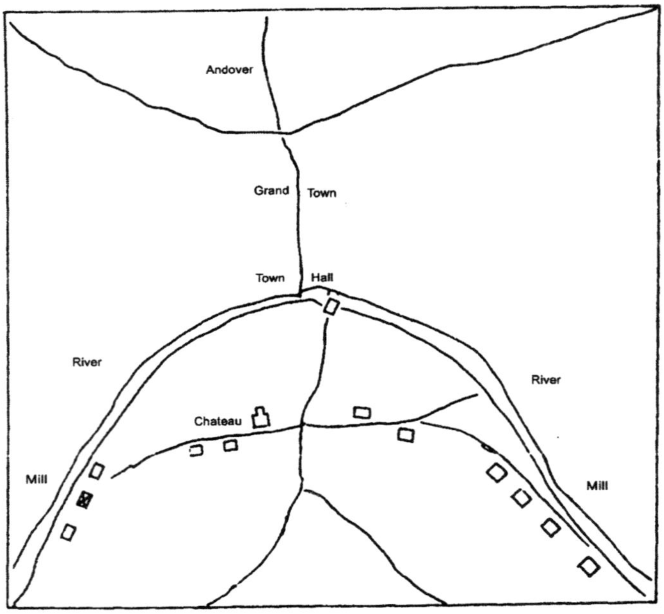

Listening Activity No. 18

1 T 2 F 3 T 4 F 5 T

Listening Activity No. 19

(Numbers shown in thousand)

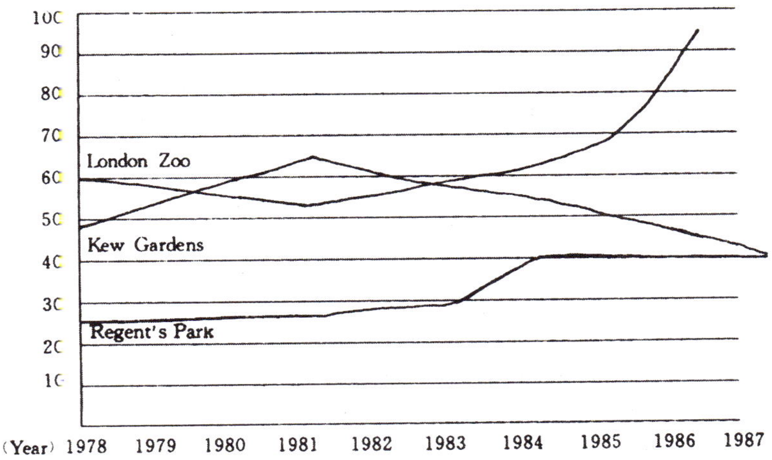

Listening Activity No. 20

(Numbers shown in thousand)

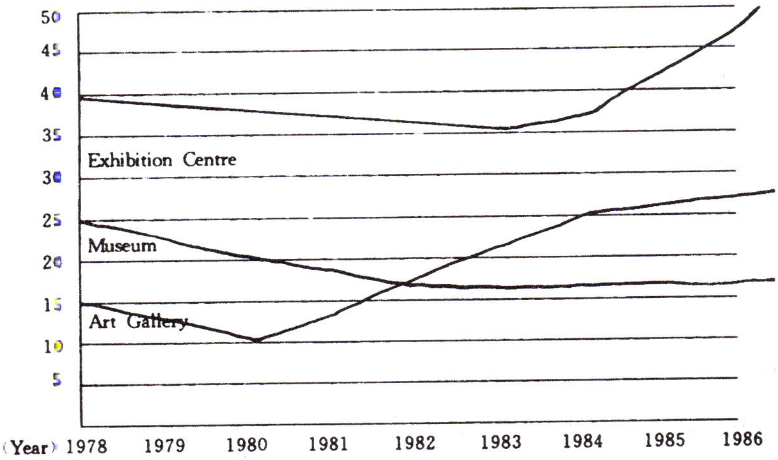

Unit Four

Listening Activity No. 1

1. F 2. T 3. F 4. F 5. F 6. F 7. T 8. T 9. N

Listening Activity No. 2

1. The final (session). 2. Room 302. 3. The reception desk.
4. C 5. D 6. C 7. D 8. A 9. N 10. I

Listening Activity No. 3

1. Jane's mother. 2. Phone bill. 3. C 4. D
5. A 6. I 7. N 8. A

Listening Activity No. 4

1. all underground stations 2. distance 3. 5 4. B, C
5. C, D 6. A 7. N 8. I

Listening Activity No. 5

1. textile company 2. a junior sales manager
3. A car. 4. A sales commission.
5. C 6. N 7. A 8. A

Listening Activity No. 6

1. Landlady. 2. Noise. 3. A 4. C 5. B
6. A 7. D 8. Tuesday 9. 29th 10. 30th

Listening Activity No. 7

1. Last week. 2. The catalogues. 3. B, C, D 4. C, D
5. B 6. I 7. A 8. A

Listening Activity No. 8

1. Italy. 2. About six months. 3. English. 4. B
5. D 6. Yes. 7. Two years. 8. Next year.

Listening Activity No. 9

1. The North Building. 2. Yes. 3. An enrolment receipt.
4. The Student Union. 5. B, D 6. A, C, D
7. C 8. A 9. I 10. A

Listening Activity No. 10

1. A counsellor.　　2. A counsellor's role/Counselling services.
3. 2　4. Yes.　5. A, D　6. C　7. N　8. A　9. I　10. I

Listening Activity No. 11

1. college　2. access　3. Instant　4. B, C　5. C
6. B　7. A　8. I　9. N　10. A

Listening Activity No. 12

1. the personnel manager　2. the present job　3. *Evening News.*
4. B　5. C　6. A　7. A　8. A　9. I　10. N

Listening Activity No. 13

1. 6 months or more　2. free　3. Register with a doctor.　4. B
5. A. From the doctor.
   B. From the receptionist.
6. I　7. A　8. A　9. I　10. I

Listening Activity No. 14

1. student-centred　2. motivation; formal qualifications
3. A, B　4. C　5. A　6. No　7. A　8. I　9. I　10. N

Listening Activity No. 15

1. non-profit-making　2. 18　3. 160　4. 70-80　5. B, C
6. B　7. I　8. N　9. A　10. I

Listening Activity No. 16

1. favor　2. London　3. a week
4. C　5. A, C　6. D　7. B　8. I　9. A　10. N

Listening Activity No. 17

1. our eating habits and lifestyles　2. information　3. B, C
4. C　5. Nibble sweet things between meals.
6. I　7. A　8. I　9. A　10. N

Listening Activity No. 18

1. part　2. 5　3. A, C　4. B　5. D
6. B, C　7. I　8. I　9. A
10. A. By post to Lunar House.
B. In person at one of the Public Enquiry Offices.

Listening Activity No. 19

1. July　2. No　3. D　4. C　5. C
6. D　7. A　8. I　9. A　10. I

Listening Activity No. 20

1. Everything Stops for Tea.　2. In the 17th century.　3. C
4. D　5. A　6. B, C, D
7. D　8. By introducing a 4 o'clock meal.　9. In 1839.
10. China; available　11. three　12. 216 Strand
13. 280　14. Richard Twining.　15. William Pitt.

Unit Five

Listening Activity No. 1

1. full-time　2. 16 or over　3. £3.90　4. 33%　5. discount
6. 10%　7. 12　8. be bought　9. Offices　10. post

Listening Activity No. 2

1. morning　2. 10:30 pm　3. those　4. agree
5. made　6. abroad　7. the name　8. speak to
9. can not be　10. left　11. available　12. 999
13. service　14. authority　15. free

Listening Acyivity No. 3

1. animal　2. upside down　3. popular　4. 600
5. (to come) back　6. F　7. F　8. T　9. T　10. F

Listening Activity No. 4

1. two weeks　2. it / the VCR　3. record　4. the guarantee certificate
5. T　6. F　7. F　8. T　9. T　10. ?

Listening Activity No. 5

1. visit	2. a couple	3. 2000	4. 500 pounds
5. 9%	6. 11.5%	7. F	8. ?
9. T	10. F		

Listening Activity No. 6

1. the proper balance	2. working	3. confront and reflect
4. the craft	5. practising	6. T
7. F	8. ?	9. F

Listening Activity No. 7

1. valuables	2. the number	3. group	4. easily
5. taken	6. F	7. ?	8. F

Listening Activity No. 8

1. Britain	2. early evening	3. Wales	4. Scotland
5. closed	6. seawalls	7. T	8. ?
9. T	10. F		

Listening Ativity No. 9

1. three	2. accident	3. avoid	4. changing
5. slow down	6. police car	7. F	8. T
9. F	10. T	11. ?	

Listening Activity No. 10

1. officer	2. helpful	3. information	4. in advance
5. instruction	6. diary	7. F	8. T
9. ?	10. F	11. T	12. F

Listening Activity No. 11

1. stamp	2. immigration	3. register	4. European
5. not have to	6. within 7 days	7. F	8. T
9. T	10. F	11. ?	12. F

Listening Activity No. 12

1. full-time	2. voting	3. access	4. affiliated
5. nationwide	6. reduced price	7. consumer	8. Discount
9. T	10. T	11. ?	

Listening Activity No. 13

1. expensive	2. freedom	3. own bedroom	4. share
5. bedsitters	6. F	7. F	8. ?

Listening Activity No. 14

1. north	2. 700	3. atmosphere	4. privileges
5. life	6. wander	7. hand	8. T
9. T	10. ?	11. F	

Listening Activity No. 15

1. respect	2. rethink	3. useful	4. rats and mice
5. pest	6. T	7. F	8. F
9. F	10. T	11. ?	12. F

Listening Activity No. 16

1. enjoyed	2. last week	3. the program me	4. the course
5. long time	6. T	7. F	8. ?

Listening Activity No. 17

1. fatty	2. a number	3. stimulate	4. circulation
5. heart	6. ?	7. T	8. F
9. F	10. T	11. F	12. T

Listening Activity No. 18

1. their summer	2. the volcano	3. frightening	4. at the foot
5. to flee	6. not enough	7. 2,000	8. T
9. F	10. T	11. ?	12. T

Listening Activity No. 19

1. advance	2. one week's	3. monthly	4. furnished
5. legally	6. paying	7. arrangement	8. tenancy
9. F	10. T	11. T	12. ?
13. T	14. F		

Listening Activity No. 20

1. lodgings	2. punctual	3. convenient	4. bath
5. late	6. save	7. key	8. T
9. F	10. F	11. ?	12. T

Unit Six

Listening Activity No. 1

1. more
2. the hotel safe
3. the serial numbers
4. pocket / a handbag
5. special care of
6. luggage office
7. the receipt
8. the airport; the station

Listening Activity No. 2

1. ports
2. historic landmarks
3. payphones
4. post offices
5. shops
6. 9:30 to 15:30
7. main airports
8. 8:00 to 20:00
9. overseas visitors
10. department stores

Listening Activity No. 3

1. late night
2. until
3. 240
4. adapters
5. post offices
6. 10-12%
7. 10-15
8. 30p-50p
9. 10-15
10. 2 pounds
11. washed
12. left
13. right
14. seat belts

Listening Activity No. 4

1. the Government
2. a bill
3. an act
4. First Reading
5. Debate
6. Committee
7. more changes
8. Third Reading
9. other House
10. Queen

Listening Activity No. 5

1. the English policeman
2. take or capture
3. first
4. the police force
5. early
6. died out
7. friendly and helpful
8. directing
9. a pistol
10. his helmet
11. servants
12. masters

Listening Activity No. 6

1. a bank
2. current
3. interest charge
4. a deposit
5. not pay
6. £50; Europe
7. check guarantee card
8. machines
9. in the wall
10. £100

Listening Activity No. 7

1. his castle
2. British home
3. customs

4. punctual
5. clean and tidy
6. a small present
7. everyone
8. their family name
9. won't normally

Listening Activity No. 8

1. golden era
2. Irish culture
3. poetic styles
4. writing
5. influence
6. collapsed
7. 19th century
8. writers
9. different
10. Anglo-Irish
11. famous
12. Nobel Prize
13. dying out
14. attactive
15. looking for
16. 10,000

Listening Activity No. 9

1. poor
2. serious problem
3. potato
4. 2 million
5. 1851
6. go down
7. America
8. emigration
9. last two
10. relatives

Listening Activity No. 10

1. hardship
2. jobs
3. discrimination
4. look after
5. politics
6. Irish politicians
7. John F. Kennedy
8. Ireland
9. self-confidence
10. 70,000,000
11. outside
12. 10,000,000
13. very difficult
14. an interest

Listening Activity No. 11

1. 45
2. 30
3. 251,200
4. overseas
5. 3
6. October to June
7. 12
8. the UCCA
9. October
10. GCE
11. equivalent
12. original

Listening Activity No. 12

1. North America
2. the midnight sun
3. never sets
4. covered
5. Eskimos
6. small
7. fishing
8. far west
9. tourists
10. beautiful forests
11. Asia
12. eastern
13. Britain and France
14. 18th century
15. over the world

Listening Activity No. 13

1. drinks
2. their orders
3. buy / get
4. are served
5. a tip
6. glass
7. both
8. apples
9. sweet
10. Spain
11. strong alcoholic
12. tomato
13. carbonated water
14. fruit
15. Value Added
16. returned

Listening Activity No. 14

1. three
2. bottled
3. a tap
4. gas/carbon dioxide
5. a pump
6. everywhere
7. the same drinks
8. cold
9. the beer better
10. bottles
11. Irish
12. sweeter
13. law
14. 11:30 to 3:00
15. Betting
16. not allowed

Listening Activity No. 15

1. 11
2. Lisbon
3. age of sail
4. two years later
5. new sail-training
6. walks of life
7. three
8. waterline length
9. 16 and 25
10. attracted
11. 250,000
12. Livepool
13. Queen Elizabeth
14. 1989
15. Tower Bridge
16. young
17. either
18. the public

Listening Activity No. 16

1. inland
2. Posting form
3. will be
4. Advice of Delivery
5. recipient
6. may be
7. money
8. speedy
9. important
10. registered letter
11. first-class
12. minimum
13. the recipient
14. address shown
15. additional fee
16. at the time

Listening Activity No. 17

1. 73%
2. 8%
3. 3%
4. informality
5. punctuality
6. competition
7. esteemed
8. key
9. their own way
10. uncomfortable
11. to the point
12. formal social
13. honesty
14. accept
15. attribute
16. present
17. exact time
18. 10 to 15
19. invited dinner
20. apology

Listening Activity No. 18

1. competitive
2. teamwork
3. own way
4. shorter
5. other cultures
6. silence
7. explain
8. Excuse me
9. in public
10. common
11. at night
12. jewelry
13. hitchhike
14. valuables
15. the robber

16. right or wrong 17. understand 18. participate

Listening Activity No. 19

1. 1917 2. 100 years 3. Harvard
4. normal schooling 5. a self-educated 6. similarities
7. congressman 8. 100 years 9. 60
10. unrest 11. assassination 12. their wives

Listening Activity No. 20

1. fought 2. four 3. 800,000
4. friction 5. issue 6. were based
7. end 8. domination 9. the Union
10. eleven 11. keep 12. The North
13. one country 14. slavery

Unit Seven

Test 1

Section 1

1. A 2. D 3. D 4. B
5. Bautisto 6. Manila
7. Development Economics 8. one year
9. UN project adviser 10. a good reputation in economics

Section 2

11. In 2 weeks. 12. One month. 13. B, C 14. B
15. D 16. A 17. No. 18. £90.
19. Yes. 20. Optimistic.

Section 3

21. sabbatical officers 22. within the Constitution 23. communications
24. B 25. A 26. I 27. A 28. A 29. I 30. N

Section 4

31. is to oversee/oversees 32. financial headaches 33. four
34. as best 35. final say 36. T 37. F 38. ?

Test 2

Section 1

1. China
2. awful
3. √
4. 2 years
5. Korea
6. late
7. ×
8. 8 months

Section 2

9. 1769
10. military
11. mathematics
12. career
13. general
14. emperor
15. December 2
16. F
17. F
18. F
19. T
20. N

Section 3

21. B
22. C
23. D
24. currents
25. back into
26. swept
27. the USA
28. 40,000
29. exchanges
30. trip/journey/ocean journey

Section 4

31. fat and sugar
32. addicted to
33. favorite
34. 400 million/400,000,000
35. eating
36. stay alert
37. medicine
38. mixing
39. C
40. D

Test 3

Section 1

1. a twin study bedroom
2. a toilet
3. shower facilities
4. towels
5. Coin-operated.
6. Once a week.
7. A common room.
8. Half board.
9. With a family/Homestay.

Section 2

10. Wolfgang Schmidt
11. German
12. 5 Franz Dieter Strausse
13. 21
14. four-month programme
15. D
16. A
17. B
18. part-time
19. √
20. girl's

Section 3

21. Film
22. Cambridge
23. 16:00

24. Wembley in London
25. Wednesday
26. 15:00
27. Football
28. Saturday morning
29. about £25
30. Student Services Office
31. today/right now
32. 8:30

Section 4

33. By plane
34. By train
35. Very quick, comfortable, regular service, nice view, nice lunch
36. To save money. It was cheap/cheaper.
37. 8:20 am.
38. Five and half hours.
39. Five a day.
40. By coach.

Test 4

Section 1

1. Mon. -Fri.
2. Petticoat
3. Aldgate
4. 9 am-4 pm
5. Brixton
6. Sundays
7. Tom and Mary.
8. By tube.
9. 9:30

Section 2

10. A
11. B
12. D
13. C
14. D
15. A
16. B
17. F
18. 5:30
19. √
20. 204

Section 3

21. an ordinary one, a twin study room
22. small and elegant
23. nice but quiet, likes reading
24. very delicious
25. 4
26. 4
27. 1
28. 1
29. 3
30. 1
31. 2
32. 3

Section 4

33. environmental
34. throwaway
35. build-up
36. artificial chemicals
37. recycled paper
38. products
39. Walking or cycling
40. parking

Appendix

A Brief Introduction to the IELTS Test

（雅思考试简介）

为了检验要去英国学习的非英语国家学生的英语能力，以英国文化委员会为主的若干英国机构近三十年来先后设计过数个考试。这些考试由于受新的语言学理论、语言教学理论和语言测试理论的影响，大多在使用一段时间后就显得过时，继而被新的考试所取代。目前在使用的最重要的此类考试是 International English Language Testing System（IELTS），被称做“雅思”考试。

IELTS 是以要在英语环境中学习或培训的母语为其他语言的人为测试对象的英语考试，它的前身是 ELTS 考试（English Language Testing Service）。ELTS 由英国剑桥大学考试委员会设计，由英国文化委员会在海外组织，对象是要去英国高等学校学习或参加技术培训的非英语国家公民。因此，考试侧重于检验考生以英语为工具从事专业学习的能力。后来澳大利亚高校国际开发署参与考试工作，因而易名为 IELTS。首份 IELTS 试卷于 1990 年 4 月开始在中国使用。在使用五年之后，IELTS 对听力、阅读和写作的题型进行了改革。新形式的 IELTS 听力、阅读和写作试卷于 1995 年 4 月开始在中国使用。2001 年 7 月 IELTS 对口语题型也做了改革。

IELTS 考试又分为 Academic IELTS（A 类，学术类）考试和 General Training IELTS（G 类，培训类）考试，前者针对留学人员和访问学者，后者针对移民申请者。两种考试的听力和口语试卷相同，阅读和写作另卷。

IELTS 考试有听力、阅读、写作、口语四个部分，每部分的满分为 9 分，总分是四部分成绩的平均。（2007 年 7 月以前，听力、阅读和总分可以有整数分和半分，而写作和口试只有整数分。自 2007 年 7 月 1 日起，写作和口语考试的分数也引入了半分制，如 5.5、6.5 等。）计算总分的方法是四个部分的成绩相加除以 4，如遇小数（0.5 除外）则或舍或入。小数为 0.25、0.375、0.75 和 0.875 时向上进一个分数段。例如：(6 + 6 + 6 + 7) ÷ 4

=6.25，总成绩为6.5分；(5.5+6+6+7) ÷4=6.125，总成绩为6分。

目前我国到英国、澳大利亚等国学习的访问学者和攻读硕士、博士学位的研究生均需参加 Academic IELTS 考试。如要申请移民澳大利亚、新西兰、加拿大等国，则要参加 General Training IELTS 考试。一般来说，访问学者要6分、研究生要6.5分方可赴英，个别学校和专业则要求7分。澳大利亚的学校在录取海外学生时要求申请人必须参加 IELTS 考试并获得5分以上的成绩，移民类考生也需达到5分以上的成绩。许多加拿大和美国大学录取海外学生时也承认其 IELTS 考试成绩。因此 IELTS 考试在我国已成为一个重要的出国考试。

IELTS 考试的听力、阅读和写作部分在上午（通常是星期六）举行，口试在下午或第二天。上午的顺序是：听力（约30分钟），阅读（60分钟），写作（60分钟）。

IELTS 考试的最大特点是对考生的英语交际能力进行测试，重点放在以英语为工具解决专业学习中的听、读、写、说实际问题方面，从而较好地避免了考生"高分低能"的现象。很多英语考试的听力、阅读，甚至写作试题均采用多项选择形式，这无疑增加了考生猜测的机会。并且由于词汇、语法题占一定比例，考生可通过在短期内大量地背单词和做语法题在考试中获得较高的"知识分"。由于有"知识"和猜测因素的作用，考生的成绩不能客观地反映其使用英语的实际能力。IELTS 考试在这方面有很大不同。

与许多主要英语考试相比，IELTS 考试的听力部分的特点亦是多项选择题数量很少，且以在数个图（而不是在数行文字）中选择为主。比如在一段听力对话中，A 告诉 B 要在某个银行门口约会，并描述赴约的路线。四个选项分别是四个街区的平面图，在每个图中银行所处的位置不同，要求考生根据录音内容指出哪一幅图是对话中所描述的图。大部分题不是多项选择题，要由考生根据录音内容填空。比如，考生要答出录音中描述的某个事件发生的时间、地点。再比如，考生要根据录音内容简要回答 which、what、why、who 等问题。很多考生的一个共同困难是，不仅要边听边读，同时还要写。如果没有做过大量的针对性很强的练习，又不熟悉这种听力考试的形式，要想获得理想的分数是比较困难的。这一部分共有40道题左右。

Academic IELTS 考试的阅读部分由3~4篇文章构成，有40个左右的问题。它的最大特点是大部分题不是传统的多项选择题。比如，试题中的一篇文章有 8 段，问题中列出 12 个小标题，要求考生根据每段的内容从 12 个小标题中挑出本段的小标题。再比如，文章描述某一过程（如打捞沉船），要求考生把问题中列出的若干个步骤按其在过程中的先后顺序排序。试题还可能要求考生从列出的十几个单词、词组中选择正确答案填入一篇短文，其中一部分词或词组为干扰性选项。由于干扰因素很多，猜对的可能性几乎为零。IELTS 考试阅读部分与其他阅读考试的另一重大区别是，IELTS 考试不仅不含语法和词汇题，反而可能会列出若干关键词和定义，以帮助考生更好地理解文章的内容。

General Training IELTS 的阅读考试主要考查考生是否具有在英语环境生存的能力，比针对留学的 Academic 考试难度小得多。一般由 6 ~ 8 篇较短的文章组成，文章虽然也选自国外报刊，但比 Academic 考试中出现的文章要短，难度也较小。General Training IELTS 阅读考试一般由三部分组成，每部分 13 ~ 15 题，共 40 题左右。考试时间为一小时，其中包括抄写答题卡的时间。第一部分的内容主要是说明性的文章，如药品说明书、操作步骤、菜单等，要求考生回答问题、排序、将示意图与文章的相应部分进行匹配及判断正误等。第二部分的常见内容有大学情况介绍（如学费、奖学金、学生会等）、旅行指南、时刻表等。第三部分则多为一些常识性文章，如环境保护、人物介绍、奥运会的起源等等，文章一般比前两部分的长。其实在真正的 IELTS 考试当中，这些类型的文章可以出现在任何一部分中。

IELTS 的写作分为 General Training 写作和 Academic 写作两种。每种分为两部分：Task 1 和 Task 2。

General Training 写作的 Task 1 一般要求考生写一封不少于 150 个词的信件，叙述对一个问题的看法或所处的一种境遇。比如：“你所居住的宿舍中的热水锅炉坏了，你已打电话通知了房主，要求对方来修理，但一周已过，对方还没有来修理。给房主写封信，说明你所处的境遇，并对此提出自己的意见。”再如：“你考试后没有与同屋打招呼就匆忙回家了。给同屋写封信，告诉对方你为什么不辞而别以及你在路上的情况，并邀请同屋有空到你家做客。”试卷建议考生在 20 分钟内完成本部分。Task 2 一般要求考生就某种观点或现象发表自己的意见或看法，同意还是不同意，原因是什么。比如：“有些机构规定在任何办公地点都禁止吸烟。一些政府也颁布了公共场所禁烟令。这是一个好的做法，但同时也剥夺了人们的一些权利。你同意还是不同意这个观点？为什么？"再如："我们越来越多地依赖计算机。计算机广泛地应用于商务、医院、案例侦察，甚至飞机驾驶中。将来还有哪些地方要用计算机？依赖计算机是好事吗？我们是否应对此产生怀疑？"试卷建议考生在40分钟内完成本部分。

Academic 写作的 Task 1 一般要求考生写一篇不少于150个词的短文描述所给的一个图（流程图、剖面图、曲线图等）或表。比如，描述一个欧洲城市分别在1995、2000和2004年中各种交通车辆的运营情况。再比如，描述某一国家若干年内人口的增减情况。试卷建议考生在20分钟内完成本部分。Task 2 一般要求考生就某个问题提出解决的方法，为某一观点辩护，比较或对比一些根据和意见，评价或反驳一些论点，或提供一般真实的报告。比如"科学技术的发展将使传统文化丧失，这是不可避免的。科学技术与传统文化是不能共存的。在多大程度上你同意或不同意这个观点？为你的回答提供论据。"再比如，你向英国一所大学申请留学生奖学金。申请书的最后部分要求你报告自己所从事的专业情况和将来的一些打算。试卷建议考生在40分钟内完成本部分。

IELTS 考试的口试部分约 11 ~ 14 分钟。口试分为三个部分。1. 一般性对话：考官提问，考生回答。内容主要是个人情况，如家庭、工作、教育等。2. 使用提示卡（topic card）：考生从桌上抽取一张卡片，根据上面所给的题目回答问题和叙述，如描述一位对你影响最大的老师，然后再回答考官提出的一两个相关的概括性的问题。3. 讨论：考官根据第二部分的谈话，向考生提出与谈话内容有关的一两个抽象性问题或就有关的内容进行讨论。考生应就此问题连续不断地发表看法。总之，口试非常注重考生的语言交际能力。

IELTS 考试的写作和口试部分的评分要参考很详细的评分标准，但在一定程度上受考官主观看法的影响。阅读和听力部分是客观题，有标准答案，一般来说有65%的正确率可得6分。

过去，由于 IELTS 考试试卷重复使用，考试部门要求考生两次考试的间隔不少于三个月。自从2006年5月1日起，IELTS 考试取消了考生90天内不能重复参加考试的规定，即考生如果感觉考试成绩不理想，可以在任一考试时间再次参加考试。

目前 IELTS 考试的费用为1450元人民币。自2005年1月起，中国大陆地区的考生报名需登陆教育部考试中心 IELTS 报名网站（http://ielts. etest. edu. cn），可在遍布全国的 IELTS 考点参加考试。北京语言大学国外考试中心不再受理考试报名事宜，北京考点仍设在北京语言大学。如果您有任何关于 IELTS 和 IELTS 网上报名的疑问，请致电教育部考试中心的 IELTS 全国服务热线：

电话：010-62798811

电子邮件：ielts@ mail. neea. edu. cn

地址：北京市海淀区清华科技园立业大厦
教育部考试中心 考试服务中心

邮编：100084

或与英国驻华使馆或北京语言大学国外考试中心联系，地址分别是：

北京东三环北路 8 号 亮马河办公楼 1 座 4 层
英国大使馆文化教育处
邮编：100004
网址：http://www. britishcouncil. org. cn/zh/china. jsp

北京市海淀区学院路 15 号
北京语言大学国外考试中心
邮编：100083
网址：http://www. blcu. edu. cn/exam-center/info. htm

北语社重点雅思图书

《IELTS 考试技能训练教程》

听力（李亚宾）	34.00 元
口语（田静先）	25.00 元
阅读（陈卫东 王冰欣）	33.00 元
写作（王玉西）	29.50 元

《IELTS 考试技能训练教程》配套用书

IELTS 应试指南（陈卫东）	37.00 元
IELTS 词汇学习手册（史宝辉）	22.00 元
雅思备考语法手册（于培文 刘悦）	29.80 元
IELTS 阅读模拟试题集（General Training）（王冰欣 王春梅）	15.00 元
IELTS 阅读模拟试题集（Academic）（尹陈毅 陈晓莹）	18.00 元
IELTS 听力模拟试题集（李亚宾 田静先）	18.00 元

《雅思直快》

听力（曾宪宇）	28.00 元
口语（王旭）	25.00 元
阅读（培训类）（王冰欣）	23.00 元
阅读（学术类）（周虹）	29.00 元
写作（陈卫东）	39.80 元

《雅思考前 15 天》

听力（夏丽萍 贺婷）	19.80 元
口语（王红霞）	25.00 元
阅读（邓和刚）	26.00 元
写作（王红霞）	24.00 元

《雅思考官教雅思》系列

跟雅思考官练口语（Tom Macri）	23.00 元
跟雅思考官练写作（Tom Macri）	19.50 元
专家点拨：如何正确备考雅思阅读（Jack Robinson）	15.00 元
专家点拨：如何正确备考雅思听力（Jack Robinson）	18.00 元

《雅思预备教程》

听力（李亚宾）	21.00 元
口语（张涓 Alison Wong）	25.00 元
阅读（张涓）	27.00 元
写作（王约西）	23.50 元

《雅思预备教程》配套用书

雅思阶梯阅读（1）（王治江）	18.00 元
雅思阶梯阅读（2）（任东升 马建龙）	18.00 元
雅思阶梯阅读（3）（王治江）	19.00 元
雅思阶梯听力（1）（王建华）	15.00 元
雅思阶梯听力（2）（王建华）	18.00 元
雅思阶梯听力（3）（王建华）	19.00 元

Sa valise de
où il venait d'accom
secrétaire qui l'ava
avait déjà commencé
écarta le battant, p
Cela devait être un rite quand quelqu'un
Avec lui le fonctionnaire avait failli ne pas oser.
Il y avait trois marches de pierre large et cirées
comme le parvis des vieilles églises. Des marches identiques,
ROYAL

COMPRENDRE
ET NE
PAS JUGER

(Le chien Jaune)

Hotel de l'Amiral | Quai de l'Aiguillon.

I

M. Cloaguen marchand de vins.

Le Docteur – Ernest Michoux.

M. Le Pommeret – vice-consul Danemark.

Jean Servières – "Le Phare de Brest."

—

Emma Grémillon.

vendredi

7 novembre

Mostaguen.

UN
PERSONNAGE
DE ROMAN

regarder ~~le vieux monsieur à qui elle devait parler. C'était~~ son client, à qui elle parlait comme une eau coule. Cela faisait sans doute ~~dans~~ partie de la partition. Elle tricotait. De la laine ~~violette~~ rouge glissait entre ~~s'échappait de~~ ses doigts.

La chienne blanche courbait l'échine sous le poids du gros mâle qui ~~sortait~~ laissait pendre une ~~grande~~ langue mouillée.

Et alors, quand tout fut en place, quand la perfection de ce matin-là atteignit un ~~e perfection~~ degré presque effrayant ~~e~~, le vieux monsieur mourut, sans rien dire, sans une plainte, sans une contorsion, en regardant ses images, en écoutant la voix de la marchande qui coulait ~~comme de l'eau~~ toujours, le pépillement des moineaux, les claxons dispersés des taxis.

Il dut mourir debout, un coude sur le rebord de pierre, et ~~il n'y eut même pas~~ pas d'étonnement dans ses yeux bleus. Il oscilla ~~la femme lui parlait toujours sans le voir~~ et tomba sur le trottoir, ~~en~~ entrainant le carton dont les images s'éparpillèrent autour de lui.

Le chien mâle n'eut pas peur, ~~et~~ ne s'arrêta pas. La femme laissa ~~tomber~~ sa pelote de laine ~~violette~~ rouge rouler de son giron et se leva précipitamment en s'écriant:

- M. Bouvet!

Il y avait d'autres bouquinistes, sur des pliants, et d'autres encore qui arrangeaient les livres dans leurs boites, car il n'était que dix heures et demie du matin. On voyait l'heure, deux aiguilles noires, sur le cadran blanc de l'horloge, au milieu du pont.

- M. Hamelin! ... Venez vite! ...

C'était le bouquiniste voisin, ~~à~~ aux grosses moustaches, vêtu d'une blouse grise. L'étudiant au Leica avait braqué son appareil sur le vieux monsieur couché parmi les images d'Epinal.

- Je n'ose pas le toucher, M. Hamelin. Vous ne voulez pas voir si...

C'EST
N'IMPORTE
QUI DANS
LA RUE

MARS

s. Benoît

Vendredi 21

8

9

10

c'est bien - Gilbert Ganne

11

Eclair journal

12

Déjeuner Labarthe - Constellation
(ici)

13

Strassova - Contrats allemands

14

45 - S. Douay

15

Gachon - Canada
Courter - 30 journaux anglais

16

P.S.

17

(si possible Cocktail Artistes
Guillot de Saix)

18

5e [redacted] - champs - élysées [redacted]

19

centre Pista. 2e étage - Paris vous parle

20

15 ou 18 Faubourg 1er angle ave Montaigne

A. Bernheim
(ici)

21

GEORGES
SIMENON

VERMONT: Waits River Village in the Fall
NOVEMBER 1966
SUN MON TUE WED THU FRI SAT
Le Voleur de Maigret
Home for the Holidays
You can be there in hours... with plenty of time to have a wonderful holiday. Substantial savings with TWA low fare services. Be sure to make your reservations early.
One Ticket—One Airline
Enjoy the convenience of traveling on one airline all the way between world centers in Europe, Africa, Asia and major cities across the U.S.A.
UNIVERSITÉ DE LIÈGE
FONDS SIMENON
S M T W T F S
MAY
JULY
PAN AM

SOMMAIRE

SIMENON
ÉCRIRE L'HOMME

Michel Lemoine

DÉCOUVERTES GALLIMARD
LITTÉRATURES

Issu d'une famille modeste, Georges Simenon est né rue Léopold, à Liège, où il passe son enfance et son adolescence à l'aube du XXe siècle. Mettant fin très tôt à ses études, il devient journaliste à la locale *Gazette de Liége* et s'y fait la main en écrivant des centaines d'articles. Manifestement doué pour l'écriture, il ne tarde pas à risquer quelques timides tentatives littéraires.

CHAPITRE 1

BALBUTIEMENTS

« J'avais l'impression de connaître, grâce à mon métier, les dessous de cette ville [à gauche, la rue Léopold] dont je parcourais les coins et les recoins […]. Sans compter les petits secrets que je découvrais à la *Gazette de Liége* sur […] les « magouilles », c'est-à-dire toutes les petites combinaisons que le public ignore. »

Simenon, *Destinées*

Hors du Poulailler

L'éternel boutade du docteur ès un tas de choses en ie, qui préfère gagner sa vie en balayant les petits papiers des rues qu'en inondant les librairies de gros bouquins nous promet des situations réjouissantes.

Le jour de la Saint-Désiré

La naissance de Georges Simenon le place sous le signe de l'ambiguïté : on ne saura jamais, en effet, s'il

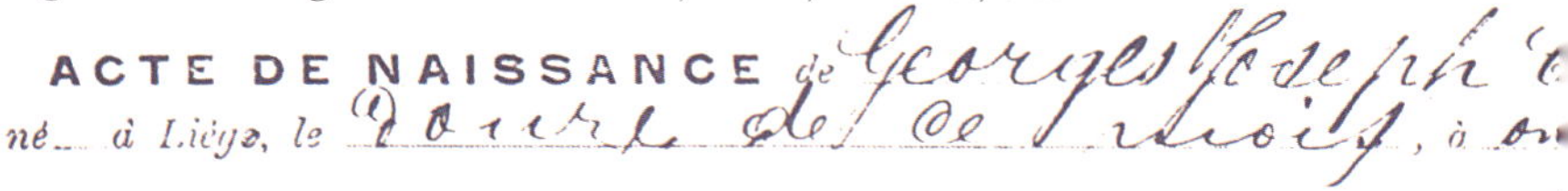

est né le 12 ou le 13 février 1903 ; le vendredi 13, dit-on, mais la mère, superstitieuse, aurait insisté pour que cette date fût officiellement modifiée. Ce qui est certain, c'est que l'événement a eu lieu au deuxième étage de la maison qui porte aujourd'hui le n° 24 de la rue Léopold, une artère commerçante du centre de Liège où Désiré et Henriette Simenon s'étaient installés peu après s'être mariés en avril 1902.

La chapellerie du grand-père paternel du petit Georges (ci-dessous au centre, avec ses parents et son frère, Christian) était le rendez-vous familial du dimanche (à gauche). Elle symbolisait aux yeux du romancier la stabilité des Simenon face au désir de changement, voire au déséquilibre des Brüll.

On était plus catégorique pour désigner la date de conception de l'enfant : le 8 mai 1902, jour de la Saint-Désiré ! À lire ceci, on pourrait se croire dans une famille de joyeux drilles un peu égrillards. Pas du tout : il s'agit de catholiques pratiquants et « il n'y a que mon père qui ose sourire en effleurant ce sujet », confiera plus tard le romancier. Ce père est comptable dans un bureau d'assurances et Henriette, née Brüll, a été vendeuse au grand magasin de l'Innovation avant son mariage. Si tous deux sont natifs de Liège, leur ascendance laisse apparaître des origines limbourgeoise, hollandaise et allemande. La famille ne s'éternise pas rue Léopold, qu'elle

La généalogie confirme cet avis : du côté paternel, on cultivait la terre ; du côté Brüll, on était plutôt dans le commerce, mais la famille avait connu des revers de fortune ; sans compter que le quintaïeul de Simenon, Gabriel Brüll, qui vivait au XVIIIe siècle, était un bandit de grand chemin et fut exécuté à ce titre, sans doute par pendaison.

quitte en juillet 1903 pour le n° 10 de la voisine rue de Gueldre, où elle demeure presque deux ans avant d'occuper en avril 1905 le deuxième étage du n° 1 de la rue Pasteur (aujourd'hui 25, rue Georges-Simenon), dans la partie petite-bourgeoise du populaire quartier d'Outremeuse. Là se trouvent les vraies racines de Simenon qui accueille avec délices, dès son jeune âge, le monde des sensations. Les jeux avec ses premiers amis, Arminio Mohr et Albert Emmerlin, les visites à l'Exposition universelle de 1905, véritable pays du rêve, chez le grand-père Simenon, chapelier rue Puits-en-Sock, chez les oncles et tantes, rompent la monotonie feutrée des jours. Le petit Georges observe tout, ignorant qu'il orne sa mémoire d'une galerie de portraits dans laquelle il puisera souvent…

Son frère Christian naît le 21 septembre 1906, tandis que lui affronte déjà le monde scolaire : il passe les années 1906-1907 et 1907-1908 à l'école gardienne des Sœurs de Notre-Dame, rue Jean-d'Outremeuse, où une sœur Adonie lui apprend à lire, puis, de 1908 à 1914, il effectue ses études primaires à l'institut Saint-André.

Entre-temps, la famille déménage en février 1911 vers le n° 53, rue de la Loi, juste en face de l'école. Là, Henriette sous-loue des chambres à des étudiants, venus parfois d'Europe centrale ou orientale, qui troublent la sérénité familiale, selon les reproches adressés plus tard à la mère par son fils. Le futur écrivain doit-il à certains de ces étudiants d'avoir découvert la littérature russe, comme il l'a souvent déclaré ? On imagine mal, en effet, un enfant de huit

Devenu adulte, Simenon a souvent dénoncé l'hypocrisie et l'élitisme constatés dans son enfance à l'institut Saint-André des Écoles chrétiennes : « Je me souviens presque avec haine, confiera-t-il en 1967, de son éducation, de ses idées sociales. » Cette photographie, où il apparaît en qualité de tambour-major dans un spectacle « engagé » monté par l'école, provoquera en outre sa colère envers les « Petits Frères qui se servaient de nous comme de pantins et nous déguisaient en soldats et en policiers. Pourquoi pas en curés aussi ? » (*Jour et nuit*)

à onze ans lisant Dostoïevski, Gogol ou Tchekhov; ces lectures ont plutôt exalté l'adolescence de Simenon, qui se souciait sans doute davantage alors de son état d'enfant de chœur.

Au nom des femmes

1914 : la guerre éclate et avec elle commencent quatre ans d'occupation et de privations. Rue de la Loi, les étudiants sont remplacés par des militaires allemands, alors que Simenon entre en sixième latine au collège Saint-Louis. Là, il subit une crise de mysticisme, tandis que ses résultats ne répondent pas aux espérances qu'autorisaient ses études antérieures. Est-ce le motif pour lequel il fréquente en 1915 la cinquième moderne au collège Saint-Servais ? L'intéressé en livre une autre raison : ayant été déniaisé durant les vacances par une fille de quinze ans, il a changé de collège pour être plus près de chez elle ou de son école – selon les versions – et on n'enseignait pas le latin à Saint-Servais (ce qui est faux). Quoi qu'il en soit, cette aventure sans lendemain sera déterminante pour lui : « La Vierge Marie allait être remplacée dans mon esprit par les femmes, par toutes les femmes, par *la* femme. » La perte de la foi a donc suivi son chemin en même

Étudiante en médecine arrivant d'un faubourg d'Odessa, Frida Stavitskaïa fut la première pensionnaire accueillie par Henriette (ci-contre). Elle laissera un souvenir très vif à Simenon, qui l'introduira sous son nom dans deux romans populaires, *La Fiancée aux mains de glace*, où elle incarne une étudiante russe nihiliste, et *L'Inconnue*, où elle se mue en artiste peintre, puis dans *L'Outlaw*, roman « dur » où, devenue polonaise, elle dirige la terrible « bande des Polonais » qui terrorise les campagnes du Nord de la France. Selon le romancier, elle aurait reçu Trotski dans sa chambre de la rue de la Loi et fut plus tard commissaire du peuple à Odessa.

temps que la primauté accordée à la sexualité. C'est aussi le sens d'un aveu à Henri Guillemin : « Je voulais baiser et l'Église me racontait que j'allais me damner. Alors j'ai tout bazardé. » Les trois ans passés au nouveau collège achèvent de le précipiter hors d'un monde catholique désormais abhorré.

Au nom du père

Trois ans ? En effet, tandis que la famille a quitté en février 1917 la rue de la Loi pour la rue des Maraîchers, n° 3 (aujourd'hui 1), de l'autre côté de la Dérivation, Simenon abandonne ses études le 20 juin 1918. Bien plus sollicité par la rue, la ville et la vie que par le collège, peut-être tire-t-il parti, comme il l'a raconté, du fait que les jours de son père, atteint d'une angine de poitrine, sont comptés et qu'il doit gagner sa vie. Sa mère a avancé une autre explication : il aurait souffert des vexations infligées par une école qui lui aurait trop souvent rappelé sa condition d'élève bénéficiant du tarif de semi-gratuité. Son goût pour les études s'était de toute façon fort émoussé depuis l'école primaire.

C'est aussi l'époque où s'affirment les sentiments qu'il porte à ses parents : tandis qu'il focalise sur

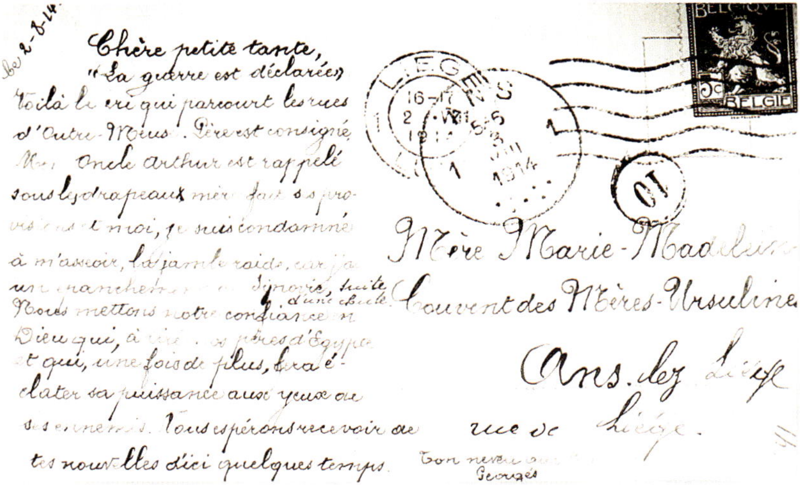

2-8-14

Chère petite tante,
« La guerre est déclarée »
Voilà le cri qui parcourt les rues d'Outre-Meuse. Père est consigné, mon oncle Arthur est rappelé sous les drapeaux, mère fait ses provisions et moi, je suis condamné à m'asseoir, la jambe raide, car j'ai un [illegible] synovie, suite d'une chute. Nous mettons notre confiance en Dieu qui, à [illegible] pères d'Égypte et qui, une fois de plus, fera éclater sa puissance aux yeux de ses ennemis. Nous espérons recevoir de tes nouvelles d'ici quelques temps.
Ton neveu [illegible]
Georges

Mère Marie-Madeleine
Couvent des Mères-Ursulines
Ans lez Liège
rue de [illegible]
Liège.

Après les vacances de 1915, c'en est bien fini de l'enfant sage et docile, de l'enfant de chœur, des bondieuseries et des émois mystiques. Un autre Simenon naît qui va rejeter ce qu'il a adoré et il est déjà loin, celui qui, au début de la Première Guerre mondiale, écrivait à sa tante religieuse ces lignes empreintes d'une foi sans faille. Ce document constitue en outre la plus ancienne trace connue de l'écriture de Simenon.

“Je vous devais la vérité : à l'origine, à la base, un NON catégorique opposé à la prétendue morale sexuelle du catholicisme.”

Simenon à Henri Guillemin, *Parcours*

une mère mesquine, cupide et larmoyante ses révoltes juvéniles, il admire au contraire la simplicité, la modestie et l'humeur égale d'un père idéalisé. Ces sentiments marqueront l'œuvre, au point qu'Alain Bertrand a montré comment le roman simenonien s'est élaboré en fonction du rejet de l'univers symbolique maternel et de la quête de l'univers symbolique paternel.

Chapeau mou et cigarette au bec… Le jeune Simenon peu avant son engagement à la *Gazette de Liége*.

Monsieur le Coq et Georges Sim

Cherchant un emploi, Simenon est engagé comme journaliste en janvier 1919, à moins de seize ans, par la *Gazette de Liége*, journal catholique conservateur. Tandis que le jeune homme accède à l'écriture par le bas de l'échelle des chiens écrasés, la famille regagne en juin Outremeuse et le n° 27 (aujourd'hui 29) de la rue de l'Enseignement. Assoiffé de vie, Simenon peut s'offrir les plaisirs qui lui avaient manqué, faute d'argent, lorsqu'il étudiait : si les journées du journaliste sont remplies, ses soirées et ses nuits sont aussi fort occupées par l'alcool et les filles. N'empêche, il se voit confier le 30 novembre un billet quotidien, *Hors du poulailler*, d'abord signé

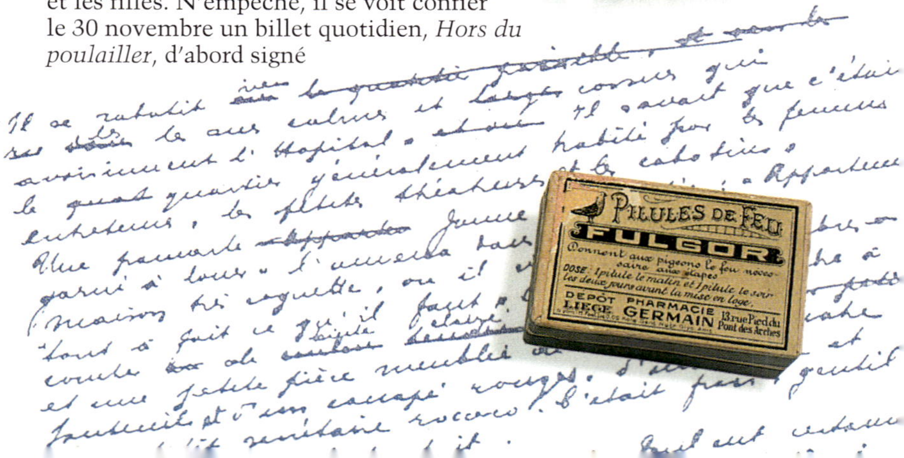

Monsieur le Coq, ce titre voulant montrer qu'il échappe à la « droite » ligne du journal.

La plume de ce Coq se plaît pourtant à des exercices personnels et la *Gazette* insère dans ses colonnes, dès 1919, l'un ou l'autre conte et un texte à l'allure surréaliste signés Georges Sim. D'autres contes sont publiés de la sorte en 1920, alors que le jeune auteur achève en septembre *Au Pont des Arches*, un roman qui se veut humoristique et se place sous l'autorité de Rabelais. Il paraît en 1921, signé Georges Sim et illustré par de jeunes peintres liégeois, dont Ernest Forgeur ou Luc Lafnet. À l'époque, Simenon fréquente en effet un groupe d'artistes baptisé la Caque.

« Comme un chien de chasse »

Il rencontre dans ce milieu Régine Renchon, une étudiante de l'Académie des beaux-arts qui devient sa fiancée. Fiancée ? Le diable se ferait-il ermite ? Certes non : « À l'époque de la *Gazette de Liége*, écrira-t-il, donc de seize ans et demi à dix-neuf ans, j'avais deux femmes à ma disposition chaque jour, et pourtant, presque chaque jour, il m'arrivait à un moment ou l'autre d'être comme un chien de chasse. » Nul doute que Régine a été alors pour lui un garde-fou l'empêchant de se noyer dans un océan de tentations.

L'intrigue du premier roman de Simenon (ci-contre), écrit à dix-sept ans, se développe autour de deux personnages : le jeune Paul Planquet et son père, Joseph, « pharmacien à l'enseigne du Pont des Arches », spécialisé dans les pilules purgatives pour pigeons. Cette spécialisation étonne moins quand on sait que l'écrivain en herbe n'a rien inventé. La pharmacie qui donne son titre au roman a en effet existé jusqu'en 1966 au n° 13 de la rue Pied-du-Pont-des-Arches sous le nom de pharmacie Germain et son pignon s'ornait d'un panneau publicitaire vantant ses « produits pour pigeons, volaille, chiens, chats et tous animaux ». Quant à Paul, il ressemble par plus d'un trait à son créateur : le roman suit notamment l'évolution de sa liaison avec une Julia Piron qui transpose celle qu'entretenait Simenon avec une Sylvie probablement nommée Noirhomme. L'adolescent avait loué un appartement pour elle boulevard de la Constitution ou boulevard Saucy, ainsi que le fit son personnage : « Il se rabattit vers les rues calmes et cossues qui avoisinent l'hôpital… » (extrait du manuscrit d'*Au Pont des Arches*, page de gauche).

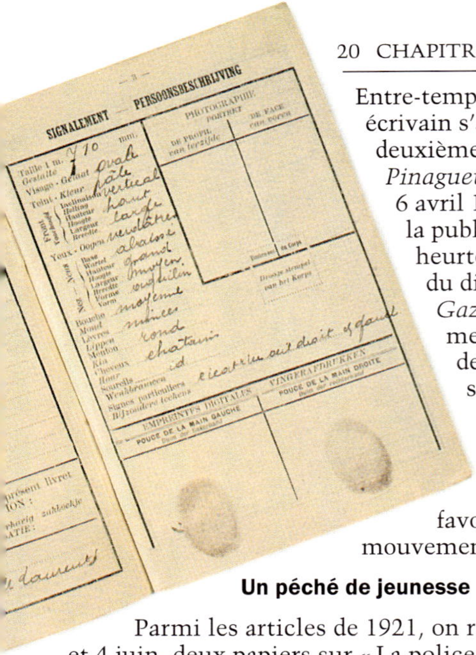

Entre-temps, l'apprenti écrivain s'attelle à un deuxième roman, *Jehan Pinaguet*, terminé le 6 avril 1921, mais dont la publication se heurte au veto du directeur de la *Gazette*. Celui-ci menace l'auteur de licenciement si paraît ce livre, qui égratigne le monde ecclésiastique et se montre favorable aux mouvements sociaux.

Un péché de jeunesse

Parmi les articles de 1921, on remarque, les 3 et 4 juin, deux papiers sur « La police scientifique », premiers témoignages d'un intérêt pour cette question chez le futur créateur de Maigret. On remarque davantage, du 19 juin au 13 octobre, une série de seize articles intitulée « Le péril juif ! », une attaque sectaire rompant avec l'habituel ton léger du journaliste. Ce faisant, Sim s'est inféodé à la ligne du journal ; bien que ces articles s'inscrivent dans une campagne antisémite internationale à laquelle la *Gazette* ne pouvait se soustraire, Simenon s'y est investi avec détermination, sinon avec conviction. Articles de commande, dira plus tard l'auteur pour se laver de ce péché de jeunesse commis à dix-huit ans. Il n'empêche que ces écrits existent, même s'il faut les replacer dans leur contexte. On peut encore observer dans la *Gazette* un article du 13 octobre où figure le « juge d'instruction Coméliau », que Simenon intégrera à plusieurs romans.
Le lendemain paraît le premier de ses articles sur « L'incurie administrative », où il s'attaque à

Simenon conservera son livret militaire (à gauche) malgré le pénible souvenir laissé par les chevaux de la caserne des Lanciers : « Certains de ces animaux étaient dociles, d'autres ruaient et cherchaient toujours à s'échapper, se souviendra-t-il dans *Point-Virgule*. Lorsque l'un d'eux y parvenait, il fallait entendre gueuler l'adjudant [...]. Je n'en veux pas particulièrement aux adjudants. Je n'en veux aux membres d'aucune profession. Je sais qu'il en faut. Et il doit exister des adjudants humains. Nous n'avons pas eu de chance. » Lors d'une longue permission du 14 au 22 août 1922, il court rejoindre sa fiancée qui passe des vacances au bord de la mer du Nord. Régine assurera le souvenir de ce moment de détente en peignant le portrait de son futur mari (ci-dessous).

La Police

l'échevin libéral de la Culture. Par la polémique suscitée, ces articles rendent le petit Sim célèbre dans le Landerneau liégeois.

Au service des chevaux

Georges n'oublie pourtant pas Régine : les 24 et 25 novembre, il écrit *Les Ridicules !*, une plaquette qui raille quatre de leurs amis peintres et dédiée « À ma Régine pour ses étrennes ». L'auteur se doute en effet qu'il ne verra plus souvent sa fiancée, puisqu'il va être appelé sous les drapeaux. Avant cela, un coup du sort s'abat sur lui : la mort de Désiré, survenue le 28 novembre, une date importante pour un fils fort attaché à son père. Le 5 décembre commence à Contich le service militaire de Simenon, qui est envoyé le 8 à la *Rote Kaserne* d'Aix-la-Chapelle, avant d'être transféré, le 2 janvier 1922, à la caserne des Lanciers de Liège. Là, le soldat est surtout au service… des chevaux, puisqu'il accomplit une tâche de palefrenier. Qu'importe ! Il retrouve au moins Gigi et poursuit sa collaboration à la *Gazette*. On ne sait quand il est admis au secrétariat de l'état-major, quai des Pêcheurs, ce qui lui permet davantage l'habit civil et des nuits hors de la caserne. Si le militaire continue à alimenter la *Gazette*, il songe, en août, à un avenir au journal bruxellois *Le Peuple*, lorsqu'un ami de la famille établi à Paris, Georges Plumier, lui conseille de tenter sa chance dans la capitale française, où il lui trouvera un emploi. Simenon est fou de joie, mais doit bien finir son service. En attendant, il rédige notamment un conte bref, *Le Compotier tiède*, attachant adieu intimiste à sa mère qui paraîtra le 15 décembre dans *La Revue sincère*.

Scientifique

Installé dans un fauteuil d'osier – symbole de son statut de chef de famille, que l'on retrouvera dans des dizaines de fictions –, Désiré Simenon est absorbé par la lecture d'un journal, sans doute la *Gazette de Liège*. Dans ses écrits autobiographiques où il l'idéalise, son fils voit en lui un homme qui savoure la vie dans les moindres de ses manifestations et ne s'embarrasse pas de problèmes superflus, contrairement à sa mère ; sous des dehors frustes et simples, il cache un amour vrai pour les siens, qu'il n'extériorise pas de manière ostentatoire, mais qui se concrétise constamment dans ses actes quotidiens.

Dans le Paris des années 1920, le journaliste se mue en un romancier populaire qui alimente de sa production les collections des maisons d'édition spécialisées; en même temps, il inonde de contes légers les feuilles lestes et colorées de l'époque, mais fournit aussi à la presse des contes plus sérieux, nettement moins nombreux: tout en effectuant son apprentissage littéraire à travers un investissement paralittéraire, Simenon en arrive ainsi, très jeune, à s'assurer des revenus considérables.

CHAPITRE 2

APPRENTISSAGE

Les romans sentimentaux du jeune Simenon sont essentiellement réservés aux éditions Ferenczi, qui accueillent dans leurs collections « Le Petit Livre... », « Mon Livre favori », « Le Livre épatant... » et « Le Petit Roman » ces fictions aux personnages le plus souvent stéréotypés, où l'amour triomphe généralement après avoir été en butte à de féroces ennemis.

À l'aube du 11 décembre 1922, Simenon arrive à Paris où l'accueille un autre écrivain liégeois émigré, Georges Ista, son aîné de près de trente ans. Il trouve une chambre minable à l'hôtel Bertha, 1, rue Darcet, puis se présente au n° 17 *ter* de l'avenue Beaucour, siège de la Ligue des chefs de section et des soldats combattants, une organisation extrémiste fondée par l'homme de lettres Binet-Valmer. Simenon trouve là le travail d'employé procuré par Plumier, mais il multiplie les démarches et les interviews, n'arrête pas d'écrire, collabore à l'occasion au *Journal* et au *Petit Parisien*. Le 13 janvier 1923, il s'installe dans une chambre meublée moins spartiate, au n° 170 du faubourg Saint-Honoré, puis déniche le 1er février deux pièces au n° 3 *ter* d'une impasse qui s'ouvre au 233 *bis* du faubourg et ne s'appelle pas encore villa Wagram-Saint-Honoré. C'est là qu'il conduit Régine le 25 mars après l'avoir épousée la veille à Liège.

Vie de château

Après son mariage, Simenon écrit les articles de la série « Mes fiches », publiés dans *La Revue sincère*. Ces portraits d'écrivains (Max et Alex Fischer, Henri

Cette toile de Régine Simenon, son épouse, laisse apparaître le souci d'élégance du jeune auteur dont la réussite matérielle, due à un travail de forçat de l'écriture, est évidente dès la fin de 1924. Sim est bientôt connu, sinon dans le monde littéraire, du moins dans celui de la presse. En témoigne ce courrier émanant de *Paris-Matinal*, le journal que se préparait à lancer Eugène Merle.

Duvernois, Claude Farrère, Paul Fort, Léon Daudet, Robert de Flers, Maurice Barrès et Tristan Bernard) résultent d'interviews. Changement de décor durant l'été : un ami de la Ligue, le marquis Raymond de Tracy, cherche un secrétaire; Binet-Valmer lui propose son employé Sim, qui voudrait gagner quelques francs de plus... Celui-ci suit donc l'aristocrate qui possède un château à Tracy, entre Sancerre et Pouilly, et un autre à Paray-le-Frésil, à une vingtaine de kilomètres de Moulins. Ces séjours parmi la noblesse marquent l'écrivain qui n'oubliera pas ce monde dans ses romans populaires ou autres et fera même de Maigret un enfant de Paray-le-Frésil, devenu Saint-Fiacre dans la fiction.

Pour autant, Simenon n'arrête pas d'écrire. Il glisse des articles dans *Paris-Centre*, le journal nivernais de son employeur qu'il accompagne parfois dans son hôtel du n° 7 de la rue Creuse. Il travaille assidûment à un roman, *Marie Ledru*, dont il attend beaucoup, mais dont on ne sait rien, sinon son refus par Colette chez Ferenczi. Il écrit surtout des contes pour les feuilles galantes où publie Ista, contes qu'il produira bientôt à un rythme prodigieux et qui lui assureront un ordinaire plus décent. Il y a pourtant moins léger, puisque Georges Sim parvient à pénétrer dès 1923 dans la rubrique des contes du *Matin*, dont la responsable est Colette.

Si Georges ne cesse d'écrire, Régine (autoportrait à gauche et caricaturée par Del ci-dessous) continue à peindre, comme elle le fera toute sa vie durant, non sans talent, et son mari ne se fait pas prier pour aller sélectionner ses modèles féminins à Montparnasse ou dans les dancings et bars miteux des rues de Lappe et de la Roquette. En décembre 1924, Simenon devant accomplir une période d'un mois de rappel militaire en Belgique, Régine en profite pour présenter à Liège une exposition de ses toiles, mais le thème choisi des « Filles publiques » scandalise peu ou prou le... public de la Cité dite Ardente.

Des contes et des romans par dizaines…

En mars 1924, Simenon quitte son emploi et regagne la capitale où le couple réside à l'hôtel Beauséjour, 42, rue des Dames, avant de louer un studio au rez-de-chaussée du 21, place des Vosges. C'est que l'écrivain s'est mis à travailler d'arrache-pied : pour cette seule année sont publiés environ deux cent trente contes légers, tandis que la collaboration sérieuse au *Matin* se poursuit avec dix-huit contes et que *Paris-Soir* en accepte trois autres. En 1924, Simenon découvre aussi le filon rémunérateur des romans populaires. Le premier, livré aux éditions Ferenczi le 30 juin, s'intitule *Le Roman d'une dactylo* et a probablement été écrit au café appelé aujourd'hui Au Rêve, 89, rue Caulaincourt. Sont proposées aux éditeurs cette année-là sept autres de ces fictions que l'auteur semble écrire comme en se jouant. Jusqu'au début des années 1930, il en écrira plus de cent quatre-vingt-dix qui relèvent de trois registres : le roman léger humoristique, le roman sentimental et le roman d'aventures aux intrigues parfois un peu policières. Avec ces romans signés de pseudonymes (Georges Sim, Christian Brulls, Jean du Perry, Georges-Martin-Georges, Gom Gut, Luc Dorsan…), Simenon fait ses gammes et met fin à la période de vaches maigres, d'autant plus que les tableaux et les dessins de Régine, qu'il rebaptise Tigy, se vendent parfois aussi.

Tandis que les premiers romans grivois – qui se teintent volontiers d'un humour facile – sont publiés dans la « Collection Gauloise » de Prima, les romans d'aventures voient plutôt le jour chez Ferenczi ou Tallandier. Les contes galants, du genre d'*Un falzar chez la colonelle*, paraissent le plus souvent, signés de pseudonymes eux aussi, dans *Froufrou*, *Sans-Gêne*, *Le Sourire*, *Paris-Flirt*, *Mon Flirt*, *L'Humour*, *Le Rire*, *Gens qui rient* et *Le Merle rose*. Jusqu'en 1932, Simenon (à sa machine à écrire, page de droite) va ainsi « déverser » mille cent contes dans cette presse, quelque six cents d'entre eux étant livrés au seul *Froufrou*.

... et une vie nocturne

Simenon écrit en 1925 treize romans, dont un *Dolorosa* qui ne manque pas d'allure, vingt-cinq contes sérieux et plus ou moins deux cent cinquante contes galants. Prélude à des milliers d'autres, le premier article consacré à Simenon dans la presse parisienne est dû à Paul Reboux et paraît le 5 juin dans *Paris-Soir*. Ce travail acharné n'empêche pas une vie nocturne intense à Montparnasse où Georges et Tigy rencontrent des peintres qui, tel Vlaminck, deviennent des amis. Le couple s'offre en été des vacances à Bénouville, village proche d'Étretat et de Fécamp, et en ramène une cuisinière de dix-huit ans, Henriette Liberge, qui sera surnommée Boule et restera sa vie durant au service de la famille Simenon, cette « servante-maîtresse » ayant été la compagne du romancier presque tout au long de son existence.

En octobre est créée au Théâtre des Champs-Élysées la Revue nègre, où triomphe Joséphine Baker. La liaison du romancier avec elle commence-t-elle alors ? Rien ne permet de l'affirmer. À la fin de l'hiver, cette vie épuisante a raison de la santé de Simenon.

“Sa production ? Soixante contes de cinquante à deux cents lignes et trois romans de trois mille lignes par mois.”

Paul Reboux, *Paris-Soir*, 5 juin 1925

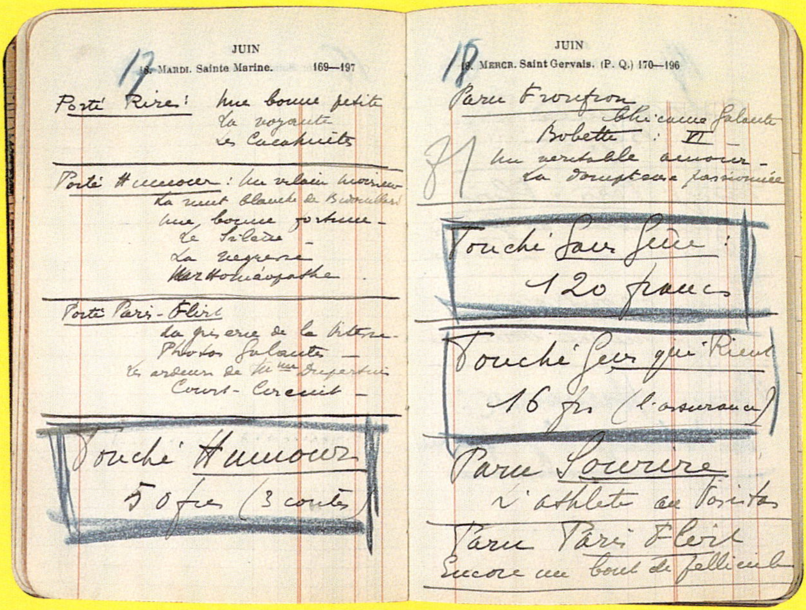
JUIN

18. MARDI. Sainte Marine. 169—197

17

Porté Rire : une bonne petite
La rozaute
les Cacahuètes

Porté Humour : un vilain monsieur
La nuit blanche de Bidouillard
une bonne fortune
Le Silatre
La négresse
Mr Homéopathe

Porté Paris-Flirt
La misère de la vitrine
Photos galantes
Les ardeurs de Mme Dupertuis
Court-Circuit

Touché Humour
50 frs (3 contes)

JUIN

19. MERCR. Saint Gervais. (P. Q.) 170—196

18

Paru Froufrou
Chicanes galantes
Bobette : VI
un véritable amour
La dompteuse passionnée

Touché Pour Lire :
120 francs

Touché Gens qui Rient
16 frs (l'assurance)

Paru Sourire
l'athlète au Pirates

Paru Paris Flirt
Encore un bout de pellicule

Tandis que parutions et rentrées d'argent sont consciencieusement notées par Simenon dans un agenda (page de gauche), l'appartement loué en 1926 au deuxième étage du 21, place des Vosges, témoigne de l'aisance acquise en quatre ans. Régine fait assaut d'élégance et le couple reçoit avec faste ses amis subjugués par le bar installé dans l'appartement.

“Un logement, au second étage, [...] se trouva libre. Je n'hésitai pas à le louer. Il était composé surtout d'une très grande pièce, plus grande que celle du rez-de-chaussée [...]. C'était le temps des Arts décoratifs. Mes murs furent peints de jaune, de bleu, de vert, dans un style cubiste. J'avais commandé un bar peint dans le même style, dont le haut était couvert de verre dépoli que rendaient lumineux des lampes se trouvant au-dessus. Les tabourets, aux longs pieds jaune citron, étaient recouverts de cuir noir. Enfin des rayonnages dans un renfoncement du mur, contenaient un nombre impressionnant de bouteilles de toutes sortes, car la mode des cocktails battait son plein.”

Destinées

C'est pourquoi il débarque en avril 1926 à Porquerolles, île qui deviendra un haut lieu simenonien où l'écrivain reviendra durant les années 1930. Vivant dans deux pièces d'une ancienne écurie, à la pointe du Langoustier, le romancier est émerveillé par les paysages de l'île. À leur retour, en plus de leur studio, les Simenon louent un appartement au deuxième étage du 21, place des Vosges et fréquentent le cabaret de Joséphine Baker, au n° 40 de la rue Fontaine. Les ennuis de santé ne freinent pourtant pas la copie qui afflue en 1926 chez Ferenczi et Prima, mais aussi chez Tallandier : vingt romans, dont *Nox l'insaisissable*, premier récit policier de Simenon, sans compter quelque deux cent cinquante contes légers et trente-quatre contes sérieux.

Écrire dans une cage de verre !

Simenon n'écrit en 1927 « que » cinq contes sérieux, environ cent vingt contes galants et treize romans, dont trois « seulement » durant le deuxième semestre. Le recours à la biographie peut-il expliquer cette baisse de régime ? Le début de l'année est marqué par l'affaire de la cage de verre. Il s'agit d'une idée d'Eugène Merle, magnat de la presse qui veut lancer un journal, *Paris-Matin*, par une opération publicitaire : faire écrire par Georges Sim enfermé dans une cage de verre durant une semaine, et sous les yeux d'un public ébahi, « un roman dont le sujet, le titre et les personnages auront été désignés par un référendum ouvert préalablement et qui lui auront été communiqués par huissier au moment de son entrée dans le local à lui assigné », roman qui serait ensuite publié dans le journal. Tels sont les termes d'un contrat du 14 janvier, Simenon devant toucher au moins 100 000 francs (le projet d'affiche parle même de 300 000 francs) dans l'aventure dont l'annonce suscite un tollé général

À côté de recueils de contes légers, sans prétention, comme *Paris leste* (ci-dessous), paraît en 1926 *Nox l'insaisissable*, modestement publié sous le n° 2 de la nouvelle collection de Ferenczi, « Le Roman policier ». C'est la première tentative de Simenon dans ce domaine. Néanmoins, la lutte à laquelle se livrent le détective Anselme Torrès et le cambrioleur Nox n'apparaît que comme une très pâle préfiguration de la lutte entre Maigret, l'intuitif, et Radek, l'intellectuel, dans *La Tête d'un homme*, que Simenon écrira en 1931. Au demeurant, le détective n'est pas plus sympathique que le talentueux bandit émule d'Arsène Lupin.

"PARIS-MATIN"

le grand quotidien d'informations qui va paraître prochainement vous présentera pour ses débuts

UN EXPLOIT SENSATIONNEL

ROMAN-RECORD

dans la presse qui pourfend ce trouble-fête pour lequel l'écriture se réduit à un exercice tout juste digne d'être exhibé dans les foires et les cirques.

C'en est fait : Simenon est un phénomène et le restera jusqu'à la fin de ses jours ; au lieu d'aider sa carrière, cette publicité nuira à sa crédibilité et lorsque, plus tard, il écrira les chefs-d'œuvre que l'on sait, il demeurera, pour certains de ses pairs, l'homme de la cage de verre…, même si le projet, finalement, n'a pas été exécuté. Pour Sim en tout cas, dans l'immédiat, l'opération n'est pas mauvaise, puisque le pactole est assuré, le contrat stipulant que l'argent dû restait dû, même si le projet capotait...

GEORGES SIM

avec lequel M. Eugène Merle, directeur de **PARIS-MATIN**, n'a pas hésité, coupant court aux pourparlers engagés avec d'autres journaux, à signer un contrat dont le *fac-simile* est ci-contre, et dont les avantages ne représenteront, pour le bénéficiaire, pas moins de

300.000 francs

L'opération « cage de verre » prévue pour le lancement de *Paris-Matin* – le jeune Sim devait y écrire en public durant une semaine – en était loin dans son élaboration, comme le montre ce projet d'affiche, quand son idée fut abandonnée. Selon Simenon lui-même, la prompte faillite du nouveau journal aurait fait échouer le projet. C'est peu plausible puisque *Paris-Matinal* – tel fut finalement le nom adopté, celui de *Paris-Matin* s'étant heurté à l'opposition du *Matin* – a tout de même paru du 13 mai 1927 au 6 avril 1928... Il est sans doute plus vraisemblable de penser que Merle n'a pas poussé l'expérience à son terme face à l'hostilité dont avait fait preuve la gent littéraire, indignée.

Non à « M. Baker »

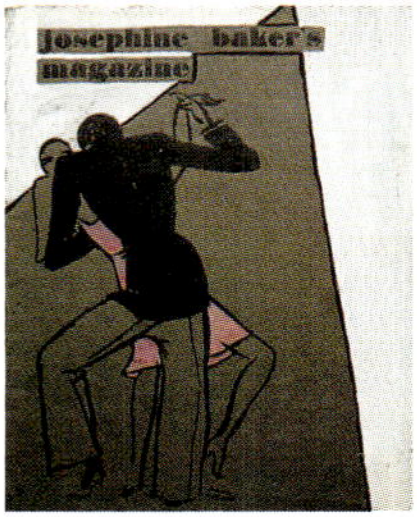

Cette affaire prend place au milieu de la liaison entre Simenon et Joséphine Baker, vedette qui le fascine au point qu'il projette de créer une feuille consacrée à l'artiste, le *Joséphine Baker's Magazine*, dont la maquette est presque réalisée, lorsque... 1927 est décidément l'année des projets avortés : prévu pour mai, le magazine ne verra pas le jour. « J'étais devenu l'*ami* [...] de Joséphine Baker que j'aurais épousée si je ne m'étais refusé, inconnu que j'étais, de devenir M. Baker », écrira Simenon. N'aurait-il pas plutôt craint de tomber dans les rets de la passion, lui qui s'est toujours voulu maître de son destin et qui regrettera amèrement la passion éprouvée ultérieurement pour sa seconde épouse ? Toujours est-il qu'en mai les Simenon quittent Paris pour l'île d'Aix, où ils restent jusqu'en septembre, séduits par la région de La Rochelle où ils viendront habiter dans les années 1930. Simenon assurera plus tard qu'il fuyait alors Joséphine et l'emprise qu'elle avait sur lui.

La relation entre la chanteuse aux deux amours et le romancier a-t-elle pourtant été aussi importante que celui-ci le prétend ? « Je ne pense pas que leur liaison ait duré aussi longtemps qu'il le dit », assure Oscar Thisse, musicien qui fit partie de 1926 à 1928 du groupe animateur du cabaret de Joséphine et de ses nuits chaudes. En tout cas, concernant la production plus réduite durant le deuxième semestre de 1927, il ne semble pas qu'elle ait un rapport avec la liaison et sa rupture, mais bien avec l'affaire de la cage de verre : même si elle n'a pas été réalisée, celle-ci n'aurait-elle pas été assez lucrative pour permettre à Simenon un relâchement dans son labeur de forçat de l'écriture ?

“C'est sans contredit la croupe la plus célèbre du monde, la plus désirée aussi. Une croupe tellement célèbre et tellement désirée qu'elle pourrait faire l'objet d'un culte, cependant que monterait vers elle en volutes plus ou moins denses, l'encens de milliers de concupiscences.”

Georges Sim, « Chez Joséphine Baker », *Le Merle rose*, 1er avril 1927

En haut et page de droite, maquettes du projet de magazine consacré à Joséphine Baker.

Entre écriture et navigation

La machine à écrire se remet sérieusement en marche l'année suivante malgré une longue absence de Paris. Simenon part en effet explorer... la France par ses voies navigables à bord d'un canot à moteur baptisé *Ginette*. Il s'agit de gagner Lyon, descendre le Rhône, puis rentrer à Paris par Bordeaux et les canaux du Centre : six mois d'une navigation au cours de laquelle Simenon écrit chaque matin. De retour à Paris, le marin d'eau douce se

J'aime

J'AIME... beaucoup, beaucoup de choses, parce que, si on n'aime pas, on déteste et détester est fatigant.
Ou alors on est indifférent et on vit comme si on était mort.

J'AIME... les bananes. C'est un vêtement pas chaud. C'est aussi le seul qui se mange.

J'AIME... les chiens, tous les chiens, les miens, les autres, parce qu'on ne peut pas les manger, ni en faire des fourrures, ou des souliers, ou des fume-cigarettes...
Rien ! Alors il leur est impossible de croire que c'est de l'amour intéressé.

J'AIME... mon cochon, parce que c'est le seul cochon dont je n'ai pas peur : il ne me donnera pas d'indigestion.

J'AIME... danser, car quand je danse je ne fais pas autre chose. Mais j'aime aussi beaucoup les danseurs, car quand ils dansent je n'ai pas besoin de danser, n'est-ce pas !

J'AIME... la musique. Une chambre vide de meubles, ou de lumière est ennuyeuse. Une chambre vide de son aussi.
Dans la rue il y a la musique des autos. Sur la mer la musique des vagues. Dans les champs la musique des oiseaux.
Mais nous avons dans notre gorge une musique plus pratique, on l'emporte partout avec soi !

À l'île d'Aix, où Simenon, ici avec son chien danois Olaf, est venu se reposer de ses soirées parisiennes, l'écrivain découvre non seulement une région qu'il affectionnera toujours, mais il s'initie aussi à la navigation en mer à bord du cotre d'un marin-pêcheur du cru, Georges Dukas. Ce n'est pas sans importance pour sa vie future, puisque ici prend une orientation décisive son rêve de posséder un jour son propre bateau et de vivre sur l'eau, rêve qu'il concrétisera dès l'année suivante.

découvre des ambitions maritimes et fait construire à Fécamp, par le chantier Georges Argentin, un cotre capable d'affronter la mer.

L'hiver 1928-1929 le voit souvent sur les quais visqueux et malfamés de Fécamp où il suit de près la construction du bateau. Ces déplacements ne nuisent certes pas à la création, comme si l'auteur, pour écrire, avait besoin d'atmosphères et de paysages différents : Simenon rédige en 1928 la bagatelle de cinquante-trois romans, parmi lesquels *Les Cœurs perdus*, *En robe de mariée*, *La Femme qui tue*, *L'Amant sans nom*, *La Fiancée aux mains de glace*, *Marie-Mystère* et *La Femme 47*, romans marquants de cette production populaire. Ainsi, après *Chair de beauté*, rédigé en 1927,

Simenon boucle en 1928, avec *La Femme qui tue*, *L'Amant sans nom* et *La Fiancée aux mains de glace*, son cycle Yves Jarry, cet aventurier proche d'Arsène Lupin devenant le premier personnage récurrent de l'œuvre si l'on oublie le juge Coméliau, apparu dès 1927 dans *Mademoiselle X...* On sait en outre qu'en décembre, le romancier a tenté de s'introduire chez Gallimard avec *Tonnerre de Brest*, première version de *La Femme en deuil*.

Maigret en gestation

La construction de l'*Ostrogoth* terminée, Simenon entreprend en 1929 une croisière qui le conduit dans le nord des Pays-Bas et de l'Allemagne, notamment à

Parmi les derniers romans populaires, certains se veulent manifestement plus ambitieux que ceux des débuts. Généralement, Simenon ne se contente plus d'une histoire sentimentale ou d'aventures, mais il y mêle les deux éléments et les pimente ici d'une intrigue policière, là d'un zeste d'espionnage. Ainsi apparaît *La Femme 47* qui reste pourtant, avant tout, un roman sentimental. Toutefois, la présence dans l'intrigue d'un espion allemand surnommé Fritz-la-Taupe suffira à faire interdire l'ouvrage sous l'Occupation, le seul autre livre de Simenon à figurer sur la « Liste Otto » étant un autre roman populaire, *Deuxième bureau*.

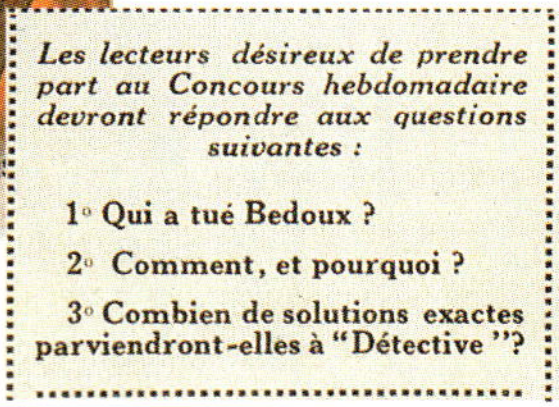
Les lecteurs désireux de prendre part au Concours hebdomadaire devront répondre aux questions suivantes :

1° Qui a tué Bedoux ?

2° Comment, et pourquoi ?

3° Combien de solutions exactes parviendront-elles à "Détective" ?

13 MYSTERES

Delfzijl, où le cotre mouille le plus longtemps et où sont écrits plusieurs romans dont, probablement, *Train de nuit*, premier récit mettant en scène un commissaire Maigret. L'*Ostrogoth* passe ensuite à Stavoren une partie du rigoureux hiver 1929-1930. Le jeune écrivain n'est jamais plus inspiré qu'en voyage, puisque sa production de 1929 s'avère quantitativement presque aussi imposante que celle de 1928 : pas moins de quarante-neuf romans dont, parmi les meilleurs, *L'Homme à la cigarette*, *Deuxième bureau*, *Matricule 12*, *Le Château des Sables Rouges*, *Katia, acrobate*, *L'Homme de proie* et *L'Inconnue*.

Simenon s'introduit par la petite porte chez Gallimard en plaçant dans l'hebdomadaire *Détective*, dirigé par Georges Kessel, des enquêtes publiées sous la forme d'un jeu-concours : *Les Treize Mystères* et *Les Treize Énigmes*. L'inspecteur Sancette naît dans les nouvelles des *Exploits de Sancette* avant de prendre son envol romanesque dans *Captain S.O.S.*, puis de poursuivre sa carrière dans *Matricule 12* et *Le Château des Sables Rouges*.

Quand Sim envoie à Georges Kessel les premières intrigues policières qui prendront place dans les « trois fois *Treize* », le directeur de *Détective* exige qu'elles soient retravaillées, ce à quoi s'emploie le romancier.

Pour *Détective*, c'est un incontestable succès : les ventes s'envolent et des centaines de réponses affluent, ce qui justifie la création d'un jury (ci-contre) composé de Pierre Mac Orlan, Maurice Garçon, Henri Duvernois, Joseph Kessel et du Dr Henri Drouin (de haut en bas).

Le voyage français de 1928 à bord du *Ginette* – ici sur le Rhône (page de gauche, en haut) – n'est pour Simenon qu'un banc d'essai préparant la grande aventure, dès l'année suivante, de l'*Ostrogoth*, baptisé en grande pompe à Paris par le curé de Notre-Dame (page de gauche, en bas) avant de prendre son élan vers le Nord début avril 1929. « Nous ne sommes jamais allés au restaurant, nous avons tenu le point d'honneur de manger toujours la tambouille que nous faisions », a déclaré Tigy (au centre sur la photo ci-contre). Simenon, en tout cas, n'est jamais plus inspiré que lors de ces voyages puisqu'il rédige en 1928 et 1929 la bagatelle de cent deux romans, soit plus de la moitié de ses œuvres de jeunesse signées de pseudonymes (ci-contre en train d'écrire à bord de l'*Ostrogoth*). Sans doute n'a-t-il jamais autant écrit, toute sa carrière durant, que pendant ces deux années-là.

Quant à Maigret, c'est d'abord un nom désignant... un médecin de Saint-Macaire dans le modeste *Une ombre dans la nuit*, mais un commissaire Maigret apparaît aussi en 1929 : s'il appartient à la police de Marseille dans *Train de nuit*, il officie à Paris dès *La Figurante* et *La Femme rousse*. Deux futurs compagnons du Maigret canonique naissent également cette année-là : Torrence dans *Train de nuit*, *L'Inconnue*, *Matricule 12* et *La Femme rousse* ; Lucas dans *L'Inconnue* et *Matricule 12*. Enfin, bien que J. K. Charles, héros de *L'Homme à la cigarette*, ne soit pas un personnage récurrent, il ressemble fort à Yves Jarry.

Durant l'hiver, Georges et Tigy prennent à Hambourg un bateau qui les conduit jusqu'en Laponie, puis ils regagnent Stavoren où les attend l'*Ostrogoth* qui les ramène en France. Simenon trouve un endroit où amarrer son cotre au lieu-dit le Gouffre, entre Seine-Port et Morsang-sur-Seine. Il reste là longtemps, ne quittant ce coin de la vallée de la Seine, devenu un des hauts lieux simenoniens, qu'à l'automne pour gagner la Bretagne. Il s'établit pour l'hiver à Beuzec-Conq, dans une villa située au lieu-dit les Sables Blancs.

Signe des temps, le rythme de production se ralentit en 1930 : vingt-neuf romans populaires tout de même d'où émergent *La Maison de l'inquiétude*, *L'Homme qui tremble*, *La Maison de la haine*, *Les Errants*, *L'Épave*, *Fièvre*, *Les Forçats de Paris*,

Durant l'été 1931, Simenon écrit à Morsang-sur-Seine quatre nouvelles destinées à la collection « Phototexte » du jeune éditeur Jacques Haumont : *L'Affaire des sept*, *La Folle d'Itteville* (projets de maquettes ci-contre), *Le Grand-Langoustier* et *L'Énigme de la « Marie-Galante »*. Il s'agissait d'une collection policière illustrée par des photos de Germaine Krull (page de droite, avec Simenon), sorte d'ancêtre du roman-photo. Seule *La Folle d'Itteville*, dont les photos ont été réalisées au château-hôtel de la Michaudière, a concrétisé ce projet ; les autres nouvelles seront publiées en volume par Gallimard en 1938 sous le titre *Les Sept Minutes*.

Simenon a rédigé à Morsang et près de Morsang ses premiers « Maigret » et il lui arrive de faire venir le commissaire sur les lieux de sa naissance, tout en lui prêtant la tendresse qu'il a conservée pour ce lieu : « Cette nuit du samedi au dimanche, à Morsang, [et] la journée du dimanche, ce fut pour Maigret la quintessence de l'été, du bord de l'eau, de la facilité de vivre, de la joie simple et bon enfant » (*Signé Picpus*).

La Fiancée du diable et *L'Évasion*, sans compter *Un crime à bord*, qui sera jugé digne, en 1932, d'être publié sous le patronyme de Simenon, mais sous le titre *Le Passager du « Polarlys »* !

Naissance de Maigret

Georges Sim, lui, continue à alimenter *Détective* de nouvelles policières, *Les Treize Coupables*, tandis que Maigret apparaît à nouveau dans *La Maison de l'inquiétude*, tout en étant cité dans *Les Forçats de Paris* et *L'Évasion*; Torrence intervient dans *La Maison de l'inquiétude, Les Amants du malheur* et *Fièvre*; Lucas est présent dans *Fièvre, Les Forçats de Paris, La Fiancée du diable* et *L'Évasion*, alors

“L'argent de « Détective » allait nous servir [...] à nous précipiter vers l'océan Glacial, non pas à bord de l'*Ostrogoth* mais à bord d'un gros bateau sur le pont duquel on embarquait aussi bien des vaches que des cochons ou des barils de morue, [...] et qui nous fit franchir le cap Nord [...]. Pour arriver là, notre étrave avait dû tracer son sillon dans la glace. Des traîneaux tirés par des rennes nous feraient parcourir la Laponie, de tente en peau de renne en tente en peau de renne, dans l'immensité blanche, et nous étions nous-mêmes vêtus en Lapons, non pour le pittoresque ou pour la photo-souvenir, mais parce que nous n'aurions pas supporté autrement des froids de quarante-cinq degrés sous zéro.”

Simenon, à propos de son voyage en Laponie [ci-dessus], *Mémoires intimes*

M. GALLET, DÉCÉDÉ,

que Sancette mène à nouveau l'enquête dans *L'homme qui tremble* et *Les Amants du malheur*. Si la production populaire s'amenuise, c'est que le jeune auteur nourrit d'autres ambitions : avec les premiers romans de Maigret « officiels » rédigés cette année-là, *Pietr-le-Letton, Le Charretier de la « Providence »*, *M. Gallet, décédé* et *Le Pendu de Saint-Pholien*, Simenon s'élève d'un échelon et songe davantage à la littérature qu'à la paralittérature.

Avec ces « Maigret », au diable les clichés et les stéréotypes ! Simenon ancre ses personnages dans le réel et encre ses paysages d'atmosphère : dans *M. Gallet, décédé*, nous transpirons avec Maigret sous le soleil estival ; dans *Le Charretier de la « Providence »*, tout comme lui, nous dégoulinons de mouillé. En osmose avec les protagonistes, nous vivons leur univers, nous sentons avec eux leur environnement. En fait, le romancier décrit des milieux qu'il a expérimentés lui-même, des décors

Constituées de fiches anthropométriques et de citations à comparaître, les invitations au Bal anthropométrique, organisé par Fayard et Simenon pour lancer Maigret, ne sont pas ordinaires. L'événement non plus puisqu'il s'agit d'un bal costumé ayant pour thème le monde de la pègre (ci-dessus). Pendant que les invités se pressent en se livrant à diverses facéties, jusqu'au lendemain matin pour certains, Simenon dédicace des centaines d'exemplaires de *M. Gallet, décédé* et du *Pendu de Saint-Pholien*.

qu'il connaît et il les rend par un procédé d'éclatement qui s'apparente au pointillisme pictural. Il s'attache principalement, en ce départ, à la peinture de déclassés, de marginaux ou de gens de peu appartenant parfois à la petite bourgeoisie dont il est issu.

REÇOIT...

Maigret au bal !...

Après quelques réticences, ces premiers romans de Maigret sont acceptés par Fayard, déjà éditeur de trente et un romans populaires de l'auteur.
Le véritable Simenon – celui que le monde entier connaît – prend réellement son essor en 1931, avec le lancement des deux premiers romans de Maigret publiés par Fayard, *M. Gallet, décédé* et *Le Pendu de Saint-Pholien*, lors du Bal anthropométrique à La Boule blanche, un cabaret de la rue Vavin où se presse le Tout-Paris dans la nuit du 20 au 21 février. Des romans de Maigret, Simenon ne cesse plus d'en écrire. Quittant la Bretagne, il s'installe à l'hôtel Aiglon, 232, boulevard Raspail, où il rédige *La Tête d'un homme*, avant de passer mars et avril au château-hôtel de la Michaudière, à Guigneville-sur-Essonne, où il écrit *Le Chien jaune* et *La Nuit du carrefour*. Il retrouve ensuite sa chère vallée de la Seine où il amarre l'*Ostrogoth* à Morsang, près

L'opération publicitaire est une réussite et les ventes suivent ; *Le Charretier de la « Providence »* paraît en mars, suivi en avril par *Le Chien jaune* et en mai par *Pietr-le-Letton*. Simenon et Maigret sont mis sur orbite. La critique, elle, est le plus souvent positive. Ainsi Odette Pannetier, dans son article sur le Bal anthropométrique, « M. Gallet, décédé, reçoit » (*Candide*, 26 février 1931), fait remarquer que les deux premiers romans de Maigret mis sur le marché auraient pu se passer de cette publicité tapageuse dont ils ont fait l'objet, tant ces livres sont « habilement mystérieux et singulièrement "prenants" ».

de l'auberge du Vieux-Garçon, pour y écrire *Un crime en Hollande* et *Au Rendez-Vous-des-Terre-Neuvas*. En été, il se rend à Deauville le 15 août pour une mémorable séance de dédicaces et rédige en chemin, à Paris, *Le Relais-d'Alsace*, un roman sans Maigret.

... et au cinéma !

Bientôt prend place le séjour à Ouistreham où, tout en fréquentant des pêcheurs, le romancier écrit en septembre *La Danseuse du Gai-Moulin* et en octobre *La Guinguette à deux sous*. Là, son ami Jean Renoir étant venu lui acheter, pour 50 000 francs, les droits

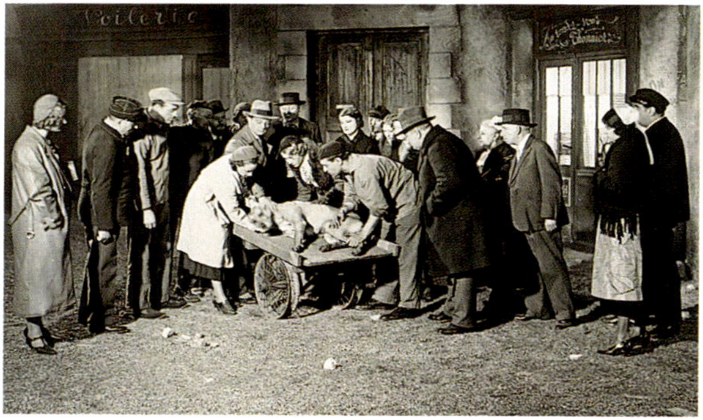

cinématographiques de *La Nuit du carrefour*, l'auteur entrevoit les bénéfices offerts par les adaptations au cinéma. Une page se tourne, marquée par la vente de l'*Ostrogoth* à Caen le 3 novembre. Simenon se dirige alors vers le sud et va passer l'hiver au cap d'Antibes, dans la villa Les Roches Grises appartenant à Henri Duvernois, où il compose *L'Ombre chinoise*, tout en travaillant avec Renoir à l'adaptation de *La Nuit du carrefour* puis bientôt, avec Jean Tarride, à celle du *Chien jaune*.

Les débuts de Simenon au cinéma – il a pris soin de faire stipuler dans le contrat avec Renoir que seuls le réalisateur et l'écrivain ont qualité pour choisir d'un commun accord les interprètes – sont donc prometteurs

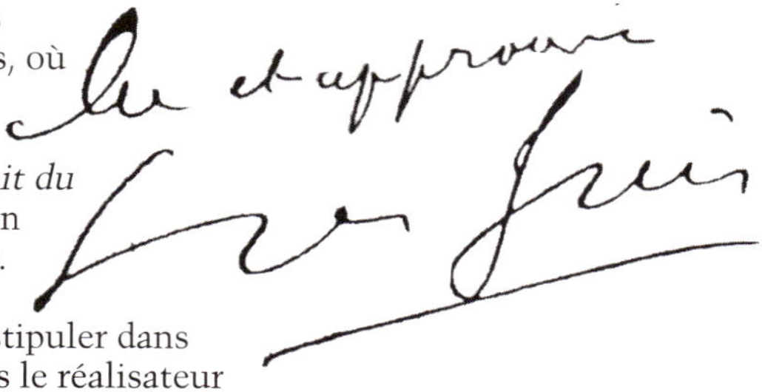

Pour tourner le premier film adapté d'une œuvre de Simenon, Jean Renoir a confié le rôle de Maigret à son frère Pierre (page de droite, en bas). Selon la majorité des spécialistes, *La Nuit du carrefour* (page de droite, en haut) reste, soixante-dix ans plus tard, « le meilleur Maigret à l'écran, et Pierre Renoir un des Maigret les plus subtils. La fameuse atmosphère simenonienne, c'est Jean Renoir, et lui seul, qui a su en donner l'exacte équivalence plastique » (Claude Gauteur, *D'après Simenon*). L'écrivain, lui, malgré l'absence manifeste de certaines séquences « oubliées », était ravi par l'interprétation de ce premier Maigret : « Pierre Renoir [...] m'a fait rêver à mon personnage comme s'il ne sortait pas de ma propre imagination », confiera-t-il dans *Paris-Midi*, le 19 avril 1932.

puisqu'il collabore à l'adaptation de ses romans. Il déchantera toutefois dès 1933 lorsque, voulant lui-même porter à l'écran *La Tête d'un homme*, son projet échouera pour tomber entre les mains de Julien Duvivier, sans compter qu'il s'estimera financièrement lésé par les producteurs. « *Le Chien jaune* et *La Nuit du carrefour* sont des films ratés, confie-t-il, amer, au journal *Pour Vous* en septembre 1932. Non par la faute de ceux qui les ont faits, mais par la faute de ceux qui les ont payés. Ou mieux : par la faute des règles et des imbéciles qui les ont édictées. » Il décide alors de ne plus accorder de droits cinématographiques et se tiendra à cette décision jusqu'en 1937, n'y renonçant qu'en fonction de ses besoins pécuniaires et des offres de plus en plus alléchantes qui lui seront proposées. Si le « pouvoir d'atmosphère » du cinéma a toujours fasciné Simenon, s'il est devenu le romancier le plus adapté, un malentendu profond subsistera entre lui et le septième art, que l'essayiste Michel Carly a résumé ainsi : « Dès qu'un roman devient un film, l'écrivain perçoit clairement que l'histoire ne lui appartient plus. [...] Lui, le créateur solitaire, individualiste [...] regarde les entrepreneurs du cinéma comme des marchands ignares. »

Reste que pour le romancier, une époque s'achève avec l'année 1931, en même temps qu'un apprentissage : à moins de trente ans, le premier Simenon a bel et bien vécu.

Dans *Le Chien jaune* (page de gauche), de Jean Tarride, le réalisateur a imposé son père, Abel, pour jouer le rôle de Maigret : « Il était plutôt destiné à faire rire qu'à représenter la Police Judiciaire », déclarera Simenon dans *Point-Virgule*.

En 1932, Simenon (ci-contre à La Richardière) travaillera lui-même au scénario de son roman *La Tête d'un homme* avec Valéry Inkijinoff, qui tiendra dans le film, réalisé finalement par

Julien Duvivier, le rôle de Radek, le tueur « intelligent » opposé à un Maigret « qui ne pense pas ». Celui-ci est interprété, dans ce troisième roman de Simenon porté à l'écran, par Harry Baur (ci-dessus), « le meilleur des nombreux Maigret de l'écran », selon Raymond Chirat (*Premier Plan*, décembre 1968).

"Harry Baur était sans doute un grand acteur, mais il avait vingt bonnes années de plus que moi à cette époque, un faciès à la fois mou et tragique."

Le commissaire Maigret,
in *Les Mémoires de Maigret*

Même si les romans de Maigret connaissent un vif succès grâce auquel le nom de l'écrivain est sur toutes les lèvres, Simenon décide dès 1932 d'abandonner ce type de récits, qu'il qualifie de semi-littéraires, pour affronter la « vraie littérature ». Dans ce domaine aussi, sa réussite est telle qu'à partir de 1934, il est édité par Gallimard tandis que, bientôt, Gide s'enthousiasme de son ton original, de son incontestable talent et d'une qualité aussi prolixe.

CHAPITRE 3

RÉUSSITE

Dans la première moitié des années 1930, Simenon parcourt le monde pour le compte de journaux et revues dont il est l'envoyé spécial. De ces voyages, dont il rapportera des centaines de photos, naissent des reportages, entre autres pour *Paris-Soir* et *Voilà*, mais aussi des romans au cadre exotique, tel *Quartier nègre*.

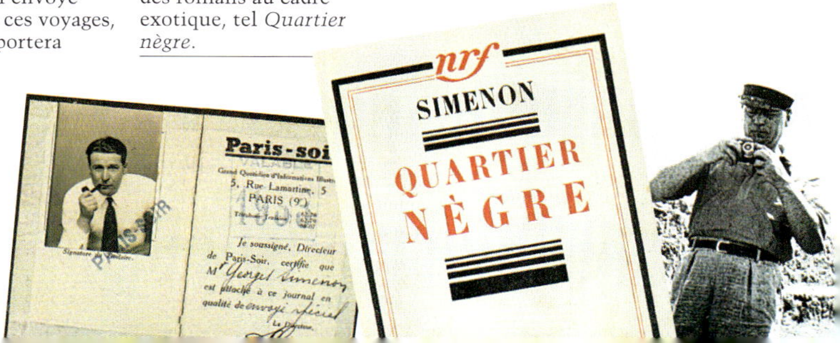

Grâce à Maigret, Simenon est connu. Ses livres s'arrachent et c'est le début d'une carrière fulgurante, d'un succès étonnant. En fait, la formule du roman « policier » simenonien est déjà prête : le commissaire s'imbibe d'une atmosphère décrite de façon impressionniste et agit davantage par intuition que par déduction, rompant avec la tradition de l'enquêteur « scientifique ». Ces romans mettent l'accent sur l'absence de méthode de Maigret qui tente de s'identifier à autrui et apporte sa sympathie aux plus démunis. Même s'ils restent des romans à énigme, on peut considérer que le romancier a créé un type romanesque nouveau.

L'accession de Simenon à sa jeune maturité se marque par l'abandon de Paris et sa région comme lieux de résidence, ainsi que par une série de grands voyages. Après son séjour au cap d'Antibes où il écrit trois « Maigret », *L'Affaire Saint-Fiacre*, *Chez les Flamands* et *Le Port des brumes*, il gagne La Rochelle où, en mars 1932, il rédige *Le Fou de Bergerac* à l'hôtel de France, puis s'installe dans une gentilhommière toute proche, La Richardière, à Marsilly, où il commence aussitôt *Liberty-Bar*. Cet emménagement n'empêche pas les Simenon, l'été venu, d'effectuer en Afrique un voyage éclair qui les amène, via l'Égypte et le Soudan, à traverser le Congo belge.

Écrit pour *Voilà* au retour du voyage de 1932 en Afrique (ci-dessus), le reportage intitulé « L'Heure du nègre » contient, en dépit de son côté décousu engendrant certaines ambiguïtés, des prises de position anticolonialistes : « L'Afrique nous dit m… et c'est bien fait. »

Des « romans durs »

De retour à Marsilly, l'écrivain compose coup sur coup trois romans importants, *Les Fiançailles de M. Hire*, *Le Coup de lune* et *L'Âne-Rouge*, qui se passent du support de Maigret, meneur de jeu considéré comme une facilité technique. Il nomme « romans durs » ces fictions que Maurice Piron a

appelées « romans de la destinée ». On y trouve généralement un héros aux prises avec un destin sur lequel il n'a justement pas de prise. Simenon y crée un autre « homme sans qualités », rappelant celui de Céline que Sartre a mis en exergue à *La Nausée* : « C'est un garçon sans importance collective, c'est tout juste un individu. » Le cadre spatial du *Coup de lune* est constitué par Libreville et la forêt équatoriale. Inspiré à Simenon par son voyage, le roman présente une vision impressionniste du paysage africain qui confine au rêve hallucinatoire, et il livre un réquisitoire contre les mœurs coloniales dont Gide a reconnu la prodigieuse exactitude. Avec *Le Coup de lune*, Simenon inaugure une série de romans « exotiques » caractérisés par l'absence de tout exotisme gratuit. Leurs héros restent des personnages typiquement simenoniens dont l'atmosphère locale ne fait qu'exacerber l'état de crise, que l'action se déroule à nouveau en Afrique (*Le Blanc à lunettes*, 1937), à Panamá (*Quartier nègre*, 1935 ; *L'Aîné des Ferchaux*, 1945), à Tahiti (*Long Cours*, 1936 ; *Touriste de bananes*, 1938 ; *Le Passager clandestin*, 1947) ou dans une île des Galápagos (*Ceux de la soif*, 1938).

En même temps, Simenon rédige à la hâte pour *Voilà* un reportage consacré à son périple africain,

À La Richardière, gentilhommière qu'il loue près de La Rochelle (ci-dessus), Simenon satisfait ses goûts pour la campagne : « Dans le grand étang qui recevait, à marée haute, sa ration d'eau de mer, barbotaient près de cinq cents canards disposant de maisonnettes peintes en vert sur un îlot. [...] Une cinquantaine de dindons blancs circulaient en paix, parmi les oies et les poules, et le dindon le plus grand, le plus massif, était surnommé Maigret, car il s'interposait avec autorité dès qu'un combat s'annonçait entre deux mâles. On aurait pu croire qu'il était chargé de la police de la basse-cour » (*Mémoires intimes*).

« L'heure du nègre ». 1932 est l'année où l'écrivain aurait pu obtenir le prix Renaudot. En effet, selon Lucien Descaves, les membres du jury tenaient pour acquis que le Goncourt irait au *Voyage au bout de la nuit* de Céline, mais son rejet par les Goncourt au profit des *Loups* de Mazeline força les jurés du Renaudot à offrir leurs lauriers à Céline plutôt qu'à Simenon, comme prévu.

Simenon enquête

Après la rédaction de *La Maison du canal,* en janvier 1933, Simenon et sa femme entreprennent un autre voyage qui les conduit notamment en Europe orientale. Au retour, le reportage intitulé « Europe 33 » est publié dans *Voilà,* tandis qu'est écrit en avril un nouveau « Maigret », *L'Écluse N° 1.* Infatigables, Georges et Tigy repartent vers la Turquie où Simenon interviewe Trotski exilé, puis accomplit une croisière en mer Noire et découvre le littoral soviétique qui lui inspire, rentré à Marsilly, *Les Gens d'en face.* Avant la fin de l'année sont écrits *Le Haut Mal, L'Homme de Londres, Le Locataire* et *Les Suicidés.* Avec ces deux derniers romans, Simenon abandonne Fayard pour Gallimard, qui l'éditera plusieurs années durant. En effet, Gaston Gallimard apprécie les écrits de Simenon et souhaite posséder dans son écurie ce talentueux poulain auquel Fayard ne donne plus entière satisfaction. En outre, Simenon a déjà un pied dans la maison grâce à ses collaborations à *Détective* et à *Voilà,* dont le directeur, son ami Florent Fels, a tôt fait de l'introduire auprès de Gaston.

1934 commence mal : à la demande de *Paris-Soir,* Simenon enquête – Maigret oblige ! –

Juin 1933 : à quoi Simenon doit-il la faveur d'être reçu par Trotski dans l'île turque de Prinkipo, « à une heure de Constantinople » ? Le prestige de *Paris-Soir* suffit-il à expliquer ce que le secrétaire de l'exilé russe ne comprend pas lui-même ? D'habitude, l'ancien commissaire du peuple « évite

les journalistes ». Seule restriction : les questions de l'envoyé spécial doivent être posées au préalable par écrit et Trotski y répondra de la même façon. Trop heureux de son scoop, Simenon obtempère et l'interview paraît dans *Paris-Soir* les 16 et 17 juin. « Je considère comme absolument inévitable une explosion guerrière du côté de l'Allemagne fasciste », y déclare entre autres le théoricien de la révolution permanente.

Chez Trotsky

La maison de Prinkipo

« HITLER S'EST FAIT LUI-MÊME, AU FUR ET A MESURE QU'IL FAISAIT SON ŒUVRE. IL A APPRIS, DEGRÉ PAR DEGRÉ, ÉTAPE PAR ÉTAPE AU COURS DE LA LUTTE... » nous déclare l'ancien leader de la Révolution russe

(De notre envoyé spécial Georges SIMENON)

sur l'affaire Stavisky et s'y ridiculise dans trois reportages. L'écrivain est davantage fait pour le roman : aussi, retrouvant avec joie Porquerolles où il loue la villa Les Robert, il y écrit *Maigret*, que lui a commandé *Le Jour*, mais il se jure que c'est le dernier roman à mettre en scène le commissaire ; à Porquerolles encore, il écrit en avril et mai *L'Évadé* et *Les Clients d'Avrenos*, un « roman turc ».

Le printemps incite au voyage : pourquoi pas un tour de la Méditerranée ? Le romancier s'assure les services de l'équipage d'un voilier, l'*Araldo*, qui le conduit à Gênes, à l'île d'Elbe où il écrit *45° à l'ombre*, en Sicile, à Malte, en Tunisie, en Sardaigne… Rentré à La Richardière, Simenon écrit un roman maritime, *Les Pitard*, qui subjugue la critique, puis parcourt à nouveau la France en vue d'un nouveau reportage, « Inventaire de la France, ou quand la crise sera finie » (*Le Jour*, octobre et novembre). Ce faisant, il en profite pour acheter à Seichebrières, dans la forêt d'Orléans, la propriété de Bois-Bezard, afin d'y construire la maison de ses rêves. En effet, La Richardière, qu'il voudrait acquérir, n'est pas à vendre.

Dans *Les Gens d'en face*, roman inspiré par ses récentes visites d'Odessa et de Batoum, Simenon se livre à une dénonciation en règle du régime soviétique stalinien (ci-contre, devant un parterre de fleurs à l'effigie de Lénine). L'ouvrage décrit un monde livré à la misère, à la famine, à la délation et à l'inertie administrative,

un monde où l'individu, écrasé par l'État, risque l'exécution sommaire s'il enfreint le mot d'ordre qui est de ne pas poser de question. Un tel témoignage, politiquement engagé contre le totalitarisme, est exceptionnel dans l'œuvre romanesque de Simenon : des ouvrages postérieurs comme *Maigret chez le ministre* (1955) ou *Le Président* (1958), qui dévoilent sans aménité les dessous du monde politique dans les régimes démocratiques et la corruption qui y règne, restent modérés à côté de celui-ci.

De ses nombreux voyages, l'écrivain ramène non seulement des reportages et de nouveaux cadres où situer ses fictions, mais aussi des centaines de photos qui témoignent de son intérêt pour la vie au quotidien, quelle que soit la région du globe traversée. Aux paysages, il préfère les visages : « Ma première préoccupation était de découvrir l'homme derrière le pittoresque qui le cachait. » (p. 52 : Tunisie ; p. 53 : Afrique ; p. 52-53 : Pologne). En rentrant de ses périples, il retrouve son havre de Porquerolles (ci-contre avec Tigy), où il se livre à la pêche (page de gauche) et organise des concours de boules (ci-dessus).

"Si mes souvenirs, mes images, étaient des cartes postales, [...] c'est Porquerolles qui fournirait le plus de ces cartes postales. Pas seulement la promenade du matin [...]; pas seulement le vin blanc à la terrasse de chez Maurice, pas seulement non plus mes interminables parties de boules avec les pêcheurs. Tout cela est un peu effacé dans ma mémoire alors que me restent avec une netteté extraordinaire les images de la mer, celles dont je ne me lassais pas."

Un homme comme un autre

Autour du monde

Ce projet est pourtant ajourné car, en décembre, *Paris-Soir* charge Simenon d'une enquête lointaine sur un fait divers qui vient de se dérouler à Floreana, une des îles Galápagos, et dont l'héroïne est l'excentrique baronne de Wagner. Cela donne au romancier et à Tigy l'occasion d'un tour du monde en bateau qui les conduit d'abord à New York, à Panamá, en Colombie et en Équateur. Le reporter ne semble pas s'être rendu aux Galápagos, mais avoir trouvé à Guayaquil les éléments nécessaires à ses articles sur « Le Drame mystérieux des îles Galápagos » qui paraissent en février 1935 dans *Paris-Soir*. Simenon aborde ensuite Tahiti, où il s'installe à Punaauia dans la maison où avait vécu Murnau. Là, il écrit *Ceux de la soif*, roman inspiré par les aventures de la baronne de Wagner, et *Faubourg*, où il mêle à son expérience du moment des réminiscences liégeoises, avant de rentrer en France.

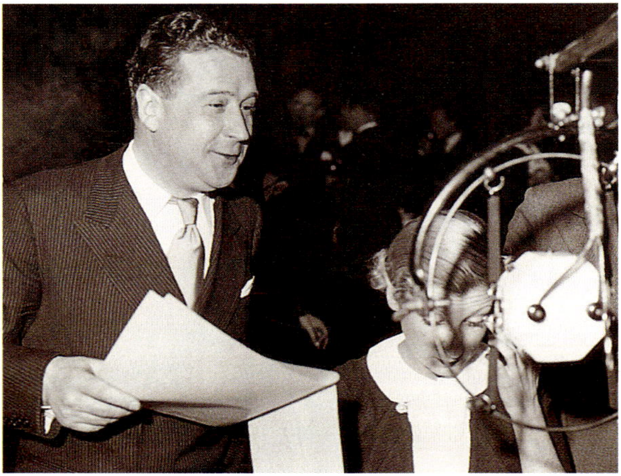

Vie mondaine

En attendant que commencent les travaux de Bois Bezard, les Simenon occupent, à six kilomètres de là, le château de la Cour-Dieu, près d'Ingrannes, où sont

❝C'était parti d'un demi-florin… L'histoire du demi-florin s'était mariée à la rancœur d'une servante… La rancœur de la servante avait rejoint le vague à l'âme d'un homme fatigué de tourner en rond… C'était tout ! Personne ne le savait ! Il était seul à connaître

ce cercle et à savoir pourquoi, chaque jour, à la même minute, il passait au même endroit. Car lui s'était évadé ! Et il était revenu aussi vite que possible, effrayé par le vide.❞

L'Assassin

Ces lignes extraites du dernier chapitre caractérisent à merveille *L'Assassin*. Médecin à Sneek, Hans Kupérus tue par désir d'évasion, mais s'aperçoit, le crime accompli, qu'il reste prisonnier de lui-même et confronté à un destin inéluctable. Simenon développera à nouveau ce thème dans *La Prison*.

écrits *Quartier nègre* et *Les Demoiselles de Concarneau*. Durant un été qui le voit souvent à Dieppe et à Paris, l'écrivain loue en outre un appartement à Neuilly, 7, boulevard Richard-Wallace, où il se met dès septembre à *Long Cours*. Il regagne ensuite la Cour-Dieu, mais que les pluies automnales sont tristes en forêt d'Orléans : les travaux de Bois-Bezard ne seront jamais entrepris… Après avoir donné à Paris une conférence sur « L'aventure » le 13 décembre, Simenon part

LE COMMISSAIRE MAIGRET REPREND DU SERVICE…

en vacances à Combloux, mais ne peut s'empêcher d'y écrire, à l'hôtel P.-L.-M., un de ses romans les plus « simenoniens », *L'Assassin*.

Séjour vacancier toujours, début 1936, à La Lézardière, villa d'Anthéor où est composé *Chemin sans issue*, en attendant que soit habitable une autre villa louée à Porquerolles, Les Tamaris. Là, Simenon écrit *Le Blanc à lunettes* et *Le Testament Donadieu*. Revenu à Neuilly en automne, le romancier livre à *Paris-Soir Dimanche* une série de neuf nouvelles qui remettent Maigret sur le métier : c'est la première partie des *Nouvelles Enquêtes de Maigret*. En décembre, retour vers les Alpes, dans le Tyrol cette fois, à la villa Sonnruh d'Igls où Simenon écrit *Les Rescapés du « Télémaque »*.

« Les Trois Crimes de mes amis »

Le séjour à Igls est suivi d'un autre au Palace Hôtel de Saint-Moritz, après quoi se situe une importante rencontre avec le philosophe Keyserling à Darmstadt.

Simenon n'avait-t-il pas proclamé en 1934 qu'il mettait définitivement son commissaire à la retraite ? Dès lors, les lecteurs de *Paris-Soir Dimanche* n'ont sans doute pas manqué d'être étonnés, le 24 octobre 1936, en découvrant dans leur journal un Maigret en belle forme aux prises avec

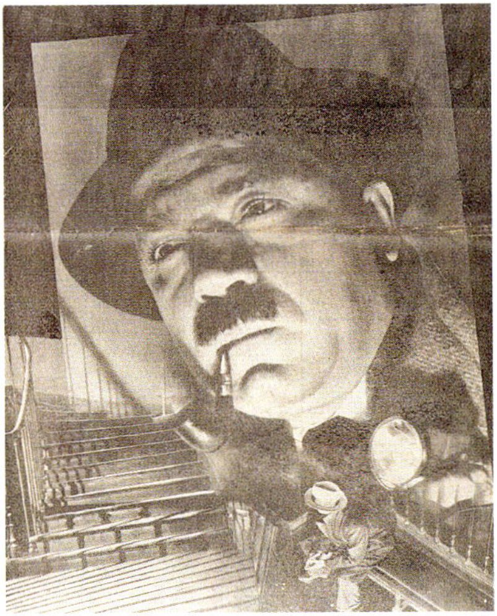

L'Affaire du boulevard Beaumarchais, un court récit publié sous forme de jeu-concours, comme les « trois fois *Treize* » de 1929-1930. Maigret reprend ainsi du service… pour assurer le train de vie de son créateur.

De retour à Neuilly, l'écrivain compose *Les Trois Crimes de mes amis*. Dès février 1937 pourtant, il regagne ses chers Tamaris où il écrit *Monsieur La Souris*, *L'homme qui regardait passer les trains* et *Touriste de bananes*. En août, durant un séjour dit de détente aux îles Borromées, *Cour d'assises* est rédigé à l'hôtel Verbano, dans l'île des Pêcheurs. La fin de l'année comporte d'autres séjours de « détente » puisque sont successivement écrits *Le Suspect* à Neuilly, *La Marie du Port* à l'hôtel de l'Europe de Port-en-Bessin, *La Maison des sept jeunes filles* à Neuilly et *Les Sœurs Lacroix* à l'hôtel de l'Étoile de Saint-Thibault, près de Sancerre.

Les « trois crimes de mes amis » ont été commis par des individus qui ont existé et que Simenon a connus durant sa jeunesse liégeoise. L'œuvre présente donc un aspect autobiographique, même si des libertés sont prises avec le réel. Les premières pages, que Gide jugeait « étourdissantes », contiennent d'ailleurs de judicieuses remarques sur les rapports entre la fiction et la réalité. À la question de savoir pourquoi ses « amis » ont tué et non lui, dont on retrouve dans les romans « les décors, les atmosphères, les états d'âme » qui mènent au crime, Simenon ne répond pas, mais

Dirigé par les frères Offenstadt, *Police-Magazine* republie en feuilletons, dès 1937 et 1938, des romans déjà anciens de Simenon : *La Guinguette à deux sous*, *La Nuit du carrefour* et *Le Passager du « Polarlys »*. À partir de 1938, leur nouveau magazine, *Police-Film*, qui deviendra *Police-Roman*, accueille les nouvelles écrites par Simenon cette année-là, à savoir la suite des *Nouvelles Enquêtes de Maigret*, les récits qui constituent *Le Petit Docteur*, *Les Dossiers de l'Agence O* et les *Nouvelles exotiques*.

laisse entendre que la période frustrante de l'Occupation les a poussés, après la guerre, à rechercher « des exaltations naturelles ou artificielles », et que l'atmosphère malsaine et veule de l'époque n'est pas étrangère aux méfaits commis par ses « amis ».

« Comprendre et ne pas juger »

Cour d'assises a pour sujet une erreur judiciaire condamnant un innocent à vingt ans de travaux forcés. Simenon met la justice en accusation dans ce texte dépouillé où le héros est écrasé par cette « machine monstrueuse, une sorte d'immense machine à broyer ». L'aspect imparfait de la justice est mis en évidence dans plusieurs autres romans de Simenon parmi lesquels figurent, entre autres, *La Tête d'un homme* (1931), où un condamné innocent sauve sa tête grâce à Maigret, *Les Témoins* (1955), où un juge se rend compte que lui aussi pourrait être condamné sur la foi de témoignages peu probants, et *Maigret aux assises* (1960), où le commissaire témoigne en faveur d'un inculpé que tout accuse. C'est le moment de rappeler la devise de Simenon : « Comprendre et ne pas juger ».

Quand il vit à Nieul-sur-Mer de 1938 à 1940, Simenon s'intègre d'autant plus facilement à la société rochelaise qu'il a déjà vécu dans les environs de La Rochelle quand il occupait La Richardière (ci-dessus, sur le port, en 1938). Pourtant, s'il fréquente la haute bourgeoisie de la ville essentiellement constituée par les armateurs locaux, il préfère aller prendre l'apéritif au café de la Paix de la place d'Armes, tenu par ses amis Caspescha et plus conforme à ses goûts. Il peint d'ailleurs fort sombrement le monde des armateurs et des notables de la ville dans deux longs romans, *Le Testament Donadieu* et *Le Voyageur de la Toussaint*. En 1982, Simenon déclarera au journal *Sud-Ouest Dimanche* (14 février) : « C'est la ville dont j'ai été le plus amoureux. »

P.S. Je lis à l'instant l'article de Thérive. Heureux certes de voir qu'il vous apprécie et ose dire (enfin !) "Quel grand romancier, ce Simenon ! " Bravo ! Mais également fort amusé de constater que nous n'apprécions pas en vous, Thérive et moi, les mêmes choses. Oh ! pas du tout...Et félicitez-vous de présenter diverses faces à la louange. Ceux-là sont vraiment forts, au sujet desquels les admirateurs ne s'entendent pas très bien entre eux. Mais je voudrais sa-

Interpellé par l'intolérance des partis extrémistes d'alors et la violence qu'elle engendre, Simenon crée avec Lucien Descaves le mouvement « Sans Haine », qui se traduit par le port d'un insigne : si la presse en fait état au début de 1938, il ne sera guère suivi d'effets… Retour aux Tamaris où Simenon rédige en mars dix nouvelles complétant la série des *Nouvelles Enquêtes de Maigret*, puis un roman attachant, *Le Cheval-Blanc*. Lors d'un séjour en avril à l'hôtel Bonnet de Beynac, il écrit *Le Coup-de-Vague*. Quant à Neuilly, l'écrivain commence à se lasser de la vie mondaine qu'il y mène.

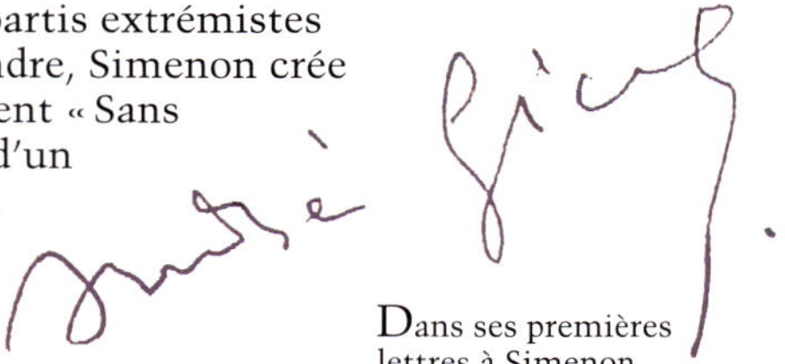

Dans ses premières lettres à Simenon (ci-dessus en date du 6 janvier 1939), André Gide ne tarit pas d'éloges envers son cadet qui, peut-être sous « l'effet naturel d'une intuition subite », écrit des romans « d'une réussite parfaite ».

À Nieul-sur-Mer, le retour de Maigret

Se mettant en quête d'un nouveau logis qu'il veut proche de la mer, Simenon trouve à Nieul-sur-Mer, près de La Rochelle, une ancienne maison du XVIIe siècle qu'il se décide à acheter. En attendant l'aménagement de cette demeure, il vit à La Rochelle, rue Jeanne-d'Albret, dans la villa Agnès, où il compose ses six *Nouvelles exotiques*, les treize qui forment *Le Petit Docteur*, les quatorze que comptent *Les Dossiers de l'Agence O*, puis, en juillet, un roman âpre, *Chez Krull*. Après quoi, le voici installé, avec Tigy et Boule, dans cette maison qu'il croit être celle où ils vieilliront ; il y écrit aussitôt *Les Inconnus dans la maison*, *Le Bourgmestre de Furnes* et *L'Outlaw*.

Marc, premier fils de l'écrivain, naît à Uccle,

dans la banlieue de Bruxelles, le 19 avril 1939, après un détour de ses parents par le château de Scharrachbergheim, près de Strasbourg, où est écrit *Malempin*. Cela ne freine pas le rythme de Simenon qui, rentré à Nieul, écrit de septembre à décembre *Bergelon*, *Oncle Charles s'est enfermé*, *Il pleut, bergère...* et *Les Caves du Majestic*. Ce dernier roman marque le retour sur la scène romanesque de Maigret, ressuscité pour des motifs pécuniaires.

Sept nouvelles sont écrites en 1939 et douze en 1940. L'écrivain, qui excelle dans ce genre, le pratique surtout pour des raisons lucratives. Il n'abandonne pas pour autant le roman, puisqu'il rédige *La Maison du juge* (un « Maigret ») et *La Veuve Couderc* avant le début de la guerre. Quand celle-ci éclate, le romancier, mobilisable, se rend à Paris où on lui déclare, à l'ambassade de Belgique, qu'il serait plus utile s'il s'occupait à La Rochelle de l'accueil des réfugiés belges. Il s'emploie activement à cette tâche jusqu'en août, puis, lorsque les bombes pleuvent sur la zone portuaire, il gagne avec Tigy, Marc et Boule, l'intérieur du pays et la Vendée.

En compagnie de son fils Marc, Simenon se plaît à arpenter la côte vendéenne et charentaise, pays des ostréiculteurs et mytiliculteurs qu'il peint – avec quelle sûreté –, dans plusieurs romans dont *Le Coup-de-Vague* : « On n'était pas dans le monde ordinaire; on n'était ni sur terre, ni sur mer, et l'univers, très vaste, mais comme vide, ressemblait à une immense écaille d'huître, avec les mêmes tons irisés, les verts, les roses, les bleus qui se fondaient comme une nacre. »

Page de gauche, en bas, publicité pour « Sans Haine », le mouvement préconisé par Simenon.

Plus que deux années à vivre ?

C'est d'abord le séjour à la ferme-moulin du Pont-Neuf, près du village de Vouvant, au nord de Fontenay-le-Comte, où il termine le 7 septembre *La Vérité sur Bébé Donge*. Durant l'automne, sa santé nécessitant une consultation, un médecin lui déclare que son cœur ne lui autorise plus que deux ans de vie. Cet avis de la faculté conduit les Simenon à abandonner Vouvant, trop isolé, pour vivre à Fontenay. Ils s'installent dans la maison du n° 12, quai Victor-Hugo, où le romancier écrit en décembre *Cécile est morte*, un « Maigret ». Il est vite rassuré sur son état de santé, mais le choc a été rude : Désiré, son père, n'est-il pas mort jeune d'une angine de poitrine ? S'il venait à mourir, lui, que saurait de sa vie son fils Marc ? C'est pourquoi il écrit à son intention le début d'un récit autobiographique, *Pedigree de Marcsimenon*.

Une « épopée des petites gens »

Après avoir écrit en février 1941 *Le Voyageur de la Toussaint*, Simenon déménage pour partager avec son propriétaire, Alain du Fontenioux, le château fontenaisien de Terre-Neuve, édifié à la fin du XVIe siècle. Là, l'écrivain travaille à son projet autobiographique qu'il entend incliner dans le sens d'une « épopée des petites gens ». Soucieux d'obtenir l'avis d'une autorité, il interrompt pourtant son récit et envoie le manuscrit à Gide, avec qui il entretient une

“Je travaillais peu ; je peux dire que je ne travaillais plus du tout, car écrire mes souvenirs d'enfance auprès de mon propre enfant qui grandissait était plutôt un passe-temps savoureux, et je crois à présent que, de t'observer, aiguisait ma mémoire et y faisait affluer les plus fraîches images.”

Mémoires intimes

Ci-dessus et page de droite, Simenon et son fils Marc au château de Terre-Neuve ; ci-contre, l'écrivain à une fête foraine en Vendée au temps de la rédaction de *Pedigree de Marcsimenon*.

correspondance littéraire. En attendant le verdict du maître, il regagne des chemins plus familiers avec *Signé Picpus* (un « Maigret »), *Le Fils Cardinaud*, *Le Rapport du gendarme* et neuf nouvelles « alimentaires ». Le rapport de Gide arrive enfin et n'est guère favorable. Qu'à cela ne tienne : Simenon reprend le projet *ab ovo*, le remanie en lui donnant une forme romanesque à la troisième personne et termine le 17 décembre la première partie de *Pedigree*. Quant à la mouture initiale, *Pedigree de Marcsimenon*, elle verra néanmoins le jour en 1945 sous le titre *Je me souviens*…

Selon les déclarations du romancier, c'est avant d'écrire *Pietr-le-Letton* qu'il a jeté quelques notes préparatoires sur une enveloppe jaune qui se trouvait à portée de main. Il a continué pour les romans suivants. Ces notes ne concernent ni l'intrigue ni la composition, mais servent de points de repère, surtout pour les noms et statuts des personnages, ainsi que pour les lieux. Les premières enveloppes conservées (la plus ancienne est celle du *Pendu de Saint-Pholien*) sont très sommaires, tandis que les renseignements se multiplient avec le temps (ci-dessous, notes pour *Pedigree*).

Sous l'Occupation

En 1942, Simenon n'écrit plus qu'une nouvelle, signe que les conditions matérielles se sont améliorées. Il sera en effet, sous l'Occupation, l'écrivain le plus adapté au cinéma qui lui offre une manne providentielle en ces temps difficiles. En outre, il obtient en 1942 une autorisation de se déplacer, notamment à Paris. Tout n'est cependant pas rose dans la vie du Simenon « occupé ». Ainsi, la santé de Marc le préoccupe et l'amène à passer deux mois au bord de

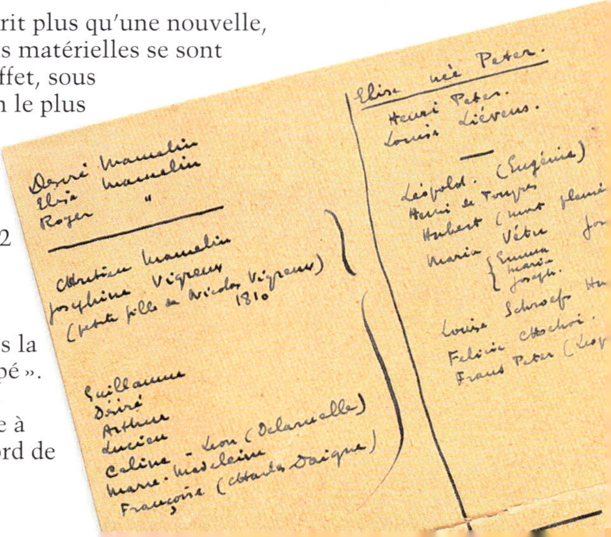

la mer, à La Faute, près de L'Aiguillon, où il écrit la deuxième partie de *Pedigree* et un savoureux « Maigret », *Félicie est là*, avant de regagner le château de Terre-Neuve et d'y rédiger *La Fenêtre des Rouet*, roman intimiste terminé le 7 juillet. Autre coup dur : en septembre, l'écrivain est soupçonné par l'occupant d'être juif – de Simenon à Simon… – et sommé de prouver qu'il ne l'est pas ; l'affaire se termine sans mal en novembre, mais décidément, il ne fait pas bon vivre à Fontenay par ces temps : mieux vaut aller s'enterrer à Saint-Mesmin, bourg vendéen proche des Deux-Sèvres où une villa est à louer, route de Pouzauges.

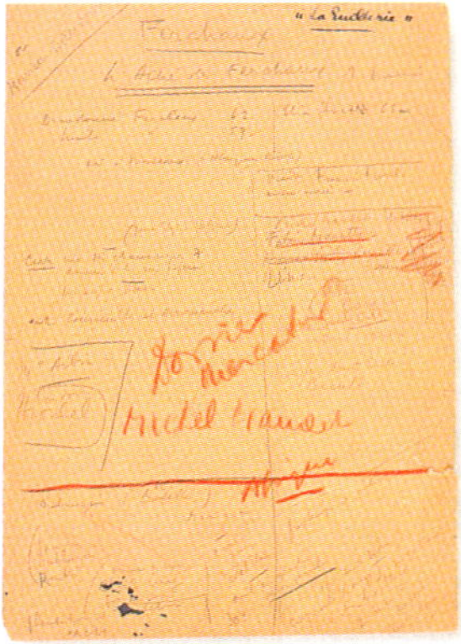

Le procédé de Maigret

L'intérêt suscité par l'intrigue de *Félicie est là* reste secondaire par rapport à la peinture d'un cas psychologiquement intéressant. Félicie est étrangère au meurtre, mais les investigations de Maigret visent essentiellement la compréhension de ce personnage. Cette jeune fille jouit en effet de la sympathie du commissaire qui a découvert en elle « cette simple palpitation humaine qui se cache sous les apparences des plus extravagants fantoches ». Certes, Félicie « se crée des vérités à son usage » et confond la réalité avec les rêves issus de ses lectures, mais elle révèle une sensibilité peu commune. Le roman met

Dans *L'Aîné des Ferchaux* (ci-dessus, enveloppe), Michel Maudet, jeune loup aux dents longues et sans scrupules, n'a rien. Il devient secrétaire du vieux et tout-puissant Dieudonné Ferchaux, qui a tout. Il finit par le tuer pour avoir tout, lui aussi. Le roman vaut principalement par les liens subtils qui se tissent entre les deux hommes, Ferchaux voyant d'abord en Maudet une image de sa propre jeunesse, et le jeune ambitieux considérant au départ son patron comme un idéal. La dégradation progressive de ces rapports forme la trame du livre.

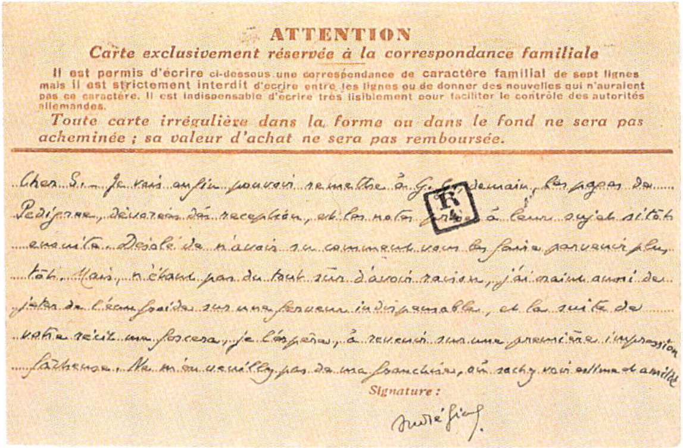

Par cette carte postale du 5 juin 1941, Gide avertit Simenon de sa réaction face à l'état initial de *Pedigree de Marcsimenon* : « première impression fâcheuse » – ce qui incitera le romancier à repenser son projet. Plus tard, Gide jugera le remaniement « incomparablement supérieur à la première version », mais pas encore suffisant. Il l'écrit à Simenon sur un ton très professoral : « En général : très bon travail, à continuer sans défaillance […]. Très bon travail, mais un peu… tranquille et l'on n'y sent pas la "transe" – où tout de même vous excellez » (lettre du 21 août 1942). Même quand *Pedigree* connaîtra sa forme définitive, Gide restera déçu par ce récit où il ne retrouvera pas le ton du romancier instinctif qui le fascine.

en relief le procédé de Maigret qui consiste à s'identifier aux personnages à propos desquels il enquête. Ce mimétisme sera à nouveau utilisé intensivement dans *Maigret au Picratt's* (1951), *Maigret et l'homme du banc* (1953) et *Maigret et la jeune morte* (1954).

Route de Pouzauges, Simenon met la dernière main à *Pedigree* dont la troisième partie est terminée le 27 janvier 1943. Il écrit ensuite un « Maigret », *L'Inspecteur Cadavre*, et un roman au sens presque « religieux », *Le Bilan Malétras*, avant de séjourner à l'hôtel de Charlannes, à La Bourboule, à nouveau à cause de la santé de Marc. À la fin de l'année, il rédige un roman où il se souvient de l'Afrique, de Panamá et… de la Normandie, *L'Aîné des Ferchaux*, achevé le 7 décembre. Est également composé en 1943 un roman radiophonique, *Le Soi-Disant M. Prou* ou *Les Silences du manchot*.

« Pedigree », les thèmes du clan et de la marginalité

Autobiographique et rédigé pour se délivrer des obsessions dues à sa jeunesse liégeoise, le plus long des romans de Simenon, *Pedigree*, n'est pas construit autour d'une intrigue. Au gré de ses souvenirs, le romancier y dépeint par petites touches la « chronique d'une famille liégeoise entre 1903 et 1918 », celle de l'auteur lui-même, qui

constitue « le plus grand roman que Liège ait jamais inspiré » (Maurice Piron). Le rôle de roman-matrice de *Pedigree* a été mis en lumière par Danièle Racelle-Latin. L'ouvrage contient en effet une thématique souvent exploitée par Simenon. On se contentera de signaler le thème du clan qui, de *La Maison du canal* (1933) à *La Mort d'Auguste* (1966), en passant par *Les Sœurs Lacroix* (1938), *Le Fils Cardinaud* (1942) ou *Tante Jeanne* (1951), parmi bien d'autres romans, alimente une bonne part de la production simenonienne. S'y profile aussi « le thème de la marginalité qui recouvre les thèmes sous-jacents de la fuite ou de la "déviance" » (Maurice Piron). De même,

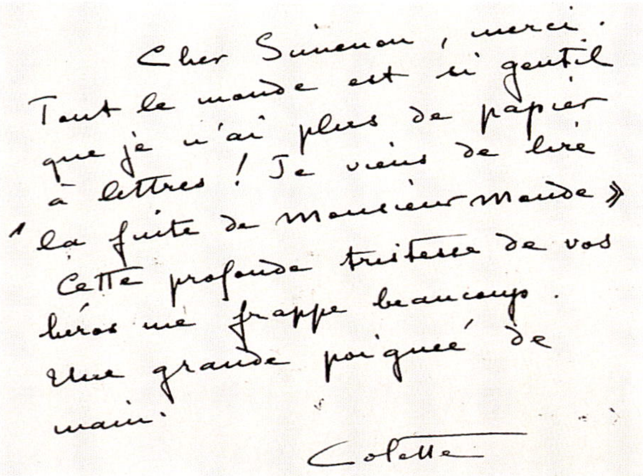
Cher Simenon, merci.
Tout le monde est si gentil
que je n'ai plus de papier
à lettres ! Je viens de lire
« la fuite de Monsieur Monde »
Cette profonde tristesse de vos
héros me frappe beaucoup.
Une grande poignée de
main.

Colette

Pedigree fournit la source de diverses histoires d'individus ou de groupes que le romancier a développées dans *Le Locataire* (1934), *Faubourg* (1937), *Chez Krull* (1939), *Il pleut, bergère...* (1941) ou *Oncle Charles s'est enfermé* (1942), entre autres ouvrages. Le roman aurait dû connaître une suite qui aurait conféré à la vision du monde des « petites gens » une portée universelle et conduit les personnages jusqu'à la veille de la Seconde Guerre mondiale. Simenon y a renoncé face aux procès dont le livre a fait l'objet lors de sa sortie, en 1948.

En 1942, les Éditions de la NRF publient à des fins publicitaires un essai anonyme d'une vingtaine de pages qui présente Simenon de manière succinte, mais fort bien documentée. Son auteur n'est autre que Raymond Queneau, qui est le premier à reconnaître la diversité spatiale de l'œuvre et a l'excellente idée d'inclure dans son étude une carte des lieux où se déroule l'action des romans de Simenon. Dans le monde littéraire de l'époque, l'auteur du *Chiendent* n'est pas le seul lecteur fervent de Simenon. Colette aussi l'appréciait (à gauche), tout comme Cocteau, Pagnol, Mauriac ou Céline, pour ne citer qu'eux.

Drames intimes et... moins intimes

En 1944, il écrit à Saint-Mesmin *Les Noces de Poitiers*, *La Fuite de Monsieur Monde* et *Le Cercle des Mahé*. Un événement d'ordre privé, capital pour la suite de sa vie, a lieu cette année-là : Tigy surprend son mari et Boule dans une position non équivoque. Elle exige aussitôt le renvoi de la cuisinière, mais, devant le refus du romancier, les époux en arrivent à un compromis : tous deux reprendront leur liberté en restant mariés. Simenon, qui, selon ses déclarations, avait trompé Tigy chaque jour depuis qu'il la connaissait, ressent un sentiment de libération : il ne sera plus obligé de se cacher, de tricher, pour assumer les besoins impérieux de sa sexualité.

Un autre événement, d'ordre historique, est moins réjouissant : à la Libération, l'écrivain a maille à partir avec la Résistance qui lui reproche d'avoir trop bien vécu sous l'Occupation, de ne pas s'être embarrassé de scrupules pour publier dans des revues collaborationnistes, d'avoir traité avec la société cinématographique Continental, d'obédience allemande, bref, on le soupçonne de

Sorti sur les écrans en 1942, le film de Henri Decoin inspiré par *Les Inconnus dans la maison*, qui bénéficie d'une adaptation, d'un scénario et de dialogues de Henri-Georges Clouzot, doit beaucoup à l'interprétation du rôle principal par Raimu (ci-dessous aux côtés de Juliette Faber) : « le colosse de l'art dramatique, l'Acteur avec une majuscule », dira Simenon (*Arts*, 18 janvier 1956). Pourtant, cette adaptation trahit le roman en se dotant d'un contenu idéologique qu'il n'a pas. Simenon n'en a cure, puisqu'il voit surtout dans le cinéma et l'argent qu'il lui procure un moyen de bien vivre en des temps difficiles.

collaboration et peu s'en faut qu'il ne soit arrêté en août. Pour comble d'adversité, il est atteint d'une pleurésie qu'il va soigner aux Sables-d'Olonne où l'accueille l'hôtel des Roches-Noires, mais où, accusé d'intelligence avec l'ennemi, il ne tarde pas à être assigné à résidence.

Dans *Les Noces de Poitiers*, Simenon analyse l'évolution d'une déchéance suivie d'une sorte de résurrection. Le roman est centré sur la vulnérabilité du héros, Gérard Auvinet, jeune ambitieux qui ne possède pas les moyens de réaliser ses rêves. Orgueilleux, d'une nervosité et d'une émotivité excessives, il souffre de ne pouvoir pénétrer dans le monde brillant qu'il ne fait qu'entrevoir. Un arrière-plan autobiographique transpose l'expérience de Simenon lors de ses débuts parisiens. Le héros ressemble comme un frère, par son mal de vivre et son immaturité, aux jeunes héros de *L'Âne-Rouge* (1933), des *Suicidés* (1934), de *Long Cours* (1936) et même de *L'Aîné des Ferchaux* (1945), quoique ces

Contrairement à son frère Christian, collaborateur notoire au sein du mouvement rexiste belge pro-nazi – il s'engagera dans la Légion en 1945, sera condamné à mort par contumace en août 1946 et tué en Indochine en 1947 –, Simenon a eu pour seul tort de trop bien vivre sous l'Occupation. Pourtant, Belge assigné à résidence en Vendée, il lui faut obtenir les autorisations qui lui permettront de mettre l'océan entre la France et lui. Son chemin passe par Paris (ci-dessus, autorisation de la Sûreté datée du 26 mars) et par Londres (ci-contre, document officiel établi le 22 août par les autorités anglaises avant son embarquement pour les États-Unis).

romans ménagent une intrigue et un dénouement différents. Les récits ultérieurs qui mettent en scène des protagonistes jeunes reçoivent une coloration plus sereine, qu'il s'agisse par exemple du *Confessionnal* (1966) ou de *La Disparition d'Odile* (1971).

Tourner la page

Guéri, Simenon écrit trois nouvelles aux Roches-Noires en janvier 1945, puis il s'installe dans l'immeuble Les Soleils, 42, promenade Georges-Clemenceau, où il rédige une quatrième nouvelle, *Les Mains pleines*, à la gloire de… la Résistance. Opportunisme ? Peut-être, mais en avril, l'écrivain retrouve sa liberté de mouvement : « aucun fait précis de collaboration ne lui est imputé » en Vendée. Néanmoins, ce climat le mine. Continuer à vivre en France dans ces conditions ? Jamais !

Je me souviens…

De l'espace ! L'Amérique ! Comme pour dire adieu à un des paysages français qui lui tiennent le plus à cœur, il se rend du côté de Morsang et de Seine-Port, à l'hôtel Beau-Rivage de Saint-Fargeau, pour écrire *Maigret se fâche*, roman promis à Pierre Lazareff pour *France-Soir* et terminé le 4 août. Avant de couper les ponts avec la France, Simenon change d'éditeur, la politique commerciale de Gallimard l'ayant déçu ; il jette son dévolu sur le jeune Sven Nielsen qui lui offre un pont d'or et auquel il ne cessera, pendant des années, de prodiguer ses conseils. Désormais, la production de Simenon en France passera par les Presses de la Cité. Son visa et celui de Tigy sont délivrés le 18 août, suivis, le 24, par un ordre de mission culturelle au Canada. En octobre, ils débarquent à New York : une nouvelle vie commence.

Le premier ouvrage de Simenon publié par les Presses de la Cité fin 1945 est ce *Pedigree de Marcsimenon*, édité sous le titre de *Je me souviens…*, que Gide avait jugé fort imparfait. L'ouvrage est illustré de très beaux dessins de Reschofsky (ci-dessous). À l'occasion d'une réédition en 1961, l'écrivain donne son avis sur le livre : « Je viens de revoir, pour l'édition définitive (?), les cinquante premières pages de *Je me souviens…* […]. Je me demande si mon style n'était pas plus nerveux, plus vivant qu'aujourd'hui. Je travaillais plus vite, en buvant une sérieuse quantité de vin. Je trouve peu à corriger, ou alors il faudrait tout récrire. C'est débraillé, certes, souvent incorrect, mais je n'ose pas y toucher par crainte de tout démolir » (*Quand j'étais vieux*).

DIRECTION
DE LA
POLICE
JUDICIAIRE
ESCALIER A
POLICE JUDICIAIRE

Dans les décennies qui suivent la guerre, Simenon devient célèbre, à la manière d'une vedette qui défraie parfois la chronique. On en parle comme d'un « cas », en se référant à son mode de vie fastueux aussi bien qu'au rythme de sa production, mais il devient aussi admis, dans les milieux lettrés, que ce phénomène est en train de bâtir une œuvre qualitativement importante et unique, en marge des modes et des écoles.

CHAPITRE 4

CÉLÉBRITÉ

En changeant d'éditeur, Simenon (ci-contre devant les locaux de la Police judiciaire, à Paris) renoue avec la production régulière de ses romans de Maigret, le nom du commissaire s'inscrivant désormais dans les cinquante-trois titres de ses enquêtes publiées par les Presses de la Cité de 1947 à 1972.

Coup de foudre à New York

“J'allais connaître […] ce qu'on appelle la passion, une véritable fièvre que d'aucuns […] assimilent à une maladie.”
Mémoires intimes
(à propos de Denyse, sa seconde épouse)

C'est un couple « séparé » qui s'installe fin octobre 1945 à Sainte-Marguerite-du-Lac-Masson (Québec), où il loue une villa et un bungalow rue Baron-Empain. L'écrivain fait souvent la navette avec New York : souhaitant développer son audience aux États-Unis, il noue divers contacts éditoriaux et cherche une secrétaire bilingue. Ainsi, le 5 novembre, une Canadienne se présente ; la passion est immédiate, Denyse Ouimet est engagée et va partager la vie du romancier à Sainte-Marguerite. Là, Simenon se remet sérieusement au travail : il écrit au début de 1946 *Trois Chambres à Manhattan*, roman qui transpose sa rencontre avec Denyse, puis *Maigret à New York*. Il rédige ensuite trois nouvelles qui prendront place dans le recueil *Maigret et l'Inspecteur Malgracieux*, avant d'aller passer l'été dans la province du Nouveau-Brunswick, à Saint Andrews, où sont composés *Au bout du rouleau*, *Le Clan des Ostendais* et trois nouvelles.

« Lettre à mon juge », un carrefour de la thématique simenonienne

Le 16 septembre, la « famille », accompagnée par l'institutrice de Marc, quitte Saint Andrews et sa Glengary House pour rouler vers le sud en suivant le rivage atlantique du Canada, puis des États-Unis. En novembre, Simenon et Denyse s'installent sur la côte ouest de la Floride, à Bradenton Beach, dans un bungalow nommé Coral Sands, tandis que Tigy et Marc se fixent à Sarasota. Ce voyage fait l'objet d'articles destinés à *France-Soir* qui seront réunis sous le titre « L'Amérique en auto ».

Fernandel et Françoise Arnoul dans une scène du *Fruit défendu* (1952), film d'Henri Verneuil d'après *Lettre à mon juge.* Ce film dénature complètement l'esprit et même la lettre du roman puisque les amants s'y séparent, tandis que l'épouse du héros du film guérit son mari de ses errements et lui pardonne sa foucade. L'intention moralisatrice tue ici l'originalité de l'écrivain.

Outre une nouvelle, le romancier écrit à Bradenton Beach *Lettre à mon juge*. Un des plus accomplis de Simenon, ce roman raconte l'histoire d'un médecin qui, après s'être marié deux fois, découvre la passion amoureuse qu'il considère comme un absolu, au point de tuer sa maîtresse, jaloux qu'il est de son passé. *Lettre à mon juge* constitue un carrefour de la thématique simenonienne. En effet, plusieurs thèmes importants s'y retrouvent imbriqués : celui de l'individu dominé par un environnement féminin envahissant (« C'est terrifiant de penser que nous sommes tous des hommes, tous à courber plus ou moins les épaules sous un ciel inconnu, et que nous nous refusons à faire un tout petit effort pour nous comprendre les uns les autres »), celui du malentendu tragique au sein du couple (« Armande, petit à petit, à son insu, a pris à mes yeux la figure du Destin. Et, révolté contre ce Destin, c'est contre elle que je me suis révolté »), celui de la sensualité comme échappatoire à la solitude (« Plus elle était mienne [...] et plus j'éprouvais le besoin de l'absorber davantage. De l'absorber. Comme, de mon côté, j'aurais

Après avoir précisé qu'il a « porté pendant douze mois » *Lettre à mon juge,* Simenon confie à André Gide (lettre du 18 janvier 1948) : « Je l'ai écrit pour me débarrasser de mes fantômes et pour ne pas faire le geste de mon héros. » C'est laisser entendre que la portée générale du livre recouvre une intention autobiographique. Écrit presque un an après *Trois Chambres à Manhattan*, le roman s'abreuve à la même source passionnelle, mais échappe à l'allégresse causée par la victoire de l'amour sur la solitude qui marquait la fin du récit new-yorkais.

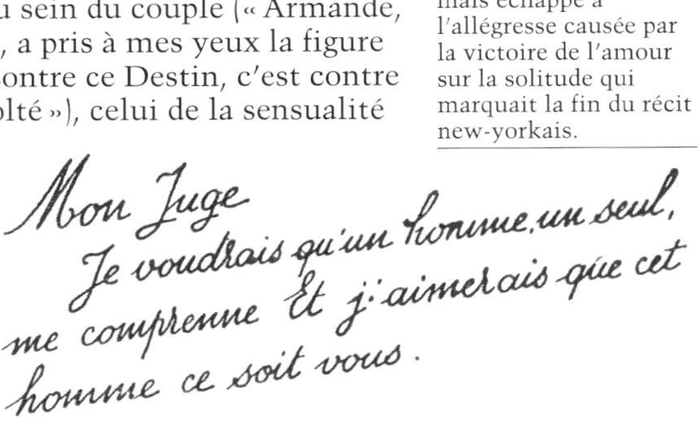
Mon Juge
Je voudrais qu'un homme, un seul, me comprenne. Et j'aimerais que cet homme ce soit vous.

voulu me fondre entièrement en elle ») ou celui de la jalousie (« Elle est tellement jalouse qu'elle ne me laisse pas un moment de liberté »)...

Fascination du désert

À Bradenton Beach, Simenon écrit encore *Le Destin des Malou* et *Le Passager clandestin*, entrecoupant son séjour par un voyage à Cuba, ainsi que par une incursion vers la Géorgie et le Tennessee. Ensuite, la randonnée à travers les États-Unis se poursuit avec Denyse et Marc vers l'ouest, où le romancier est séduit par l'Arizona. Il s'installe en septembre à Tucson, au n° 325 de West Franklin Street. Tigy, qui est rentrée en France mettre de l'ordre dans la gestion des affaires de son mari, en revient avec Boule qui n'avait pu, jusque-là, obtenir un visa. C'est donc en compagnie de trois femmes que vit alors l'écrivain, ce qui n'empêche pas ses visites aux prostituées de Nogales, au Mexique. La nouvelle de la mort de son frère le trouble sans déranger son rythme de création, puisqu'il écrit *La Jument-Perdue*, *Les Vacances de Maigret* et *Maigret et son mort*.

Il y a loin de New York à l'Arizona, de la ville par excellence aux étendues désertiques de l'Ouest. Pourtant, Simenon (ci-dessous avec son fils Marc) est fasciné par l'une comme par les autres et l'espace américain, avec ses spécificités, envahit son œuvre. Ses romans de l'Arizona, *La Jument-Perdue*, *Le Fond de la bouteille* et *Maigret chez le coroner*, témoignent de son émerveillement pour ce « pays aux vastes espaces, à l'herbe bleue et aux chevaux en liberté dans la nature » (*Mémoires intimes*), celui qu'il recherchait depuis son arrivée en Amérique pour l'avoir vu photographié dans une revue.

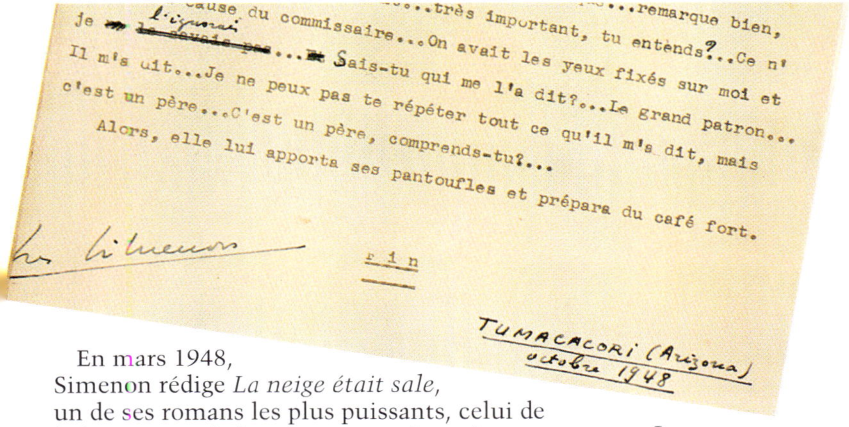
...cause du commissaire...très important, tu entends?...remarque bien,
je l'ignorais...On avait les yeux fixés sur moi et...Ce n'
Il m'a dit...Sais-tu qui me l'a dit?...Le grand patron...
Je ne peux pas te répéter tout ce qu'il m'a dit, mais
c'est un père...C'est un père, comprends-tu?...
Alors, elle lui apporta ses pantoufles et prépara du café fort.

Fin

TUMACACORI (Arizona)
octobre 1948

En mars 1948, Simenon rédige *La neige était sale*, un de ses romans les plus puissants, celui de l'abjection et de la rédemption, du rachat par la souffrance. Ensuite, soucieux de ses droits cinématographiques, il se rend à Hollywood, où il ira souvent durant son séjour en Arizona. En juin, il déménage à Tumacacori, entre Tucson et Nogales, où il a trouvé à louer une maison proche d'un ranch, Stud Barn. Là sont composés, avant la fin de l'année, *Le Fond de la bouteille*, où rôde l'ombre du frère disparu, *La Première Enquête de Maigret* et *Les Fantômes du chapelier*.

La Première Enquête de Maigret (ci-dessus, dernière page du tapuscrit) se déroule en 1913, alors que Maigret n'est pas encore commissaire, et a pour cadre principal la parisienne rue Chaptal. En effet, Simenon a beau vivre aux États-Unis, Paris continue à imprégner son œuvre.

« Un nouveau dans la ville »

Début 1949, *Mon Ami Maigret* est rédigé alors que Denyse est enceinte, état qui provoque en juin un repli vers Tucson, où les amants s'établissent au n° 4 325 d'East Whitman Street. Durant ce temps, en avant-garde, Tigy et Boule gagnent Carmel, où Marc les rejoint bientôt. À Tucson cependant, Simenon, qui vient d'achever, le 4 juillet, *Les Quatre Jours du pauvre homme*, est rattrapé par son passé ; en France, le 19 juillet, le Comité d'épuration des gens de lettres proclame sa sanction à son égard : interdiction de publication et d'activités annexes pendant deux ans.

L'intéressé est atterré – ce qui ne l'empêche pas, sur-le-champ, d'écrire *Maigret chez le coroner* –, mais, grâce à son avocat Maurice Garçon et à des relations, la condamnation n'aura pas de suite. Le 29 septembre, l'écrivain accueille avec joie son deuxième fils, John, dont la première demeure sera un appartement de l'immeuble Desert Sands, 3 805, East Fifth Street. Là est composé un roman sombre au titre symbolique saluant l'événement, *Un nouveau dans la ville*, terminé le 20 octobre. Après quoi, le père, la mère et l'enfant rejoignent l'avant-garde à Carmel (dans une autre villa, toutefois, Ocean View Avenue), où Simenon écrit avant la fin de l'année *Maigret et la vieille dame* et *L'Amie de madame Maigret*.

Jean Renoir, qui continue lui aussi à édifier son œuvre, reste admiratif devant la production de son ami (lettre ci-dessous).

À Shadow Rock Farm

Carmel est aussi le lieu de rédaction, au début de 1950, de deux excellents romans : *Les Volets verts* et *L'Enterrement de monsieur Bouvet*. Simenon régularise ensuite sa situation : le divorce d'avec Tigy est prononcé le 21 juin à Reno, où le mariage avec Denyse a lieu le lendemain. À la recherche d'un domicile, le nouveau couple officiel le trouve et l'achète à Lakeville, dans l'Est du pays, parmi les collines du Connecticut : une vaste maison du XVIIIe siècle, Shadow Rock Farm, dans une propriété de vingt hectares. Il emménage en juillet, tandis que Tigy, Marc et Boule s'installent non loin de là, à Lime Rock : Simenon pourra voir

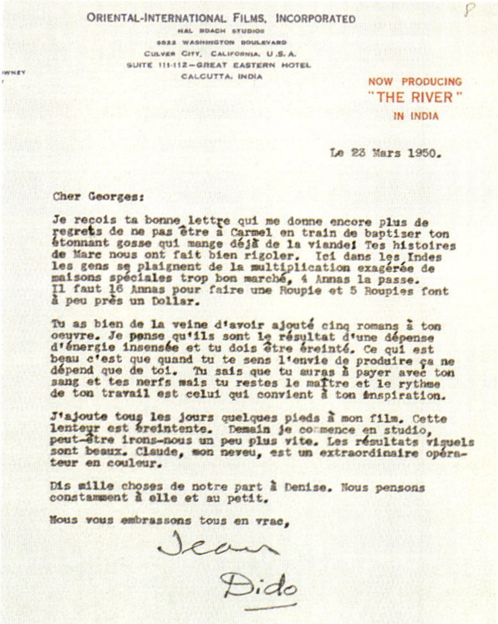

ORIENTAL-INTERNATIONAL FILMS, INCORPORATED
HAL ROACH STUDIOS
8822 WASHINGTON BOULEVARD
CULVER CITY, CALIFORNIA, U.S.A.
SUITE 111-112 – GREAT EASTERN HOTEL
CALCUTTA, INDIA

NOW PRODUCING "THE RIVER" IN INDIA

Le 23 Mars 1950.

Cher Georges:

Je recois ta bonne lettre qui me donne encore plus de regrets de ne pas être à Carmel en train de baptiser ton étonnant gosse qui mange déjà de la viande! Tes histoires de Marc nous ont fait bien rigoler. Ici dans les Indes les gens se plaignent de la multiplication exagérée de maisons spéciales trop bon marché, 4 Annas la passe. Il faut 16 Annas pour faire une Roupie et 5 Roupies font à peu près un Dollar.

Tu as bien de la veine d'avoir ajouté cinq romans à ton oeuvre. Je pense qu'ils sont le résultat d'une dépense d'énergie insensée et tu dois être éreinté. Ce qui est beau c'est que quand tu te sens l'envie de produire ça ne dépend que de toi. Tu sais que tu auras à payer avec ton sang et tes nerfs mais tu restes le maître et le rythme de ton travail est celui qui convient à ton inspiration.

J'ajoute tous les jours quelques pieds à mon film. Cette lenteur est éreintente. Demain je commence en studio, peut-être irons-nous un peu plus vite. Les résultats visuels sont beaux. Claude, mon neveu, est un extraordinaire opérateur en couleur.

Dis mille choses de notre part à Denise. Nous pensons constamment à elle et au petit.

Nous vous embrassons tous en vrac,

Jean

Dido

Marc lorsqu'il le voudra; quant à Boule, elle retournera bientôt au service des nouveaux mariés et sera heureuse de retrouver son « petit monsieur joli ».

Alors que le nouveau couple Simenon s'installe dans l'imposante demeure de Lakeville (ci-dessus), Thomas Narcejac publie la première étude littéraire portant sur l'œuvre du romancier. Entre autres mérites, elle analyse la portée « philosophique » de cette masse déjà hors du commun et établit, ce faisant, que les romans dits policiers de l'auteur n'ont de policier que le nom. Ils s'intègrent au contraire à un ensemble dont les romans « durs » constituent certes le noyau, mais, fondamentalement, ils participent d'une même vision du monde, avec une thématique et une finalité semblables, procédant d'« un identique sentiment de l'humain ». Un demi-siècle plus tard, l'essai n'a pas pris une ride et reste un des meilleurs commentaires de l'œuvre.

« Le Cas Simenon » et la célébrité universelle

Simenon demeure à Lakeville jusqu'en 1955, tandis que s'affirme sa notoriété aux États-Unis. *Le Cas Simenon*, de Thomas Narcejac, premier ouvrage consacré au romancier, paraît en 1950 aux Presses de la Cité. Avec trois millions d'ouvrages vendus chaque année dans le monde, la célébrité de l'auteur est universelle et son secrétariat, géré par Denyse, est comparé à une activité industrielle. Sont encore écrits en 1950 *Tante Jeanne*, *Les Mémoires de Maigret*, *Le Temps d'Anaïs* et *Maigret au Picratt's*; en 1951, *Maigret en meublé*, *Une vie comme neuve*, *Maigret et la Grande Perche*, *Marie qui louche*, *Maigret, Lognon et les gangsters* et *La Mort de Belle*.

1952 est l'année du voyage triomphal de Simenon en Europe en compagnie de Denyse : Paris, Milan, Rome, Liège, qui l'accueille dans la joie, Bruxelles où il est reçu à l'Académie royale de langue et de littérature françaises de Belgique.

En 1952, le voyage qu'effectue l'écrivain en Europe a plusieurs motivations : Simenon veut montrer à sa femme l'Ancien Continent et lui présenter ses relations ; il doit être reçu à l'Académie royale de langue et de littérature françaises de Belgique ; enfin, sa présence est souhaitée à Verviers où un procès lui est intenté par un ancien pensionnaire de sa mère qui s'est reconnu dans *Pedigree*. Si le monde de l'édition, de la presse et du cinéma le fête à Paris (ci-dessous avec son fils John lors de leur arrivée à Paris le 18 mars), si ses amis le revoient avec plaisir, Liège lui réserve début mai un accueil populaire délirant (ci-contre). Est-ce l'homme phénoménal, dont parlent les journaux, qu'est venu admirer

et applaudir la foule ? Le romancier ? Le créateur du commissaire Maigret ? Ou tout simplement l'enfant du pays qui a réussi ?

“18 avril. Réception officielle au 36, quai des Orfèvres, le siège de la Police judiciaire, avec un grand déjeuner à la clef. L'écrivain est accueilli par le préfet, des commissaires et des inspecteurs comme s'il était de la famille. Visite des locaux. Odeurs, couleurs, ambiance. Il se croirait dans ses romans. À ceci près que ses différents « modèles » de Maigret sont à la retraite; quant au poêle que son héros aimait tisonner, il a été remplacé par le chauffage central. Au moment du départ, remise solennelle d'une plaque de commissaire n° 0000 au nom de Maigret. Simenon en fera un porte-clefs.”

Pierre Assouline, *Simenon*

Simenon doit sa connaissance du Quai des Orfèvres à une rencontre avec le commissaire Massu, un des modèles de Maigret (page de gauche, en haut). En outre, peu après la sortie des premiers « Maigret », le directeur de la PJ, Xavier Guichard, l'avait invité à visiter les locaux de l'institution en compagnie du commissaire Guillaume. Ces deux policiers, Marcel Guillaume surtout, inspireront à leur tour la personnalité de Maigret.

Malgré ce triomphe, rentré en juin à Lakeville, il écrit : « Je ne pourrais plus m'habituer à l'existence de là-bas où il reste comme des relents d'esclavage », tandis qu'il vante « l'atmosphère de réelle démocratie qui règne ici ». En 1952, Simenon rédige encore *Le Revolver de Maigret*, *Les Frères Rico*, *Maigret et l'homme du banc* et *Antoine et Julie*.

Lorsque « Maigret a peur »

À la joie de son père, Marie-Jo, troisième enfant de Simenon, naît à Sharon le 23 février 1953. Après la naissance, il écrit cette année-là *Maigret a peur*, *L'Escalier de fer*, *Feux rouges*, *Maigret se trompe*, *Crime impuni* et *Maigret à l'école*. L'action de *Maigret a peur* se déroule à Fontenay-le-Comte. L'ouvrage met en évidence l'antagonisme entre la classe des nantis et le peuple, auquel va la sympathie du commissaire, comme dans *L'Inspecteur Cadavre* (1944), autre roman vendéen. Pourtant, Maigret a peur de la foule prête à se faire justice, tout comme il a peur quand il apprend qu'une erreur dans son enquête mène à un suicide. Sa carrière de policier est émaillée d'autres fautes, depuis *Pietr-le-Letton* (1931) et *Le Pendu de Saint-Pholien* (1931), où il provoque deux suicides, jusqu'à *Maigret aux assises* (1960), où il favorise un meurtre, en passant par *L'Inspecteur Cadavre*, où il n'arrête pas les coupables, et *Une confidence de Maigret* (1959), où il ne peut disculper un innocent condamné à mort.

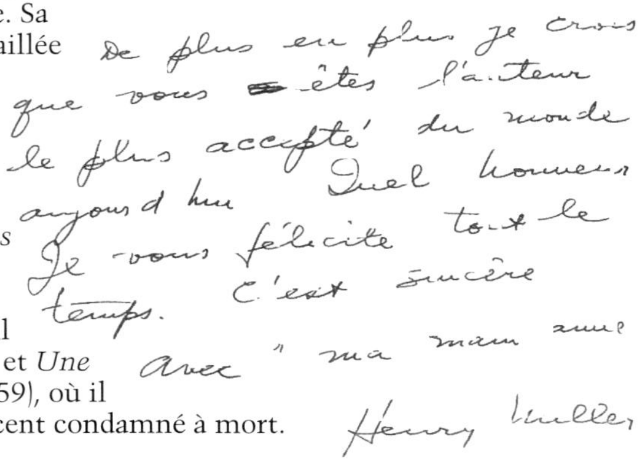

L'admiration d'écrivains aussi différents que Miller et Cocteau traduit la portée universelle de l'œuvre. D'Amado à Mac Orlan, d'autres partagent ce sentiment, faisant écho à l'opinion de Gide qui voyait en Simenon « un grand romancier, le plus grand peut-être et le plus vraiment romancier » de son temps.

La nostalgie de l'Europe

En 1954 sont rédigés *Maigret et la jeune morte*, *L'Horloger d'Everton*, *Le Grand Bob*, *Maigret chez le ministre* et *Les Témoins*. Simenon se sent vieillir et perçoit des fissures entre Denyse et lui. À la fin de l'année, il effectue pourtant avec elle un voyage en Angleterre prolongé par quelques jours à Paris. Ces indices laissent deviner l'attrait que l'Europe conserve pour lui. En effet, Simenon termine le 25 janvier 1955 *Maigret et le corps sans tête*, puis décide d'abandonner définitivement les États-Unis. Ayant débarqué le 26 mars, la famille s'installe début avril dans une villa de Mougins, La Gatounière, où sont écrits *La Boule noire*, *Maigret tend un piège* et *Les Complices*, avant d'occuper en octobre une demeure imposante à Cannes, Golden Gate. Là, Simenon termine le 8 novembre *En cas de malheur*. Quant à Tigy, fuyant la vie mondaine et les lumières du vedettariat, elle retourne vivre à Nieul.

21 mai 1955
Santo Sospir
251-28
— à Jean

Silence intolérable

venez déjeuner n'importe quel jour et à n'importe quelle heure.

Télégraphiez la veille

j'arrive demain avec épouse et famille

Je t'embrasse

Jean Cocteau

En 1951, Simenon est l'écrivain de langue française le plus traduit (31 traductions). En 1955, il a comptabilisé la sortie dans le monde de 80 de ses titres, soit plus d'un par semaine, l'édition française ne constituant plus qu'un cinquième de son chiffre d'affaires. Les tirages des Presses de la Cité sont en moyenne de 47 000 exemplaires par titre, mais les « Maigret » se vendent mieux que les autres romans. (*Maigret à New York* : 92 000 ; *Maigret chez le coroner* : 77 000 ; contre 35 000 pour *Lettre à mon juge*, 36 000 pour *La neige était sale*.) (Page de gauche, publicité NRF métro, Rue du Bac, 1951.)

En 1956 sont achevés à Cannes, en mars, *Un échec de Maigret*, puis, en avril, sur la lancée d'un voyage aux Pays-Bas et à Liège, *Le Petit Homme d'Arkhangelsk*, un roman très élaboré. Après des vacances en Suisse et quelques escapades à Paris, Simenon termine le 13 septembre *Maigret s'amuse* et, le 28 décembre, *Le Fils*. Denyse, elle, commence à donner des signes de dérèglement psychique. En réalité, le couple est en train de se déchirer, miné en outre par des abus de boisson.

Simenon et Gabin sur le plateau de tournage de *Maigret tend un piège*, de Jean Delannoy, en 1957. L'écrivain a beau prétendre à maintes reprises qu'il ne voit jamais les films adaptés de ses romans, il n'en déclare pas moins qu'il ne pourra plus « voir Maigret que sous les traits de Gabin » (*L'Express*, 6 février 1958). Ce sera encore le cas avec *Maigret et l'affaire Saint-Fiacre* (1959) du même Jean Delannoy et dans *Maigret voit rouge* (1963) de Gilles Grangier.

Un roman feutré, tout en pointillisme

Le « petit homme d'Arkhangelsk », Jonas Milk, natif de Russie et établi dans le Berry, a épousé Gina, qui fait des fugues. Lors d'une de celles-ci, on le soupçonne de l'avoir fait disparaître. Rejeté par la population qui lui reproche aussi d'être d'origine russe et juif de surcroît, Milk se pend. La petite ville où s'inscrit le drame est évoquée avec maîtrise : Simenon procède par pointillisme pour rendre son atmosphère et peindre ses habitants souvent mesquins, médiocres et conformistes. De même, la tragédie de Milk est contée sur un mode mineur dans ce roman feutré où règnent la résignation et l'accablement.

Les fictions de Simenon sont régies par un art consommé qui fait oublier la technique. On se rend vite compte, en effet, que le romancier manie avec brio les structures temporelles du récit, entre anticipations et retours en arrière où les émergences d'un passé contraignant conditionnent le présent. De même, le traitement de l'espace reçoit tous

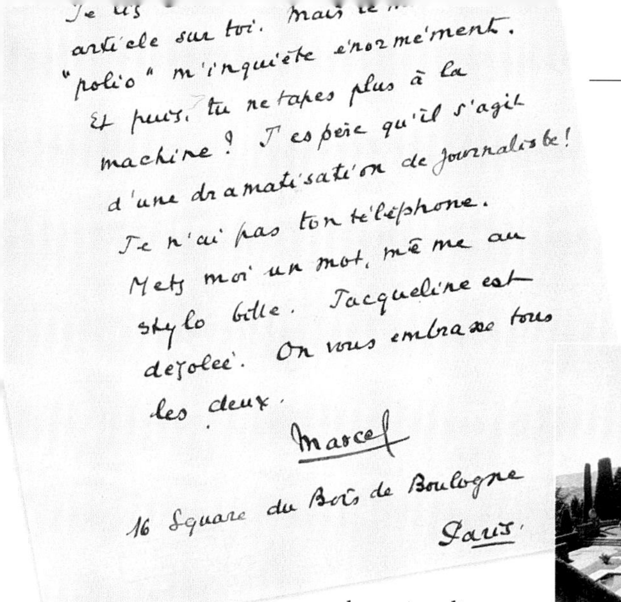
Je lis … Mais le …
article sur toi.
"polio" m'inquiète énormément.
Et puis, tu ne tapes plus à la
machine ? J'espère qu'il s'agit
d'une dramatisation de journaliste !
Je n'ai pas ton téléphone.
Mets moi un mot, même au
stylo bille. Jacqueline est
désolée. On vous embrasse tous
les deux.
Marcel
16 Square du Bois de Boulogne
Paris

Cette lettre de Pagnol atteint Simenon à l'époque où il occupe à Cannes l'opulente villa Golden Gate, avenue de la Reine-Élisabeth (ci-dessous). Durant cet intermède azuréen, l'inspiration ne tarit certes pas. Sur un plan personnel toutefois,

le luxe et la grande vie n'empêchent pas les fêlures du couple de devenir déchirures ; à cet égard, les titres des deux premiers romans rédigés à Cannes, *En cas de malheur* et *Un échec de Maigret*, prennent une valeur prémonitoire.

les soins d'un auteur qui, loin d'épuiser le réel à la façon d'un Balzac dont on l'a trop souvent indûment rapproché, le reconstitue par petites touches, qu'il s'agisse de noter tels détails descriptifs ou d'évoquer les sons, les odeurs, la luminosité, domaine des sensations dans lequel Simenon excelle. « On dit que je suis un écrivain réaliste, s'insurge-t-il. C'est absolument faux parce que, si j'étais réaliste, j'écrirais exactement les choses comme elles sont. Or il faut les déformer pour leur donner une plus grande vérité. »

L'utilisation de ces structures n'est pas la seule à témoigner de la virtuosité technique de Simenon. Ainsi, tout en portant à son maximum d'efficacité narrative le procédé de la focalisation interne, il ne néglige pas les domaines de l'intrigue et de la composition : même s'il a souvent déclaré qu'en commençant un roman il en ignorait la fin, on constate souvent la présence de divers motifs récurrents jalonnant le récit en fonction de son dénouement, au point que ces échos et ces reprises font penser aux subtils arcanes du nouveau roman.

AMIARD

Depuis la fin de la guerre, le cinéma ne cesse d'adapter Simenon : pas moins de trente-trois films entre 1945 et 1972, dont *Panique* (page précédente, à gauche), *L'Homme de la Tour Eiffel* (page précédente, à droite), *Maigret tend un piège* (page de gauche, en haut), *En cas de malheur* (page de gauche, en bas), *Le Bateau d'Émile* (ci-contre) et *La Vérité sur Bébé Donge*.

“Les personnages de Simenon sont tellement vivants, tellement burinés, tellement décrits qu'il n'y a pas de difficulté à travailler [...]. Les personnages vous sont apportés sur un plateau, il n'y a qu'à les saisir. C'est un écrivain cinématographique, le plus important, le plus riche que nous ayons eu en France.”

Claude Autant-Lara in *Simenon-Travelling*

“Lorsqu'on lit un de ses bouquins, trois choses sont très évidentes : la qualité de l'atmosphère – formidablement décrite –, la justesse des dialogues et la densité des personnages. Tous éléments indispensables et presque suffisants pour faire un bon film.”

Claude Chabrol, in *Le Vif-l'Express*, 11 juin 1993

Le style ascétique d'un grand romancier

Enfin, il serait erroné de tenir pour négligeable le style simple de Simenon, qui résulte davantage d'une ascèse scripturale que d'une volonté délibérée de facilité. Couramment qualifié de blanc, gris ou neutre, ce style sobre, sans fioritures, aux constructions simples, au vocabulaire limité, relève en effet d'une quête de dépouillement visant à bannir l'artifice, le pathos et, d'une manière générale, tout romantisme de bas étage. On a d'ailleurs peine à imaginer le travail d'émondage que s'est infligé pour parvenir à ce stade un auteur qui a montré dans ses écrits de jeunesse qu'il pouvait écrire tout autrement. Ce type d'écriture, qui n'empêche pas Simenon d'obtenir quand il le faut une émotion de type lyrique, a certainement contribué au succès universel d'un romancier qui n'a jamais caché l'influence de la musique sur le rythme de sa composition.

En dépit des apparences, la mésentente entre l'écrivain et sa femme règne le plus souvent au château d'Échandens (ci-dessus et ci-dessous, article du *MD Pictorial*).

Au bord du lac

Denyse étant devenue amoureuse du lac Léman, les Simenon font la navette, au début de 1957, entre Cannes et Lausanne où ils résident au Lausanne Palace. C'est pourtant à Golden Gate, à un moment où l'écrivain envisage un voyage en Israël qui ne se réalisera pas, que sont écrits en avril et juin *Le Nègre* et *Strip-Tease*. En juillet enfin, ils quittent Cannes pour s'établir au château d'Échandens, près de Lausanne, où ils demeurent jusqu'en décembre 1963. Là sont rédigés, dès 1957, *Maigret voyage*, *Le Président* et *Les Scrupules de Maigret*.

Dans la catégorie des romans « durs », *Le Nègre*, qui n'a rien d'exotique puisqu'il se passe en Picardie, met en scène un caractère velléitaire. « Un jour, je leur montrerai » : telle est la raison de vivre de l'insignifiant Théo Doineau. L'occasion se présente, mais le faible Théo n'a pas les moyens de se mettre en avant et il retombe dans ses ornières routinières.

Roman très dense racontant une ascension sociale finalement peu valorisante, *Le Passage de la ligne* est terminé le 27 février 1958, année durant laquelle Simenon préside le festival du film de Bruxelles du 28 au 31 mai. Il revient en juillet dans la capitale belge visiter l'Exposition internationale après avoir achevé *Dimanche* le 3 juillet et avant d'effectuer une croisière aux Pays-Bas, puis de séjourner à Venise. Retour en octobre vers la Belgique où Simenon prononce à Bruxelles, Charleroi et Liège une conférence intitulée « Le roman de l'homme » : s'y fait jour l'idée selon laquelle l'acte créateur, donc artistique et romanesque, trouve son origine, depuis la nuit des temps, dans l'éternelle peur de l'homme. Le 23 octobre, le romancier boucle *Maigret et les témoins récalcitrants*. En janvier 1959, il dissèque *La Vieille*, puis *Une confidence de Maigret* émouvante est achevée le 3 mai. Quatrième enfant de l'écrivain, Pierre Simenon naît le 26 mai. Son père termine *Maigret aux assises* le 23 novembre.

Au Festival de Cannes

Simenon se débarrasse, début 1960, d'un texte sur Balzac promis à la télévision, puis passe quelques jours à Londres avant d'écrire *L'Ours en peluche*. En mai, il préside le Festival de Cannes où il contribue à faire primer *La Dolce Vita* de Fellini, y rencontre celui-ci qui devient un ami, ainsi qu'Henry Miller, avec lequel il correspond depuis plusieurs années. En juin, il écrit *Maigret et les vieillards*, puis commence un journal qu'il tiendra jusqu'en 1963 et qui sera publié sous le titre *Quand j'étais vieux*. Après des vacances à Venise fin juillet et début août, Simenon subit une appendicectomie, puis passe sa convalescence au Trianon Palace de Versailles. Rentré chez lui, il termine le 12 octobre *Betty*, inspiré par une expérience versaillaise.

1961. Sont écrits en janvier *Maigret et le voleur paresseux*, en mars *Le Train*, un roman que Simenon porte en lui depuis la guerre, en juin *La Porte*, un drame de la jalousie vécu par un handicapé, et, après des vacances familiales suisses au Bürgenstock en juillet, *Maigret et les braves gens* en septembre. Au retour d'un voyage à Liège en octobre, le romancier rédige *Les Autres*. Le 14 décembre, une femme de chambre italienne de 35 ans, Teresa Sburelin, entre au service des Simenon : elle deviendra l'ultime compagne de l'écrivain.

Montrer l'« homme nu »

La rédaction de *Maigret et le client du samedi*, terminée le 27 février 1962, précède un voyage à Londres en mars. *Maigret et le clochard* et *La Colère de Maigret* sont achevés

Au lendemain d'une visite d'Henry Miller, entre la rédaction du *Train* et celle de *La Porte*, Simenon est photographié à Échandens par Robert Doisneau le 28 avril 1961. Le document montre l'écrivain face à une partie de sa nombreuse production.

Si l'écrivain accepte de présider en 1958 le festival du film de Bruxelles, puis en 1960 celui de Cannes (ci-contre, avec Jeanne Moreau et Federico Fellini), il ne s'implique pas davantage pour autant dans l'adaptation cinématographique de ses romans. Ainsi, lorsque Henri Verneuil, après *Le Fruit défendu*, se mêle d'adapter *Le Président* (1960) et dénature la sobre grandeur du roman, transformant la réflexion du héros sur le pouvoir et la vieillesse en un spectacle aux allures démagogiques et poujadistes, glorifiant en la personne du Président le pouvoir d'un seul, de l'homme fort qui refuse et méprise le jeu démocratique des partis, Simenon ne se formalise pas de cette trahison. Il sait depuis longtemps que le cinéma est coutumier du fait.

le 2 mai et le 19 juin, avant les vacances passées à nouveau au Bürgenstock. En septembre, un voyage à Paris permet à Simenon de se documenter pour son prochain roman, *Les Anneaux de Bicêtre*, écrit du 2 au 25 octobre, c'est-à-dire durant une période plus longue que d'habitude. Dans ce dernier roman, le directeur d'un grand journal parisien est atteint d'une thrombose qui entraîne une hémiplégie. À la faveur de son immobilité, le héros opère un retour sur lui-même qui le conduit à juger sans aménité sa vie professionnelle et privée. Étayé par une solide documentation médicale, le roman mêle à la méditation métaphysique et existentielle du héros une évocation réaliste de l'univers hospitalier perçu par le patient. Jamais peut-être Simenon n'est allé aussi loin dans sa tentative de montrer l'« homme nu ». Cette expérience du dénuement qui fait prendre conscience de la vanité d'une position sociale élevée était déjà présente, à divers niveaux, dans *Les Volets verts* (1950), *Le Président* (1958) ou *L'Ours en peluche* (1960) et sera évoquée à nouveau dans *La Prison* (1968) ou dans *Il y a encore des noisetiers* (1969).

« Descendre, spirale après spirale, l'escalier de l'être » : cet extrait de Bachelard figure en tête du manuscrit. Bien que l'écrivain l'ait fait disparaître de la version définitive, la citation, qui confère au titre son sens second, éclaire aussi le propos de celui qui n'a cessé de poursuivre une quête de l'homme dans ce qu'il a de plus profond. À cet égard, Simenon aurait pu reprendre à son compte cette réflexion qu'il prête dans *Maigret voyage* au plus célèbre de ses personnages : « Toute sa vie, il s'était efforcé d'oublier les différences de surface qui existent entre les hommes, de gratter le vernis pour découvrir, sous les apparences diverses, l'homme tout nu. » Il s'agit là d'une constante de l'œuvre, qui doit être perçue avant tout comme une recherche de la condition humaine. Même dans les romans dits policiers – où Simenon n'a pas hésité à infléchir les lois du genre en fonction de cette recherche –, il importe moins de savoir qui a tué que de savoir quel homme est l'assassin, quel homme était la victime et… qui nous sommes.

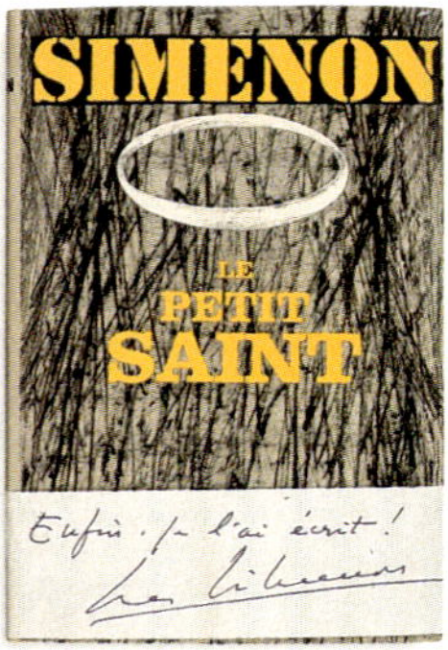

Le Petit Saint raconte surtout la jeunesse, pauvre mais heureuse, d'un peintre de génie pour qui tout est sujet d'émerveillement. Le roman s'attarde sur l'enfance et l'adolescence, période de maturation à laquelle ne cessera de se référer l'artiste, dont la carrière n'est évoquée que brièvement. Ce procédé illustre la théorie de l'auteur selon laquelle l'enfance explique l'homme. De même, le héros et son créateur appréhendent pareillement la réalité : « Ma mémoire, dira l'écrivain, est celle d'un impressionniste pour qui la vibration de l'air et ses ondulations déforment les images. » La création d'un personnage aussi serein est unique dans l'œuvre simenonienne. *L'Enterrement de Monsieur Bouvet* (1950) présente certes une autre vie réussie, mais elle est basée sur la fuite et le refus, non sur l'acceptation.

« Quand la maison est achevée, le malheur y pénètre »

Dans *Les Nolépitois*, deux êtres qui s'aiment sont séparés et se retrouvent ; en rédigeant cette nouvelle inspirée par un rêve de Denyse en janvier 1963, Simenon espère-t-il sauver son propre couple ? En mai et juin, il écrit *La Chambre bleue* et *Maigret et le fantôme* avant de passer les vacances au traditionnel Bürgenstock et d'écrire en septembre *L'Homme au petit chien*. Dès 1961, l'écrivain avait caressé le projet de faire construire une maison à sa convenance. Ce projet se concrétise par la vaste demeure d'Épalinges, dominant Lausanne, où Simenon vivra jusqu'en octobre 1972.

« Quand la maison est achevée, le malheur y pénètre », écrira Simenon à un ami. La dégradation de ses rapports avec Denyse s'accélère. Dès juin 1962,

celle-ci avait fréquenté une clinique psychiatrique. Son état continuant à se détériorer, elle y avait fait d'autres séjours en 1963. Elle y retourne le 21 avril 1964 pour ne plus résider à Épalinges, et les époux finiront par se séparer sans pourtant jamais divorcer. La production du romancier se ressent de ce malstrom d'amour-haine; deux romans seulement sont écrits en 1964, *Maigret se défend* en juillet et *Le Petit Saint* en octobre. Cette année-là, Denyse n'est pas la seule à quitter Épalinges : elle insiste pour que le romancier se sépare aussi de Boule, qui se met au service de Marc et de sa famille.

La demeure démesurée construite à Épalinges (à gauche), qui convoque tous les superlatifs avec ses vingt-six pièces, ses interphones, ses vingt et un téléphones, son infirmerie, son imposante piscine, aurait dû être celle du bonheur retrouvé. « Nous y avons bâti la maison de nos rêves », écrit Simenon à Jean Mambrino le 11 janvier 1965. Ce sera celle des rêves brisés puisque Denyse n'y vivra pratiquement pas.

Consécration : « Œuvres complètes » pour Simenon, statue pour Maigret

En janvier 1965, Simenon fait une chute, se fracture plusieurs côtes et est soigné par Teresa. C'est avec

Ci-dessous, Simenon à nouveau photographié par Doisneau en 1962.

elle, après avoir écrit en février et mars *La Patience de Maigret*, que l'écrivain part en avril à Florence pour faire découvrir la ville à Marie-Jo, dont l'adolescence s'avérera psychologiquement difficile. Après un séjour aux Pays-Bas en mai, *Le Train de Venise* est achevé le 3 juin. Une croisière en mer Noire fait retrouver à Simenon des lieux qu'il a connus jadis, mais le cœur n'y est plus.

Après *Le Confessionnal*, terminé le 21 octobre, puis des vacances à Crans-sur-Sierre, Simenon rédige *Maigret et l'affaire Nahour*, achevé le 8 février 1966, et *La Mort d'Auguste*, le 17 mars. Le mois suivant, il montre Paris à Marie-Jo et Pierre, puis accepte en mai la publication de ses œuvres complètes par les éditions suisses Rencontre – ce qui représente pour lui une consécration, mais n'implique nullement un quelconque pressentiment d'un prochain abandon de l'écriture. Un séjour estival à Royan précède le voyage à Delfzijl où est inaugurée le 3 septembre la statue de Maigret due à Pieter d'Hont. À l'époque, les chaînes de télévision envahissent Épalinges pour consacrer des émissions

Le 3 septembre 1966, quatre acteurs interprètes de Maigret à la télévision ont pris place aux côtés de Simenon lors de l'inauguration de la statue du commissaire à Delfzijl : l'Anglais Rupert Davies, l'Allemand Heinz Rühmann, l'Italien Gino Cervi et le Hollandais Jan Teulings. « C'est Rupert Davies [...] que j'ai trouvé le meilleur, confiait Simenon à Fenton Bresler. Je le mettrais à égalité avec Michel Simon. [...] C'était un homme charmant et il faisait tout pour se mettre dans la peau du rôle. »

à l'auteur qui écrit encore en 1966 *Le Chat*, évocation d'un enfer conjugal terminée le 5 octobre, et *Le Voleur de Maigret*, achevé le 11 novembre.

« Maigret hésite », ou la mise en abyme de l'œuvre

Le repos hivernal à Crans est suivi en 1967 d'un enchaînement d'obligations, notamment, en avril, une série de rencontres culturelles en Italie, signe de

Comme Balzac, tu réussis à nous plonger dans une réalité indéniable, une réalité résultant de ton don d'observer la vie sans t'arrêter à la surface

l'importance intellectuelle que lui accordera toujours ce pays. C'est du monde entier pourtant que Simenon reçoit un important courrier admiratif, curieux, critique ou importun. Il répond patiemment à chaque lettre, aux questions sur la narrativité d'un docte professeur norvégien comme à la naïve admiration d'une adolescente californienne ou d'un ouvrier marseillais. C'est donc le 27 juin seulement qu'est terminé *Le Déménagement* avant des vacances d'été à Vichy qui inspirent *Maigret à Vichy*, achevé le 11 septembre. C'est le moment où la télévision va populariser davantage encore le commissaire en diffusant le 14 octobre le premier épisode de la série des « Maigret » avec Jean Richard dans le rôle-titre. Simenon, pour sa part, boucle *La Prison* le 12 novembre, achève la rédaction de *Maigret hésite* le 30 janvier 1968 et le 29 avril, celle de *La Main*. Le romancier applaudit en mai l'action étudiante, puis se remet au travail : le 24 juin est terminé *L'Ami d'enfance de Maigret* et, le 13 octobre, *Il y a encore des noisetiers*, alors que les vacances d'été ont eu pour cadre La Baule.

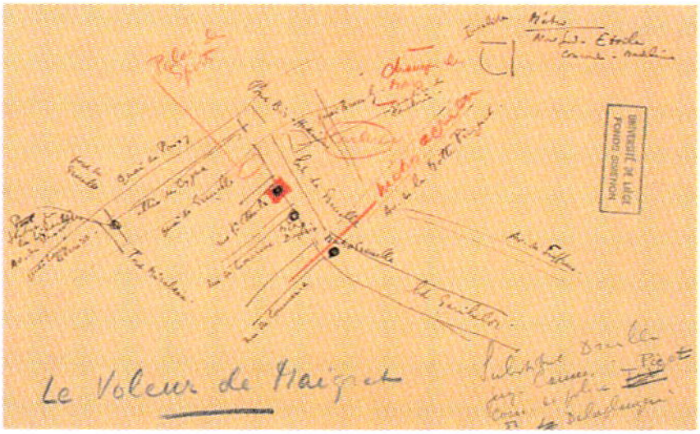

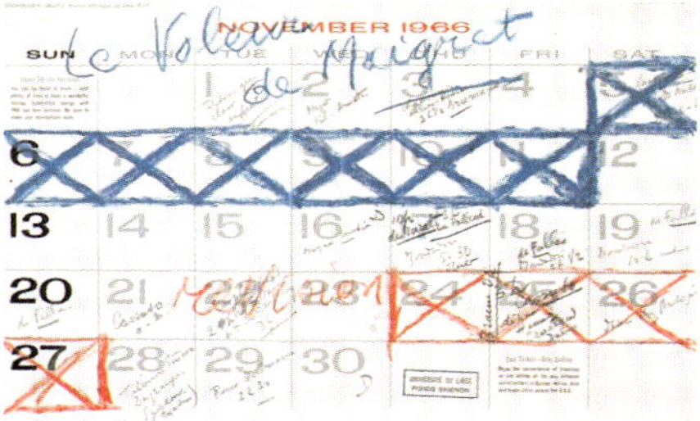

Le principal intérêt de *Maigret hésite* réside dans les discussions entre le héros et le commissaire au

Contrairement à Balzac auquel le compare son ami Renoir dans une lettre du 5 septembre 1967 (ci-dessous), Simenon boucle ses corrections le plus rapidement possible et corrige très peu ses écrits. La rédaction elle-même connaît un rythme pour le moins soutenu : un chapitre par jour, de bon matin. En témoignent les calendriers de ses romans (ci-dessus, celui du *Voleur de Maigret* et son plan préparatoire) où les croix bleues et rouges correspondent aux dates d'écriture et de révision.

THE CRIME OF INSPECTOR MAIGRET
GEORGES SIMENON

Мегрэ и Долговязая
Смерть Веллы
ЖОРЖ
СИМЕНОН

MAIGRET AND THE
SATURDAY CALLER
SIMENON

סימנון
מגרה
על פרשת
דרכים

Impressionnant et ingénieux, ce montage photographique réalisé par *Paris-Match* en juin 1970 ! Simenon semble y passer en revue divers interprètes de Maigret. Encore ne sont-ils pas tous ici… Il découvre ainsi successivement Pierre Renoir, Heinz Rühmann, Gino Cervi, Jean Richard, Jean Gabin, Albert Préjean, Michel Simon, le Russe Boris Tenine, Jan Teulings, Harry Baur et Charles Laughton.

Les traductions témoignent du succès universel du plus célèbre des personnages de Simenon, devenu mythique. Dès le début des années 1930, les premiers « Maigret » parus chez Fayard furent traduits aux États-Unis, en Angleterre, en Italie – qui avait déjà traduit des romans populaires des années 1920 –, en Espagne, en Norvège, au Portugal et au Japon. En 1939, des traductions de Simenon existent en dix-huit langues. L'estimation actuelle est d'une soixantaine de langues.

sujet de l'article du code pénal qui traite de la responsabilité des criminels. Ces entretiens laissant entendre que l'auteur du meurtre n'est pas coupable prolongent certaines conversations entre Maigret et son ami, le docteur Pardon, dans *Maigret tend un piège* (1955) ou *Une confidence de Maigret* (1959) par exemple. Ils font du roman la « mise en abyme » d'une bonne partie de l'œuvre où est souvent posé le problème de la responsabilité en matière criminelle, comme en témoignent notamment *Les Scrupules de Maigret* (1958) et *Maigret et le tueur* (1969). *Maigret hésite* n'est pas le seul roman de Simenon où la police, avertie d'un meurtre imminent, ne parvient pas à l'éviter ; cette carence jalonne l'œuvre, de *L'Affaire Saint-Fiacre* (1932) à *La Folle de Maigret* (1970), en passant par *Signé Picpus* (1944), *Maigret et son mort* (1948) et *Les Scrupules de Maigret*.

Maigret, encore et toujours...

Après avoir terminé *Maigret et le tueur* le 21 avril 1969, Simenon rend visite à sa mère malade dans la maison de repos de Fouron-le-Comte,

Les notes préparatoires concernant les personnages de *Victor* (ci-dessous) laissent à jamais le témoignage de la fin de carrière du romancier.

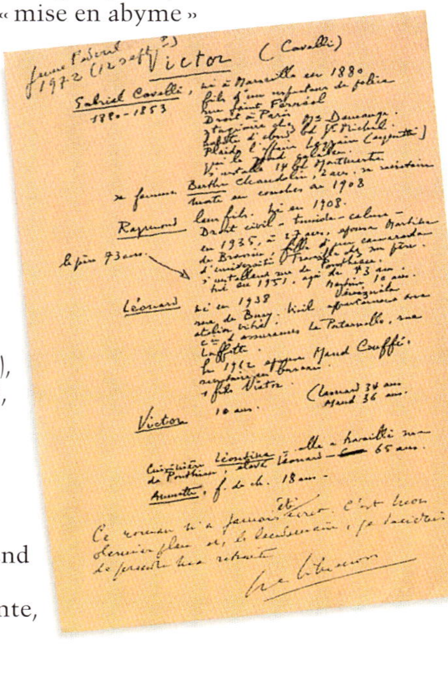

près de Liège, où elle a été admise l'année précédente. Il achève *Novembre* le 19 juin, avant de reprendre le chemin de Fouron-le-Comte en août et de mettre la dernière main à *Maigret et le marchand de vin* le 29 septembre. *Le Riche Homme* est terminé le 9 mars 1970 ; *La Folle de Maigret*, le 7 mai ; *La Disparition d'Odile*, le 4 octobre. Henriette Simenon meurt le 8 décembre à l'hôpital de Bavière, alors que son fils est à son chevet depuis plusieurs jours. Après le traditionnel séjour à Crans-sur-Sierre, *Maigret et l'homme tout seul* est achevé le 7 février 1971 ; puis viennent *La Cage de verre* le 17 mars, *Maigret et l'indicateur* le 11 juin et *Les Innocents* le 11 octobre, suivant des vacances d'été à La Baule.

De tous ces interprètes de Maigret, au cinéma puis à la télévision, Simenon dira : « Jean Richard est […] franchement le pire. » (De gauche à droite, Harry Baur, Charles Laughton, Michel Simon, Jean Gabin, Jean Richard, Bruno Crémer, et ci-dessous, le Maigret japonais, Kinya Aikana.)

… jusqu'au dernier

Quand il termine, le 11 février 1972, *Maigret et Monsieur Charles*, Simenon vient de rédiger l'ouvrage marquant la fin de sa prolifique production romanesque : cent quatre-vingt-douze romans et cent cinquante-cinq nouvelles signés de son nom. Le 18 septembre, voulant entreprendre *Victor*, il se rend dans son bureau où il prend des notes sur une traditionnelle enveloppe jaune. Il ne commencera jamais la rédaction du roman, et le lendemain, il annonce à Teresa sa décision de ne plus écrire. Peu après, il fait supprimer sur ses papiers d'identité sa profession de romancier.

La femme est au centre de la recherche humaine à laquelle s'est livré Simenon, tout comme elle occupe une position primordiale dans sa vie et son univers. Lors des voyages des années 1930, il braque partout sur elle son objectif, qu'il s'agisse de travailleuses de Charleroi (ci-contre) ou de filles faciles de Guayaquil (ci-dessous). De même, ses photos fixent le souvenir de jolies Slaves d'Odessa, d'Africaines à la fascinante beauté altière ou d'envoûtantes Tahitiennes.

En posant la dernière pierre de son imposant édifice romanesque, ce prodigieux raconteur d'histoires est-il conscient d'avoir bâti un univers imaginaire hors du commun par son étendue et sa profondeur, un univers où chaque roman répond à un autre à la façon d'un écho prolongé à l'infini ?

Un théâtre d'ombre et de lumière

L'univers de Simenon, c'est celui de la fuite, de la marginalité, du drame, du suicide, du meurtre ; c'est un espace tragique où les humiliés côtoient les offensés ; c'est le domaine du malaise, du vide intérieur, de la solitude, des échappatoires.

L'univers de Simenon, c'est celui de protagonistes qui vont jusqu'au bout d'eux-mêmes, un théâtre d'ombre et de lumière où la chute avoisine parfois la rédemption, un monde où le héros, dépouillé de sa façade sociale artificielle, apprend, parfois au prix de sa vie, que « le métier d'homme est difficile ».

L'univers de Simenon, c'est, nouvelle Anabase, celui de ces dix mille… personnages enfantés dans la douleur de la création, depuis le plus modeste d'entre eux jusqu'au plus illustre, ce commissaire

“Au fond, à part deux exceptions, je n'ai jamais été ce qu'on appelle d'habitude amoureux d'une femme déterminée. J'étais amoureux de toutes, curieux de toutes.”

La Femme endormie

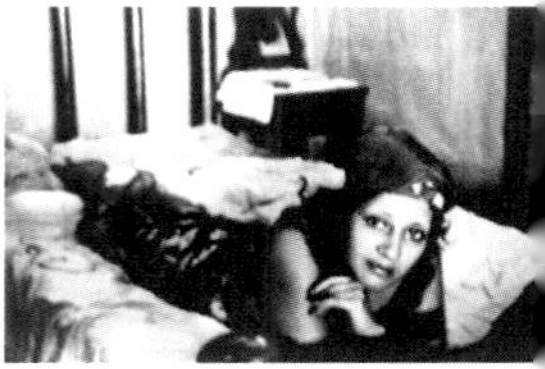

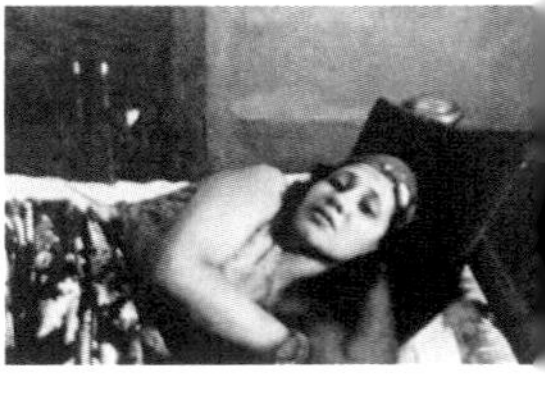

Maigret, notre prochain, ce policier des âmes, avec ses défauts et ses qualités, avec son intuition, sa morale de la compréhension, son sens inné de la justice immanente et sa manière d'enquêter qui semble calquée sur la façon d'écrire de son créateur, ce Maigret auquel l'écrivain a fini par ressembler.

L'univers de Simenon, c'est celui de l'inconscient, inconscient des personnages et d'un créateur qui proclame que tous ses romans sont des fantasmes de son enfance. C'est enfin le monde où le romancier nous entraîne, en un perpétuel mouvement du réel à l'imaginaire, du souvenir à la (re)création, du terreau fécond d'Outremeuse aux collines du Connecticut, des rues à arcades de La Rochelle aux lagons polynésiens, des bouges de Fécamp à ceux de Panamá, des brumes du Nord à l'éclat méditerranéen, de la pluie nivernaise à celle de Buenaventura, du pétillant soleil ligérien à celui, écrasant, de l'Arizona, du quai des Orfèvres au boulevard des Batignolles, de la quiétude feutrée du Marais à la fièvre des Grands Boulevards... Lieux de la mémoire devenus, par une étrange alchimie, lieux de notre mémoire mentale et livresque.

De sa naissance au bord de la Meuse à sa mort sur les rives du lac Léman, la vie de Simenon est imprégnée d'eau. Faut-il rappeler son rêve de jeunesse concrétisé par ses bateaux, le *Ginette* et l'*Ostrogoth* ? Présent dans ses romans sous de multiples formes, de la pluie aux canaux, de la mer aux larmes, l'élément liquide fait de la plupart d'entre eux des histoires d'eaux. Aussi cette photo prise par l'écrivain dans le port de Concarneau au début des années 1930 est-elle emblématique d'un motif dominant de l'œuvre, voire du plus marquant.

La décision de 1972 d'abandonner l'écriture romanesque n'est pas un refus de s'exprimer : à partir de l'année suivante, Simenon enregistre devant un magnétophone des textes de souvenirs et de réflexions qui constitueront les vingt et un volumes de *Dictées* et la matière d'une *Lettre à ma mère*. Pour des raisons d'ordre privé, il se met ensuite à écrire en 1980 ses *Mémoires intimes*, le plus long de ses ouvrages. S'établit alors un long silence jusqu'à sa mort, en 1989.

CHAPITRE 5

RETRAITE

Même si le romancier est retraité, ses œuvres continuent à être adaptées au cinéma, parfois de manière excellente, comme avec *Équateur* (1982) de Gainsbourg, adaptation du *Coup de lune*, voire exemplaire avec *Les Fantômes du chapelier* (1981) et *Betty* (1991) de Chabrol qui respectent l'esprit et la lettre de Simenon.

« Dictées » dans la « petite maison rose »

La décision d'abandonner l'écriture s'accompagne d'une autre : celle de quitter la maison d'Épalinges : le 27 octobre 1972, Simenon s'installe avec Teresa et son fils Pierre au huitième étage d'une tour de Lausanne, au n° 155 de l'avenue de Cour, avant d'occuper, le 6 février 1974, une maison située au pied de la tour, au n° 12 de l'avenue des Figuiers. Cette habitation, qu'il appelle sa « petite maison rose », sera son dernier domicile.

La carrière du romancier s'est donc terminée en 1972, mais peut-on renoncer à s'exprimer quand on s'appelle Simenon ? Le 13 février 1973, à soixante-dix ans et un an après *Maigret et Monsieur Charles*, il commence à enregistrer des réflexions inspirées par sa vie quotidienne, l'actualité ou ses souvenirs. Jusqu'au 19 octobre 1979, il se livre ainsi de manière intermittente, n'écrivant plus, mais parlant. Ces propos ont été publiés en vingt et un volumes sous le titre général *Mes dictées*. La critique a souvent été dure envers ces textes parfois répétitifs et exprimés sans grand souci esthétique, au sujet desquels Angelo Rinaldi a pu parler du « niveau zéro de la pensée ». En réalité, il faut prendre les *Dictées* pour ce qu'elles sont : un « document humain » (Maurice Piron) où un homme veut montrer ce qu'il est. On y voit Simenon s'élever contre le nationalisme, le patriotisme, le capitalisme, la bureaucratie, l'autorité, les institutions, la papauté, le mariage, la technologie ou l'industrialisation : bref, on prend conscience, à la lecture de ces volumes, de l'existence d'un Simenon anarchiste non violent. En avril 1974, dans *Lettre à ma mère*, il tente de définir les rapports ambigus qu'il a entretenus avec elle.

Si l'écrivain ne revient plus dans sa ville natale, il lègue à l'université de Liège, le 8 juin 1976, ses archives littéraires, qui forment aujourd'hui le Fonds Simenon. Ce legs est dû à l'action du professeur Maurice Piron : sur sa proposition, Simenon était devenu le 22 mai 1973 docteur

❝Nous ne nous sommes jamais aimés de ton vivant, tu le sais bien. Tous les deux, nous avons fait semblant.❞

Lettre à ma mère

«JE N'ÉCRIRAI PLUS»

honoris causa de l'université, les deux hommes s'étaient rencontrés, appréciés et un Centre d'Études Georges Simenon avait été créé.

Vivre avec Simenon

Durant cette période, Simenon ne s'éloigne guère de Lausanne. Il passe souvent ses vacances dans une maison de repos proche de Montreux ou à l'hôtel du Débarcadère de Saint-Sulpice, non loin de chez lui, exception faite, en 1976, d'un séjour au Royal-Palace d'Évian, de l'autre côté du lac. Quelques problèmes de santé le troublent sans doute moins que la parution, en 1978, d'*Un oiseau pour le chat*, un livre polémique dans lequel Denyse raconte – ou fait raconter – à sa façon sa vie avec l'écrivain.

La vieillesse de Simenon est plus ébranlée encore par le suicide de sa fille, qui met fin à ses jours à

La presse annonce au monde entier la décision de 1972. Même après cette date, Simenon, qui a toujours

entretenu les meilleurs rapports avec les journalistes, considérés comme des confrères, ne refuse jamais d'être interviewé, fût-ce dans sa « petite maison rose » (ci-contre). En 1977, *L'Express* organise notamment une rencontre entre Fellini et Simenon, qui s'estiment frères. Au cours de cet entretien paru le 21 février, Simenon lâche : « J'ai eu 10 000 femmes depuis l'âge de 13 ans et demi », déclaration qui fera aussi le tour du monde. On retiendra moins que l'écrivain y confie avoir pleuré en voyant *Casanova*, ou encore cette phrase : « Ce n'est pas parce qu'on cherche un contact humain qu'on le trouve. On trouve surtout le vide. »

Paris le 19 mai 1978. Ce suicide et l'attaque portée par Denyse amènent Simenon à reprendre la plume – oui : la plume, lui qui s'est toujours voulu un adepte de la machine à écrire ! – en février 1980 et à rédiger pendant presque un an ses *Mémoires intimes*, publiées à la fin de 1981.

Cet ouvrage autobiographique retraçant la vie familiale et privée de l'auteur n'est pourtant pas seulement une œuvre de circonstance. Outre le Simenon époux et père attentionné envers ses enfants, on y découvre un homme amoureux de la vie sous toutes ses formes, un homme à la curiosité insatiable, aux activités inlassables, à l'appétit démesuré, au point que l'on se demande où il a pris le temps d'écrire tellement. Même si ce qui est raconté par le mémorialiste ne correspond pas toujours à une vérité objective, le document est exceptionnel dans la mesure où Simenon, qui se voulait « un homme comme un autre », entend se montrer dans toute sa vérité, tel qu'il se croit être.

Cependant, la part d'ombre qui entoure le « mystère Simenon » ne disparaît pas avec les *Mémoires intimes* : certes, l'homme s'explique sur son comportement, mais son moi profond, avec ses obsessions et ses fantasmes, se révèle davantage au lecteur des romans qu'à celui de l'autobiographie. De plus, celle-ci ne permet en aucune façon de comprendre en quoi l'homme se double d'un romancier exceptionnel. Simenon eût-il consacré une telle somme à expliquer comment, près de deux cents fois, il a créé des histoires « où se reconnaît l'humanité » entière, peut-être

❝J'ai couru après un rêve que je savais impossible : je me sentais « femme » pour toi, mon but de « devenir » n'était que par rapport à toi. Te retrouver plus jeune, jeune homme d'avant ma naissance, ou petit garçon que j'aurais conçu. J'aurais pu me reconnaître en toi, m'épanouir dans le reflet de tes yeux. « Save me Daddy » – I'm dying […].❞

Marie-Jo, la fille de Simenon, en 1978

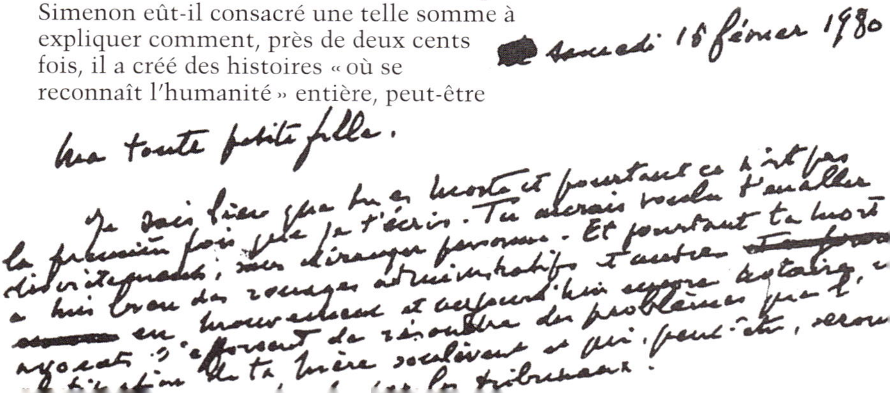
samedi 16 février 1980

Ma toute petite fille.

Je sais bien que tu es morte et pourtant ce n'est pas la première fois que je t'écris. Tu aurais voulu t'en aller sans déranger personne. Et pourtant ta mort …

aurions-nous eu la chance de percer du même coup « l'un des secrets de cette force mystérieuse qui s'appelle le génie » (Maurice Piron). Mais l'écrivain était-il capable d'un tel détachement par rapport à son œuvre, d'une telle analyse de son acte créateur ?

« Enfin, je vais dormir »

Peu avant la sortie des *Mémoires intimes* paraît un autre ouvrage pamphlétaire de Denyse, *Le Phallus d'or*, signé Odile Dessane. Cette fois, son mari se tait : la postérité jugera et ses *Mémoires intimes* seront son testament public, « la plus belle des biographies qu'on écrira jamais sur Simenon » (Paul Mercier).

> Je demande beaucoup de choses à Dieu, mais je suis incapable d'atteindre l'égalité entre toutes ces prières. Il y a toujours, quand je pense à notre destinée humaine, un article qui surnage. C'est celui de notre commune amitié.

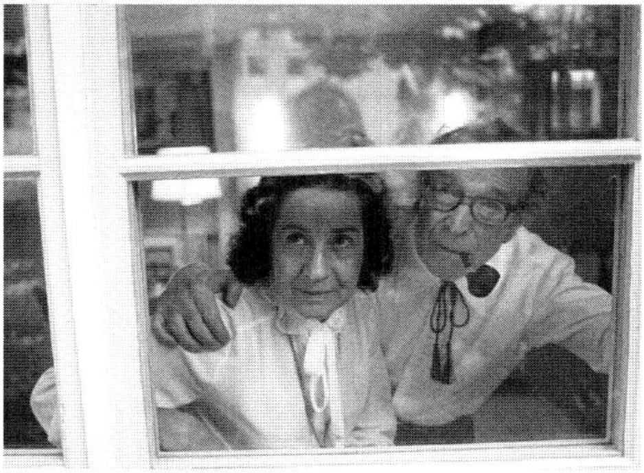

Rien ne dit pourtant que, le livre publié, l'écrivain retrouve sa sérénité, ne fût-ce que partiellement.

Le 17 décembre 1984, il est opéré avec succès d'une tumeur au cerveau. On ne sait comment il réagit, l'année suivante, au décès de Tigy, morte le 24 juin. Sa propre santé, cependant, se détériore : en 1987, il doit se résoudre à se déplacer en fauteuil roulant. C'est le début de la fin ; une vie tourbillonnante se clôt dans un repli sur soi-même. Le 4 septembre 1989, la main dans celle de Teresa, Simenon lui murmure : « Enfin, je vais dormir », le dernier mot, avant l'éternel silence, de celui qui en a tant écrit. Ses cendres rejoindront celles de Marie-Jo sous le grand cèdre du jardin, alors qu'éclate dans le monde entier, en guise d'éloge funèbre, un étonnant concert unanime de louanges médiatiques.

Alors que Renoir, dans sa dernière lettre du 17 mars 1978, insiste sur leur « commune amitié », Simenon tente de définir ce qu'il éprouve pour Teresa : « Je cherche le nom à donner au contraire du mot solitude. J'aimerais en trouver un qui ne soit pas le mot amour, par trop galvaudé et trop incomplet. [...] On vit ensemble tous les moments de la journée et de la nuit. On pourrait presque se passer de parler car chacun a compris avant que l'autre ait ouvert la bouche. N'être plus seul au monde ! » (*Un homme comme un autre*)

Prise par Daniel Filipacchi dans une rue du quartier d'Outremeuse lors du bref séjour à Liège de mai 1952, cette photographie suggère la permanence de l'esprit d'enfance chez l'adulte à laquelle Simenon était très sensible.

“Je sais, comme tout le monde, que c'est de l'enfance et de l'adolescence que nous tirons le principal de notre acquis.
Mais, en ce qui me concerne, ce ne sont pas tant les souvenirs qui comptent.
En réalité, je suis resté, à soixante-dix ans, le petit garçon et l'adolescent que j'ai été, et je continue à penser, à sentir, à comprendre comme un petit garçon. [...]
Certes, j'ai de multiples souvenirs d'enfance, d'une précision peut-être assez exceptionnelle.
Mais ce ne sont pas ces souvenirs-là qui comptent : c'est l'être que je suis resté. [...]
L'important, à mes yeux, c'est que je ne sois jamais devenu une grande personne et que mes réactions soient les mêmes que lorsque j'avais moins de quinze ou seize ans. [...] À soixante-dix ans j'agis, je pense, je me comporte comme l'enfant d'Outremeuse.”

Un homme comme un autre

TÉMOIGNAGES ET DOCUMENTS

« J'écrirai mon premier vrai roman à 40 ans »

Très touché par deux lettres consécutives d'André Gide dans lesquelles celui-ci exprime son intérêt et sa curiosité pour une œuvre qui suscite son admiration, Simenon répond, en janvier 1939, par une longue lettre-confession, où il fait état de son apprentissage de l'écriture romanesque. On en trouve le prolongement dans la plupart de ses lettres écrites après 1945 et son installation aux États-Unis.

« Écrire le roman de ceux qui vivent et ne pensent pas »

[Nieul-sur-Mer, mi-janvier 1939]

Mon cher Maître et grand ami,

[…] Est-ce que le seul terrain défendu de la connaissance n'est pas soi-même ? C'est souvent ma pensée, en tout cas, et c'est ce qui fait que souvent je triche avec moi-même. Je fais semblant de ne pas savoir pour ne pas défier le destin.

[…] À douze ans, je voulais être prêtre ou officier – le seul moyen, me semblait-il, d'écrire tout en gagnant sa vie. Je finirais Xavier de Maistre et Massillon.

À seize ans j'annonçais en traversant le pont des Arches une nuit de brouillard : à quarante ans je serai ministre ou académicien (il n'en a jamais été question, bien entendu).

Et depuis l'âge de dix-huit ans, je sais que je veux être un jour un romancier complet et je sais que l'œuvre d'un romancier ne commence pas avant quarante ans au bas mot – je dis d'un romancier et non d'un poète.

Dès cet âge-là j'ai choisi ma voie, en toute connaissance de cause, d'accord avec ma femme qui seule a connu cette progression régulière.

D'abord le métier. *Gâcher du plâtre*. Je me suis donné dix ans pour cela. Au début, il m'arrivait, après journée, c'est-à-dire après mes romans populaires, que j'écrivais à la cadence d'un par trois jours, de *me mettre en transes* et d'écrire un conte ou une nouvelle. Je n'ai jamais essayé de les publier. J'en ai de pleins dossiers. Je savais ce qu'il y manquait. Et je savais ce que je voulais faire un jour – *ce que je n'ai pas encore fait.*

Je me permets de vous adresser ci-joint une petite nouvelle de cette époque, « M. Gustave », que je vous demande de me retourner car c'est un souvenir. Vous verrez que j'étais déjà hanté par un problème que je poursuis toujours : les trois dimensions – le passé, le présent et l'avenir nouant étroitement une seule action – avec une densité d'atmosphère et de vie complète que je n'atteignais pas et que je n'ai pas atteinte encore.

[…] [Ces nouvelles] m'ont montré ce qui me manquait. Entrer dans la peau de *n'importe quel homme*. Certains m'étaient perméables, d'autres pas. Et tandis que dans mes romans populaires (je me demande comment ils ont été acceptés) je m'ingéniais à apprendre ici le dialogue, là tel raccourci, là tel genre d'action… je me promettais que la seconde étape serait d'apprendre à vivre.

J'ai attendu près de dix ans. Pour vivre beaucoup de vies, très vite, il me fallait beaucoup d'argent.

À vingt ans j'avais écrit : – Je publierai mon premier roman à trente ans.

À trente ans je décidais : – Je vais écrire pour vivre, pour apprendre la vie, des romans semi-littéraires et j'écrirai mon premier vrai roman à quarante ans.

J'en ai trente-six aujourd'hui. Je suis un tout petit peu en avance, mais pas tant qu'il y paraît car je suis encore loin du compte.

La formule policière me permettait de toucher et le grand public et l'argent – et d'étudier mon métier dans les conditions les plus faciles c'est-à-dire avec un *meneur de jeu*.

Troisième période. Après dix-huit romans policiers, j'en suis las – je me crois plus fort et je supprime le meneur de jeu, soit Maigret. Ce sont : *Le Coup de lune*, *L'Âne-Rouge*, *Les Gens d'en face*, *Le Haut Mal*, etc.

Mais je suis encore dans un cadre étroit. J'ai besoin de *support* ; d'une grosse action. Je ne peux retenir l'attention que par une histoire dramatique.

Et surtout je n'arrive à porter qu'un personnage à la fois ! Je crois que c'est ici la clé de tout mon effort et, parfois, de préférences qui peuvent paraître étranges. Avant d'écrire les grands romans que je me propose d'écrire, je *veux* être en pleine possession de mon métier et j'imagine mal Sébastien Bach ayant à lutter contre des questions techniques. Or, elles sont aussi complexes pour le roman (à mon sens) que pour la musique ou la peinture. On dit en peinture *qu'un bras ne vit pas*. Il y a tant de bras et même de têtes qui ne vivent pas en littérature.

[…] Je m'emballe. Je parle ex-cathedra, mais c'est toute ma vie que je défends de la sorte, car si j'ai tort je l'ai perdue. j'ai perdu en tout cas les dix ans pendant lesquels, avec le roman populaire, j'ai eu l'illusion d'apprendre mon métier de gâcheur de plâtre – et les dix autres années ou presque pendant lesquelles j'ai voulu vivre coûte que coûte *toutes les vies possibles*.

Pour ne pas faire de documentaire. Pour ne pas avoir à étudier le personnage qui me manque. Pour qu'au moment voulu, dans mon bureau, dix personnages pour un soient là le moment venu.

Et surtout pour ne pas les avoir *observés*. J'ai horreur de l'observation. Il faut *essayer*. *Sentir*. Avoir boxé, menti, j'allais écrire volé. Avoir tout fait, non à fond mais assez pour comprendre.

[…] Il y a un mot qui nous est familier à ma femme et à moi : « me mettre en transes ».

C'est-à-dire me neutraliser d'abord, oublier tout mon moi, tous mes soucis pour trouver soudain, dans le fatras du souvenir, le personnage qui va m'intéresser. Cela dure quelquefois une heure, quelquefois deux jours, selon les tracas du moment, le climat, etc. Plus vite l'hiver que l'été, je ne sais pas pourquoi.

Le roman peut commencer car je pars sur un minimum d'action. Mais la difficulté c'est, pendant le nombre de jours que durera l'action, de rester *dans le bain*.

Plus de vie intérieure ni extérieure. Rien qu'une vie physique. Et, du matin au soir, la hantise, avec de rares oasis que sont des parties de cartes qui *neutralisent*.

Une sorte d'abrutissement volontaire, intégral.

Encore un mot du ménage : *l'État de Grâce*. Y rester, coûte que coûte. Si je suis parti sur un air de Bach, il faut qu'on me le joue chaque jour à la même heure. Rien ne peut plus changer dans l'ordonnance des journées. Le moindre imprévu risque de flanquer tout par terre. Plus de courrier ni de téléphone.

Deux heures seulement, le matin, à jeun, pour écrire. Mais la discipline, la manie le reste du temps.

[…] Sacrebleu ! Je me crève depuis des années à essayer de faire dire un mot juste à un fermier, à un pêcheur, à n'importe qui. Il m'aurait été facile de faire parler des gens comme moi. Le personnage compliqué est le plus facile puisque l'écrivain, étant a priori compliqué, le sent et le comprend mieux que n'importe quel autre.

Mais écrire le roman de ceux qui vivent et ne pensent pas – ce que nous appelons penser !

[…] Le roman commencé, je suis mon personnage, je vis sa vie. Je travaille deux heures par jour. Je vomis encore comme à mes débuts quand j'écrivais M. Gustave. J'en suis abruti et *vidé*. Je dors. Je mange. J'attends le moment de me replonger dans le bain.

C'est tout.

Après, il m'est impossible de changer une page. On me l'a assez reproché. J'aurais voulu, moi aussi, être capable de fignoler. Mais, comme je ne sais pas comment c'est fait, je sais encore moins comment ça peut se réparer.

C'est réussi ou raté. Mais c'est comme ça et je n'y peux rien.

[…] La preuve c'est qu'un roman fini j'oublie jusqu'au nom des personnages et que je n'en garde que quelques visages – comme le lecteur sans doute.

L'intelligence me fait, m'a toujours fait horriblement peur. Il m'arrive de penser que c'est par vengeance que les dieux l'ont donnée à l'homme. Je m'en méfie, j'essaie de sentir plutôt que de penser. Ou plutôt de penser avec… (?) et voilà ! Je serais bien en peine de dire avec quoi ! Un tableau de Rembrandt, de Renoir… Une petite pièce pour clavecin ou pour violon que Bach *pissait* pour apprendre la musique à ses enfants.

Vous voyez combien c'est vague, encore informe. Et que j'ai besoin encore d'années et d'années pour mettre tout cela au point […].

Georges Simenon André Gide,
… sans trop de pudeur. Correspondance
1938-1950, Omnibus, Paris, 1999

« Je ne cherche, au fond, que l'homme tout nu »

Tucson – Arizona
Lundi 29 mars 1948

Mon cher Maître,

[…] J'ai terminé il y a juste une semaine mon roman sur le titre duquel j'hésite encore. J'avais écrit : *La Neige sale*. Cela me paraît trop romantique. Je crois que je me déciderai pour *M. Holst*. Trois cents pages dactylographiées. Donc un *long* roman. Mais est-ce un grand roman ? Une fois encore j'y suis pas à pas un personnage principal et je me rends compte que, ce faisant, je décourage beaucoup de ceux qui veulent bien me faire confiance. Mais c'est plus fort que moi. Il m'arrive de commencer autrement et de bifurquer tout de suite. Mon seul essai, en somme, a été justement *Le Testament Donadieu* et, justement, à cause de ça, je l'ai toujours considéré comme un roman raté.
Me permettez-vous d'essayer de m'expliquer à ce sujet – je sais que

mes explications sont toujours un peu confuses, un peu naïves, mais j'aimerais essayer de faire le point. Je l'avais déjà essayé dans un numéro de *Confluences* consacré au roman. Je distinguais, comme tout le monde sans doute, dans le domaine du roman pur (non didactique, non philosophique, historique, etc.) deux tendances : le roman-chronique et le roman-crise. Le roman-chronique à la façon de Proust, de Zola, de Martin du Gard, des

Américains du début du siècle (Dreiser, etc.) et le roman-crise qui, à mon avis, se rapproche davantage de la tragédie, à la façon de Steinbeck et de tant d'autres (dont assez peu de Français). Mais tout cela doit avoir déjà été dit et si je ne le sais pas c'est que je ne lis pas les revues. Or, si j'ai toujours rêvé d'écrire un roman-chronique – et si tous les critiques m'y poussent – je ne m'y sens pas à l'aise. J'éprouve inconsciemment le besoin de ramasser, de concentrer, de pousser tout de suite mon ou mes personnages au paroxysme. Peut-être par faiblesse ? Peut-être aussi parce que le roman-chronique est fatalement un roman d'époque, un roman de « mœurs », et que cela ne m'intéresse pas, que je ne cherche, au fond, que l'homme tout nu, malgré la fameuse atmosphère, qui est d'ailleurs aussi indifférente au temps que possible.

J'ai l'air de plaider, mon cher Maître, mais je ne fais en réalité que chercher. Et justement – on me le reproche aussi –, si je prends des hommes très quelconques, c'est que pour moi ils représentent davantage *l'homme* qu'un normalien, un général, un dictateur, un savant, un génie quelconque. Et si mes personnages *ratent*, c'est que l'homme rate, fatalement. Il rate consciemment ou inconsciemment. C'est même à mes yeux, le seul drame : la disproportion entre ce que l'homme voudrait, pourrait être, entre ses aspirations et ses possibilités. […] La seule issue, c'est la sérénité – ou la sainteté. Et je n'y suis pas encore. J'ai cependant hâte de connaître vos réactions à la lecture du dernier roman écrit et, si vous le permettez, je demanderai à Nielsen de vous en envoyer un jeu d'épreuves, comme le faisait Gallimard.

[…] Au cas – je ne l'ose pas l'espérer – où vous aimeriez vraiment ce livre, je vous demanderais la permission de vous le dédier. C'est une chose que je n'ai jamais faite – sauf pour les toubibs qui m'ont rassuré quand j'ai cru que mon cœur flanchait. C'est peut-être passé de mode. Ce serait pourtant un honneur pour moi – et une joie sentimentale – d'écrire votre nom en tête d'un de mes livres. J'attendrai pour cela que l'un d'eux soit à point… Et que vous me le disiez […].

Ibidem

De Max Jacob à Federico Fellini

Retenus parmi des milliers de lettres reçues tout au long de sa carrière par Simenon, ces affectueux témoignages expriment certes l'admiration, mais caractérisent en même temps l'art du romancier tel qu'il est ressenti par d'autres créateurs. Quand Mac Orlan évoque la « poésie humaine » de l'œuvre ou quand Martin du Gard voit en Simenon « un fastueux vagabond », ils apportent une fois de plus la preuve que l'artiste est le mieux placé pour apprécier un autre artiste.

Max Jacob, 13 avril 1933

Monsieur,
Ne me croyez pas grand clerc en littérature. Je n'ai jamais pu savoir à quoi l'on reconnaît un roman bien fait (comme on dit) d'un roman mal fait. Le dernier livre que vous publiez me plaît énormément comme tout ce que vous publiez. Je retrouve le même enthousiasme qui, il y a deux ou trois ans, me fit vous prôner partout et vous faire lire autour de moi. Ce qui me plaît en vous c'est « l'homme dans la foule », cette manière unique de voir l'être dans la fourmilière humaine, qui ne peut venir que d'un très grand esprit, supérieur encore à son ouvrage, pour grand que soit celui-ci.

Je me suis beaucoup informé de vous : on m'a dit que vous étiez de haute stature, qu'après un traité, devenu riche, vous aviez acheté deux autos au lieu d'une, loué deux appartements au lieu d'un et que vous étiez toujours en voyage. Je ne sais de quoi vous louer. J'ai admiré que vous ayez campé toute la Bretagne en quelques lignes (et je la connais à fond) mieux que tous les pseudo-Loti en cent volumes. J'admire la sobriété colorée et forte de vos descriptions, votre goût, votre compréhension du détail expressif, votre documentation juste, la réalité et le réalisme de vos livres que l'on coudoie dans la rue, rue dont vous faites du pathétique, pathétique contenu souvent dans un petit silence, un petit regard, etc. Je ne suis pas un critique mais j'aime à admirer et plus encore à dire que j'admire.

Merci de m'avoir envoyé ce nouveau et beau livre. Votre dédicace est un événement dans ma vie et un événement heureux. Ils sont rares pour moi. Merci et croyez-moi votre lointain « ami ».

« Simenon », *Cistre essais*, nº 10, L'Âge d'Homme, Lausanne, 1980

Émile Henriot, 26 mars 1937

Eh bien, Monsieur et cher confrère, vous pouvez vous vanter de choisir vos adverbes, dans vos dédicaces ! « À Émile Henriot – Timidement… », quand vous m'envoyez un chef-d'œuvre ! – Ce n'est pas la première fois que je vous lis : mais *Le Testament Donadieu*, il y a longtemps que je n'ai eu un pareil livre entre les mains – et, toute affaire cessante, articles en retard, et nuit sans sommeil, il m'a fallu poursuivre ma lecture sans arrêt, avec un intérêt, une excitation, et une admiration sans réserve. Cette rapidité de récit, cette variété de personnages, cette exactitude de détails, cette création, ce secret suspendu, ces paysages, cette atmosphère, ce romanesque, cette vérité, cette alacrité, et cet esprit, en outre : je suis sous le charme, quoique vos héros ne soient pas charmants. Et vous êtes intimidé, en m'offrant à lire ce livre parfait ? Ne sauriez-vous donc pas ce que vous faites ? Quand vous êtes un merveilleux conteur, et un maître romancier ? Laissez-moi vous dire merci de m'avoir envoyé ce beau et riche livre, et vous dire ma sincère admiration et ma particulière sympathie. [...]. Je serais heureux de vous connaître un jour, de parler avec vous de votre art, de vous demander vos secrets.

En attendant, mon cher confrère, permettez-moi de vous serrer la main, et Croyez, je vous prie, à mes sentiments de complète sympathie, et à ma vive gratitude.

Ibidem

François Mauriac, 23 avril 1937

Cher Georges Simenon,
Je ne saurais dire combien votre lettre me touche : vous avez l'humilité des grands talents. Il suffit de jeter les yeux sur les romans de Robert Brasillach pour comprendre ce qu'il déteste en vous : tout ce qu'il n'a pas, le don de créer des êtres vivants dans une atmosphère vivante.

Je ne vous ferai pas de phrases : je crois que je connais presque toute votre œuvre. Je ne vous ai jamais beaucoup apprécié au point de vue policier, mais dans beaucoup de vos romans policiers j'ai aimé un don qui se manifeste magnifiquement dans *Le Testament Donadieu*. Toute la première partie me paraît *admirable*. Vous avez à travailler beaucoup, non pas votre style au sens profond (vous avez le « style ») mais du point de vue « correction », quand ce ne serait que pour décourager les chercheurs de poux.

Je vous serre bien cordialement la main.

Ibidem

André Gide, 31 décembre 1938

[...] Vous obéissez, en écrivant, à un instinct des plus sûrs et des mieux éduqués ; la justesse des notations, du ton des dialogues, des moindres propos ; et jamais d'insistance inutile ; vous passez outre : tant pis si le lecteur n'a pas compris.

Mais ce que je voudrais dire, précisément, dans mon article, c'est le curieux malentendu qui s'établit à votre sujet ; vous passez pour un auteur populaire et vous ne vous adressez nullement au *gros public*. Les sujets mêmes de vos livres, les menus problèmes psychologiques que vous soulevez, tout s'adresse aux délicats ; à ceux qui, précisément, pensent, tant qu'ils ne vous ont pas encore lu : « Simenon n'écrit pas pour nous. » Et, dans mon article, je voudrais leur dire qu'ils se trompent. Mais je me sens encore trop abruti, trop obtus, pour exposer cela comme il faudrait. En tout cas, et en attendant, persuadez-vous que vous n'avez pas de lecteur plus attentif et plus épris.

Georges Simenon André Gide, ... sans trop de pudeur. Correspondance 1938-1950, Omnibus, Paris, 1999

Roger Martin du Gard, 9 août 1945

Cher Monsieur, revenu chez moi, j'inventorie mes souvenirs, et je songe avec gratitude à la bonne soirée que je vous dois. Je désirais depuis longtemps comparer l'homme à l'œuvre. Je les confonds maintenant dans une même sympathie. L'un éclaire l'autre, et l'authentifie. Je sais que vous êtes un fastueux vagabond, mais je veux espérer que nos relations ébauchées l'autre soir n'en resteront pas là, et qu'à votre retour en France vous me laisserez faire naître des occasions de vous revoir.

Je vous souhaite beau et profitable voyage, bon travail, et vous prie de croire à mes sentiments les plus sincèrement cordiaux,

lettre conservée au fonds Simenon, université de Liège

André Gide, 12 à 16 février 1948

Bien cher Simenon,
[…] Il y a dix jours nous étions, ici, tous atteints d'une simenonite aiguë ; et vous auriez ri sans doute à nous voir, dans la même pièce, plongés, Richard Heyd dans la *Lettre à mon juge*, Jacqueline H. dans *Il pleut, bergère…*, Jean Lambert, mon gendre, dans *Le Haut Mal*, Catherine, ma fille, dans *Le Bourgmestre de Furnes* et moi-même, dans [en marge : Douze de vos anciens : relus en quinze jours] Oh ! c'était la pleine crise. Elle me prend une fois par an ; mais maintenant je ne vous lis plus sans prendre de notes […]. Gallimard avait eu la gentillesse de nous envoyer quatorze volumes de vous et, de plus, nous avons cherché dans les librairies d'ici tous les « Fayard » disponibles (dire que je n'avais pas encore lu *Les Fiançailles de M. Hire* !) Ajoutez les volumes de la nouvelle série, soit achetés ici, soit envoyés par vous (Merci !) dévorés aussitôt. Là-dessus vos deux longues lettres… j'étais plein de vous – le suis encore.

Georges Simenon André Gide, … sans trop de pudeur, *op. cit.*

Henry Miller, 23 avril 1954

Cher Monsieur Simenon,
Avec cette lettre, je vous envoie des salutations amicales d'une bonne douzaine d'amis à moi, tous des lecteurs dévoués de Simenon. Pour nous Américains qui viennent [*sic*] de vous découvrir (grâce aux traductions), c'est comme une nouvelle étoile qui s'est levée à l'horizon. Vous êtes absolument unique parmi les auteurs qui connaissent un grand succès auprès du public. Avec ce raccourcissement (?) que vous employez, vous ne perdez rien. Tout est là dans vos œuvres, et au-dessus tout le sens de l'humanité et la connaissance de la vie. Pour moi, qui ne connais rien de votre vie, hélas, c'est comme si vous avez fait vos préparations dans une vie antérieure. On parle souvent (et même trop, à mon avis) de la grande connaissance de Balzac. La vôtre est pour moi plus réelle, plus substantielle, et vous la nous servez d'une manière plus appétissante. Il y a une « tendresse » chez vous que je ne trouve pas assez souvent chez les écrivains français. Est-ce le côté belge ?

[…] Je vous salue très cordialement en espérant que vous nous donnerez au moins une centaine de plus de vos livres si séduisants.

« Simenon », *Cistre essais*, n° 10, *op. cit.*

Pierre Mac Orlan, 16 juin 1965

Cher Georges Simenon,
La dédicace que vous avez inscrite de votre main sur la première page de votre admirable roman : « LE PETIT SAINT » me touche profondément, plus que vous ne pouvez le penser. Je pourrais vous le dire si nos routes pouvaient se rencontrer ; mais l'écriture obéit trop souvent à la sentimentalité littéraire. C'est un domaine où l'affection et le

respect, quand ils sont sincères, se trouvent un peu dépaysés. Votre livre est un des meilleurs aspects de cette poésie humaine qui est la vôtre et qu'il est difficile de commenter dans les laboratoires universitaires. La dernière phrase de votre roman est magnifique… C'est ça la poésie. Pour ma part, je pense en avoir fini avec la littérature, pour le meilleur et aussi pour le pire. Je vais avoir 84 ans mais je n'imagine pas la fin de mon propre roman. Cher ami je vous suis reconnaissant pour tout ce que vous avez écrit et pour la dédicace placée sur la première page du « PETIT SAINT ». Encore une fois c'est un livre d'une intelligence et d'une dignité l'une et l'autre parfaites.

« Simenon », *Cistre essais*, nº 10, *op. cit.*

Marcel Achard, 12 avril 1967

Mon cher Georges,
Tu ne peux pas savoir le plaisir que tu m'as causé en me faisant envoyer, et numérotés et imprimés spécialement, les deux premiers volumes de la merveilleuse collection de tes œuvres complètes.

Je t'ai dit ce que je pensais du *Chat*, qui est une des œuvres les plus atroces, mais aussi les plus extraordinaires que tu aies écrites. Seuls, peut-être, *Les Anneaux de Bicêtre* pourrait tenir la comparaison.

Mais quelle joie de relire les premiers Maigret, de me retrouver subitement en 1930, à l'époque d'Eugène Merle (« nous autres, les chacals, nous n'avons pas de scrupules »…) et de notre jeunesse qui commençait à triompher !

[…] Plongé dans l'univers Simenon je rêve debout. Cette atmosphère Simenon n'est pas la même en 1930 qu'en 1966 et quelqu'un qui s'appliquerait à suivre – comme je vais le faire – le développement de ton œuvre sentirait la différence profonde qui existe entre le monde de 1930 et celui d'aujourd'hui. Pas seulement à cause des différences de monnaie mais ta science du détail, cet extraordinaire pouvoir que tu as de créer la vie t'ont fait recréer celle de 1930 et, j'en suis sûr, les années intermédiaires jusqu'en 1966.

[…] Tu es un grand bonhomme.

[…] Je ne vais pas me livrer ici à une étude complète de ton œuvre, mais je tiens à te dire l'enchantement de tes premiers Fayard. On a bien fait de les rééditer : il aurait été bien dommage qu'ils se perdissent. On y voit grandir peu à peu Simenon.

lettre conservée au fonds Simenon, université de Liège

Federico Fellini, 22 septembre 1969

Cher Simenon
Eh bien, votre lettre, de temps en temps, je me la relis. Il n'y a pas de doute que j'ai un fort complexe à votre égard et la seule idée que peut-être décembre vous verra à Rome et que nous pourrons y bavarder ensemble me transforme en un petit garçon émotionné dès maintenant. C'est vrai que votre talent et vos possibilités surhumaines de discipline dans le travail créent une intimidation et un émerveillement. Il faut penser à vos qualités humaines pour rétablir un rapport d'équilibre et voilà que tout de suite et avant toute autre chose on découvre que l'on vous aime et vous devenez une présence familière, l'ami le plus grand que chacun voudrait avoir, un compagnon de travail et de vie, un point de repère qui ne déçoit jamais et donne de la force. Excusez-moi si je me laisse un peu aller. Je sais très bien que certaines choses, à se les entendre dire, tapent un peu sur les nerfs. Pourtant c'est tout à fait comme cela, cher Simenon.

lettre conservée au fonds Simenon, université de Liège

Débuts de romans

« Le "commencement" de chacun des romans de [Simenon] est un faux début : nous prenons – je l'ai dit – le discours en marche. Comme si soudainement, lisant la première ligne, nous commencions à nous soucier d'une voix qui parlait déjà, mais à laquelle, jusqu'alors, nous ne prêtions pas l'oreille. Un roman de Simenon ne débute pas par une naissance […], mais par l'apparition abrupte […] d'un discours qui se continue, qui se poursuit, venu de plus avant. Il en va de même pour la fin. »

Hubert Juin, « Un roman ininterrompu », *Simenon*, Plon, 1973

Le Chien jaune, mars 1931

Vendredi 7 novembre. Concarneau est désert. L'horloge lumineuse de la vieille ville, qu'on aperçoit au-dessus des remparts, marque onze heures moins cinq.

Liberty-Bar, mai 1932

Cela commença par une sensation de vacances. Quand Maigret descendit du train, la moitié de la gare d'Antibes était baignée d'un soleil si lumineux qu'on n'y voyait les gens s'agiter que comme des ombres. Des ombres portant chapeau de paille, pantalon blanc, raquette de tennis. L'air bourdonnait, il y avait des palmiers, des cactus en bordure du quai, un plan de mer bleue au-delà de la lampisterie.

L'Écluse nº 1, avril 1933

Quand on observe des poissons à travers une couche d'eau qui interdit entre eux et nous tout contact, on les voit rester longtemps immobiles, sans raison, puis, d'un frémissement de nageoires, aller un peu plus loin pour n'y rien faire qu'attendre à nouveau.

Quartier nègre, juin 1935

– Je ne vois que des nègres, avait murmuré Germaine, alors que le navire manœuvrait encore et que, du haut du pont-promenade, elle voyait se rapprocher lentement un quai où attendaient deux rangs de dockers noirs. Et son mari avait murmuré sans conviction : – Évidemment !

Pourquoi évidemment, puisqu'ils étaient à l'entrée du canal de Panamá, c'est-à-dire en Amérique centrale ? N'auraient-ils pas dû apercevoir des Indiens ?

L'Assassin, décembre 1935

Le mélange était si intime entre la vie de tous les jours, les faits et gestes conventionnels et l'aventure la plus inouïe, que le docteur Kupérus, Hans Kupérus, de Sneek (Frise néerlandaise), en ressentait une excitation quasi voluptueuse qui lui rappelait les effets de la caféine par exemple.

***Chemin sans issue*, mars 1936**

Ce n'est qu'après coup, bien sûr, que les heures prennent leur importance. Cette heure-là, sur le moment, avait la couleur du ciel, un ciel gris partout : en bas, où couraient des nuages poussés par le vent d'est ; en haut, où l'on devinait des réserves de pluie pour des jours et des jours encore.

***L'homme qui regardait passer les trains*, printemps 1937**

En ce qui concerne personnellement Kees Popinga, on doit admettre qu'à huit heures du soir il était encore temps, puisque, aussi bien, son destin n'était pas fixé. Mais temps de quoi ? Et pouvait-il faire autre chose que ce qu'il allait faire, persuadé d'ailleurs que ses gestes n'avaient pas plus d'importance que pendant les milliers et les milliers de jours qui avaient précédé ?

***Le Cheval-Blanc*, mars 1938**

– Tu devrais le poser par terre, Maurice… Pourquoi cette phrase-là plutôt qu'une autre ? Et pourquoi cette minute-là plutôt que n'importe laquelle des minutes de ce dimanche de Pentecôte ?

***La Veuve Couderc*, mai 1940**

Il marchait. Il était seul sur trois kilomètres au moins de route coupée obliquement, tous les dix mètres, par l'ombre d'un tronc d'arbre, et, à grandes enjambées, sans pourtant se presser, il allait d'une ombre à l'autre. Comme il était près de midi et que le soleil approchait du zénith, une ombre courte, ridiculement ramassée, la sienne, glissait devant lui.

***La Vérité sur Bébé Donge*, septembre 1940**

N'arrive-t-il pas qu'un moucheron à peine visible agite davantage la surface d'une mare que la chute d'un gros caillou ? Ainsi en fut-il ce dimanche-là à la Châtaigneraie. D'autres dimanches, pour les Donge, sont restés en quelque sorte historiques, comme le dimanche de l'orage, quand le hêtre s'est abattu « trois minutes après le passage de maman » ou encore le dimanche de la grande dispute, celle qui a brouillé les deux ménages pour plusieurs mois.

***Cécile est morte*, décembre 1940**

La pipe que Maigret alluma sur son seuil, boulevard Richard-Lenoir, était déjà plus savoureuse que les autres matins. Le premier brouillard était une surprise aussi plaisante que la première neige pour les enfants, surtout que ce n'était pas ce méchant brouillard jaunâtre de certains jours d'hiver, mais une vapeur laiteuse dans laquelle erraient des halos de lumière. Il faisait frais. Le bout des doigts, le bout du nez picotaient et les semelles claquaient sur le pavé.

***Félicie est là*, mai 1942**

Ce fut une seconde absolument extraordinaire, car cela ne dura probablement qu'une seconde, comme, assure-t-on, les rêves qui nous paraissent les plus longs. Maigret, des années plus tard, aurait pu montrer l'endroit exact où cela s'était produit, la portion de trottoir où il avait mis les pieds, la pierre de taille sur laquelle se profilait son ombre, il aurait pu, non seulement reconstituer les moindres détails du décor, mais retrouver l'odeur éparse, les vibrations de l'air, qui avait un goût de souvenir d'enfance.

L'Aîné des Ferchaux, décembre 1943

Le train s'ébranlait d'une secousse brutale et Maudet, interrompu dans sa course, était collé, l'espace d'une seconde, contre la cloison du couloir, près de l'accordéon noir d'un soufflet. Alors, la viscosité de cette cloison, qui semblait suer gras et froid par une nuit pluvieuse d'octobre, lui entra dans les doigts, dans la peau, dans la mémoire ; elle devait à tout jamais s'associer pour lui à la notion de train de nuit.

Maigret se fâche, août 1945

Mme Maigret, qui écossait des petits pois dans une ombre chaude où le bleu de son tablier et le vert des cosses mettaient des taches somptueuses, Mme Maigret, dont les mains n'étaient jamais inactives, fût-ce à deux heures de l'après-midi par la plus chaude journée d'un mois d'août accablant, Mme Maigret, qui surveillait son mari comme un poupon, s'inquiéta :
– Je parie que tu vas déjà te lever…

Les Fantômes du chapelier, décembre 1948

On était le 3 décembre et il pleuvait toujours. Le chiffre 3 se détachait, énorme, très noir, avec une sorte de gros ventre, sur le blanc cru du calendrier fixé à la droite de la caisse, contre la cloison en chêne sombre séparant le magasin de l'étalage. Il y avait exactement vingt jours, puisque cela avait eu lieu le 13 novembre – encore un 3 obèse sur le calendrier – que la première vieille femme avait été assassinée, près de l'église Saint-Sauveur, à quelques pas du canal.

Un nouveau dans la ville, octobre 1949

Il se trouva installé dans la ville sans que personne l'eût vu arriver, et on en ressentit un malaise comparable à celui d'une famille qui apercevrait un inconnu dans un fauteuil de la salle commune sans que personne l'ait entendu entrer, ni que la porte se soit ouverte.

L'Amie de Madame Maigret, décembre 1949

La poule était au feu, avec une belle carotte rouge, un gros oignon et un bouquet de persil dont les queues dépassaient.

Feux rouges, juillet 1953

Il appelait ça entrer dans le tunnel, une expression à lui, pour son usage personnel, qu'il n'employait avec personne, à plus forte raison pas avec sa femme. Il savait exactement ce que cela voulait dire, en quoi consistait d'être dans le tunnel, mais, chose curieuse, quand il y était, il se refusait à le reconnaître, sauf par intermittence, pendant quelques secondes, et toujours trop tard. Quant à déterminer le moment précis où il y entrait, il avait essayé, souvent après coup, sans y parvenir.

Crime impuni, octobre 1953

Des cris d'enfants éclatèrent dans la cour de l'école d'en face, et Élie sut qu'il était dix heures moins le quart. Certaines fois, il lui arrivait d'attendre avec une impatience qui frisait le malaise ce déchirement brutal de l'air par les voix des deux cents gamins jaillissant des classes pour la récréation. On aurait juré que, chaque matin, quelques instants avant ce feu d'artifice sonore, le silence régnait plus profondément sur le quartier, comme si celui-ci tout entier était dans l'attente.

Les Complices, septembre 1955

Ce fut brutal, instantané. Et pourtant, il resta sans étonnement et sans révolte comme s'il s'y attendait depuis toujours. D'une seconde à l'autre, dès le moment où le klaxon se mit à hurler derrière lui, il sut que la catastrophe était inéluctable et que c'était sa faute.

Le Nègre, avril 1957

« Un jour, je leur montrerai... »

Depuis combien d'années se répétait-il ça dans sa tête, quelquefois entre ses dents, surtout le soir, quand son teint devenait violacé et ses gros yeux humides ? Peut-être le pensait-il déjà sur les bancs de l'école, à Versins-Haut, lorsque les Van Straeten, les fermiers, Ferdinand et Emma à la voix criarde, chez qui l'Assistance publique l'avait placé, le traitaient de fainéant et de propre-à-rien.

Maigret et les vieillards, juin 1960

C'était un de ces mois de mai exceptionnels comme on n'en connaît que deux ou trois dans sa vie et qui ont la luminosité, le goût, l'odeur des souvenirs d'enfance. Maigret disait un mois de mai de cantique, car cela lui rappelait à la fois sa première communion et son premier printemps à Paris, quand tout était pour lui nouveau et merveilleux.

Maigret et le clochard, mai 1962

Il y eut un moment, entre le quai des Orfèvres et le pont Marie, où Maigret marqua un temps d'arrêt, si court que Lapointe, qui marchait à son côté, n'y fit pas attention. Et pourtant, pendant quelques secondes, peut-être moins d'une seconde, le commissaire venait de se retrouver à l'âge de son compagnon.

Le Petit Saint, octobre 1964

Il avait entre quatre et cinq ans lorsque le monde commença à vivre autour de lui, lorsqu'il prit conscience d'une vraie scène se jouant entre des êtres humains qu'il était capable de distinguer les uns des autres, de situer dans l'espace, dans un décor déterminé. Il n'aurait pas pu préciser, plus tard, si c'était en été ou en hiver, bien qu'il eût déjà le sens des saisons. Probablement en automne, car une légère buée ternissait la fenêtre sans rideau et la lumière du bec de gaz d'en face, seule à éclairer la chambre jaunâtre, semblait humide.

La Prison, novembre 1967

Combien de mois, d'années, faut-il pour faire d'un enfant un adolescent, d'un adolescent un homme ? À quel moment peut-on affirmer que cette mutation a eu lieu ? Il n'existe pas, comme dans les études, de proclamation solennelle, pas de distribution de prix, pas de diplôme.

Alain Poitaud, à trente-deux ans, ne mit que quelques heures, peut-être quelques minutes, pour cesser d'être l'homme qu'il avait été jusqu'alors et pour en devenir un autre.

Maigret et Monsieur Charles, février 1972

Maigret jouait dans un rayon de soleil de mars encore un peu frileux. Il ne jouait pas avec des cubes, comme quand il était enfant, mais avec des pipes.

Il y en avait toujours cinq ou six sur son bureau, et chaque fois qu'il en bourrait une, il la choisissait avec soin selon son humeur.

Son regard était flou, ses épaules tassées. Il venait de décider du reste de sa carrière. Il ne regrettait rien, mais il en gardait une certaine mélancolie.

Extraits des « Dictées »

« On plaidera ici, comme l'a fait François Truffaut, pour l'intérêt de ces volumes […]. L'oralisation de la prose la rend transparente à qui n'a jamais lu un livre d'un point de vue littéraire, et c'est là un bel éloge littéraire qu'on puisse lui faire. Les pauvres en argent y liront leur situation ; les pauvres en esprit trouveront chez ce nouveau riche l'esprit de la pauvreté. »

Jacques Lecarme, « Les cinq voies de l'autobiographie simenonienne », *Traces*, n° 11, 1999

Du ministère de la Culture [9 avril 1973]

Picasso est mort hier. Depuis le début de l'après-midi, des gens s'en sont donné à cœur joie, à la radio, à la télévision, et ce matin dans les journaux.

La France possède un ministre de la culture. Culture de quoi ? Ce n'est pas précisé dans le titre. Mais on a choisi pour ce poste, dans le nouveau gouvernement, l'écrivain le plus arriviste, le plus bête de toute sa génération. Si ses livres sont mauvais, il n'en est cependant pas responsable, car il les a fait écrire par des nègres.

Cela l'a mené à l'Académie française.

Et, hier, on a pu le voir prononcer, sur Picasso, un discours ampoulé qui, récité de la même manière à Bobino ou dans n'importe quel music-hall, aurait été considéré comme un excellent numéro comique.

Bien entendu, comme toujours, on a eu soin, à peu près partout, de souligner le prix atteint par les toiles de Picasso, le nombre d'œuvres qu'il a produites pendant sa carrière, le prix aussi des moindres croquis griffonnés sur une table de café.

Est-ce vraiment ce qui intéresse le public ? Est-ce le genre de nécrologie auquel un homme de l'envergure de Picasso avait droit ?

Cela me met en boule. J'avoue que je suis indigné. Je ne me compare pas au peintre. J'espère cependant que ni Druon ni tous ceux qui ont parlé de Picasso n'auront l'idée de parler de moi. Si seulement on pouvait laisser les gens mourir et être enterrés en paix !

Un homme comme un autre, 1975

Petit homme [15 octobre 1973]

Homme, pauvre et merveilleux petit homme, plein d'aspirations héroïques, plein d'espoir et si souvent plein d'un courage quotidien que rien ne parvient à user !

Je ne comprends pas que, depuis qu'il existe, il n'ait pas balayé une bonne fois toutes les forces qui se liguent contre lui, qui font de lui ce qu'on appelait jadis un manant, maintenant un OS, c'est-à-dire un esclave.

Heureusement pour son équilibre relatif qu'il ne le sait pas. Chaque matin, on lui dit ce qu'il faut penser et l'on reprend ce travail de dressage à chaque heure de la journée.

Pour quoi ? Pour qui ? Pour quelques individus qui ont un peu moins de scrupules que les autres, un peu moins d'idéal que les autres. Ceux-là n'hésitent pas à tricher, à tricher en tout, à montrer les guerres comme le sursaut d'un peuple alors qu'il ne s'agit que de livraisons de chars ou d'avions.

Comme jadis on entraînait les paysans à aller se battre au Moyen-Orient pour sauver le tombeau du Christ. Mon œil ! comme dirait Pierre.

Des traces de pas, 1975

Humilité [1er décembre 1974]

S'il y a un mot que je voudrais voir inculquer aux enfants, c'est-à-dire aux petits d'hommes, aux futurs hommes, c'est le mot *humilité*.

Ce mot-là, plutôt que les mots Liberté, Égalité, Fraternité, je le voudrais voir gravé dans la pierre de nos monuments éphémères.

Vent du nord vent du sud, 1976

Les voyous [13 mars 1975]

– Il faut en finir avec les voyous.

Eh bien, ce mot voyou, pas plus que je ne l'admettais dans mon enfance, ce qui a créé beaucoup de frictions entre ma mère et moi, je ne l'accepte pas plus aujourd'hui qu'alors.

D'autant plus que ceux qui l'emploient sont d'anciens voyous eux-mêmes. Mais des voyous qui n'avaient pas l'excuse de la misère, ni d'un horizon bouché.

– Il faut que jeunesse se passe…

C'était le mot pour excuser les fils de famille, les fils de riches, de se faire les dents, d'exprimer leur impatience de vivre.

On ne les appelait pas des voyous. On les appelait des étudiants.

Aujourd'hui, les collégiens, les lycéens, beaucoup de leurs professeurs eux-mêmes, sont devenus des voyous.

Pour ma part, je serais avec les jeunes, avec ceux qu'ils appellent les voyous, pour déboulonner les vrais voyous, les voyous dignes, les voyous qui se donnent une bonne conscience et qui s'arrogent, chaque jour, le droit de montrer leur image à la télévision, ce qui m'apparaît comme un vrai défi à l'ensemble de la population.

Ibidem

Racisme ordinaire [21 mars 1975]

On parle beaucoup en ce moment de racisme, surtout en France, et même en Suisse, pays de refuge, pourtant, dit-on toujours, mais où les ouvriers étrangers sentent leur position menacée, sans compter ceux qui ont déjà été renvoyés dans leur pays et les saisonniers dont un petit nombre seulement reviendra cet été.

Le racisme me fait grincer des dents. Je déteste toute distinction entre les hommes et mon antiracisme s'étend, si je puis dire, jusqu'aux animaux.

Ibidem

« Plutôt gauchiste » [8 mai 1975]

Je ne me suis jamais occupé de politique. C'est en vain qu'on épluchera mes deux cent vingt et quelques romans pour y trouver des traces d'idéologie. Néanmoins, tout au long de ma vie, j'ai passé par des alternatives de révolte aiguë et d'enthousiasme.

Je m'en suis rendu compte cette semaine. Pendant deux jours, j'ai répondu à des questions qui m'étaient posées pour un numéro spécial qu'un magazine littéraire veut me consacrer à l'automne. On m'a demandé, bien entendu, quelles étaient mes idées politiques. Je crois que j'ai assez surpris mon interlocuteur en lui disant que, comme à l'âge de seize ans, je suis ce qu'on pourrait appeler un anarchiste.

Pour moi, en effet, les partis qui cherchent à créer une évolution progressive de la société humaine ne font que le jeu des profiteurs. Ils se sont peu à peu embourgeoisés et aujourd'hui se trouvent prêts à prendre la relève du bon vieux capitalisme, avec peut-être d'autres méthodes, mais les mêmes résultats.

Je crois avoir dit : – Je serais plutôt gauchiste. Pas un gauchiste violent. Pas un lanceur de bombes, pas plus que je n'aspirais à devenir lanceur de bombes lorsque j'avais seize ou dix-huit ans. Gauchiste, non pas non plus dans le sens de groupuscule plus ou moins organisé et plus ou moins clandestin.

J'emploie ce mot dans le sens d'individualisme. J'ai toujours eu la volonté de devenir un individu et j'ai caressé le rêve que, un jour, le monde ne serait plus composé que d'individus.

Un banc au soleil, 1977

Distinction ? [5 juin 1976]

Toute ma vie, j'ai eu horreur de ce mot « distingué », comme j'ai eu l'horreur de la découpe de la population d'un pays en classes sociales. Je ne parle pas d'un autre mot, beaucoup plus scandaleux :
– C'est un homme de bonne famille.

Ce qui implique *a contrario* que tous les autres sont de mauvaise famille.

Classes dirigeantes, gentilshommes, personnalités distinguées, classes sociales sont des mots que je hais depuis mon enfance, parce que, depuis mon enfance je n'arrive pas à les comprendre. Ou plutôt je ne comprends que trop bien que, même en république, même en démocratie, il existe une sorte de « cour » semblable à celle de Versailles où chacun a son rang bien déterminé qui dépend surtout du bon vouloir du pouvoir [...].

Post-scriptum. Pour en revenir à l'Académie française, elle se considère elle-même comme un club, un club restreint, où l'on n'entre qu'en remplissant certaines conditions dont celle d'être un personnage de bon ton. Car il y a aussi le bon ton. Celui d'une exquise politesse pour exprimer les pires vacheries, de promesses généreuses et prétendues amicales à un candidat pour qui l'on sait que l'on ne votera jamais.

Pour bien faire, pour être admis d'emblée dans ce club, il est bon de posséder un titre, vrai ou faux, de descendre d'un personnage plus ou moins illustre, fût-ce par le valet de chambre ou par une des femmes de chambre.

[...] J'ai eu plus de dix amis intimes qui ont été pris soudain, passé l'âge mûr, de ce qu'Isorni appelle la « fièvre verte ». Ils s'y présentaient, disaient-ils, pour faire « sauter la baraque », je crois que je l'ai déjà dit. Je crois aussi avoir dit que, de moutons enragés qu'ils avaient été, ils sont devenus les plus dociles, sinon les plus pointilleux de ce club de gens distingués.

Tant que je suis vivant, 1978

Le pape Paul VI [6 juin 1976]

[...] De toutes les dictatures dont on parle ou qu'on craint à présent, celle du Pape, et particulièrement de celui en fonctions, m'apparaît comme la plus inhumaine.

[...] La plupart des dictatures, ou, encore une fois, des idéologies, demandent, exigent, que l'on vive d'une certaine façon.

Mais rares sont celles qui s'adressent, non seulement à vos actes, à vos attitudes envers autrui, mais à vos moindres pensées.

[...] La religion, le pape Paul VI vient de le confirmer solennellement à deux reprises, prétend contrôler, non seulement nos instincts les plus normaux, mais aussi nos pensées secrètes.

[...] Des dictateurs empêchent leurs concitoyens de franchir les frontières du pays, ou de s'exprimer librement.

Le Pape, lui, prétend contrôler notre vie la plus personnelle et franchir les frontières qu'il a fixées à nos propres pensées, sinon à nos rêves de la nuit.

Ibidem

Les chefs d'État [28 septembre 1976]

[...] « De mon temps ». Pour ma part, c'est un mot que je ne prononce jamais. Parce qu'il n'y a pas de temps. Le temps, c'est nous qui l'avons créé à notre mesure, une mesure infinitésimale.

[...] Nous oublions qu'il y a eu les mêmes enfances à Rome, en Grèce, en Égypte, en Chine, et dans toutes les régions du globe. Nous oublions aussi qu'il y a eu, partout, des ambitieux, des avides, qui, pour une gloire passagère, n'hésitaient pas à sacrifier des centaines de milliers d'hommes.

[...] Il reste de faux Napoléon, de faux César, de faux Alexandre aujourd'hui aussi. Je serais tenté de les considérer, à la façon de ceux d'autrefois, comme des irresponsables. Je ne parviens pas à leur en vouloir. Si leurs manœuvres et leur politique m'irritent, je serais plutôt apitoyé sur leur personnalité.

Pour ne prendre que Napoléon, ses dernières années à l'île de Sainte-Hélène étaient d'un ridicule qui tenait des comédies bourgeoises de Labiche.

Il en sera de même, quand l'Histoire aura ouvert ses vrais dossiers, des sous-Napoléon plus proches de nous, et même de ceux qui nous gouvernent encore.

Est-ce une maladie ? Je ne serais pas surpris que l'on découvre un jour que c'en soit une. À mon avis, c'est un complexe d'infériorité poussé à l'extrême qui oblige certains individus à se donner coûte que coûte l'illusion d'une supériorité sur leurs semblables. Je les déteste, certes, pour tout le mal qu'ils font aux autres. En même temps, j'en ai pitié pour l'existence qu'ils ont à mener.

La Main dans la main, 1978

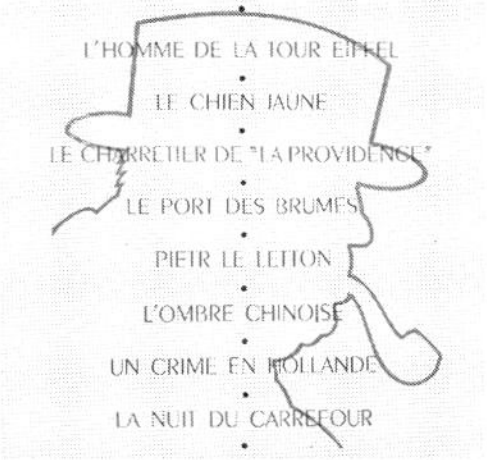

Le roman se meurt [11 juillet 1977]

Le roman se meurt ? Le roman est mort ?

À mon sens, c'est surtout une question de commerce. Il est évident qu'un film qui s'intitule « Watergate » ou qui nous parle de la vie intime de l'ex-président Nixon éveillera davantage la curiosité qu'un film qui s'intitule tout bêtement :
– *Les Yeux Verts*.

[...] Il faut qu'un livre soit un best-seller et un best-seller ne s'obtient qu'en chatouillant la curiosité du grand public. Ce n'est pas le roman qui se meurt. Ce sont les véritables romanciers qui commencent à nous manquer. Les quelques-uns qui restent ne sont évidemment pas aussi bien reçus par les bureaux d'un éditeur qu'un ancien bagnard ou qu'une ancienne tenancière de maison close.

Qu'arrive-t-il alors ? C'est que les rares romanciers dont je parle, se prostituent et écrivent sagement ce qu'on leur demande.

À quoi bon jurer ?, 1979

GÉOGRAPHIE DES ROMANS

*Sont ici sélectionnés les cadres spatiaux des romans et nouvelles (précédées par *) pour autant qu'ils atteignent un minimum de vingt pages dans l'édition des* Œuvres complètes *(Rencontre). Dans cette liste, le quai des Orfèvres n'est pas retenu dans la mesure où il sert de cadre spatial à la majorité des « Maigret ».*

PARIS

• 1er arrondissement
Place Dauphine : *La Colère de Maigret* – Rue de la Grande-Truanderie : *La Mort d'Auguste* – Halles : *Le Petit Saint* – Quai de la Mégisserie : *La Folle de Maigret* – Place Vendôme : *Monsieur La Souris, Il y a encore des noisetiers.*

• 2e arrondissement
Rue Montmartre : *Pedigree* – Avenue de l'Opéra : *Une vie comme neuve* – Rue des Petits-Champs : *L'Outlaw* – Boulevard Saint-Denis : *Le Veuf* – Rue Thorel : *Le Veuf.*

• 3e arrondissement
Rue des Arquebusiers : *L'Homme au petit chien* – Boulevard Beaumarchais : *L'Homme au petit chien, Les Innocents* – Rue Béranger : *Marie qui louche* – Rue des Minimes : *La Porte* – Place de la République : *Maigret s'amuse* – Rue de Sévigné : *Les Innocents* – Rue de Turenne : *L'Amie de Madame Maigret, Marie qui louche, La Porte.*

• 4e arrondissement
Quai d'Anjou : *En cas de malheur, Maigret et le tueur* – Rue de Birague : *L'Outlaw* – Quai de Bourbon : *La Vieille* – Quai des Célestins : *Maigret et le clochard* – Rue de Jouy : *La Vieille* – Rue Neuve-Saint-Pierre : *Maigret et le voleur paresseux* – Quai d'Orléans : *En cas de malheur* – Rue du Pas-de-la-Mule : *Les Suicidés* – Rue du Roi-de-Sicile : *Maigret et son mort* – Rue Saint-Antoine : **Stan le Tueur* – Place des Vosges : *L'Ombre chinoise, *L'Amoureux de Madame Maigret, Maigret et le marchand de vin*

• 5e arrondissement
Rue de l'Abbé-de-l'Épée : *Le Petit Saint* – Rue des Feuillantines : *Le Chat* – Rue de la Harpe : *La Disparition d'Odile* – Rue Lhomond : *Maigret en meublé* – Rue Mouffetard : *Maigret et le voleur paresseux, Le Petit Saint* – Rue Saint-Jacques [désignant par méprise la rue du Faubourg-Saint-Jacques, 14e arr.] : *Maigret en meublé* – Quai de la Tournelle : *L'Enterrement de Monsieur Bouvet*

• 6e arrondissement
Quai des Grands-Augustins : *Maigret, Maigret s'amuse* – Quai Malaquais : *Les Quatre Jours du pauvre homme* – Rue Notre-Dame-des-Champs : *Maigret et les braves gens* – Rue Saint-André-des-Arts : *La Folle de Maigret.*

• 7e arrondissement
Rue de Bourgogne : *Maigret et les vieillards* – Rue Saint-Dominique : *Maigret et les vieillards* – Boulevard Saint-Germain : **Le Client le plus obstiné du monde, Maigret chez le ministre, Maigret tend un piège, Maigret et Monsieur Charles* – Rue des Saints-Pères : **Le Client le plus obstiné du monde* – Rue de Varenne : *Maigret et les vieillards.*

• 8e arrondissement
Boulevard des Batignolles : *Signé Picpus* – Rue de Berri : *Le Veuf* – Avenue des Champs-Élysées : *Pietr-le-Letton, Le Testament Donadieu, Les Caves du Majestic, Les Quatre Jours du pauvre homme* – Boulevard de Courcelles : *Un échec de Maigret, L'Ours en peluche* – [Impasse Daru (transposition de l'avenue Beaucour)] : *Les Noces de Poitiers* – Rue Daru : *Antoine et Julie* – Rue du Faubourg-Saint-Honoré : *La Fenêtre des Rouet* – Avenue George-V : *Les Volets verts, Maigret voyage* – Avenue de Marigny : *Maigret hésite* – Rue de Ponthieu : *Les Caves du Majestic, En cas de malheur, Le Déménagement*

• 9e arrondissement
Rue Ballu : *Maigret et l'indicateur* – Cité Bergère : *La Cage d'Émile, Le Ticket de métro, Le Chantage de l'Agence O* – Rue Chaptal : *La Première Enquête de Maigret* – Boulevard de Clichy : *L'Escalier de fer* – Rue de Clichy : *Maigret et la jeune morte* – Rue Fontaine : *Maigret, La Patience de Maigret, Maigret et l'indicateur* – Rue La Bruyère : *La Colère de Maigret* – Rue La Rochefoucauld : *La Première Enquête de Maigret* – Rue Laffitte : *Le Fils* – Rue Notre-Dame-de-Lorette : *Le Grand Bob, L'Ami d'enfance de Maigret* – Rue Pigalle : *L'Ombre chinoise, Maigret au Picratt's, La Colère de Maigret* – Rue Victor-Massé : *La Colère de Maigret*

• 10e arrondissement
Quai de Valmy : *Maigret et le corps sans tête*

• 11e arrondissement
Rue d'Angoulême [devenue rue Jean-Pierre-Timbaud] : *Maigret et l'homme du banc* – Rue Popincourt : *Le Revolver de Maigret* – Boulevard Richard-Lenoir : *Maigret et son mort, La Première Enquête de Maigret, *Un Noël de Maigret, Maigret, Lognon et les gangsters, Maigret et la jeune morte, Maigret et le corps sans tête, Maigret s'amuse, Les Scrupules de Maigret, Maigret et le voleur paresseux, Maigret et les braves gens, Maigret et le client du samedi, Maigret et le clochard, La Colère de Maigret, Maigret se défend, L'Ami d'enfance de Maigret, Maigret et le tueur, Maigret et le*

marchand de vin, *La Folle de Maigret*, *Maigret et l'homme tout seul*, *Maigret et l'indicateur*
– Boulevard Voltaire : *Une confidence de Maigret*
– Place Voltaire : *Maigret s'amuse.*

• 13e arrondissement
[Square Sébastien-Doise (impasse inventée donnant « sur la rue de la Santé, à mi-chemin entre la prison et l'hôpital Cochin »)] : *Le Chat.*

• 14e arrondissement
Avenue de Châtillon : *Les Scrupules de Maigret* – Rue Delambre : *Les Quatre Jours du pauvre homme* – Rue du Faubourg-Saint-Jacques : *La Cage de verre* – Boulevard du Montparnasse : *La Tête d'un homme* – Avenue du Parc-de-Montsouris [devenue avenue René-Coty] : *Maigret et l'affaire Nahour* – Rue du Saint-Gothard : *La Cage de verre.*

• 15e arrondissement
Rue Blomet : **Le Vieillard au porte-mine*
– Boulevard de Grenelle : *Le Voleur de Maigret*
– Boulevard Pasteur : *Maigret chez le ministre*
– Rue Saint-Charles : *Le Voleur de Maigret.*

• 16e arrondissement
Avenue Henri-Martin : *Le Testament Donadieu*, *L'Ours en peluche* – Rue Laurent-Pichat : *Marie qui louche* – Avenue des Tilleuls : *L'Ours en peluche.*

• 17e arrondissement
Rue des Acacias : *Maigret, Lognon et les gangsters*, *Maigret se défend*, *La Patience de Maigret* – Rue de l'Arc-de-Triomphe : *La Patience de Maigret* – Avenue Carnot : *Maigret se trompe*
– Rue de l'Étoile : *Les Noces de Poitiers*
– Rue Fortuny : *La Prison* – Rue Legendre : *Le Train de Venise* – Avenue Mac-Mahon : *Le Fils* – Avenue des Ternes : *L'Escalier de fer.*

• 18e arrondissement
Rue Caulaincourt : **Mademoiselle Berthe et son amant*, **Les Petits Cochons sans queue*, *Maigret et le voleur paresseux*, *Maigret et le fantôme*
– Place Constantin-Pecqueur : *Monsieur La Souris*, *Maigret et le fantôme* – Avenue Junot : *Maigret et le fantôme* – Rue Lamarck : **Maigret et l'Inspecteur Malgracieux*, **Les Petits Cochons sans queue*, *Le Grand Bob* – Place du Tertre : *Maigret s'amuse*
– Rue Tholozé : *Maigret et le client du samedi.*

FRANCE

Les noms de lieux créés par Simenon figurent entre crochets, la région étant donnée entre parenthèses.

• Région parisienne
– Asnières : **La Nuit des sept minutes*
– Avrainville [(et le proche) carrefour des Trois-Veuves] : *La Nuit du carrefour*
– Bourg-la-Reine : *Cécile est morte*
– Charenton : *L'Écluse no 1*, *Maigret et son mort*, *Maigret et le marchand de vin*
– Chelles : **La Pipe de Maigret*
– [Clairevie (proche d'Orly)] : *Le Déménagement*
– Coudray (Le) : **Menaces de mort*
– Courbevoie : *Le Suspect*
– [Givry-les-Étangs (inspiré par Ville-d'Avray)] : *Novembre*
– Issy-les-Moulineaux : *Lettre à mon juge*
– Itteville : **La Folle d'Itteville*
– Ivry : *Maigret et les témoins récalcitrants*
– [Jeanneville (proche d'Orgeval)] : *Félicie est là*
– Juvisy : *L'homme qui regardait passer les trains*
– Kremlin-Bicêtre (Le) : *Les Anneaux de Bicêtre*
– Moret-sur-Loing : **L'Étrangleur de Moret*
– Morsang-sur-Seine : *La Guinguette à deux sous*
– Neuilly : *Maigret et la Grande Perche*, *Le Revolver de Maigret*, *Le Train de Venise*
– Orgeval : *Félicie est là*
– [Orsenne (inspiré par Le Coudray-Montceaux)] : *Maigret se fâche*
– Puteaux : *L'Homme au petit chien*
– Saint-Cloud : *Les Caves du Majestic*
– Saint-Fargeau : *M. Gallet, décédé*, *La Guinguette à deux sous*
– Sceaux : *La Mort d'Auguste*
– Versailles : *L'Ours en peluche*, *Betty*
– Vésinet (Le) : *Le Fils*
– Villejuif : *Les Fiançailles de M. Hire*

• Centre
– Châteauneuf-sur-Loire : **Le Notaire de Châteauneuf*
– [Gué-de-Saulnois (Le) (proche de Saint-Amand-Montrond)] : *La Veuve Couderc*
– [Louvant (Berry)] : *Le Petit Homme d'Arkhangelsk*
– Meung-sur-Loire : **Ceux du Grand-Café*
– Sancerre : *M. Gallet, décédé*, *Une vie comme neuve*

• Auvergne
– Moulins : *L'Affaire Saint-Fiacre*, *Les Inconnus dans la maison*
– [Saint-Fiacre (inspiré par Paray-le-Frésil)] : *L'Affaire Saint-Fiacre*
– Vichy : *Maigret à Vichy*

• Bourgogne
– [Bugle (en bord de Loire)] : *Bergelon*
– Cézy : **La Sonnette d'alarme*
– [Malouville (proche d'une ville inspirée par Nevers)] : *Le Destin des Malou*
– Nevers : *Les Suicidés*, **Une femme a crié*, **Le Doigt de Barraquier*, *Pedigree*
– Pouilly-sur-Loire : *Le Cheval-Blanc*

• Alsace
– Schlucht (La) : *Le Relais-d'Alsace*

- **Champagne-Ardennes**
– [Bissancourt (proche de Vitry-le-François)] : *Le Baron de l'écluse
– Dizy : *Le Charretier de la « Providence »*
– Fumay : *Le Train*
– Givet : *Chez les Flamands*
– [Ornaie (Aube)] : *La Vérité sur Bébé Donge*
– Reims : *Le Pendu de Saint-Pholien*
– Vitry-le-François : *Le Charretier de la « Providence »*
- **Nord-Pas-de-Calais**
– Boulogne-sur-Mer : *Les Mariés du 1er décembre*
– Dunkerque : *L'Aîné des Ferchaux*
- **Picardie**
– [Versins-Haut (inspiré par Pont-Rémy)] : *Le Nègre*
– [Versins-Station] : *Le Nègre*
- **Normandie**
– Bayeux : *Les Sœurs Lacroix*
– Bénouville : *Le Président*
– Caen : *La Maison des sept jeunes filles*, *La Vieille Dame de Bayeux, L'Aîné des Ferchaux*
– Cherbourg : *La Marie du Port*, *Le Vieux Couple de Cherbourg, Le Passage de la ligne*
– Deauville : *La Fleuriste de Deauville*
– Dieppe : *L'Homme de Londres*, *Tempête sur la Manche*
– Étretat : *Maigret et la vieille dame*
– Fécamp : *Pietr-le-Letton*, *L'Énigme de la « Marie-Galante », Au Rendez-Vous-des-Terre-Neuvas, Les Rescapés du « Télémaque »*, *Le Bateau d'Émile*
– Havre (Le) : *Le Bilan Malétras*
– Ouistreham : *Le Port des brumes*
– Port-en-Bessin : *La Marie du Port*
– Riva-Bella : *Bergelon*
– Rouen : *Les Rescapés du « Télémaque », Oncle Charles s'est enfermé*
– [Saint-Saturnin (proche de Bayeux)] : *Le Passage de la ligne*
- **Bretagne**
– Concarneau : *Le Chien jaune, Les Demoiselles de Concarneau*
- **Pays de Loire**
– Aiguillon (L') : *La Maison du juge*
– [Chantournais (inspiré par Fontenay-le-Comte)] : *Au bout du rouleau*
– Fontenay-le-Comte : *Maigret a peur*
– Nantes : *L'Âne-Rouge, Lettre à mon juge*
– [Ormois (proche de La Roche-sur-Yon)] : *Lettre à mon juge*
– [Pont-du-Grau (Le) (inspiré par Le Pont-du-Brault)] : *Vente à la bougie
– [Pont-Saint-Jean (inspiré par Fontenay-le-Comte)] : *Tante Jeanne*
– [Quatre-Bras (Les) (proche de Coulonges-sur-l'Autize)] : *Valérie s'en va
– Roche-sur-Yon (La) : *Lettre à mon juge*
– Sables-d'Olonne (Les) : *Le Fils Cardinaud, Les Vacances de Maigret, La Chambre bleue*
– [Saint-Aubin-les-Marais (proche de Benet)] : *L'Inspecteur Cadavre*
– [Sainte-Odile (inspiré par Souil)] : *Le Rapport du gendarme*
– [Saint-Hilaire (inspiré par Saint-Mesmin)] : *Le Cercle des Mahé*
– [Saint-Justin-du-Loup (inspiré par Saint-Mesmin)] : *La Chambre bleue*
– [Triant (inspiré par Pouzauges)] : *La Chambre bleue*
- **Poitou-Charentes**
– Charron : *Le Clan des Ostendais*
– Coup-de-Vague (Le) : *Le Coup-de-Vague*
– [Dion (proche de Rochefort)] : *Le Mort tombé du ciel
– Esnandes : *Le Testament Donadieu*
– Fouras : *Marie qui louche, Le Grand Bob*
– Marsilly : *Le Coup-de-Vague*, *Le Flair du petit docteur, Le Riche Homme*
– Nieul-sur-Mer : *Le Haut Mal*
– Niort : *Le Passage de la ligne*
– Pallice (La) : *Le Clan des Ostendais*
– Poitiers : *La Chambre bleue*
– Pré-aux-Bœufs (La) : *Le Haut Mal*
– Rochelle (La) : *Le Haut Mal, L'Évadé, Le Testament Donadieu*, *Annette et la dame blonde, Le Voyageur de la Toussaint, Le Clan des Ostendais, Les Fantômes du chapelier, Le Fils, Le Train, Le Riche Homme*
– Royan : *La Demoiselle en bleu pâle
– [Saint-André-sur-Mer (inspiré par Marsilly)] : *Maigret à l'école*
- **Aquitaine**
– Bergerac : *Le Fou de Bergerac*
– Bordeaux : *Le Passager et son nègre
- **Provence-Alpes-Côte d'Azur**
– Antibes : *Liberty-Bar*
– Bandol : *Maigret et l'indicateur*
– [Bastide (La) (proche de Mouans-Sartoux)] : *Dimanche*
– Cannes : *Liberty-Bar*, *L'Improbable Monsieur Owen, Strip-Tease, Dimanche, Le Confessionnal*
– Cap-d'Antibes : *Liberty-Bar, Les Volets verts*
– Golfe-Juan : *Chemin sans issue*, *Le Fantôme de Monsieur Marbe*
– Hyères : *Le Passage de la ligne*
– Juan-les-Pins : *Liberty-Bar*
– Lavandou (Le) : *Cour d'assises*, *Les Trois Bateaux de la calanque*
– Marseille : *La Fuite de Monsieur Monde*

– Nice : *Cour d'assises*, *La Fuite de Monsieur Monde*, *Le Confessionnal*
– Porquerolles : **Le Grand-Langoustier*, *Cour d'assises*, *Le Cercle des Mahé*, *Mon Ami Maigret*
– Saint-Raphaël : *Le Testament Donadieu*
– Super-Cannes : *Chemin sans issue*

DANS LE MONDE

EUROPE
• **Monaco**
– Monte-Carlo : *Maigret voyage*
• **Suisse**
– Lausanne : *Maigret voyage*, *La Disparition d'Odile*
• **Angleterre**
– Londres : *Le Revolver de Maigret*, **Les Nolépitois*
– Tottenham Corner : *Le Passage de la ligne*
• **Belgique**
– Anvers : *Bergelon*
– Bruxelles : *Le Locataire*, **Émile à Bruxelles*
– Charleroi : *Le Locataire*
– Embourg : *Pedigree*
– Furnes : *Le Bourgmestre de Furnes*
– Liège : *Le Pendu de Saint-Pholien*, *La Danseuse du Gai-Moulin*, *Les Trois Crimes de mes amis*, *Pedigree*, *Crime impuni*
– Neeroeteren : *La Maison du canal*
– Ostende : *Le Bourgmestre de Furnes*
– Schaerbeek : *Le Suspect*
• **Pays-Bas**
– Delfzijl : *Un crime en Hollande*
– Groningue : *L'homme qui regardait passer les trains*
– Sneek : *L'Assassin*
• **Allemagne**
– Brême : *Le Pendu de Saint-Pholien*
– Hambourg : *Les Pitard*
• **Norvège**
– Kirkenes : **Le Docteur de Kirkenes*
• **Pologne**
– Vilna : **Les Mystères du Grand-Saint-Georges*

TURQUIE
– Istanbul : *Les Clients d'Avrenos*, **Le Policier d'Istanbul*

URSS
– Batoum : *Les Gens d'en face*

AFRIQUE
• **Gabon**
– Libreville : *Le Coup de lune*, **Un crime au Gabon*
• **Congo belge**
– Nyangara : *Le Blanc à lunettes*

AMÉRIQUE
• **États-Unis**
– [Aconda (proche d'El Centro)] : *Les Frères Rico*
– Bisbee : *La Jument-Perdue*
– [Brentwood (inspiré par Lakeville)] : *La Main*
– [Carlson-City (inspiré par Bisbee)] : *Crime impuni*
– El Centro : *Les Frères Rico*
– [Everton (inspiré par Millerton)] : *L'Horloger d'Everton*
– [Hayward (inspiré par Narragansett)] : *Feux rouges*
– Indianapolis : *L'Horloger d'Everton*
– Liberty : *L'Horloger d'Everton*
– Litchfield : *La Mort de Belle*
– New York : *Trois Chambres à Manhattan*, *Maigret à New York*, *Les Frères Rico*, *La Main*
– Oldbridge : *La Boule noire*
– [Santa Clara (inspiré par Sarasota)] : *Les Frères Rico*
– Tucson : *La Jument-Perdue*, *Maigret chez le coroner*
– Tumacacori : *Le Fond de la bouteille*
– [Williamson (inspiré par Lakeville)] : *La Boule noire*
• **Panamá**
– Colon : *Quartier nègre*, *Long Cours*, **La Tête de Joseph*, *L'Aîné des Ferchaux*
– Panamá : *Quartier nègre*, **L'Escale de Buenaventura*
• **Colombie**
– Buenaventura : *Long Cours*
• **Équateur**
– Floréana (île de l'archipel des Galápagos) : *Ceux de la soif*

OCÉANIE
• **Tahiti**
– Papeete : *Long Cours*, *Touriste de bananes*, *Le Passager clandestin*
– Taiarapu : *Le Passager clandestin*

MERS ET OCÉANS
• **Manche** : *Les Pitard*
• **Mer du Nord** : *Le Passager du « Polarlys »*, *Les Pitard*
• **Mer de Norvège** : *Le Passager du « Polarlys »*
• **Océan Atlantique** : *45° à l'ombre*, *Les Pitard*, *Long Cours*
• **Océan Pacifique** : *Touriste de bananes*, **L'Enquête de Mlle Doche*, **Little Samuel à Tahiti*, *Le Passager clandestin*

BIBLIOGRAPHIE

ÉTUDES ET ESSAIS

– *Album Simenon*, iconographie choisie et commentée par Pierre Hebey, Gallimard, Album de la Pléiade, Paris, 2003.
– Bernard Alavoine, *Georges Simenon. Parcours d'une œuvre*, Encrage, Amiens, 1998.
– Bernard Alavoine, *Les Enquêtes de Maigret de Georges Simenon*, Encrage, Amiens, 1999.
– Pierre Assouline, *Simenon. Biographie*, Julliard, Paris, 1992 ; rééd. revue et augmentée : *Simenon*, Gallimard, Folio, Paris, 1996.
– Danielle Bajomée, *Simenon, une légende du XXe siècle*, la Renaissance du Livre, Tournai, 2003.
– Jean-Baptiste Baronian, *Simenon ou le roman gris*, Paris, Éditions Textuel, coll. Passions, 2002.
– Lucile Becker, *Georges Simenon*, Twayne, Boston, 1977 ; rééd. remaniée : *Georges Simenon revisited*, Twayne, New York, 1999.
– Jules Bedner, *Simenon et le jeu des deux histoires. Essai sur les romans policiers*, Institut de Romanistique, Amsterdam, 1990.
– Alain Bertrand, *Georges Simenon*, La Manufacture, Lyon, 1988 ; rééd. revue et augmentée : *Georges Simenon : de Maigret aux romans de la destinée*, CÉFAL, Liège, 1994.
– Alain Bertrand, *Maigret*, Labor, Bruxelles, 1994.
– Marie-Paule Boutry, *Les Trois Cents Vies de Simenon*, Claire Martin du Gard, Paris, 1990 ; rééd. L'Arsenal, Paris, 1994.
– Fenton Bresler, *L'Énigme Georges Simenon*, Balland, Paris, 1985.
– Michel Carly, *Le Pays noir de Simenon*, CÉFAL, Liège, 1996.
– Michel Carly, *Simenon, la vie d'abord !*, CÉFAL, Liège, 2000.
– Michel Carly, *Sur les routes américaines avec Simenon*, Omnibus, Paris, 2002.
– Michel Carly et Michel Lemoine, *Les Chemins belges de Simenon*, CÉFAL, Liège, 2003.
– Salvatore Cesario, *Su Georges Simenon*, Edizioni Scientifiche Italiane, Naples, 1996.
– Pierre Deligny et Claude Menguy, *Simenon au fil des livres et des saisons*, Omnibus, Paris, 2003.
– Stanley G. Eskin, *Simenon. Une biographie*, Presses de la Cité, Paris, 1990.
– Jean Fabre, *Enquête sur un enquêteur. Maigret. Un essai de sociocritique*, Études sociocritiques, Montpellier, 1981.
– Bernard de Fallois, *Simenon*, Paris, Gallimard, 1961 ; rééd. Gallimard, Tel 2003.
– Jean Forest, *Notre-Dame de Saint-Fiacre, ou l'affaire Maigret*, Presses de l'Université de Montréal, Montréal, 1994.
– Didier Gallot, *Simenon ou la comédie humaine*, France-Empire, Paris, 1999.
– Francis Lacassin, *Conversations avec Simenon*, La Sirène/Alpen, Genève, 1990 ; rééd. Éditions du Rocher, Monaco, 2002.
– Michel Lemoine, *Index des personnages de Georges Simenon*, Labor, Bruxelles, 1985.
– Michel Lemoine, *L'Autre Univers de Simenon*, CLPCF, Liège, 1991.
– Michel Lemoine, *Paris chez Simenon*, Les Belles Lettres/Encrage, Paris/Amiens, 2000.
– Michel Lemoine, *Liège couleur Simenon*, CÉFAL/Centre d'Études Georges Simenon, Liège, 2002.
– Paul Mercier, *La Pulsion d'écrire. Approche psychologique de la création romanesque chez Georges Simenon*, PUFC et Belles-Lettres, Besançon, 2003.
– Thomas Narcejac, *Le Cas Simenon*, Presses de la Cité, Paris, 1950 ; rééd. Le Castor astral, Bordeaux, 2000.
– Maurice Piron, avec la collaboration de Michel Lemoine, *L'Univers de Simenon. Guide des romans et nouvelles (1931-1972) de Georges Simenon*, Presses de la Cité, Paris, 1983.
– Anne Richter, *Simenon malgré lui*, Pré aux sources/Les Amis de Georges Simenon, Bruxelles, 1993 ; rééd. La Renaissance du Livre, Tournai, 2002.
– Mathieu Rutten, *Simenon. Ses origines. Sa vie. Son œuvre*, Wahle, Nandrin, 1986.
– Roger Stéphane, *Le Dossier Simenon*, Laffont, Paris, 1961.
– Henri-Charles Tauxe, *Georges Simenon. De l'humain au vide*, Buchet-Chastel, Paris, 1983.
– Denis Tillinac, *Le Mystère Simenon*, Calmann-Lévy, Paris, 1980.
– Pol Vandromme, *Georges Simenon*, Pierre De Méyère, Bruxelles, 1962 ; rééd. : *Georges Simenon romancier russe de langue française*, L'Âge d'Homme, Lausanne, 2000.
– André Vanoncini, *Simenon et l'affaire Maigret*, Honoré Champion, Paris, 1990.
– Hendrik Veldman, *La Tentation de l'inaccessible. Structures narratives chez Simenon*, Rodopi, Amsterdam, 1981.

OUVRAGES COLLECTIFS

– *Magazine Littéraire*, nº 107, Paris, décembre 1975.
– *Lire Simenon, Réalité/fiction/écriture*, Nathan/Labor, Bruxelles, 1980.
– *Nord'*, nº 7, Lille, juin 1986.
– *Simenon*, « Cistre essais », nº 10, L'Âge d'Homme, Lausanne, 1980.

– *Simenon* (sous la direction de Francis Lacassin et Gilbert Sigaux), Plon, Paris, 1973.
– *Simenon Travelling*, 11e Festival international du roman et du film noirs, Grenoble, 1989.
– *Télérama hors-série*, nº 41, Paris, janvier 1993.
– *2003. Année Simenon*, Bruxelles, *W + B*, n° 80, octobre 2002.
– *Simenon. L'Homme, l'univers, la création* (sous la direction de Michel Lemoine et Christine Swings), Complexe, Bruxelles, 1993 ; rééd. augmentée, 2002.
– *Le Roman de Simenon* (ouvrage consacré à l'analyse de *Pedigree,* sous la direction de Jacques Dubois et Jean-Louis Dumortier), La Renaissance du Livre, Tournai, 2003.

Simenon fait aussi l'objet d'études éditées dans deux publications annuelles :

– *Cahiers Simenon*, Les Amis de Georges Simenon, Bruxelles, depuis 1987.
– *Traces* (Travaux du Centre d'études Georges Simenon), Université de Liège, Centre d'études Georges Simenon, depuis 1989.

À PROPOS DES ADAPTATIONS CINÉMATOGRAPHIQUES ET TÉLÉVISUELLES

On trouvera une filmographie abondamment commentée dans Claude Gauteur, *D'après Simenon*, Carnets Omnibus, Paris, 2001, et des compléments dans Dick Tomasovic, « Le petit cinéma de Georges Simenon », in *W + B*, n° 80, octobre 2002, p. 35-43. Voir aussi Michel Carly, *Moteur ! Monsieur Simenon*, CÉFAL, Liège, 1999.

TABLE DES ILLUSTRATIONS

COUVERTURE

OUVERTURE

CHAPITRE 1

lisant son journal, Liège, vers 1918-1920. FS/UL.

CHAPITRE 2

22 Simenon à l'époque des romans populaires, vers 1925-1928. FS/UL.
23 Romans de Simenon publiés sous divers pseudonymes dans la collection « Le Petit Roman », Ferenczi. FS/UL.
24h Portrait de Simenon, par Régine Renchon, huile sur toile. Collection particulière.
24b Enveloppe de *Paris-Matinal*. FS/UL.
24h Autoportrait de Régine Renchon, huile sur toile. Collection particulière.
24b Caricature de Régine Renchon, par Del. Collection particulière.
26hg 1ers plats de couv. d'*Orgies bourgeoises* (Prima, « Gauloise », 1926) et de *Défense d'aimer* (Ferenczi, « Le Petit Livre », 1927). FS/UL.
26hm 1er plat de couv. du *Roi du Pacifique*, Ferenczi, « Le Livre de l'aventure », 1929.
26hd 1ers plats de couv. d'*Histoire d'un pantalon* (Prima, « Gauloise », 1926) et d'*Amour d'Afrique* (Ferenczi, « Le Petit Livre », 1927). FS/UL.
26b « Un falzar chez la colonelle », signé Gom Gut, *Paris-Flirt*, automne 1925. FS/UL.
27h et **27m** Simenon à sa machine à écrire, à l'époque des romans populaires. FS/UL.
28 Double page de l'agenda 1924 de Simenon. FS/UL.
28b Simenon au bar de son appartement, 21, place des Vosges, à Paris. FS/UL.
29 *Idem*, avec Tigy (à gauche) et Suzy Solidor. FS/UL.
30g 1er plat de couv. de *Nox l'insaisissable* (Ferenczi, « Le Roman policier », 1926). FS/UL.
30d 1er plat de couv. de *Paris leste*, Paris-Plaisir, 1927.
31g Projet d'affiche de *Paris-Matin* relatif à l'exploit de la « Cage de verre ». FS/UL.
31d Caricature relative à la « Cage de verre », *Le Canard enchaîné*, 23 février 1927. FS/UL.
32h Maquette de couverture du *Josephine Baker's Magazine*, illustration de Paul Colin. FS/UL.
32b Simenon à Paris, entre Tigy et Joséphine Baker. FS/UL.
33h Simenon en 1927 à l'île d'Aix. FS/UL.
33b Page de maquette du *Josephine Baker's Magazine*, illustrations de Paul Colin. FS/UL.
34h 1er plat de couv. de *La Femme 47*, Fayard, « Le Livre populaire », 1930. FS/UL.
34md Questions du concours hebdomadaire des « 13 énigmes », *Détective*, 3 octobre 1929.
34m « Les 13 énigmes », *ibidem*.
35h « Les 13 mystères », *Détective*, 28 mars 1929.
35m Les membres du jury du concours de *Détective*, *ibidem*.
35d 1er plat de couv. des *13 Mystères*, Fayard, 1932.
36h À bord du *Ginette*, sur le Rhône, 1928. FS/UL.
36b Photographies du baptême de l'*Ostrogoth*, à Paris, par le curé de Notre-Dame, 1929. FS/UL.
37h Simenon et Tigy en pique-nique, 1928-1929. FS/UL.
37b Simenon en train d'écrire à bord de l'*Ostrogoth*, 1929. FS/UL.
38g et **38d** Projets de couverture de *La Folle d'Itteville* et de *L'Affaire des 7*, par Georges Simenon et Germaine Krull, pour les éditions Jacques Haumont, 1931. FS/UL.
39h Simenon et Tigy en Laponie, hiver 1929-1930. FS/UL.
39b Georges Simenon et Germaine Krull à Morsang-sur-Seine, été 1930. FS/UL.
40h Au Bal anthropométrique, cabaret de la *Boule blanche*, 20-21 février 1931. FS/UL.
40-41m « M. Gallet, décédé, reçoit… », titre d'un article de *Candide*, 26 février 1931. FS/UL.
41h 1ers plats de couv. du *Pendu de Saint-Pholien*, *M. Gallet décédé*, *Pietr-le-Letton* et *Le Chien jaune*.
42h Scène du *Chien jaune* de Jean Tarride, 1932. FS/UL.
42m Signature du contrat passé entre Jean Renoir et Simenon pour l'adaptation cinématographique de *La Nuit du carrefour*, 31 octobre 1931. FS/UL.
43hg et **43hd** Scènes de *La Nuit du carrefour*, de Jean Renoir, 1931. FS/UL.
43b Pierre Renoir dans le rôle de Maigret, dans *La Nuit du carrefour*, de Jean Renoir, 1931. FS/UL.
44-45 Simenon à La Richardière (Marsilly), en train de travailler au scénario de *La Tête d'un homme*, avec l'acteur Valéry Inkijinoff, 1932, reportage *Pour Vous*, 19 mai 1932. FS/UL.
45m Scène de *La Tête d'un homme*, avec Valéry Inkijinoff dans le rôle de Radek et Harry Baur dans celui de Maigret, adaptation de Jean Duvivier, 1933. FS/UL.

CHAPITRE 3

46 Simenon, photographie Raymond Voinquel, 1939.
47g Carte de presse de Simenon, *Paris-Soir*. FS/UL.
47m 1er plat de couv. de *Quartier nègre*, Gallimard, 1935.
47d Simenon en train de photographier. FS/UL.
48h Simenon en Afrique, été 1932. FS/UL.
48b Une du magazine *Voilà*, 15 octobre 1932.
49h Simenon à La Richardière (Marsilly). FS/UL.
50d 1er plat de couv. de *Maigret*, Fayard,

CHAPITRE 4

Maigret et le corps sans tête, Presses de la Cité, 1955. FS/UL.
83b Lettre de Jean Cocteau à Simenon, 21 mai 1955. FS/UL.
84 Simenon et Jean Gabin aux studios d'Épinay, 1957. FS/UL.
85hg Lettre de Marcel Pagnol à Simenon, mars 1957.
85md La villa de Simenon à Cannes. FS/UL.
85bd Simenon à sa machine à écrire, Cannes, photographie E. Quinn, 1956.
86 Michel Simon dans *Panique*, de Julien Duvivier, 1947. FS/UL.
87 Scène de *L'Homme de la tour Eiffel*, de Burgess Meredith, 1949.
88h Scène de *Maigret tend un piège*, de Jean Delannoy, 1958. FS/UL.
88b Jean Gabin et Brigitte Bardot dans *En cas de malheur*, de Claude Autant-Lara, 1958. FS/UL.
89h Scène du *Bateau d'Émile*, de Denys de la Patellière, 1962. FS/UL.
89b Affiche de *La Vérité sur Bébé Donge*, de Henri Decoin, 1952. FS/UL.
90h Simenon, Denyse et leurs enfants à Échandens, près de Lausanne, vers 1960.
90b *« Simenon's Castle »*, article sur Simenon dans *MD Pictorial*, juillet 1960. FS/UL.
91 1er plat de couv. du *Nègre*, Presses de la Cité, 1957. FS/UL.
92 Simenon à Échandens, photographié par Robert Doisneau, 28 avril 1961.
93h Simenon, Jeanne Moreau et Federico Fellini au festival de Cannes, mai 1960.
93m Affiche du *Président*, d'Henri Verneuil, 1961. FS/UL.
94g 1er plat de couv. du *Petit Saint*, Presses de la Cité, 1965. FS/UL.
94d Simenon devant sa maison d'Épalinges, dominant Lausanne.
95 Simenon photographié par Robert Doisneau, 1962.
96 Inauguration de la statue de Maigret de Pierre Hondt, à Delfzijl, 3 septembre 1966, en présence d'interprètes du commissaire Maigret, photographie de Sergio del Grande. FS/UL.
97h Lettre de Jean Renoir à Simenon, 5 septembre 1967. FS/UL.
97m Enveloppe du *Voleur de Maigret*. FS/UL.
97b Calendrier de rédaction du *Voleur de Maigret*, novembre 1966. FS/UL.
98h De gauche à droite, Harry Baur Charles Laughton et Michel Simon dans le rôle de Maigret. FS/UL.
98b Enveloppe de *Victor* (roman jamais rédigé), 18 septembre 1972. FS/UL.
99hg Jean Gabin dans le rôle de Maigret.
99hm Jean Richard *idem*. FS/UL.
99hd Bruno Crémer *idem*. FS/UL.
99b L'acteur japonais Kinya Aikawa dans le rôle de Maigret. FS/UL.
100h 1ers plats de couv. de : édition américaine du *Pendu de Saint-Pholien* (Covici Friede Publishers, New York, 1932) ; édition russe de *Maigret et la grande perche* (Moscou, 1991) ; édition anglaise de *Maigret et le client du samedi* (Hamish Hamilton, Londres, 1964) ; édition en hébreu de *La Nuit du carrefour* (1966). FS/UL.
101h 1ers plats de couv. de : édition hongroise du *Chien jaune* (Ifjùsàgi Könyvkiado, Bucarest, 1966) ; édition croate de *Maigret et le clochard* (Matica Hrvatska, Zagreb, 1966) ; édition espagnole de *L'Inspecteur cadavre* (Ayma, Barcelone, 1951) ; édition japonaise de *La Tête d'un homme* (Shonyûsha, Tokyo, 1945). FS/UL.
100-101 Simenon et ses Maigret, juin 1970.

Chapitre 5

104 Simenon, 20 décembre 1976.
105 Affiches de *L'Étoile du Nord*, *Les Fantômes du chapelier*, *Le Train*, *Monsieur Hire*. FS/UL.
106h La dernière demeure de Simenon à Lausanne, avenue des Figuiers.
106b 1er plat de couv. de *Lettre à ma mère*, Omnibus, 1999.
107 Première de couverture de *L'Express*, 21 février 1977. FS/UL.
108g 1er plat de couv. de *Mémoires intimes*, Presses de la Cité, 1981. FS/UL.
108d Marie-Jo Simenon.FS/UL.
108b Première page du manuscrit de *Mémoires intimes*. FS/UL.
109h Dernière lettre de Jean Renoir à Simenon, 17 mars 1978. FS/UL.
109d Simenon et Teresa, sa dernière compagne.
110-111 Simenon à Liège en 1952, photographié par Daniel Filipacchi.
112 Simenon à Épalinges en 1972.

TÉMOIGNAGES ET DOCUMENTS

113 Simenon à Paris, photographie Pierre Vals, 1952.
117 Simenon et sa production romanesque, Lakeville. FS/UL.
129 4e de couv. du *Coup de Lune*, Fayard, 1953.

INDEX GÉNÉRAL

A

INDEX DES ŒUVRES DE SIMENON

Ne sont retenus ici que les titres faisant l'objet d'une mise en situation ou d'un développement.

CRÉDITS PHOTOGRAPHIQUES

Les documents iconographiques reproduits dans cet ouvrage proviennent des collections du Fonds Simenon de l'Université de Liège, à l'exception de : Collection Claude Menguy 16h. Collection Gallimard 66h, 82h. Archives Mylène Demongeot-Simenon 20b, 24h, 24h, 55b. Collection Viollet 62b, 79b, 93h, 94d. Keystone 6, 8, 101hg. Kharbine Tapabor 26hg, 34md, 34m, 35h, 35m, 35d, 41h, 48b, 57, 58-59, 58b, 76h, 100hg. Magnum/René Burri 109d. Mission du patrimoine photographique/Raymond Voinquel, Paris 46. Opale/Pierre Vals 70, 113. Paris-Match/E. Quinn 4h, 85bd, 90h. Paris-Match/Habans 98-99. Paris-Match/Jeannelle 104. Paris-Match/Pierre Vals 1er plat de couv. Paris-Match/Habans 11. Paul Buisson 80. Photos Douze 87. Rapho/Doisneau 92. Rapho/Pepe Dimiz 112. Rapho/Goursat 56g. Rapho/R. Doisneau 92, 95. Roger-Viollet 64b. Rue des Archives 78-79. Sergio del Grande, Epoca 96. © ADAGP/Paul Colin 32h, 33b. © Estate of Georges Simenon pour les photographies prises par Simenon 52-53, 102-103.

REMERCIEMENTS

L'auteur remercie Madame Christine Swings-Deliège, Messieurs Alain Bertrand, Michel Carly et Claude Menguy. L'éditeur remercie à son tour Madame Christine Swings-Deliège, Monsieur Claude Menguy, ainsi que Jean-Pierre Dauphin, Alban Cerisier, Dominique Jochaud et Isabelle Flamigni. Il est particulièrement reconnaissant à John Simenon pour son soutien.

ÉDITION ET FABRICATION

DÉCOUVERTES GALLIMARD
COLLECTION CONÇUE par Pierre Marchand. DIRECTION Élisabeth de Farcy.
COORDINATION ÉDITORIALE Anne Lemaire.
GRAPHISME Alain Gouessant.
COORDINATION ICONOGRAPHIQUE Isabelle de Latour.
SUIVI DE PRODUCTION Fabienne Brifault-Dandé.
SUIVI DE PARTENARIAT Madeleine Gonçalves.
PROMOTION & PRESSE Flora Joly et Pierre Gestède.

SIMENON, ÉCRIRE L'HOMME
ÉDITION et ICONOGRAPHIE Caroline Larroche.
MAQUETTE ET MONTAGE Pascale Comte.
LECTURE-CORRECTION Emmanuel de Saint-Martin et Jocelyne Marziou.
PHOTOGRAVURE Graphic Productions, Chambéry.

Michel Lemoine, professeur honoraire, est spécialiste de l'écrivain liégeois. Il a notamment dirigé jusqu'en 1999 la revue *Traces* (Travaux du Centre d'études Georges Simenon de l'université de Liège), devenue au fil du temps un véritable carrefour des études simenoniennes. Outre sa collaboration à *L'Univers de Simenon* (Presses de la Cité, 1983), on lui doit un monumental *Index des personnages de Georges Simenon* (Labor, 1985), *L'Autre Univers de Simenon* (CLPCF, 1991), *Le Liège de Simenon en cartes postales d'époque* (CÉFAL, 1993), *Paris chez Simenon* (Encrage, 2000), *Liège couleur Simenon* (CÉFAL et Centre d'études Georges Simenon, 2002) et *Les Chemins belges de Simenon* (en collaboration avec Michel Carly; Liège, CÉFAL, 2003). Il prépare actuellement deux autres ouvrages sur le romancier, *Lumières sur le Simenon de l'aube* et *La France de Simenon*, ainsi qu'un essai sur les sites simenoniens (en collaboration avec Claude Menguy).

À Marie-France Léonard.

1er dépôt légal: janvier 2003
Dépôt légal : février 2003
Numéro d'édition : 123479
ISBN : 2-07-076696-9
Imprimé en France
à l'Imprimerie Moderne de l'Est
Numéro d'impression : 16562

DERNIERS TITRES PARUS

326/ LE LANGAGE
327/ LA RÉVOLUTION RUSSE
328/ ARAGON
329/ GEORGES DE LA TOUR
330/ LUTÈCE
331/ LE MONT ATHOS
332/ LA DANSE MODERNE
333/ SHERLOCK HOLMES
334/ LA BEAT GENERATION
335/ LES ÉCHECS
336/ LES PIERRES PRÉCIEUSES
337/ FERRARI
338/ LES ROUX
339/ COUPERIN
340/ LEWIS CARROLL
341/ VICTOR HUGO
342/ UN JOUR EN FRANCE
343/ L'EXPÉDITION D'ÉGYPTE
344/ RAMSÈS II
345/ DE L'INDIGÈNE À L'IMMIGRÉ
346/ VERS LA TERRE D'ISRAËL
347/ DELACROIX
348/ DON JUAN
349/ LA MÉMOIRE
350/ MAI 68
351/ LES CHEVALIERS DE MALTE
352/ LE PHARE D'ALEXANDRIE
353/ LES MÉGALITHES
354/ SAINT FRANÇOIS D'ASSISE
355/ LES STADES
356/ SAINT-EXUPÉRY
357/ LA GRANDE GUERRE 1914-1918
358/ LES PHÉNICIENS
359/ LE THÉÂTRE DE BOULEVARD
360/ LA REDÉCOUVERTE DE LA CHINE ANCIENNE
361/ NAPOLÉON
362/ LE JAPON ÉTERNEL
363/ L'HISTOIRE DU LIVRE, VOL. 2
364/ LES JUMEAUX
365/ LA GÉNÉALOGIE
366/ L'INQUISITION
367/ L'EUROPE
368/ LES PRÉRAPHAÉLITES
369/ LE PAPIER
370/ LA DOULEUR
371/ HEMINGWAY
372/ PÉTRA
376/ BONNARD
377/ CHARDIN
378/ L'EUROPE À L'ÂGE DU BRONZE
379/ L'EURO
380/ L'IMMIGRATION
381/ PROUST
382/ L'ILLUSION BAROQUE
383/ LES MATÉRIAUX DE LA COULEUR
388/ LE CONSEIL D'ÉTAT
389/ VIVE L'EAU
392/ LA BIBLE
393/ LES ARTS PREMIERS
394/ BERLIN
395/ L'ÉGYPTE COPTE
396/ VENISE
397/ DARWIN
398/ LA SCIENCE-FICTION
399/ LE VERRE
400/ LE CALENDRIER
401/ LA VIERGE
402/ MARIE-ANTOINETTE
403/ LA POLICE JUDICIAIRE
404/ SIGNAC
405/ LE CHEVEU
406/ L'ALIMENTATION
407/ CÉLINE
408/ GAUDÍ
409/ SALADIN
410/ LA VILLE
411/ LES ARCHÉOLOGUES EN ASIE CENTRALE
412/ ALEXANDRIE
413/ LA BIOSPHÈRE
414/ L'INVENTION DE LA PHOTOGRAPHIE
415/ HENRI IV
416/ SAINT AUGUSTIN
417/ LA LONGUE MARCHE DES GAYS
418/ TOUAREGS
419/ LA LÉGION D'HONNEUR
420/ LA PEAU
421/ FLAUBERT
422/ GENGIS KHAN
423/ LES DROGUES
424/ MOÏSE
425/ GENET
426/ LA SYRIE ANTIQUE
427/ LE TIBET
428/ LES ABORIGÈNES D'AUSTRALIE

UNE AUTRE HISTOIRE DES RELIGIONS (6 VOL.)
373/ L'HÉRITAGE DES RELIGIONS PREMIÈRES
374/ LE DIEU DU CROISSANT FERTILE
384/ LES SPIRITUALITÉS INDIENNES
385/ LES RELIGIONS EXTRÊME-ORIENTALES
390/ L'ESPRIT DES SAVOIRS
391/ LE SACRE DES POUVOIRS

UNE AUTRE HISTOIRE DE L'ESPACE (3 VOL.)
375/ L'APPEL DU COSMOS
386/ HOMMES ET ROBOTS DANS L'ESPACE
387/ LE VILLAGE INTERPLANÉTAIRE

Romancier prolixe, Georges Simenon a réussi cette double gageure de devenir l'un des écrivains les plus populaires de son siècle et d'être considéré par ses contemporains à l'égal des meilleurs, à commencer par André Gide, qui voyait en lui « le plus grand peut-être que nous ayons en littérature française aujourd'hui ». Son nom est indissociable de celui de Maigret, ce policier des âmes héros de plus de cent romans et nouvelles. Mais Simenon est aussi l'auteur d'une œuvre purement romanesque, au sein de laquelle il s'est livré à une quête de l'homme prisonnier de sa condition, une quête de l'« homme nu », inlassablement scruté à l'aune de sa devise : « Comprendre et ne pas juger ». Tout en suivant au jour le jour la formidable production de ce prodigieux raconteur d'histoires, Michel Lemoine analyse cet univers de la fuite et du drame, où les protagonistes vont au bout d'eux-mêmes, ce théâtre d'ombre et de lumière où le romancier nous entraîne en un perpétuel mouvement du souvenir à la recréation, du terreau fécond d'Outremeuse aux collines du Connecticut, des rues de La Rochelle aux lagons polynésiens, de la quiétude du Marais au quai des Orfèvres.

Simenon apprenti journaliste à Liège, Simenon auteur de romans légers à Paris, Simenon père de Maigret, Simenon reporter, marin, photographe, Simenon en famille, en voyage, Simenon en Amérique, Simenon traduit, adapté au cinéma, célébré, plus de 200 documents qui mettent en scène l'univers de ce romancier de génie qui, un jour de 1972, décidait de ne plus écrire...

A 76696
ISBN : 2-07-076696-9
9 782070 766963
catégorie 4